SOCIALISM, CAPITALISM AND ECONOMIC GROWTH

EDITORIAL BOARD

SOCIALISM, CAPITALISM AND ECONOMIC GROWTH

ESSAYS PRESENTED TO MAURICE DOBB

EDITED BY

C.H.FEINSTEIN

Fellow of Clare College, and Lecturer in Economics,
University of Cambridge

CAMBRIDGE
AT THE UNIVERSITY PRESS
1967

Published by the Syndics of the Cambridge University Press
Bentley House, 200 Euston Road, London, N.W.1.
American Branch: 32 East 57th Street, New York, N.Y. 10022

Printed in Great Britain
at the University Printing House, Cambridge
(Brooke Crutchley, University Printer)

EDITOR'S PREFACE

One of the pleasures of editing this Festschrift for Maurice Dobb has been the warmth of the response—from so many people, in so many parts of the world—to all my requests for contributions, advice and assistance. I have had the invaluable co-operation of the Editorial Board and of Piero Sraffa in the planning of this volume; Ezra Bennathan, Ruth Feinstein, Michele Salvati and Bob Rowthorn have helped me with translations from German, Russian, Italian and matrix algebra; and Jennifer Warren did most of the work for the compilation of the bibliography.

C. H. F.

Cambridge
August 1966

CONTENTS

CONTRIBUTORS

E. H. Carr, Fellow of Trinity College, University of Cambridge.

R. W. Davies, Professor and Director of the Centre for Russian and East European Studies, University of Birmingham.

P. Erdös, Institute of Economics, Hungarian Academy of Sciences, Budapest.

R. M. Goodwin, Reader in Economics and Fellow of Peterhouse, University of Cambridge.

L. J. Hejl, Econometric Laboratory of the Institute of Economics, Czechoslovak Academy of Sciences, Prague.

E. J. Hobsbawm, Reader in History, Birkbeck College, University of London.

C. Hill, Master of Balliol College, University of Oxford.

R. H. Hilton, Professor of Medieval Social History, University of Birmingham.

L. Johansen, Professor of Economics, University of Oslo.

M. Kalecki, Professor of Economics, School of Planning and Statistics, Warsaw.

A. A. Konüs, Gosplan U.S.S.R., Moscow.

O. Kýn, Econometric Laboratory of the Institute of Economics, Czechoslovak Academy of Sciences, Prague.

O. Lange, Late Professor of Political Economy, University of Warsaw.

S. J. Patel, Staff Member, United Nations Conference on Trade and Development, Geneva.

A. Pesenti, Professor of Public Finance, University of Pisa.

T. Prager, Economist, Chamber of Labour for Vienna.

K. N. Raj, Professor of Economics, University of Delhi.

J. V. Robinson, Professor of Economics, University of Cambridge.

K. W. Rothschild, Austrian Institute for Economic Research, Vienna.

R. A. J. Schlesinger, Lecturer, Institute of Soviet and East European Studies, University of Glasgow.

B. Sekerka, Econometric Laboratory of the Institute of Economics, Czechoslovak Academy of Sciences, Prague.

A. K. Sen, Professor of Economics, University of Delhi.

O. Šik, Professor and Director of the Institute of Economics of the Czechoslovak Academy of Sciences, Prague.

R. M. Solow, Professor of Economics, Massachusetts Institute of Technology, Cambridge, Mass.

J. Steindl, Austrian Institute for Economic Research, Vienna.

P. M. Sweezy, Co-editor *Monthly Review*, New York.

J. Tinbergen, Professor of Economics and Development Planning, Netherlands Institute of Economics, Rotterdam.

Sh. Ya. Turetsky, Professor of Economics, Moscow Institute of Economics named G. V. Plekhanov.

MAURICE DOBB

It is not easy to recall for how long Maurice Dobb has been a part of the intellectual universe of both Cambridge and the British left. I think I first heard of him in 1932 from an Oxford student, who talked (with the superiority of undergraduates over schoolboys) about that then extremely rare species, the socialist economist. There was G. D. H. Cole, of course, and Maurice Dobb, whom he described as a Marxist, an even rarer and indeed at the time virtually unique species in British academic life. I was a Marxist too, naturally, or thought I was. There was little enough to read on the subject in this country, other than the works of the founding fathers, for John Strachey had hardly yet begun his brief career as the cicerone of the far left. (He acknowledged his debt to Dobb's short and now forgotten *Introduction to Economics* handsomely.) Schoolboys like myself must have read Dobb simply because there were so few intellectual Marxists that we could hardly miss him. As I write, there lies before me, heavily marked, visibly re-read and inscribed with the date 1934, his Hogarth Press pamphlet *On Marxism Today*. In how many small discussion groups at school, in suburban back rooms, in the cafés of Parton and Houghton Streets, were its arguments used and re-used by boys of my generation? Probably at that time not in very many as yet, though I distinctly remember putting Trinity and Downing on my list of college preferences in the scholarship examination, the one because it contained F. R. Leavis, the other because it had at least some connection with Maurice Dobb.

The object of this otherwise irrelevant and presumptuous excursus into autobiography is to suggest not merely how long Dobb has been with us, but how unique his position was for a very considerable period. For several generations (as these are measured in the brief lives of students) he was not just the only Marxist economist in a British university of whom most people had heard, but virtually the only don known as a Communist to the wider world. After the 1930s he ceased to be quite so unusual a figure, but he ante-dated them. When young intellectuals began to turn towards Marxism in significant numbers, and for the first time in British history, he was already there to guide, to instruct, to provide the assurance which we, in spite of our ostensible readiness to dismiss the official authorities, badly needed. His very existence as a Marxist academic was itself an achievement. It is not easy to recall the Siberian climate in which the plant of intellectual Marxism then attempted to put out its feeble shoots in this country, the

casual dismissal—so much more wounding than the impassioned pole-
mics of the cold war era—with which our elders passed over Marx. If he
was really so eminent a thinker, why then (I still recall the question of a
Cambridge supervisor) were there no intellectually interesting contemporary Marxists to read? There were, though Cambridge, then as later
an exaggerated example of avoidable Anglo–Saxon insularity, did not
know them. Yet even by the criteria of the British educational system of
the 1930s, there was Dobb, a trebly unusual figure. 'The 1930s' Paul
Sweezy has remarked, 'were not a period of substantial progress in
Marxist economics.' Britain was a country in which barely any significant native contribution to Marxist theory had ever been made. But
Dobb's was such a contribution, he was English, and he was a man who
was at least marginally accepted as an academic.

Dobb's isolation was in many ways characteristic of the situation of
socialist, and *a fortiori* of Marxist, intellectuals until the 1930s. The traditional habitat of the progressive intellectuals in this country had been
the radical wing of liberalism. The major intellectual effort of the left,
which on the continent came from socialists, in Britain came from
liberals. It was not a Hilferding, Luxemburg or Lenin who produced the
British analysis of the imperialist phase of capitalism, but a J. A. Hobson;
not a Jaurès who rewrote the history of the crucial phenomenon in
national history—in our case the industrial revolution—'from below',
but writers like J. L. and Barbara Hammond. Even the relatively few
socialist intellectuals of the era from 1890 to 1914, which was everywhere
else a golden age of Marxism, owed little to Marx. The first world war
and the collapse of the Liberal Party produced a migration of radical
intellectuals towards Labour, but neither their formation nor their new
environment encouraged any great development of Marxism among
them, at all events until the slump and the rise of Hitler. However, shortly before the war the first numerically significant groups of university
socialists came into existence, largely under the initial auspices of the
Fabians against whom they subsequently rose in revolt. The labour unrest of 1911–14, the war, and the inspiration of the October Revolution
drove them to the left, and the profound and lively sense of class division and class struggle led them towards radical ideologies—revolutionary syndicalism and guild socialism—and thence to Marxism. It was a
slender enough basis for the theory, though it was in this setting—
notably in the summer schools of the Fabian (later Labour) Research
Department—that Maurice Dobb made his ideological début.

'Like Douglas Cole' writes one of his seniors in this milieu, 'the
young Dobb was singularly good-looking, while less like a "spoiled
darling" in his behaviour. He was (also like Cole) exceedingly well-
dressed in those days.' (Both the modesty and the touch of informal

dandyism in the choice of shirts and ties have, as his friends know, survived the intervening decades.) He was probably a slightly unexpected figure even then, the product of a respectable Daily Mail-reading suburban family and of Charterhouse, a school not notably productive of revolutionary intellectuals, but to which he has always maintained the loyalty due from an Old Carthusian. Such patently bourgeois appearances were not usual. Dobb himself remembers his first attempt to join the small band of Cambridge University socialists, and being intensively interrogated by H. D. Dickinson (later Professor of Economics in Bristol), who was clearly under the impression that so spruce and conventional-looking a young man must be a provocateur. (There was some excuse for caution in those days, when the bullies of athletic conservatism were only too likely to break the rooms and heads of the unconforming minority.) Nor was Dobb at this stage the most extremist of Cambridge left-wingers. He did not in fact join the Communist Party until 1921. Yet he proved to be the most persistent of his contemporaries.

He had become a socialist in the last phase of the war, while waiting for the apparently inevitable call-up into the army, from which only the armistice of November 1918 saved him. The next year he entered Pembroke College as a historian and shocked the authorities by the decision to read economics, a subject for which the college was entirely unprepared, though J. M. Keynes advised it on how best to deal with this eccentric young man. There were then not many economists and considerably fewer socialists: Kingsley Martin, R. B. Braithwaite (now Professor of Philosophy at Cambridge), Dickinson, Kitto (later Professor of Classics at Bristol), the slightly senior Lancelot Hogben, the rather junior J. D. Bernal and one or two others. Socialist economists were even scarcer, though a few years later P. Sargant Florence (before his translation to Birmingham) presided over the economic left, and Keynes—this was the period of the 'Economic Consequences'—advertised a sympathy for radical oppositionists. Dobb recalls his support against bitter attacks by other undergraduates at one of the meetings of the Political Economy Club, though the older man had little contact with the younger, and certainly neither sympathy with nor understanding of Marx. (However, he was later to commission Dobb's small work on *Wages* for the Cambridge Economic Handbooks.) Nor had Dobb any sympathy for Keynes' efforts. 'Keynes is certainly,' he wrote to a correspondent in 1925, 'departing from the assumptions of orthodoxy sufficiently to be anti-*laissez-faire* (quite the fashion now in Camb.) to wish to displace anarchic by *controlled* economic operations—but with the class basis of the whole thing still untouched. If you told him that he is neglecting this, he will simply misunderstand you, or else say that

you are introducing "sentimental" considerations which do not concern him & do not seem to him important.'

The postgraduate years at the London School of Economics (1922–
24) gave Dobb a slightly less constricted political environment, but in
1924 he accepted the invitation to return—as we now know for good—
to a teaching post in Cambridge, and to a situation which was probably
as uncongenial for revolutionary intellectuals as any to be found in the
1920s. It was not merely that, as he wrote in a letter shortly after, 'I find
it rather distasteful teaching embryo exploiters how to exploit the workers
in the most up-to-date and humane way.' Cambridge lacked any significant minority of radical students, and any industrial working-class in
the town. It did not have even Oxford's traditional penchant for the
wider world of national politics, or a permanent local headquarters for
dissidents such as the G. D. H. Cole household provided. Its rebels were
isolated, often even from each other. When the General Strike emptied
the lecture-rooms, the young Marxist lecturer was left confronting a
scattering of students who had refused to go strike-breaking. Yet as he
himself recalls, he did not realize that they were on his side, that they
were probably waiting for his words, and attacked them as blacklegs and
reactionaries. After the General Strike what little movement of the
left there was in Cambridge, collapsed entirely. For several years Dobb
was virtually the only Communist in either university or city. Not until
1931 did a new generation of student Marxists begin to revive the left
both in the town and among the undergraduates.

Inevitably, part of Dobb's life therefore lay outside Cambridge: in
London, in the Labour Research Department, or in the classes of the
National Council of Labour Colleges, which was the main organization
for Marxist education in the trade unions between the wars, and to
which he gave up weekends and vacations. Much, and at times most,
of his non-academic writing is to be found in the pages of its journal
Plebs, of which he was *de facto* editor for some years. Dobb was and remains primarily a teacher and writer. Though a devoted and loyal
member of the Communist Party almost since its foundation, neither
his situation in Cambridge nor perhaps his personality and intellectual
style qualified him markedly for the work of political organization and
propaganda which absorbed most of the few intellectuals who threw in
their lot with the Party before the 1930s. Conversely, though his gifts
were appreciated—an old Communist recalls mentioning the young
Dobb to Eugene Varga in Moscow as the ablest Marxist economist in
Britain as early as 1922—before the 1930s there was not a great deal for
a man of his kind to do in the Communist movement, except to take
his share of the adult teaching which has always been so central an
activity in the British labour movement. We may not regret that Dobb

was thus left free to write *Capitalist Enterprise and Social Progress* (1925) and the pioneer study of *Russian Economic Development since the Revolution* (1927); probably the first work of its kind by a British economist. Curiously enough, it was written without a knowlege of the Russian language, which Dobb only acquired after the second world war; though of course he had the constant assistance of a translator.

Within Cambridge he soon came to occupy the characteristic position which he has retained ever since. Totally isolated as a Marxist in his faculty for so long, he did not initially suffer much discrimination, though the late King George V is reported to have expressed some anxiety about the presence of a bolshevik in an institution likely to educate royalty. The decision by Pembroke College to withdraw its economics undergraduates from his dangerous influence in 1928 was due to his divorce rather than to his Marxism, though there may well have been dons who (as in the case of Bertrand Russell) made no clear distinction between varieties of what they regarded as immorality. Thanks to the late D. H. Robertson, whose political sentiments had not yet been exacerbated by the rise of the Keynesians, he was soon attached to Trinity, though he did not actually become a Fellow of this (or any) college until after the second world war.

Economics students knew him as a devoted supervisor and lecturer, initially on any and every subject required by the syllabus—even, at one stage, Public Finance—later increasingly on the congenial topics of the history of economic thought and on social problems. They did not know, and could not appreciate, the immense care and trouble he brought to his teaching, which made him into the most painstaking and sympathetic of examiners. The undergraduate left, which developed in the 1930s, saw little of him in the ordinary course of events, partly because its activities were sharply distinct from those of the post-graduates and dons—the ones living, then as later, in an academic limbo, the others in a permanent world quite different from the rapidly revolving universe below them—partly because Dobb's punctilious refusal to use his position as a teacher for political purposes, tended to confine his contacts with the student Marxists to the extra-curricular. I remember him, most charactistically, at student summer schools during vacations, where he introduced us, with remarkable lucidity and a flattering assumption of intellectual equality, to the Marx of volumes 2 and 3 of *Capital* and of the *Theories on Surplus Value*. He probably taught us more about Marx' analysis on such occasions than we ever learned in an equally brief space of time before or since.

For post-graduates, colleagues and friends he became a less elusive figure, though, even after his final establishment in Neville's Court, Trinity, he still escaped to the rural isolation of Fulbourn and to his

wife Barbara Nixon. In Cambridge his friends see him perhaps most
typically sitting in an armchair, rosy-faced, still elegant in an informal
but carefully colour-checked shirt and disclaiming, against all probability, any special competence on any subject under discussion, diffi-
dently intervening in conversation, with a natural and deep-seated
courtesy which once led a visiting foreigner to say that he had always
heard about English gentlemen, but he had never met one until he met
Maurice Dobb. Or else we think of him on those long discussion-laden
walks through Backs, Fellows' Gardens or the woods near Fulbourn,
which are so inseparable from the intellectual life of the older universi-
ties. Outside Cambridge we recognize the characteristic square hand-
writing, getting perhaps even more regular and legible as the years
pass, with which he fills his pages. As time has passed the number of
people who have thus come to know Dobb—few of them can have failed
to become his friends—has grown larger. It is only natural that some
of them have decided to commemorate in this volume his contribution
to the science and the cause to which he has devoted his life.

His position among the economists was for a long time anomalous. A
Marxist who could express himself fluently in the Marshallian idiom of
his formal economic schooling was odd enough; so strange that this
bilingualism has led even able observers to suggest sometimes, against
all evidence, that he was not really a Marxist at all, but only a bolshevik
among the neo-classicists. Moreover, British economists long found it
difficult enough to grasp what Marx (and Dobb) were after, even
though—thanks largely to Dobb—they were eventually to learn not to
underestimate his analytical capacity as grossly as they had habitually
done in the 1920s. The combined force of the Vienna–London and
Cambridge schools made it difficult to accept the Marxist contention
that a historical abstraction in economics was, at best, of strictly limited
usefulness, and at worst, 'exclude(d) a large tract of economic territory
which to any realistic view is of great importance for understanding the
economic shape, and especially the larger movement of society',† risked
narrowing an increasingly refined analysis to the vanishing point of
tautology, and in practice presented the specific features of the capitalist
mode of production as the universal requirements of rational economic
activity. It even made it difficult, at some periods, to distinguish the
Marxist approach clearly from the institutionalist or historicist one,
associated with other minority trends in the subject. The argument that
the methodology of the economics which became dominant in the half-
century after the 1870s 'has tended to make economics essentially a

---

† Dobb's essay On Some Tendencies in Modern Economic Theory (reprinted in *On
Economic Theory and Socialism*, London, 1955) is, with his *Political Economy and Capitalism*
(London, 1937) the best guide to his thought in these matters.

theory of exchange—a determinate theory of price relationships between things which appear on the market as objects of sale and purchase' might be accepted. The contention that, 'insofar as he introduces "sociological" factors as "data", the economist justifies his method of handling them by the assumption that they are independently determined from an outside sphere, and that any interaction between that sphere and the circle of economic relations proper is too small to impugn the postulated independence of the latter' might strike home. Yet an entire tradition of economic thought still reinforced resistance to the view that 'it becomes increasingly doubtful whether any propositions of substantial importance can be made about exchange relations without introducing "social" or "institutional" data.'

Under these circumstances there was—perhaps until the 1950s—little enough contact between the writing of Dobb and his British colleagues. His first book was politely received, though so acute and usually unflattering a judge as Schumpeter later drew attention to its arguments. *Russian Economic Development* seemed to be of purely descriptive interest. It is doubtful whether any British economist in 1928 had so much as heard of the discussions on economic development in the U.S.S.R., which are in many ways the foundation of modern development economics, and even if he had, would have been prepared to make much of them for another twenty-five years. *Political Economy and Capitalism* was clearly a much more 'relevant' work, and both the power and tenacity of its critique of the then dominant subjective utility school and the defence of Marx as the logical successor to the classical political economists, could not be overlooked; at least by writers of a more recent generation. Nevertheless, its critique of the economic orthodoxy of the time ran parallel to the more influential Keynesian one, but hardly touched it except perhaps in the common rejection of both of theories whose refinement was bought at the cost of gross unrealism. Nor did either side make much effort to approach the other. The Keynesian pre-occupation with controlling economic fluctuations within the capitalist economy was one which Marxists in the 1930s were not likely to share, and conversely, Dobb's argument, intellectually able as it unquestionably was, seemed quite remote from the practical policy questions which British economists, always potential Treasury advisers at heart, sought to influence.

As soon as academic interest shifted from the study of fluctuations to that of economic development and planning, the Marxists' theoretical interests became much more obviously relevant. The trend of Dobb's own writings in the post-war period encouraged this *rapprochement*. His *Studies in the Development of Capitalism* (1946) helped to re-open the discussion on the origins of capitalist industrialization, which has increasingly occupied economic historians. The revised edition of *Soviet Economic Development Since 1917* (1948) did not perhaps appear at an ideal moment for the study of this subject, but both it and the articles periodically reviewing the processes of Soviet planning and the expert discussions to which these gave rise in the U.S.S.R., drew attention to problems which were now of concrete importance far beyond the frontiers of that country. Above all, Dobb's increasing interest in the economic development of pre-industrial countries, which found a first expression in the admirable Delhi lectures of 1951 (*Some Aspects of Economic Development 1951*) (1960) allowed him to combine the results of both his analysis of capitalist historical development and of the Soviet economy with considerable profit. This aspect of his work was carried forward with the influential essays of 1954 and 1956 on the choice of technique, and was further developed with the appearance in 1960 of *An Essay on Economic Growth and Planning*. Despite the modest title this is a study of considerable importance and shows very clearly Dobb's profound understanding of the central problems of economic growth. It was also fortunate that the great monument to that classical political economy which Dobb had so long championed was unveiled at a time when it was more likely to be appreciated than in earlier decades. Sraffa's and Dobb's great edition of Ricardo was finally published in 1951–55.

This is neither the time nor the place to attempt a criticial assessment of Dobb's work, if only because it is as yet far from complete. Yet even if he were to write nothing more it would be difficult to find many other economists of the present time who could match Dobb's major studies with work of comparable quality and originality over such a wide range: from the broad historical sweep of the *Studies in the Development of Capitalism* through to the highly abstract economic theory of his analytical essay on economic growth. In any case the very existence of a volume such as this, and the range and quality of its contributors, provides at least a provisional clue to the respect in which he is today held in many countries, and the extent to which his fields of interest are also those of other workers who have drawn stimulation from his work, his friendship, his long and lonely championship of Marxism, or all of these. It contrasts—the point is worth making only incidentally, but it ought not to be omitted—with the modesty, indeed the marginality, of his position in the official academic world. There can be no doubt that his official career has suffered from his long association both with Marxism and the Communist Party, especially as his period of maximum literary output—roughly, the decade following the end of the second world war—coincided with the worst years of the ideological cold war. Perhaps Cambridge has less to reproach itself with in this respect than other academic institutions which could have at one time or another had or retained the services of a man whose intellectual distinction is beyond any doubt, and in 1959 he was one of a group of distinguished Cambridge economists (the others included Joan Robinson and Nicholas Kaldor) who were elected Readers in Economics. In any event, the stature and influence of a writer is rarely determined by the eminence of his official positions. This is particularly true in the case of a man like Maurice Dobb and a truer indication of the esteem and affection in which he is held in so many parts of the world may be seen in this testimony of those who have united to honour him on the occasion of his retirement.

E. J. HOBSBAWM

PART I

PROBLEMS IN THE THEORY OF
ECONOMIC GROWTH

A CLASSICAL MODEL
OF ECONOMIC GROWTH

LEIF JOHANSEN

I. INTRODUCTION

The purpose of the present paper is to analyse some of the fundamental questions raised by Adam Smith, David Ricardo and other classical economists within the framework of a model which I think is a fair, though simplified, representation of their thinking. I do not claim to have obtained any original or surprising conclusions; the analysis corroborates the logic of classical analysis. The advantage of the present approach is that conclusions which were stated in qualitative terms by classical economists can be given in terms of the parameters of the model.

Since I shall use only well known and often quoted chapters and paragraphs, mainly from Smith and Ricardo, I do not find it necessary to give many references to the literature.

The main questions on which we shall concentrate are the following two:

A. Is growth in the long run possible or is stagnation inevitable?
B. Will the wage rate remain above subsistence level in the long run?

These were central questions in classical thinking on economic development. We shall be less concerned with other questions which have a more special flavour of earlier centuries.

The basic assumptions in classical growth theory which we shall retain throughout are the following:

I. Employment is determined by the amount of capital.
II. Population growth depends upon the wage rate.
III. Current wage rate is high when labour is scarce, and low when labour is abundant.
IV. Savings and investments are determined by profits.

I think these assumptions—which will be given more precise forms below—are obligatory in an analysis of economic growth on classical premises.

With respect to returns to scale and technical progress, which are also important for questions A and B, we shall try some different assumptions.

2. THE BASIC MODEL

We shall proceed on the basis of a one-commodity model. I think this is permissible for analysing the main questions mentioned in the introduction, but of course it prevents us from analysing some other questions which are also prominent in classical writings on growth or development.

We shall use the following notations:

X = total production per period of time;
K = capital stock;
N = total population;
L = employed labour;
w = wage rate in terms of goods; it corresponds with Ricardo's 'market price of labour';
w^* = natural wage rate, corresponding to Ricardo's 'natural price of labour'; its meaning will be clarified below;
π = total profits.

The natural wage rate w^* is assumed to be a given constant. The other symbols represent variables that are functions of time. When necessary we indicate this by $X(t)$, $K(t)$ etc., t being 'continuous time'.

We assume production and employment to be determined by capital by the following two equations:

$$X = f(K) \qquad (1)$$

$$L = bK, \qquad (2)$$

where f is a function and b is the (constant) labour/capital ratio. With constant returns to scale (1) is simply

$$X = aK, \qquad (1')$$

where a is a constant.

Equations (1) and (2) seem to imply capital having infinite life. However, we may let X be output net of depreciation, and the labour necessary for repair work to offset depreciation may be accounted for through b.

Equation (2) means that demand for labour is determined by capital stock. The momentary supply function for labour is written as

$$L = Ng(w - w^*), \qquad (3)$$

where function g is the *per capita* supply function for labour. We assume the supply of labour to increase with the wage rate, i.e. $g' > 0$. (3) can be inverted so as to be written

$$w = w^* + G(L/N), \qquad (4)$$

where we have introduced G for the inverse of the function g.

Here L/N measures the momentary scarcity of labour, and (4) gives the 'supply price' of labour. It represents Ricardo's expression: 'Labour is dear when it is scarce and cheap when it is plentiful.' (*Principles*, Chapter V.)

In the longer run labour supply is influenced by population growth, which is a function of the wage rate:

$$dN/dt = Nh(w - w^*). \tag{5}$$

We shall put

$$h(0) = 0, \quad \text{i.e. } dN/dt = 0 \quad \text{when } w = w^*, \tag{6}$$

which may be interpreted as an implicit definition of w^*; compare Ricardo's definition: 'The natural price of labour is that price which is necessary to enable the labourers, one with another, to subsist and to perpetuate their race, without either increase or diminution.' (*Principles*, Chapter V.)

We shall assume h to increase with $w - w^*$. The function $h(w - w^*)$ is obviously non-linear, but in some connections we shall employ the linear approximation

$$dN/dt = N\lambda(w - w^*) \quad (\lambda = h'(0)), \tag{7}$$

which will be valid when w is not too far away from w^*.

Profits are

$$\pi = X - wL. \tag{8}$$

In most cases we shall for simplicity assume that all profits are invested:

$$dK/dt = \pi. \tag{9}$$

However, we shall in some connections consider the effects of replacing (9) by

$$dK/dt = \alpha(\pi/K)\pi \tag{10}$$

where α, the ratio of profits invested, is assumed to be a function of the profit rate. It may be assumed that $\alpha(\pi/K) = 0$ for some critical value of π/K, and increases with π/K, approaching unity for large values of the profit rate.

Counting unknowns and equations, we now have six of both. A given initial capital stock $K(0)$ and population $N(0)$ is necessary to complete the system and to start it moving. Given $K(0)$, we see from (1) and (2) that $X(0)$ and $L(0)$ are determined. Then from (3) and the given $N(0)$, $w(0)$ is determined. Profits are determined by (8). The transition to 'the next moment of time' then follows from (5) and (9) or (10), and so the system moves.

3. THE CASE OF CONSTANT RETURNS TO SCALE

Let us first consider the case of constant returns to scale, i.e. the special case (1′) of (1). This may be approximately valid for a newly opened country, rich in natural resources, as exemplified by the classical economists by North America.

We define *a steady growth path* as one along which the wage rate w and the proportions between X, K, N, L and π remain constant, these latter variables growing at a common rate per period of time. Let $\bar{w}$ be the wage rate on such a path, and let the common growth rate for the other variables be r, i.e.

$$X(t) = X(0)\,e^{rt}, \quad K(t) = K(0)\,e^{rt}, \text{ etc.}$$

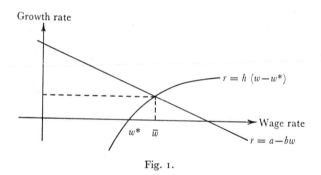

Fig. 1.

Now insert these assumptions in (1′), (2), (3), (5), (8) and (9). It is then easy to see that with appropriate proportions between the variables initially, a steady growth path will exist with a growth rate r and a wage rate $\bar{w}$ determined by the following two equations:

$$r = a - b\bar{w}, \tag{11}$$

$$r = h(\bar{w} - w^*). \tag{12}$$

The solution is shown in fig. 1.

It follows immediately that we have positive growth if and only if

$$a - bw^* > 0, \tag{13}$$

and furthermore, this condition also ensures a wage rate on the steady growth path permanently above the natural wage rate.

Condition (13) is easily interpreted: it simply says that production should yield a profit if labour were paid the natural wage rate. The difference $a - bw^*$ is simply the surplus, in terms of product, per unit of labour, above the natural wage rate.

With the linearized function (7) for the growth of population the solution of (11–12) is:

$$\bar{w} = \frac{a + \lambda w^*}{\lambda + b} = w^* + \frac{a - bw^*}{\lambda + b}, \tag{14}$$

$$r = \frac{a - bw^*}{1 + \frac{b}{\lambda}}. \tag{15}$$

Let us consider some classical conclusions in the light of these formulae. First observe that (14) and (15) imply

$$\bar{w} = w^* + \frac{r}{\lambda}, \tag{16}$$

i.e. for given w^* and λ the wage rate on the steady growth path is higher the higher is the growth rate. Compare this with Chapter VIII, Book I of *Wealth of Nations*: 'It is not the actual greatness of national wealth, but its continual increase, which occasions a rise in the wages of labour. It is not, accordingly, in the richest countries, but in the most thriving, or in those which are growing rich the fastest, that the wages of labour are highest.'† Furthermore, see Chapter V of Ricardo's *Principles*: 'Notwithstanding the tendency of wages to conform to their natural rate, their market rate may, in an improving society, for an indefinite period, be constantly above it; for no sooner may the impulse which an increased capital gives to a new demand for labour be obeyed, than another increase of capital may produce the same effect; and thus, if the increase of capital be gradual and constant, the demand for labour may give a continued stimulus to an increase of people.'

Next consider the role played by λ, which measures the effect of higher wages on population growth. A lower λ means a higher wage rate on the steady growth path, and a slower growth. The effect is of course that labour by making labour supply react more slowly to higher wages extracts a greater share of the surplus $(a - bw^*)$, and thereby also decreases accumulation.

It is also interesting to observe the effects of the natural wage rate w^*. This can be interpreted as a strictly defined subsistence wage rate, and then alternative levels are perhaps not interesting. But at least in Ricardo's work one finds the suggestion that w^* is not a subsistence wage rate in this sense, but rather a magnitude determined by 'habits and customs', and by sociological factors. Then one may ask: what is the effect upon

† It is usually assumed that the expression 'a rise in the wages' in the first period refers to a comparison between levels of wages rather than the rate of change through time. This would conform with (16).

the actual wage on a steady growth path of a higher natural wage rate?
From (14) we see that

$$\frac{d\overline{w}}{dw^*} = \frac{\lambda}{\lambda + b},\tag{17}$$

that means $\overline{w}$ increases with an increase in the natural wage rate, though
only by a fraction of the increase in w^*. It is interesting, particularly in
the light of later developments, to compare this with Ricardo's wishes
expressed in Chapter V of *Principles*: 'The friends of humanity cannot
but wish that in all countries the labouring classes should have a taste for
comforts and enjoyments, and that they should be stimulated by all legal
means in their exertions to procure them. There cannot be a better
security against a super-abundant population.'

All conclusions drawn above could be drawn also for the case (11–12)
without linearizing the function for the increase in population. A proportional shift in the function $h(\overline{w} - w^*)$ would correspond to a change in λ.

Replacing (9) by (10) we would still have a steady growth path in the
model, with (13) as a condition for positive growth. Instead of (11) we
would now get

$$r = \alpha(\pi/K)(a - b\overline{w}),\tag{18}$$

where the profit rate π/K is constant on the steady growth path. If α is
independent of π/K, it is obvious from fig. 1 that a value of α less than
unity would result in both a lower growth rate and a lower wage rate on
the steady growth path. If α does in fact depend on π/K, (18) and (12)
cannot be solved for r and $\overline{w}$ independently of the rest of the system, but it
is nevertheless clear that the same conclusion holds if only $\alpha(\pi/K) < 1$.

All conclusions above concerning r and $\overline{w}$ are independent of the form
$g(\ )$ of the momentary labour supply function. In fact, on the steady
growth path this function only serves to determine the ratio L/N. If we
study the stability of the steady growth path, this function is, however,
important.

Let us imagine a starting point at $t = 0$ with arbitrary values of $N(0)$
and $K(0)$ which do not correspond to the proportions on the steady
growth path. Let us assume that $N(0)$ is 'too big' in proportion to $K(0)$.
Total employment would be $L(0) = bK(0)$, which inserted in (3) or (4)
would yield a wage rate $w(0) < \overline{w}$. This would on the one hand make
population growth slower than on the steady growth path, and on the
other hand through higher profits give a faster accumulation. We would
by this get an increasing value of L/N, and by (4) an increasing w. The
same type of argument could be applied for an initial situation with 'too
small' population in proportion to capital. It appears that there is a convergence to the steady growth path. Furthermore, it is clear that the
momentary labour supply function, which does not influence $\overline{w}$ and r on

the steady growth path, does influence the wage rate and the growth rate when the economy is not on the steady growth path, and thereby also the speed with which it approaches this path.

4. DECREASING RETURNS TO SCALE

Clearly the classical economists believed that constant returns to scale would be prevalent only up to a certain level of production, after which one would encounter decreasing returns. Let us now analyse the working of the model for the general case (1) of the production function, where, at least for K above a certain level, average productivity $f(K)/K$ decreases with increasing K.

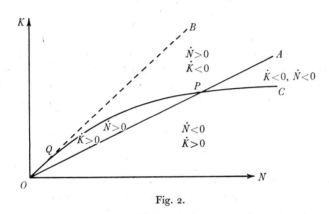

Fig. 2.

By insertion the model can now (using (9), not (10)), be reduced to the following two differential equations in N and K:

$$\frac{1}{K}\frac{dK}{dt} = \frac{f(K)}{K} - b\left[w^* + G\left(\frac{bK}{N}\right)\right],\tag{19}$$

$$\frac{1}{N}\frac{dN}{dt} = h\left(G\left(\frac{bK}{N}\right)\right).\tag{20}$$

We can draw some conclusions from this by means of fig. 2, in which N and K are measured along the two axes.

Consider first equation (20). Clearly $(1/N)(dN/dt)$ is constant for a constant ratio K/N. For a certain ratio K/N we will have $G(bK/N) = 0$, and accordingly $(1/N)(dN/dt) = 0$ (compare (6)). We can thus draw a beam OA from the origin in the diagram along which $(1/N)(dN/dt) = 0$. Furthermore, since both h and G are increasing functions, we will have $(1/N)(dN/dt) > 0$ above this line and $(1/N)(dN/dt) < 0$ below.

Next consider (19). If $f(K)/K$ were constant as in the previous section, $(1/K)(dK/dt)$ would be constant for a constant ratio K/N. We could then draw another beam OB through the origin along which $(1/K)(dK/dt) = 0$. Now $(1/K)(dK/dt)$ would be negative above this line and positive below. Evidently growth in both N and K would be possible if OB is above OA, and there would be a beam between OB and OA which would correspond to the steady growth path of the previous section. The condition that OB should be above OA is the same as condition (13).

However, we are now assuming that $f(K)/K$ will decrease with K, at least for values of K above a certain level. By implicit differentiation in the equation obtained by setting (19) equal to zero it is easy to verify that for points with such values of K the curve for $(1/K)(dK/dt) = 0$ will be less steep than a beam from the origin to the same point—i.e.

$$0 < (dK/dN) < K/N.$$

In fig. 2 we have drawn a curve OC for $(1/K)(dK/dt) = 0$ which first follows OB, representing constant returns to scale up to some value of K, and then (from Q) falls below OB as we encounter decreasing returns. $(1/K)(dK/dt)$ will be negative above OC and positive below OC.

In the diagram we have now four areas delimited by OA and OC, with different combinations of signs of $(1/N)(dN/dt)$ and $(1/K)(dK/dt)$. These are indicated by $\dot{N}$ and $\dot{K}$ being >0 or <0. P is evidently a stable equilibrium point, representing a stationary state. From any initial situation in the area $OQPO$ we will have continuous growth in both K and N, but the growth will slow down as we approach P. Asymptotically when $t \to \infty$ K and N will approach the values $\bar{K}$ and $\bar{N}$ which are obtained by setting both (19) and (20) equal to zero. These correspond to

$$\frac{f(\bar{K})}{\bar{K}} = bw^* \qquad\qquad (21)$$

$$G\left(\frac{b\bar{K}}{\bar{N}}\right) = 0. \qquad\qquad (22)$$

The first condition gives $\bar{K}$, which inserted in (22) gives $\bar{N}$.

Also from starting points outside the region $OQPO$ we would have convergence towards the same stationary state. From an economic point of view, situations above the curve for $\dot{K} = 0$ in the diagram are, however, implausible.

Condition (21) means that average capital productivity is just sufficient to pay the normal wage rate to the labour employed. Evidently $w = w^*$ in this stationary state.

During the growth process, i.e. when we are moving in the interior of $OQPO$, the wage rate will be above w^*. But it inevitably approaches w^* when we move towards P.

All this confirms the logic of the classical vision of an inevitable stationary state when there are decreasing returns to scale.

For completeness it should be mentioned that we may of course have a production function which does not obey the law of constant returns to scale, but nevertheless gives a curve OC which does not cross through OA. This is true when average productivity $f(K)/K$ decreases with K, but in such a way that it never reaches a value as low as bw^*.

Employing (10) instead of (9) will not change the reasoning about the approach to a stationary state in any essential way. It will, however, result in a stationary state at a lower level for N and K if $\alpha(\pi/K)$ reaches zero for a profit rate above zero. The same would be true if we introduced some marginalistic considerations into capitalists' investment decisions instead of the simple mechanism that they automatically invest the whole or a fraction of profits. As the formulae stand above, capitalists go on investing out of their profits even when this causes profits to be reduced. I think Ricardo is on some occasions reasoning *hypothetically* on the basis of such an assumption, but he hardly believed it to be realistic.

5. NEUTRAL TECHNICAL PROGRESS

In classical writings one can find some suggestions about technical progress postponing stagnation, perhaps for an infinite future. We shall consider two types of technical progress; first, in the present section, neutral technical progress, and thereafter labour-saving technical progress.

By neutral technical progress we shall simply mean positive shifts in the production function (1) which leave the labour/capital ratio b in (2) unaffected.

In the case of constant returns to scale a once-and-for-all technical change of this type would be represented by a positive shift in the constant a in (1'). It is seen from fig. 1 that this would shift the steady growth path to one with both a higher wage rate $\bar{w}$ and a higher growth rate r. The stability property of the steady growth path ensures that the actual development would gradually approach this new steady growth path after the shift in the productivity coefficient a.

Now consider technical progress going on continually according to

$$X(t) = a(t)K(t), \quad \dot{a} = \frac{da(t)}{dt} > 0, \tag{23}$$

where a is now an increasing function of time.

In this case we can reduce the system to the following two equations

$$\frac{1}{K}\frac{dK}{dt} = a - b\left[w^* + G\left(\frac{bK}{N}\right)\right] \qquad (24)$$

$$\frac{1}{N}\frac{dN}{dt} = h\left(G\left(\frac{bK}{N}\right)\right). \qquad (25)$$

Now steady growth in the sense defined in section 3 is no longer possible. This follows directly from (23). From the reasoning about the once-and-for-all change in productivity, it seems intuitively obvious that the growth rate of the economy and the wage rate will now be increasing in the long run.

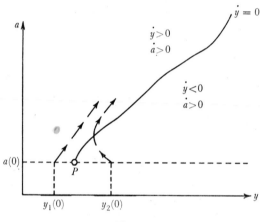

Fig. 3.

This can be more clearly seen by transforming (24) and (25) into a differential equation for capital per head, say y:

$$\frac{1}{y}\frac{dy}{dt} = a - [bw^* + bG(by) + h\{G(by)\}], \quad \text{where } y = K/N. \qquad (26)$$

The development generated by (26) can be studied by means of fig. 3. In this diagram y is measured along the horizontal axis and a along the vertical axes. Any initial situation $a(0)$, $y(0)$ is represented by a point in this diagram. Since $a(t)$ is increasing with t we are only interested in the part of the diagram lying above $a(0)$, the initial value of the productivity coefficient.

Now for any value of y there is a certain value of a which would make $\dot{y} = 0$, obtained by setting the expression in (26) equal to zero. This value of a would increase with y; it is represented by the curve starting from P in the diagram. Above this curve $\dot{y} > 0$, and below it $\dot{y} < 0$.

Now assume that $\dot{a} > 0$ everywhere in the diagram and that $a(t)$ increases beyond any limit with increasing t. We can then distinguish two cases. First assume that $y(0) = y_1(0)$ to the left of P. Then clearly y would be increasing with t right from the beginning. Next assume that $y(0) = y_2(0)$ to the right of P. Then y will first decrease; but the point must inevitably pass through the curve for $\dot{y} = 0$, and from then y will increase. (Also for the special case where $y(0)$ corresponds to the point P, one would clearly move into the region of $\dot{y} > 0$.) In the long run therefore y will increase, whatever initial value we start from. When y increases, the wage rate will also increase since we have

$$ w = w^* + G(by) \quad \text{with } G' > 0. $$

With the favourable combination of assumptions which we have now been considering, conditions for the workers could thus improve continually.

A more interesting question is perhaps whether technical progress can, in the long run, offset the effects of decreasing returns to scale so as to prevent the eventual approach of wages to the normal wage level in this case. The answer will of course depend on the more precise assumptions made. Let us consider the case of a logarithmic linear production function with a technical progress term, i.e.

$$ X = aK^{\mu}e^{\epsilon t}, \tag{27} $$

where μ is a constant, $0 < \mu < 1$, and ϵ is a positive constant.

By insertions we reduce the system to three equations in K, N and w:

$$ \frac{1}{K}\frac{dK}{dt} = aK^{\mu-1}e^{\epsilon t} - bw, \tag{28} $$

$$ \frac{1}{N}\frac{dN}{dt} = h(w - w^*), \tag{29} $$

$$ w = w^* + G\left(b\frac{K}{N}\right). \tag{30} $$

We cannot in this case reduce the number of equations by introducing capital per head, y, as we did in (26) since K appears separately on the right hand side of (28).

Is steady growth now possible? Try again

$$ \frac{1}{K}\frac{dK}{dt} = \frac{1}{N}\frac{dN}{dt} = r, \quad w = \bar{w}, \tag{31} $$

r and $\bar{w}$ being constant.

For this to satisfy (28) it is evident that the growth rate r must be such that the term $K^{\mu-1}e^{\epsilon t}$ remains constant through time, which requires

$$r = \frac{\epsilon}{1-\mu}. \tag{32}$$

The wage rate on the steady growth path is then, from (29),

$$\bar{w} = w^* + h^{-1}(r) = w^* + h^{-1}\left(\frac{\epsilon}{1-\mu}\right), \tag{33}$$

provided that the function h allows this solution, i.e. that there is a wage rate that makes population grow at the rate $\epsilon/(1-\mu)$.

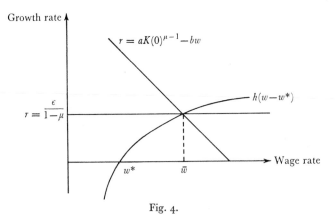

Fig. 4.

This steady growth requires a certain proportion between K and N as is seen from (30) when $\bar{w}$ is inserted from (33). Furthermore, it also requires that the economy starts at a certain level at $t = 0$. It is seen from equation (28) that $K(0)$ must satisfy

$$aK(0)^{\mu-1} - b\bar{w} = r, \tag{34}$$

where r and $\bar{w}$ are given by (32) and (33).

The whole situation is depicted in fig. 4, which corresponds to fig. 1 in the simpler situation with constant returns and no technical progress.

As is seen a solution for r and $\bar{w}$ will exist only if the function $h(w - w^*)$ reaches the level $\epsilon/(1-\mu)$ for some value of w.

The value of $K(0)$ is determined by the requirement that the straight line representing (34) shall pass through the solution point for r and $\bar{w}$. Such a value will always exist.

In contrast to the steady growth path studied in §3, we now have a steady growth path with a growth rate determined completely by parameters characterizing production conditions (provided that this is not so high that population cannot follow up). The wage rate on this steady growth path will be higher the faster is the growth, i.e. the higher is the rate of technical progress and the less marked is the decrease in returns.

Will this growth represent a stable growth path? I think a full mathematical treatment would prove that it does. Here we shall however be content with a more intuitive reasoning.

We assume initially that $K(o)/N(o)$ is lower than it would be on the steady growth path, which implies $w(o) < \bar{w}$. Furthermore we assume that $K(o)$ is smaller than it should be according to (34). Then it is seen from (28) that K would start growing at a higher rate, and from (29) that N would start growing at a lower rate than on the steady growth path. This would through (30) make for w to increase, which would again make $(1/K)(dK/dt)$ and $(1/N)(dN/dt)$ approach each other.

Alternatively, let us start with a ratio $K(o)/N(o)$ equal to what it should be on the steady growth path, and accordingly $w(o) = \bar{w}$, but with a lower initial capital stock than what we should have, according to (34), for steady growth. Then initially N would grow at a rate r, while K would grow at a higher rate. It is clear from (28) however that the growth rate for K would have to decline again, since with K growing at a rate higher than $r = \epsilon/(1-\mu)$, the term $K^{\mu-1}e^{\epsilon t}$ in (28) will decline. Also the movements of w would of course influence the development of K, and it would help to pull up the size of the population so as to approach the 'right' proportion again between K and N.

Such reasoning for different initial conditions seems to indicate that the steady growth path is indeed stable in the sense that we would approach such a growth path from an arbitrary initial situation.

The same conclusion can alternatively be obtained by trying to let K/N increase or decrease in the long run, both attempts leading to contradictions in the system (28–30).

The above discussion assumes that population can grow at a rate $\epsilon/(1-\mu)$. Let us briefly consider the case when $\epsilon/(1-\mu)$ is so high that population can not follow up. We then reasonably assume that population will in the long run grow at a maximal rate, say ν, so that

$$N(t) = N(o)e^{\nu t}. \tag{35}$$

Introducing now $y = K/N$ as we did in connection with (26), we get from (28) and (30):

$$\frac{1}{y}\frac{dy}{dt} = a[N(o)]^{\mu-1}y^{\mu-1}e^{[\epsilon+\nu(\mu-1)]t} - b[w^* + G(by)] - \nu. \tag{36}$$

In a similar way as for (26), it can be seen from (36) that y, and then also the wage rate, will increase in the long run on the assumptions now made.

6. LABOUR-SAVING TECHNICAL PROGRESS

This section is inspired by Ricardo's Chapter XXXI, '*On Machinery*'. The main problem raised there is whether 'such an application of machinery...as should have the effect of saving labour' could be 'injurious to the interests of the class of labourers.' And, as is well known, Ricardo's answer was affirmative.

From the standpoint of modern theory one would be inclined to investigate this question on the basis of a growth model with a shifting two-factor production function. However, I think we remain closer to classical assumptions by simply introducing the possibilities of 'labour saving' as shifts in the labour/capital ratio.

We shall do this within the framework of the model as used in § 3, i.e. we shall assume constant returns to scale. The interactions between labour-saving progress and the problems treated in §§ 4 and 5 would hardly give any further insight.

Let us first consider a once-and-for-all change in technology which can immediately be introduced in all production. In this we follow Ricardo: 'To elucidate the principle, I have been supposing that improved machinery is *suddenly* discovered and extensively used...'

We assume then that the economy has for a time been growing along the steady growth path, as explained in § 3, with technical coefficients a and b. Then suddenly the coefficients change to a' and b', with $b' < b$ so that the new technology implies less labour per unit of capital. We may have $a' > a$, $a' = a$ or $a' < a$; that means the introduction of new labour-saving technology may increase, leave unchanged or decrease the amount of production per unit of capital.

On the growth path before the switch in technology, the wage rate is $\bar{w}$, given by formula (14). With the sudden switch the wage rate must necessarily fall since the momentary wage rate is determined by (2) and (3), and N and K need time to change. Thus the immediate effect of the labour-saving switch in technology is detrimental to the wage-workers.

Because of the stability property of the steady growth path, the wage rate will however start moving towards a new level which will in general be different from $\bar{w}$. This new level will be

$$\bar{w}' = \frac{a' + \lambda w^*}{\lambda + b'}. \tag{37}$$

(For simplicity we use the linearized form (7) of (5).)

This new level is higher than the wage rate on the previous steady growth path if and only if the following condition is fulfilled:

$$\lambda[w^*(b - b') + (a' - a)] + ba' - ab' > 0. \tag{38}$$

This is always fulfilled if $a' \geqq a$. However, a more general and more interesting conclusion can be given.

Consider the profitability of the new technique. Being on the old steady growth path and considering the question of introducing the new technique (a', b') it is natural to evaluate the profitability of this technique by means of the current wage rate $\bar{w}$. Evaluated in this way the expected profit rate by the new technique will be

$$m' = a' - b'\bar{w} = a' - b' \frac{a + \lambda w^*}{\lambda + b}. \tag{39}$$

Consider now the condition for this expected profit rate by the new technique to be higher than the profit rate on the old steady growth path, i.e. the condition for

$$a' - b'\bar{w} > a - b\bar{w}. \tag{40}$$

This condition turns out to be equivalent to (38). Thus we have the conclusion: A labour-saving switch in technology causes an immediate fall in the wage rate, but in the long run the wage rate will increase towards a higher level than before the switch if the new technology is profitable. The effect is of course that, in spite of reduced demand for labour per unit of capital, the *rate of increase* of demand for labour will be higher after the switch because of faster accumulation.†

These results hold for the case of a once-and-for-all change in technology. If we now consider a never-ceasing flow of technological changes, the economy will evidently be chasing, but never reaching, a steadily moving target. The total effect of the technological changes on the wage level at a certain point of time, will then consist of two different tendencies: the positive long-term effects of labour-saving changes in a distant past, and the negative short-run effects of changes in the more immediate past. An interesting question is then: Is it possible that a continuous flow of labour-saving changes can produce a flow of negative short-run effects which will always dominate the positive long-run effects, i.e. that the latter will never catch up with the former?

We shall consider this question by assuming that $b = b(t)$ is a decreasing function of time, i.e.

$$\frac{db(t)}{dt} = \dot{b}(t) < 0, \tag{41}$$

while a remains constant. In this case we are sure that new technology will always appear more profitable than old technology, and consequently be preferred by capitalists.

---

† It should be noted that if the technology (a', b') is more profitable than (a, b) evaluated by means of the wage rate $\bar{w}$, it is also more profitable when evaluated by means of the wage rate $\bar{w}'$ on the new steady growth path, i.e. $a' - b'\bar{w}' > a - b\bar{w}'$.

It is convenient in this case to consider again the differential equation governing the development of capital per head, $y = K/N$. The equation now appears as

$$\frac{1}{y}\frac{dy(t)}{dt} = a - [w^* + G(b(t)\,y(t))]b(t) - h[G(b(t)\,y(t))]. \qquad (42)$$

We can study the properties of this equation in fig. 5 where y is measured along the horizontal axis and b along the vertical axis.

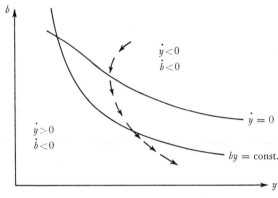

Fig. 5.

In this diagram we have drawn a curve representing b, y—points which give $\dot{y} = 0$. It is obtained by setting (42) equal to zero. This curve must evidently be falling with increasing y. From the way b and y enter the formula it is, furthermore, clear that the product by is increasing along this curve, which means that the curve in any point is less steep than the hyperbola $by = $ const. through the point.

Above this curve $\dot{y} < 0$, and below it $\dot{y} > 0$.

From any starting point $y(0), b(0)$, the economy will evidently enter upon a path of increasing y—after a temporary decline in y if $y(0), b(0)$ is above the curve for $\dot{y} = 0$.

What happens now to the wage rate? The wage rate is

$$w(t) = w^* + G(b(t)\,y(t)),$$

which means that it increases/decreases with increases/decreases of the product $b(t)\,y(t)$. The question then is whether the path followed by the y, b-point in the diagram will cut through hyperbolas $by = $ const. from above or from below. Apparently, it is possible that $\dot{b}$ is everywhere so big in absolute value that the y, b-point follows a path which cuts through these hyperbolas from above. Then $w(t)$ will be a decreasing function of time. This is the case indicated in the diagram.

Logically such a development could go on forever. It is thus theoretically possible that a continuous flow of labour-saving technological changes can produce a declining wage rate even in the long run.

Some of the arguments of this section could, I think, by changing the interpretation of the model, be related to the recent debate on choice of technique in economically underdeveloped countries. Furthermore, I think the arguments about the effects of a continuous flow of labour-saving technological changes could be related to some of Marx's ideas about the laws of development under capitalism. To pursue these matters would, however, be beyond the purpose of the present exposition.

THE INTEREST RATE
AND TRANSITION BETWEEN
TECHNIQUES†

ROBERT M. SOLOW

1. INTRODUCTION

Recent discussion of the pure theory of interest and capital‡ has elucidated such matters as the 'switching of (discrete) techniques' when the
rate of interest changes, the possibility that the same technique or set of
techniques should 'recur' at different rates of interest, and the accompanying variation in 'degree of mechanization', value of capital, and
net output or consumption. In this discussion, the rate of interest has
generally been treated as a parameter, whose exogenous variation
sweeps out alternative steady states. One consequence of this approach is
that an important property of the interest rate has been overlooked:
through all vicissitudes of 'normal' and 'perverse' cases, however the
rate of interest is actually determined, so long as full employment and
competitive pricing prevail, the interest rate is an accurate measure of
the social rate of return to saving. There follows a proof of this basic
proposition, and a few comments on its implications.

2. TECHNOLOGICAL ASSUMPTIONS

The economy produces n commodities and uses one primary unpro-
ducible input called labour. There is no joint production; thus one can
speak unambiguously of n industries, one for each commodity. Each
industry knows a finite number of activities; an activity of the i-th
industry, when operated at unit level, produces one unit of the i-th
commodity, uses up specified stocks of each of the n commodities which
must be made available in advance, and requires a specified input of

† I owe the origin of this paper to correspondence with my former student, Professor
Edwin Burmeister of the University of Pennsylvania, and to conversations with my colleagues
Paul A. Samuelson and Michael Bruno.

‡ M. Dobb, *Economic Growth and Planning* (New York, 1960); D. Levhari, 'A Non-substitu-
tion Theorem and Switching of Techniques', *Quarterly Journal of Economics*, February 1965;
M. Morishima, *Equilibrium, Stability, and Growth* (Oxford, 1964), p. 126; L. Pasinetti, 'Changes
in the Rate of Profit and Switches of Technique', *Quarterly Journal of Economics*, November
1966; J. Robinson, *The Accumulation of Capital* (London, 1956), pp. 109–10 and 417–18;
P. Sraffa, *Production of Commodities by Means of Commodities* (Cambridge, 1960); J. Stiglitz,
'Notes on the Switching of Techniques', February 1966, unpublished.

labour. Each activity is subject to constant returns to scale, and different activities combine additively. This is a circulating-capital technology. (The introduction of fixed capital would involve a certain kind of joint production, but the results can be extended easily to that case.) A single activity is fully described by a column vector giving its input requirements and its labour requirement at unit level; one must also remember which commodity it produces. A selection of one activity for each industry is called a technique of production. It is fully described by its $n \times n$ matrix of non-negative input coefficients and its $1 \times n$ row vector of non-negative labour-requirement coefficients. One might describe this as a generalized Leontief technology.

3. PRICING ASSUMPTIONS

Consider a particular technique of production, its input matrix a and its labour requirement vector a_0. Let r be the rate of interest, w the wage in any unit of account, and p a row vector of commodity prices in the same unit of account. They are a long run competitive equilibrium provided

$$p = (1+r)pa + wa_0. \tag{1}$$

It is assumed that all commodities are actually produced, and that wages are paid at the end of the production process—otherwise it is necessary merely to replace w by $w(1+r)$.

The system (1) is discussed in many places in the literature; I shall not bother with details here. The technique a is 'viable' at the interest rate r if (1) has a non-negative solution for p/w. If a is viable at r, it is viable for any non-negative interest rate less than r. Assume the technology is sufficiently productive that some techniques are viable for positive r. Now consider a non-negative interest rate at which there is a viable technique. It is known† that at that interest rate there will be one or more viable techniques yielding a p/w unambiguously—component by component—less than or equal to the p/w corresponding to any other viable techniques. If there is only one such technique, it is the only one that can survive competition at the given interest rate, because it can offer the highest real wage in terms of any and every commodity. If there are two or more such techniques, they have exactly the same price vector p/w. They can coexist. Suppose that at the interest rate r only a is competitive, but that as we consider slightly lower interest rates there comes a point r^* at which both a and b are competitive, while for still smaller r only b is competitive. Then we say that r^* is a 'switching point' for a and b; at the interest rate r^*, (1) and its analogue for b give the same p/w.

† Levhari, *op. cit.*, p. 98; Morishima, *op. cit.*, p. 126; Sraffa, *op. cit.*, Ch. XII.

4. THE RATE OF RETURN IN A SIMPLE CASE

Suppose the available labour force is constant, equal to L, and imagine an economy in competitive equilibrium in a steady state using technique a. If x is the $n{\times}1$ column vector of activity levels (or outputs) and c the vector of consumption, then

$$x = c + ax. \qquad (2)$$

I write (2) in that form to emphasize that out of this period's output x must come this period's consumption c and the circulating capital ax necessary to repeat the performance next period. Now imagine the economy tries by next period to get into a new steady state using technique b, with output y and consumption c^*, where

$$y = c^* + by. \qquad (3)$$

I am assuming that a and b are neighbouring techniques in the sense that there is an interest rate at which they are both capable of surviving competition from all other techniques, i.e. an efficient switching-point between them. I am not worrying how the economy decides to change from one steady state to another. For my purposes it is enough to think of the economy as centrally planned; but it would be interesting to study how the thing might be done in a decentralized capitalist economy. Michael Bruno has made a start in that direction.†

To get from (2) to (3) in one period, the economy will have to provide circulating capital (by) out of its current output (x). Thus consumption will have to be reduced temporarily to $\bar{c}$, where

$$x = \bar{c} + by. \qquad (4)$$

Here it is tacitly assumed that $\bar{c}$ is non-negative, i.e. that x is component by component not less than by. There is no particular reason for that to be so; if it is not so, the economy can not get from x to y in one period. Alternative slow transitions are discussed later. If the transition is accomplished, the economy will have sacrificed consumption $c - \bar{c}$ during one period to achieve a perpetual gain in consumption $c^* - c$. (The sacrifice and the gain could be a gain and a sacrifice, but that makes no difference.) The sacrifice and the gain have to be valued before they can be compared. Set $w = 1$, let r^* be the interest rate at which a and b both compete, and let p^* be the corresponding price vector. Then the natural definition of the social rate of return to saving, R, is the ratio of the perpetual consumption gain to the initial one-time sacrifice:

$$R = \frac{p^*(c^* - c)}{p^*(c - \bar{c})}. \qquad (5)$$

† M. Bruno, *On Growth, Duality and Choice of Technique'*, unpublished notes, 1966.

Note that if only one of the commodities is ever consumed, the prices drop out of the definition of R, leaving a purely physical concept. If only the fixed-composition basket of commodities were consumed, then a new composite commodity could be introduced in place of one of the natural commodities, and exactly the same thing could be accomplished.

From (2) and (4) it follows that $c - \bar{c} = by - ax$; from (2) and (3) it follows that $c^* - c = (I-b)y - (I-a)x$. Thus

$$R = \frac{p^*(I-b)y - p^*(I-a)x}{p^*by - p^*ax}.$$

Now, from (1), $p^*(I-a)x = r^*p^*ax + a_0x = r^*p^*ax + L$. Since b also competes at (r^*, p^*) analogously $p^*(I-b)y = r^*p^*by + b_0y = r^*p^*by + L$. Therefore

$$R = \frac{r^*p^*by + L - r^*p^*ax - L}{p^*by - p^*ax} = r^*.$$

This is the basic proposition I set out to prove. The interest rate at which a and b can both compete is equal to the social rate of return on saving in passing from a steady state with technique a to a steady state with technique b.† If a is competitive at interest rates r_a slightly higher than r^*, and b is competitive at interest rates r_b slightly lower, then in general

$$r_a \geqq R \geqq r_b,$$

which is as much as one can hope for in a discrete technology. As the number of techniques becomes larger and the gaps between them shrink, every interest rate becomes a switching point and this minor indeterminacy vanishes in the limit.

5. SLOWER TRANSITIONS

This theorem is not limited to the case where the transition from one steady state to another is made in one period. Indeed, if x is not component-by-component greater than by, the transition can not be made in one period. I sketch the argument for a slow—asymptotic—transition which is always possible if every commodity enters, however slightly, into consumption, and is sometimes possible even if the consumption vector c contains zero elements.

Return to (2) and (4) and suppose that it is not true that $x \geqq by$, so that one cannot write (4) with non-negative $\bar{c}$. It may yet be true that

$$x = \bar{c} + gby + hax \quad (\bar{c} \geqq 0), \tag{6}$$

† Mr Eytan Sheshinski has pointed out to me that a and b may be the *same* technique throughout this argument. So the rate-of-return property of the interest rate is proved also for variations in the consumption-bundle within the same technique, i.e. at every point on the factor-price frontier.

where g and h are positive numbers adding to one. The point is that the case $g = 0$, $h = 1$ is simply (2); the case $g = 1$, $h = 0$ is (4). If the transition from (2) to (3) in one step is impossible, the transition from (2) to some weighted average of (2) and (3) in one step is always possible if $c > 0$ and may be possible in other cases as well. If (6) is possible, then in the next period output will be $gy + hx$. This makes possible consumption $gc^* + h\bar{c}$, and circulating capital $g(1 + h)by + h^2ax$ (one little sub-economy like (3) at scale g, and one like (4) at scale h, with the labour force allocated accordingly). The resulting output is $g(1 + h)y + h^2x$, which can be made to yield consumption $g(1 + h)c^* + h^2\bar{c}$ and circulating capital $g(1 + h + h^2)by + h^3ax$. The limit of this process is obviously consumption of $(g/1 - h)c^* = c^*$ and circulating capital of $(g/1 - h)by = by$. That is, the process goes from (2) asymptotically to (3) along a kind of geometric path.

The k-th term in the consumption path is $g(1 + h + \dots + h^{k-1})c^* + h^k\bar{c}$. If the transition is not attempted, consumption stays at c. For comparison purposes, value all consumption at the switching-prices p^*. (If there is a fixed bundle of consumption goods this is unnecessary.) Now the natural definition of the social rate of return to saving, R, is the discount rate that gives the two alternative consumption streams the same present value. Some calculation with geometric series shows that

$$R = g \frac{p^*(c^* - c)}{p^*(c - \bar{c})},$$

which becomes the one-period transition of the previous section, as it should, when $g = 1$. Together (2) and (6) imply that $c - \bar{c} = g(by - ax)$. From this point, the procedure used in the preceding section leads directly to the conclusion that $R = r^*$.

That this result is quite general is shown by the following line of argument, whose scope goes well beyond the model used in this paper.† Consider any path along which prices and interest rate are constant and appropriate to the a and b techniques. Let C_t and V_t be the values of consumption and stock of capital goods at those prices. Then the collection of normal competitive price relationships will guarantee that

$$wL_t + rV_t = C_t + V_{t+1} - V_t.$$

Consider any other path with the same prices, interest rate, and employment: $wL_t + rV_t^1 = C_t^1 + V_{t+1}^1 - V_t^1$. By subtraction,

$$V_{t+1} - V_{t+1}^1 = (1 + r)(V_t - V_t^1) + (C_t^1 - C_t).$$

† Paul Samuelson convinced me that this kind of proof would clarify the meaning of the basic proposition.

Therefore

$$V_t - V_t^1 = (1+r)^t(V_0 - V_0^1) + \sum_{j=0}^{t-1} (1+r)^{t-j-1}(C_t^1 - C_t).$$

Let $t = 0$ be the last period in which $V_t = V_t^1$, and divide by $(1+r)^t$. The result is

$$\frac{C_0^1 - C_0}{1+r} + \frac{C_1^1 - C_1}{(1+r)^2} + \dots + \frac{C_{t-1}^1 - C_{t-1}}{(1+r)^t} = \frac{V_t - V_t^1}{(1+r)^t}$$

Now let $t \to \infty$ and suppose that the two paths are such that

$$(1+r)^{-t}(V_t - V_t^1) \to 0$$

(this will surely be the case if V_t and V_t^1 are eventually constant, e.g. if both paths tend to steady states). Then clearly r is the rate of return associated with the transition in question. It is easy to apply this procedure to the specific technology of this paper.

6. THE CASE OF A SINGLE CONSUMPTION GOOD AND AN APPARENT PARADOX

There are cases where even (6) is not possible. In particular, if there is only one consumer good—or at least one commodity that is not consumed —a difficulty may arise. For instance, if some element of by exceeds the corresponding element of x, and if the corresponding element of c is zero, then (6) is impossible with non-negative $\bar{c}$ and positive g and h. The y steady state requires more of some pure intermediate good than the x steady state produces (and requires). Any weighted average of x and y will also require more of that input than is available. I shall simply assume without investigating further that there is some feasible path leading from x to y which preserves full employment of labour and uses only the a and b techniques *en route*.

Now a paradox appears. There is only one consumption good, so the social rate of return, as I have defined it in the preceding section, is independent of commodity prices. Now suppose that techniques a and b are competitive at two or more distinct interest rates. Then I seem to be asserting that whenever a transition occurs from a to b, the social rate of return is equal to the competitive interest rate; but the physical act of transition from a to b is exactly the same whatever the interest rate. How can the rate of return on that transition be equal to two or more different interest rates?

The answer reveals something about the 're-switching' or 'recurrence' phenomenon. It has long been a familiar fact that a one-dimensional time-sequence of net benefits can be reduced to zero by more than one discount rate, i.e. such a sequence can have more than one 'marginal efficiency' or rate of return. It seems to be the case that if a and b are competitive at more than one interest rate, the feasible consumption paths between them must admit more than one rate of return. Any interest rate at which the two techniques can compete will serve as a rate of return.

Consider an artificially simple case. Suppose it is possible to get from x to y in three steps: the first step uses technique a at level x^1 and technique b at level y^1; the second step goes to levels x^2 and y^2; the third step goes to the (b, y, c^*) steady state, always with full employment and full use of circulating capital. Then

$$x = ax + c,$$

$$x = ax^1 + by^1 + c^1,$$

$$x^1 + y^1 = ax^2 + by^2 + c^2, \qquad (7)$$

$$x^2 + y^2 = by + c^3,$$

$$y = by + c^*.$$

In (7), the c vectors have only their first components different from zero (denoted c_0, c_1, c_2, c_3, c_*). Let $s = 1 + R$. A little calculation shows that if R is a rate of return for this transition-path, then s must be a root of

$$(c_0 - c_1)s^3 + (c_1 - c_2)s^2 + (c_2 - c_3)s + (c_3 - c_*) = 0. \qquad (8)$$

No harm can come from valuing the consumption vectors at any set of prices satisfying (1) or its analogue for b, because all the components of each consumption vector vanish except the first, leaving just a scalar multiple of (8). Now use of (1), (7), and full employment in (8) shows that (8) vanishes whenever $s = 1 + r^*$. If a and b admit several distinct values of r^*, then the transition-paths must be such as to admit the same distinct values of R. The connection between 'recurrence' and multiplicity of marginal efficiencies† is very close indeed. And there is no paradox any more. (If, as may be the case, all feasible paths from a to b require some inequalities in (7), then only an inequality relation between r^* and R can be established.)

7. GROWING LABOUR FORCE

There is no need to limit this analysis to stationary states. All the reasoning goes through if the labour force is growing geometrically at the rate m per period, and all comparisons are between steady states growing at this same natural rate. To show this, I return to the simple one-period transi-

† M. Bruno, E. Burmeister, E. Sheshinski, *The Nature and Implications of the Reswitching of Techniques*, *Quarterly Journal of Economics*, November 1966; Stiglitz, *Notes on the Switching of Techniques*.

tion of § 4. Because the whole system is growing at rate m, (2) to (4) become·

$$x = c + (1+m)ax, \qquad (2')$$

$$y = c^* + (1+m)by, \qquad (3')$$

$$x = \bar{c} + (1+m)by. \qquad (4')$$

Hence $\qquad p^*(c - \bar{c}) = (1+m)(p^*by - p^*ax)$

and $\qquad p^*(c^* - c) = p^*(y - x) - (1+m)(p^*by - p^*ax).$

From (1) and its analogue for technique b,

$$p^*(y - x) = (1+r^*)(p^*by - p^*ax).$$

Thus $p^*(c^* - c) = (r^* - m)(p^*by - p^*ax)$. (Which, by the way, proves the 'Golden Rule'.)

In the growing economy, the one-period transition amounts to a sacrifice of $c - \bar{c}$ in consumption in the current period in return for a stream of consumption gains equal to $(1+m)(c^* - c)$ next period, $(1+m)^2(c^* - c)$ in the period after that, and so on. The social rate of return is the discount rate R which discounts the value of this stream to the value of the current consumption foregone. Naturally the values are calculated at prices p^*; this operation is unnecessary if there is a fixed consumption bundle. It is easily calculated that

$$R = m + (1+m)\frac{p^*(c^* - c)}{p^*(c - c)} = m + (1+m)\frac{(r^* - m)}{(1+m)} = r^*$$

exactly as before.

8. SOME IMPLICATIONS

The literature mentioned earlier gives major attention to the possibility that a technique may disappear as the interest rate falls, and then reappear as the interest rate falls further. In the notation of this paper, it is possible that technique a should give way to b at interest rates slightly less than r^*, and that b should then give way to a at interest rates slightly less than $r^{**} < r^*$. A rather more important phenomenon has been less studied: in models with a single (perhaps composite) consumption good, it is possible that steady-state consumption per head should be lower in a steady state with a lower interest rate. This cannot be true for all interest rates; the Golden Rule tells us that steady-state consumption per head must be a decreasing function of the interest rate for interest rates slightly greater than the natural rate of growth. This phenomenon is related to 'recurrence', but they are not the same: in a technology with smoothly diminishing returns to variable proportions (or perhaps if only one commodity using labour and at least one other input in an indecomposable system has that kind of technology), it is not possible for a whole technique to 'recur', but it is possible for steady-state consumption per head to be an increasing function of the steady-state interest rate for some range or ranges.

Both phenomena, 'recurrence' of technique and perverse behaviour of consumption per head with the interest rate, point to a weakness in the 'neoclassical parable'. Evidently there are situations in which one can not speak safely of 'capital deepening' as the concomitant of both lower interest rate and higher steady-state consumption per head. But neither phenomenon, so far as I can see, subverts neoclassical capital theory in its full generality. They do suggest some further investigation of the microeconomics of the perverse cases.

The proposition proved in this paper pinpoints the nature of the problem, or of one of the problems. Equation (5) tells us that, come what may, the sign of $p^*(c^* - c)$ is the same as the sign of $p^*(c - \bar{c})$, so long as the interest rate is positive. Society always earns extra consumption later in return for consumption foregone now. If steady state b involves lower consumption than steady state a, society can pass from a to b without saving, in fact by splashing itself with some extra consumption in the transition. If b also involves a lower interest rate than a, the paradox resides in the fact that society can get from a steady state with higher interest rate to a steady state with lower interest rate without saving, in fact by splashing itself with some extra consumption in the transition. This paper shows directly how a planned economy could in fact make those transitions; it remains an open question whether the perverse cases are peculiar in other respects in the context of decentralized profit-maximizing capitalism.

The argument of this paper also provides an answer to a question once asked by Mr Dobb:†

'An initial question that arises concerns the practical meaning to be given ...to the "rate of transformation of present goods into future goods", or "the marginal productivity of investment". This is quite commonly treated as being analogous (if not identical) with the rate of profit that the investment would earn in a capitalist economy: i.e. with the future product of investment after first deducting the values of *other* factors of production such as labour, employed along with the capital goods in question. But when we are looking at the matter from the social standpoint, why should profitability be the criterion, even if we ignore external effects? Why should not the *social* return on investment be regarded as being the *total* resulting addition to national output, without any such deduction of the values of other factors?'

† Dobb, *op. cit.*, p. 16.

The answer is that it is both, so long as the 'addition to national out-put' is understood as the addition to national consumption. And so long as other factors are valued at their competitively-imputed shadow prices.

If the prices and interest rate are those at the 'switching point' then the result is exact if labour continues to be paid its old wage; it holds for small. finite changes in consumption in either direction. If the initial prices and interest rate are not those at the switching point, then the in-equality at the end of section 4 above is all one can assert; the rate of return will differ for small increases and decreases in consumption. As the number of techniques gets 'dense', the inequalities become a limiting equality; the difference between infinitesimal forward and backward movements—and the accompanying change in the real wage—become second-order small quantities. Of course for finite changes, one is back to inequalities.

TERMINAL CAPITAL
AND OPTIMUM SAVINGS†

AMARTYA K. SEN

I. THE FUNDAMENTAL RELATIONS

There are at least three political elements in the formulation of an optimum savings exercise in terms of maximizing the sum of utilities within a finite horizon, viz. (i) the choice of the utility function, (ii) the choice of the time horizon, and (iii) the choice of the terminal stock of capital. Of this the first problem is an inevitable part of any optimization exercise, but the latter two are the results of confining our attention to a finite time period. However, such finite programmes fit in more easily with the convenience of planning, and the question is not really one of a completely arbitrary break in the future, since the terminal stock of capital provides an adjustable link between the period within the horizon and the period beyond. It could even be argued that if problem (iii) is well solved, the arbitrariness of problem (ii) can be satisfactorily eliminated.

Much of this note is concerned with problem (iii). We shall assume that the problems (i) and (ii) have already been solved in a simple manner, so that the exercise has already been reduced to one of maximizing the sum of utilities given by a specified utility function, over a given time period T. The utility function depends only on consumption, $C(t)$, and is taken to be of the constant elasticity type, beyond a 'subsistence' consumption, $\bar{C}$.

$$U(t) = A.[C(t) - \bar{C}]^\alpha. \tag{1}$$

For a concave utility function with diminishing marginal utility, we assume $\alpha < 1$. The marginal utility is given by:

$$u(t) = \frac{dU(t)}{dC} = A.\alpha.[C(t) - \bar{C}]^{\alpha-1}. \tag{1A}$$

To simplify our calculations, we choose our units such that $(A.\alpha)$ equals unity. There is no loss of generality involved here, and it is only a problem of normalization. Thus modified, the marginal utility can be taken to be:

$$u(t) = [C(t) - \bar{C}]^{\alpha-1}. \tag{1B}$$

† An earlier version of this note was written in 1964 when the author was Visiting Professor of Economics at the University of California at Berkeley. I have benefited from the comments of Sukhamoy Chakravarty, Richard Goodwin, Jan Graaff, and Stephen Marglin. I am also very grateful to Maurice Dobb for clarifying some of the issues discussed in this note.

We assume a constant output-capital ratio (b), so that the rate of accumulation is given by:

$$\dot{K}(t) = b.K(t) - C(t), \tag{2}$$

The sum of utility over the period up to T, we call 'period welfare', or simply welfare, denoted by W.

$$W = \int_0^T U[C(t)].dt. \tag{3}$$

The problem is to maximize W, subject to the initial condition:

$$K(0) = K_0 \tag{4}$$

and a terminal stock, K_T, the decisions on which will be our primary concern, in what follows.

With $\overline{C}$ subsistence consumption, we can define a subsistence capital stock ($\overline{K}$), such that

$$\overline{K} = \frac{\overline{C}}{b}. \tag{5}$$

We can define over-subsistence capital stock, $S(t)$, as the capital stock over and above $\overline{K}$.

$$S(t) = K(t) - \overline{K}. \tag{6}$$

The terminal capital stock, K_T, can be specified in terms of the initial stock, as Chakravarty† does. Since he takes $\overline{C} = 0$, $K(t)$ can be expressed as simply an accumulated value of K_0 at the exponential rate (g) to be chosen. This is not convenient in our exercise, however, since $\overline{C} \geqq 0$, but we can use the same device for $S(T)$.

$$K_T = S(0).e^{gT} + \overline{K}. \tag{7}$$

We know of course, from (6), that

$$S(0) = K_0 - \overline{K}. \tag{6A}$$

Since over-subsistence capital cannot grow faster than at the rate b (corresponding to zero over-subsistence consumption), we require $g \leqq b$.

Within these conditions, the optimal time path of capital can be obtained by solving the Euler–Lagrange equation, and checking that the second-order conditions are also satisfied.‡

$$S(t) = A_1.e^{bt} + A_2.e^{bt/(1-\alpha)}. \tag{8}$$

The two constants, A_1 and A_2, are solved by using the initial and the terminal conditions, i.e. equations (4) and (7), taken with equation (6A).

† S. Chakravarty, 'Optimal Savings with Finite Planning Horizon', *International Economic Review*, September 1962.

‡ See Chakravarty, p. 343. Note that the case $\alpha = 0$ is avoided, when we get multiple roots.

Then by using equation (2), and remembering that $\dot{K}(t) = \dot{S}(t)$, we obtain the following optimal time path of consumption:

$$C(t) = \frac{S(0) \cdot \alpha \cdot b \cdot (e^{bT} - e^{gT})}{(1 - \alpha)(e^{bT/(1-\alpha)} - e^{bT})} \cdot e^{bt/(1-\alpha)} + \bar{C}. \qquad (9)$$

The political difficulties in choosing K_T, or what comes to the same thing here, g, has been discussed extensively by Graaff.† We would like to go into this problem, but before that we must examine a result of Chakravarty that 'the best consumption profiles are, in general, insensitive to changes in terminal capital stock within a wide range' (p. 342). Chakravarty obtains the result on the basis of some numerical examples. We shall instead try first to get an algebraic formula for 'sensitivity' and then apply his numerical values and other ones.

2. SENSITIVITY OF BEST CONSUMPTION PROFILES TO VARIATIONS IN TERMINAL CAPITAL

It is readily seen from equation (9) that the optimum consumption profiles all have an exponential component and a constant component. It is, naturally, the former component that is dependent on the assumption of the terminal capital stock. But it will also be noticed that the exponential growth rate of over-subsistence consumption is given simply by $b/(1-\alpha)$, which is independent of g, i.e. of our terminal assumption. In fact writing $x(t)$ for over-subsistence consumption at time t, we can easily check that:‡

$$x(t) = x(0) \cdot e^{bt/(1-\alpha)} \qquad (9A)$$

This means that an idea of the sensitivity of the whole path of $x(t)$ can be obtained by examining the sensitivity of $x(0)$ to the terminal assumption. We define a 'sensitivity indicator', η, by the following:

$$\eta = \left| \frac{dx(0)}{dg} \middle/ \frac{x(0)}{g} \right| \qquad (10)$$

We take the absolute value of the elasticity of $x(0)$ with respect to g, since we are interested in the magnitude of the elasticity and not in its sign, which, incidentally, will be always negative.

From (9), (9A) and (10), we get:

$$\eta = \frac{g \cdot T \cdot e^{gT}}{e^{bT} - e^{gT}}. \qquad (11)$$

† J. de V. Graaff, *Theoretical Welfare Economics* (Cambridge, 1957), Chapter VI.
‡ This corresponds to the Ramsey result that marginal return to capital must equal the rate of fall of marginal utility, in an optimal path. (See F. P. Ramsey, 'A Mathematical Theory of Saving', *Economic Journal*, December 1928.)

Following Chakravarty,[†] we take $T = 20$, and $b = 0\cdot33$. We try out the following ten values of g. The sensitivity is seen to be quite great for high values of g.[‡]

Table 1. *Terminal capital assumption (g) and the sensitivity of over-subsistence consumption (η)*

g	η	g	η
0·05	0·004	0·29	4·733
0·10	0·020	0·30	7·300
0·15	0·084	0·31	12·610
0·20	0·321	0·32	28·920
0·25	1·265	0·325	61·759

Since Chakravarty took values of g within the closed range $(0\cdot05, 0\cdot15)$, the sensitivity was very small. So his result is entirely correct. But since this low sensitivity result is not generally valid, i.e. is not independent of the numerical assumption, the question arises as to what is the relevant range for g. As higher values of g are taken, the sensitivity indicator rises abruptly, and with g approaching b, grows without bound.

How big a change is one from $g = 0\cdot05$ to $g = 0\cdot15$? It shifts the size of final over-subsistence capital from being 2·7 times the initial level to 20 times the initial level. But in the same period, over-subsistence consumption (in his model total consumption) grows about sixty thousand times, given by $e^{bT/(1-\alpha)}$, when $b = 0\cdot33$, $T = 20$, $\alpha = 0\cdot4$. If we treat this as total consumption, a shift of capital stock from 2·7 times to 20 times the initial level is not really very big. If, instead, we assume the existence of a considerable subsistence level, the proportionate growth of *total* consumption will of course be very much less; the phenomenally high rate of growth of over-subsistence consumption is coupled with starting at a level very near zero. But in that case a shift from $g = 0\cdot05$ to $g = 0\cdot15$ does not change the *total* terminal capital stock very much. Indeed assuming that 90 per cent of the initial output represents subsistence requirement (as seems to be the case in some underdeveloped countries), that shift changes total capital stock from being 1·2 times the original value to 2·9 times that, which is a much narrower change.

Thus while Chakravarty's insensitivity result is entirely correct for the range of values he confined his attention to, it does not eliminate the

† Chakravarty, *op. cit.*

‡ Since this paper was written, a similar point has been made by A. Maneschi, in his 'Optimal Savings with Finite Planning Horizon: A Note', *International Economic Review*, Vol. 7, January 1966. See also Chakravarty's 'Reply' in the same number.

need for facing Graaff's problem† of the determination of the terminal capital stock. In the sections that follow, we concern ourselves with this question.

3. DEFINITION AND USE OF A 'TERMINAL MARGIN'

What consistitutes a 'proper' terminal stock? It is reasonable to argue that if the stock $K(T)$ does not succeed in producing an output equal to the terminal consumption $C(T)$, there is trouble immediately after the period, for even at zero saving, the economy has to take on a decline in the consumption level. This is in fact what does happen in models of the kind discussed, since the optimality problem as posed there does imply considerable 'eating up' of capital for consumption purposes, in the last few moments. $K(T)$ can, however, be so selected as to prevent this. In fact, we may go further and assume that $K(T)$ should be sufficient to produce enough output to invest a certain proportion of it, say λ, and still be left with $C(T)$ consumption as determined by the optimum path. We require that $1 > \lambda \geqq 0$. In fact, $\lambda = 0$, corresponds to the first case of no investment.

We can call λ the 'terminal margin'. If $\lambda = 0\cdot1$, this means that the terminal capital should be big enough to allow 10 per cent saving of the output in year T, and even after that there would be enough output left to meet the entire requirement of consumption as given by the optimal path for period T. The terminal margin being positive prevents the possibility of an immediate drop in consumption just beyond the horizon. The value judgment about how much of a margin over and above this should be left for the society at point T, is expressed pithily by the choice of a λ from the interval $(0, 1)$.

We now follow up the optimization problem in terms of such a margin. We retain, however, equations (8) and (9A), giving us the optimal growth rules for capital and consumption. As in the previous exercise:

$$K_0 - \bar{K} = S(0) = A_1 + A_2. \tag{12}$$

We know from (2), (8), and (12), when $\dot{S}(0)$ refers to the right-hand derivative of $S(t)$ with respect to time at $t = 0$:

$$x(0) = S(0).b - \dot{S}(0)$$
$$= A_2.b.z \tag{13}$$

putting
$$z = \frac{\alpha}{\alpha - 1}. \tag{13A}$$

† Graaff, *op. cit.*, Chapter VI.

Since $\alpha < 1$, z is negative when $\alpha > 0$ and positive when $\alpha < 0$. The case $\alpha = 0$ is avoided (see footnote ‡, p. 41). From (13) and (9A), we have:

$$A_2 = \frac{x(T) . e^{(b.T)/(\alpha-1)}}{b.z} \tag{14}$$

In view of the postulated terminal condition:

$$x(T) = S(T).(1-\lambda).b \tag{15}$$

From (6A), (8), (13), (14), and (15), the value of $x(0)$ is found to be:

$$x(0) = \frac{b.z.(1-\lambda).e^{bzT}}{z+(1-\lambda)(e^{bzT}-1)} [K_0 - \bar{K}]. \tag{16}$$

Note that for $\lambda < 1$, $x(0) > 0$, no matter whether $z > 0$, or < 0. And this, coupled with (9), gives the optimum consumption profile:

$$C(t) = \bar{C} + x(0).e^{(b.t)/(1-\alpha)} \tag{17}$$

The augmentation of the over-subsistence capital stock in this period is given by:

$$J = \frac{S(T)}{S(0)} = \frac{z.e^{bT}}{z+(1-\lambda)(e^{bzT}-1)}. \tag{18}$$

To put it in our old terms, we can convert the relation into an exponential one at the rate g:

$$J = e^{gT}. \tag{19}$$

Incidentally for our old values of $b = 0.33$, $\alpha = 0.4$, and putting the 'terminal margin' $\lambda = 0.1$, we get $g = 0.288$, and the corresponding value of sensitivity, η, is around 4.

The method of fixing the terminal stock through a 'terminal margin' may, in fact, be quite useful in practical decision making. The optimal time profile in our solution satisfied the condition of maximizing utility within the horizon, and ends up in a situation where the new level of consumption is (a) sustainable for $\lambda \geq 0$, and (b) further expandable with a leeway determined by the 'terminal margin' λ for $\lambda > 0$.

The method used here is a cross between Radner's Problems I and II,† for $\delta = 1$, and $T < \infty$. Radner's Problem I consists of maximizing total welfare within a horizon; and Problem II is the maximization of one-period welfare of the final stock at T. Here we have instead the problem posed as maximizing total welfare within the horizon subject to a boundary condition that makes the final stock exceed the requirement of the last period optimal consumption by a specific margin. The closest to our presentation is that of Goodwin,‡ in terms of maximizing total welfare

† R. Radner, *Optimal Growth in a Linear-Logarithmic Economy*, Center for Research in Management Science, U.C. (Berkeley), Technical Report No. 18.

‡ R. M. Goodwin, 'The Optimum Growth Path for an Underdeveloped Economy', *Economic Journal*, December 1961.

within the horizon subject to having a specified terminal rate of growth. Indeed our presentation can be readily translated into his, though the method used here is probably simpler, and may allow us to see perhaps more clearly what issues are involved.†

4. SOME QUANTITATIVE EXERCISES

Before taking up some specific numerical values, we may introduce a measure of over-all growth achieved during the period T. J gives the growth rate of over-subsistence capital. We can define a corresponding growth-ratio of all capital, and call it the Over-all Growth Ratio.

$$G = \frac{S(T) + \bar{K}}{S(0) + \bar{K}} = \frac{J + m}{1 + m}, \qquad (20)$$

where m is the ratio of subsistence consumption to over-subsistence output in the initial period. If s is the share of subsistence consumption in initial output, we can check that:

$$m = \frac{s}{1 - s}. \qquad (21)$$

It is to be noted that in this model G is not specified from outside, but (given λ) is determined by the internal logic of utility maximization. It is, thus, a result of optimization in this model.

We take a time horizon of 20 years, a subsistence consumption ratio of 0·9, and the following set of numerical assumptions.‡

$$b = \begin{bmatrix} 0·33 \\ 0·25 \end{bmatrix}, \quad \alpha = \begin{bmatrix} 0·4 \\ 0·1 \end{bmatrix}, \quad \text{and} \quad \lambda = \begin{bmatrix} 0·2 \\ 0·1 \\ 0·0 \end{bmatrix}.$$

The results are presented in table 2.§ The optimal growth ratio shows considerable variation, but even the lower ratios are relatively high. For

---

† However, Goodwin in *The Optimum Growth Path for an Underdeveloped Economy*, bases his notion of welfare on individual utility and per capita consumption, and as such catches the impact of a changing population, which makes his analysis more interesting than ours, in many ways. See also S. Chakravarty and L. Lefeber, 'An Optimizing Planning Model', *Economic Weekly*, Annual Number, February 1965, for a terminal constraint in the shape of post-terminal rates of growth in a multi-sector model.

‡ The assumption of $s = 0·9$ fits many underdeveloped countries but not the developed ones, unless subsistence is defined in some special way, e.g. in terms of habitual standard of living. However, this is not an especially limiting assumption here, for in any case the use of a constant capital-output ratio is not easily justifiable for a developed country. Even for the underdeveloped countries it may be a bad assumption as discussed in B. Horvat, 'The Optimum Rate of Investment', *Economic Journal*, December 1958; T. N. Srinivasan, 'Investment Criteria and Choice of Techniques of Production', *Yale Economic Essays*, 1962; A. K. Sen, 'A Note on Tinbergen on the Optimum Rate of Saving', *Economic Journal* December 1957; but see also J. Tinbergen, 'Optimum Savings and Utility Maximization Over Time', *Econometrica*, April 1960,; and Goodwin, *The Optimum Growth Path for an Underdeveloped Economy*.   § Miss Edita Tan did the numerical computations.

example even if we take (i) $b = 0.25$ (i.e. a capital-output ratio of 4), (ii) $\alpha = 0.1$ (i.e. a 10 per cent increase in over-subsistence consumption increases utility by only 1 per cent), (iii) $\lambda = 0$ (i.e. we do not leave the people 20 years from now with any 'terminal margin'), even then the optimal growth ratio requires a 4-fold expansion of the country's productive capital stock in 20 years. This is equivalent to a compound rate of growth of 7 per cent per period; though of course the optimal path of the capital stock is not an exponential one (see equation (8)).

Table 2. *Optimal growth ratio with alternative numerical assumptions*

Assumptions			Results		
b	α	λ	J	g	G
0.33	0.4	0.2	336.4	0.29	34.5
		0.1	315.0	0.29	32.4
		0	296.2	0.29	30.5
	0.1	0.2	155.0	0.25	16.4
		0.1	141.1	0.25	15.0
		0	129.4	0.24	13.8
0.25	0.4	0.2	69.2	0.21	7.8
		0.1	64.5	0.21	7.3
		0	60.7	0.21	7.0
	0.1	0.2	36.5	0.18	4.5
		0.1	33.3	0.18	4.2
		0	30.7	0.17	4.0

5. SENSITIVITY TO THE TERMINAL CONDITIONS

We noted earlier that while in some regions the optimal growth path was rather insensitive to the assumption of terminal capital, in other regions the sensitivity was quite high. As the value of g rose, the path became more and more sensitive. Now that the problem has been redefined in terms of a 'terminal margin' (λ), it is relevant to ask how the sensitivity aspects look in terms of the terminal margin. The problem is, however, not very well-defined. In the case of terminal capital as expressed by the equivalent compound accumulation rate (g), we considered the variation of the path in response to a given percentage change in g. But λ being itself defined as a percentage of income, its percentage variations do not give a very meaningful measure.

One consideration to pose is to continue to take the earlier definition of sensitivity (η) in terms of g, and to translate any λ into the corresponding g. Looking at table 2 this way, we find that for terminal margins varying from 0 to 0.2, the value of g is fairly high almost throughout. That is, while the correspondence does depend on the capital–output ratio assumed and the elasticity of the utility function, for the values assumed here, g lies mostly in the 'sensitive' range (as can be seen by examining table 1).

The above, however, is a somewhat different question from the one concerning the sensitivity of the optimal path to changes in the assumption of the terminal margin. One indicator of the latter is the variation in J, the over-all growth rate of over-subsistence capital, or in G, the over-all growth ratio of total capital, with respect to variations in λ. Unlike in the previous exercise, J and G are not the assumptions of the exercise but their results, and as such the sensitivity of J and G to changes in λ is interesting. One of the remarkable aspects of table 2 is the strikingly small size of the variation in J and G as the value of λ is raised from 0 per cent to as much as 20 per cent. Since the terminal margin is simply the saving rate in the terminal year, it is very likely to be contained within this region. However, even if we consider wider variations of λ within the entire region of 0 to 100 per cent, the variations in J and G are not very great. Table 3 gives the values of J and G as λ is raised from 0 to 1. As the elasticity of the utility function is changed from 0·1 to 0·4, the response becomes even smaller. Compared with the phenomenal scale of the growth possibility, it is interesting to note the relatively limited variation of J and G in the optimal path as λ is varied from one extreme of 0 to the other of 1.

Table 3. *Sensitivity of over-all growth to the terminal margin*

λ	$\alpha = 0\cdot1$		$\alpha = 0\cdot4$	
	J	G	J	G
0·0	129·4	13·8	296·2	30·5
0·1	141·1	15·0	315·0	32·4
0·2	155·0	16·4	336·4	34·5
0·5	220·2	22·9	422·3	43·1
1·0	735·1	74·4	735·1	74·4

Assumptions: $T = 20$, $b = 0\cdot33$.

We do not intend to go much further into the sensitivity question here. Obviously much depends on the precise numerical values and we have not given here anything more than some specific results in some specific regions that we find empirically relevant. Others might prefer to take different assumptions. But one relatively interesting aspect of the entire sensitivity question is worth emphasizing. The sensitivity of the optimal path to the terminal margin can be split into two questions, viz. (i) the sensitivity of the terminal capital stock (or of g) to the terminal margin, and (ii) the sensitivity of the optimal path to the terminal capital stock (or to g). Chakravarty† discussed the latter question, and for his range of values found the response to be insensitive. By taking values outside this range, we found that the sensitivity was quite great. Furthermore, it is seen that to make economic sense, i.e. to avoid 'eating up' of capital, λ has to be specified to be non-negative,‡ and this puts g (for Chakravarty's quantitive assumptions) in the sensitive region rather than in the insensitive one.§

However, even in this region the sensitivity of type (i) is low, so that over-all sensitivity of the optimal path to the terminal margin, which depends on both (i) and (ii), may not be high. In table 2 itself it can be seen that the three alternative values of g, varying the terminal margin (terminal saving rate) from 0 per cent to 20 per cent, changes the value of g remarkably little. The value of g is seen to vary greatly with changes in the assumption of the output-capital ratio and considerably with changes in the assumption about the utility function elasticity, but not with changes in the terminal margin. And this is found to be so for all the alternative combination of b and α considered here.

From these quantitative values, it becomes possible to argue the following. While the optimal path is sensitive to variations in the terminal capital in the relevant region, the terminal capital stock implied by the economically meaningful assumptions about the terminal margin is itself rather insensitive to the variations in the margin. Thus the sensitivity of the path to the terminal condition newly defined may not be very high even when the path is sensitive to the terminal capital stock as such. This lends support to Chakravarty's insight into the sensitivity question, once the terminal condition has been appropriately redefined.

6. TERMINAL CAPITAL AND TERMINAL MARGIN

The precise relationship between solving a finite-horizon, optimum savings problem with (a) a postulated terminal capital stock, and that with (b) the use of a postulated terminal margin as outlined here, is somewhat intricate, and some technicalities may be cleared up. Given the initial capital stock, problem (a) states: Maximize W, subject to $K(T) = K_T$. Given the existence of an optimal solution to this problem and its uniqueness, both of which can be easily established given our

---

† Chakravarty, *op. cit.*

‡ Note that in this model $\lambda > 0$ is sufficient for there being no eating up of capital any time during the entire period up to the horizon if $1 > \alpha > 0$. See section 7 below.

§ For all values of g considered by Chakravarty, viz. 0·05 to 0·15, we have $\lambda < 0$ for his assumptions of output-capital ratio ($b = 0.33$) and elasticity for the utility function ($\alpha = 0.4$), and indeed for all alternative values of b and α considered in Table 2. With $\lambda \geqq 0$, g is higher and yields a higher value of sensitivity.

assumptions, this will define a unique savings ratio $v(T)$ for the terminal point.† What is more important in this optimality-relationship is that not only is $v(T)$ a function of K_T, but the inverse function also exists, i.e. given a value of the terminal savings ratio $v(T)$ we can find out the corresponding K_T. Furthermore, the domain of the inverse function, i.e. of $K_T = f[v(T)]$, includes the closed interval $(0, 1)$, as is obvious from (18). Hence we can specify a given λ, between 0 and 1, and corresponding to it the proper value of K_T can be found, i.e. a K_T such that problem (a) when solved will yield an optimum solution with $v(T) = \lambda$.

We did not define problem (b) as: Maximize W, subject to $v(T) = \lambda$. We defined it instead as: Maximize W, subject to $K(T) = f(\lambda)$. Hence all the properties of optimum solutions of problem (a) are preserved in problem (b). The trick of stating the problem in terms of λ is simply to restrict the range of the terminal capital stock in terms of which the classical exercise of problem (a) can be carried out, without the danger of having an inevitable prospect of a drop in the level of consumption in the period beyond the horizon.

7. MONOTONICITY OF SAVINGS RATE AND NON-NEGATIVITY OF SAVINGS

One interesting feature of both problems (a) and (b) is that the savings rate $v(t)$ will be either monotonically decreasing, or monotonically increasing, or constant throughout the period. It is easy to check that by differentiating $v(t)$ with respect to time we get:

$$\dot{v}(t) = (A_1 . A_2) . H(b, \alpha, t), \qquad (22)$$

where H is a function of b, α, and t, but is always positive for $\alpha < 1$, i.e. given diminishing marginal utility. So the sign of $\dot{v}(t)$ is independent of time.

From (12), (13), and (16), we obtain:

$$A_2 = \left[\frac{R}{1-R}\right] A_1, \qquad (23)$$

where

$$R = \frac{(1-\lambda)e^{bzT}}{z + (1-\lambda)(e^{bzT} - 1)} \qquad (24)$$

Now, for $1 > \alpha > 0$, we have $z < 0$, and $R < 0$. Thus A_1 and A_2 will have opposite signs, and $\dot{v}(t) < 0$, so that the savings rate will be monotonically decreasing. However, if the utility function is bounded on top, and $\alpha < 0$, then $1 > z > 0$, and $R > 0$. It is evident that:

† We define $v(t)$ as the ratio of savings to over-subsistence income,

$$\text{i.e.,} \quad v(t) = \frac{\dot{S}(t)}{S(t) . b}.$$

$\dot{v}(t)$ $\{\gtreqless\}$ o, according as $R\{\gtreqless\}$I, which is according to λ $\{\gtreqless\}$ $\dfrac{\text{I}}{\text{I}-\alpha}$.

Thus if the terminal margin is chosen to be equal to $\dfrac{\text{I}}{\text{I}-\alpha}$, the optimum profile of the savings ratio will be a stationary one. If the terminal margin is chosen to be lower, the savings rate will monotonically fall, and if higher, will monotonically rise. Since $(b.\lambda)$ and $\left(\dfrac{b}{\text{I}-\alpha}\right)$ are respectively the postulated terminal rate of growth and the optimum rate of growth of oversubsistence consumption prior to the horizon, the critical values can also be stated in terms of these two magnitudes, making greater intuitive sense.

One important corollary of the monotonicity result is that if we take a utility function with $\text{I} > \alpha > 0$, which is what we have done with our numerical illustrations, then the non-negativity of the terminal margin will automatically ensure positivity of the savings ratio throughout the period. Thus a separate non-negativity constraint on savings, if imposed,† will be redundant. Even when the utility function is bounded from the top provided the terminal margin λ is not above $\left(\dfrac{\text{I}}{\text{I}-\alpha}\right)$, the constraint will be redundant. Since the phenomenon of 'eating up' of capital in these finite-horizon, one-commodity Ramsey-type models is rather disturbing, this result is important. Our method of posing the problem in terms of a postulated terminal margin also provides a method of eliminating this irritating feature of the simple optimum savings exercises.

Finally, we might comment on the relevance of a problem on terminal conditions raised by Diamond‡ and Cass.§ With the possibility of free disposal, it makes obvious sense to pose problem (a) in terms of an inequality constraint on the terminal capital, i.e. as: Maximize W, subject to $K(T) \geqq K_T$. Since problem (b) is simply a suitably truncated problem (a), the same question will apply to our presentation also. It is easy to check, however, that with the possibility of 'eating up' capital, the value of period welfare W must be a *decreasing* function of K_T in the equality-constrained problem. Under these circumstances, the terminal condition even if imposed as a weak inequality, will bind as a strict equality. Hence nothing is lost here in defining the problem in terms of equality-constraints.

† Cf. Alan Manne, 'Numerical Experiments with a Finite Horizon Planning Model', *Indian Economic Review* (forthcoming).

‡ P. A. Diamond, 'Optimal Growth on a Model of Srinivasan', *Yale Economic Essay*, Spring 1964.

§ D. Cass, 'Optimum Economic Growth in an Aggregative Model of Capital Accumulation: A Turnpike Theorem', Cowles Foundation Discussion Papers, No. 178.

It might, however, look as if we have leaped from the frying pan to the fire, since the prospect of 'eating up' of capital with which we avoid the Diamond–Cass problem is itself very disturbing. However, our last result shows that even when the technical *possibility* of 'eating up' of capital exists, an *optimum* solution will not actually involve such an operation provided the terminal margin is chosen from the appropriate range.

8. CHOICE OF THE TERMINAL MARGIN

The problem of determination of the terminal capital stock is of course a political one. It includes the problem of determination of inter-generation distribution of consumption, various aspects of which have been discussed by Pigou, Dobb, Graaff, Baumol, Horvat, Eckstein, Sen, Marglin, and Feldstein,† among others. These problems cannot be eliminated. However, in this presentation, we have narrowed down the range of choice considerably by posing the problem in terms of the terminal margin λ, and by imposing the boundary conditions $1 > \lambda \geq 0$. This makes K_T dependent on optimal $C(T)$ and optimal $C(T)$ in its turn is of course dependent on K_T, so that the two problems have been simultaneously solved. The justification of the narrowing down of the range of choice of K_T is a value judgment that can be expected to be shared by most people, viz. that there should not be the necessity of a drop in the absolute level of consumption immediately beyond the horizon. (This requires $\lambda \geq 0$; the other boundary condition $\lambda < 1$ follows from the fact that terminal investment cannot exceed output.) The value judgement in question narrows down the field of choice considerably. Indeed the terminal capital stock is found to be not sensitive to the terminal margin for the empirical values considered.

If my hypothesis is right, i.e. if people would subscribe to the value judgement that the *necessity* of a future fall in consumption immediately beyond the horizon should be avoided, the problem of choice of terminal capital stock becomes considerably simpler. In fact for the numerical assumptions used in table 2, the optimum values of G seem to be quite close to each other even when the terminal margin is varied from 0 to 20 per cent.

---

† A. C. Pigou, *Economics of Welfare* (London, 1932), pp. 24, 30; M. H. Dobb, *An Essay on Economic Growth and Planning* (London, 1960), Chapter 2; Graaff, *op. cit.*; W. J. Baumol, *Welfare Economics and the Theory of the State* (Cambridge, Mass., 1952), Chapter 6; Horvat, *op. cit.*; Eckstein, 'Investment Criteria for Economic Development and the Theory Of Intertemporal Welfare Economics', *Quarterly Journal of Economics*, February 1957; A. K. Sen, 'On Optimising the Rate of Saving', *Economic Journal*, September 1961; S. A. Marglin, 'The Social Rate of Discount and the Optimal Rate of Investment', *Quarterly Journal of Economics*, February 1963; M. S. Feldstein, 'The Social Time Preference Discount Rate in Cost-Benefit Analysis', *Economic Journal*, June, 1964.

The method of optimization used here is a combination of Ramsey's rule† about distribution of consumption *within* the horizon, and relating the terminal capital stock (for the period *beyond*) to the experience within the horizon. The latter relation is, however, not a unique one; but it rules out a variety of possible terminal stock assumptions (those that give $\lambda < 0$) by making use of a widely held value judgement. The problem of determining λ from the interval $(0, 1)$ however remains, and this is where the present paper merges with the literature (cited above) on the political questions behind the optimum rate of saving.

† Ramsey, *op. cit.*

A GROWTH CYCLE†

R. M. GOODWIN

Presented here is a starkly schematized and hence quite unrealistic model of cycles in growth rates. This type of formulation now seems to me to have better prospects than the more usual treatment of growth theory or of cycle theory, separately or in combination. Many of the bits of reasoning are common to both, but in the present paper they are put together in a different way.

The following assumptions are made for convenience:

(1) steady technical progress (disembodied);

(2) steady growth in the labour force;

(3) only two factors of production, labour and 'capital' (plant and equipment), both homogeneous and non-specific;

(4) all quantities real and net;

(5) all wages consumed, all profits saved and invested.

These assumptions are of a more empirical, and disputable, sort:

(6) a constant capital-output ratio;

(7) a real wage rate which rises in the neighbourhood of full employment.

No. (5) could be altered to constant proportional savings, thus changing the numbers but not the logic of the system. No. (6) could be softened but it would mean a serious complicating of the structure of the model.

Symbols used are:

q is output;

k is capital;

w is wage rate;

$a = a_0 e^{\alpha t}$ is labour productivity; α constant;

σ is capital-output ratio (inverse of capital productivity);

w/a is workers' share of product, $(l - w/a)$ capitalists';

Surplus = profit = savings = investment = $(l - w/a)q = \dot{k}$.

Profit rate = $\dot{k}/k = \dot{q}/q = (l - w/a)/\sigma$.

$n = n_0 e^{\beta t}$ is labour supply, β constant;

$l = q/a$ is employment.

Writing $(\dot{q}/l)$ for $d/dt(q/l)$, we have

$$(\dot{q}/l)/q/l = \dot{q}/q - \dot{l}/l = \alpha,$$

so that
$$\dot{l}/l = (l - w/a)/\sigma - \alpha.$$

† Presented at the First World Congress of the Econometric Society, held in Rome, 1965.

Call
$$u = w/a, \quad v = l/n,$$

so that
$$\dot{v}/v = (l-u)/\sigma - (\alpha+\beta).$$

Assumption (7) may be written as

$$\dot{w}/w = f(v)$$

as shown in fig. 1.

The following analysis can be carried out using such an $f(v)$, with a change in degree but not in kind of results. Instead, in the interest of lucidity and ease of analysis, I shall take a linear approximation (as shown in fig. 1),

$$\dot{w}/w = -\gamma + \rho v$$

and this does quite satisfactorily for moderate movements of v near the point $+1$. Both γ and ρ must be large. Since

$$\dot{u}/u = \dot{w}/w - \alpha, \quad \dot{u}/u = -(\alpha+\gamma) + \rho v.$$

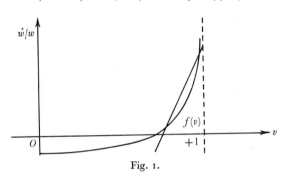

Fig. 1.

From this and the equation above for v, we have a convenient statement of our model.

$$\dot{v} = [(1/\sigma - (\alpha+\beta)) - 1/\sigma u]v. \tag{1}$$

$$\dot{u} = [-(\alpha+\gamma) + \rho v]u. \tag{2}$$

In this form we recognize the Volterra case of prey and predator (*Théorie Mathématique de la Lutte pour la Vie*. Paris, 1931). To some extent the similarity is purely formal, but not entirely so. It has long seemed to me that Volterra's problem of the symbiosis of two populations—partly complementary, partly hostile—is helpful in the understanding of the dynamical contradictions of capitalism, especially when stated in a more or less Marxian form.

Eliminating time and performing a first integration we get

$$(1/\sigma)u + \rho v - [1/\sigma - (\alpha+\rho)] \log u - (\gamma+\alpha) \log v = \text{constant}.$$

Letting
$$\theta_1 = 1/\sigma; \quad \eta_1 = 1/\sigma - (\alpha+\beta),$$
$$\theta_2 = \rho; \quad \eta_2 = \gamma+\alpha,$$

we can transform this into

$$\phi(u) = u^{\eta_1} e^{-\theta_1 u} = H v^{-\eta_2} e^{\theta_2 v} = H\psi(v),\qquad(3)$$

where H is an arbitrary constant, depending on initial conditions, since $1/\sigma > (\alpha+\beta)$, all coefficients are positive. By differentiating,

$$d\phi/du = (-\theta_1 + \eta_1/u)\phi,\quad d\psi/dv = (\theta_2 - \eta_2/v)\psi,$$

so that we can see that these functions have the sorts of shapes given in fig. 2.

Our problem as stated in (3) is to equate $\phi(u)$ to $\psi(v)$ multiplied by a constant H. This can be done neatly in the four quadrant positive diagram in fig. 3. We draw through the origin a straight line, A, with the

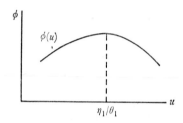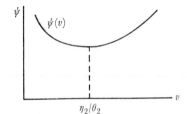

Fig. 2.

slope $\phi/\psi = H$ (arbitrary since dependent on the given initial condition). Then in symmetrical quadrants we place the two curves ϕ and ψ and equating these two through the constant of proportionality gives a possible pair of values for u and v. All possible pairs of u and v constitute a solution, which may be plotted in the remaining quadrant. It can be shown, and indeed is quite obvious, that these solution points lie on a closed, positive curve, B, in u, v space. By going back to equations (1) and (2) we can find in what order the points succeed each other and hence in what direction we traverse curve B, as indicated by arrows in fig. 3. A second integration will yield u and v as functions of time, thus allowing us to determine the second arbitrary factor, the point on B at which we start. By varying the slope of A we can generate a family of closed curves broadly similar to B, thus yielding all the possible solutions. One initial condition selects the curve, a second fixes the starting point, and then we traverse some particular curve B in the direction of the arrows for ever, in the absence of given outside changes. There remains only to spell out the meaning of the motion.

Hence we may classify our model as a non-linear conservative oscillator of, fortunately, a soluble type. As the representative point travels around the closed curve B, u vibrates between ξ_1 and ξ_2, and v between

ζ_1 and ζ_2. Both u and v must be positive and v must, by definition, be less than unity; u normally will be also but may, exceptionally, be greater than unity (wages and consumption greater than total product by virtue of losses and disinvestment). Over the stretch 0 to $+1$ on the u axis, the

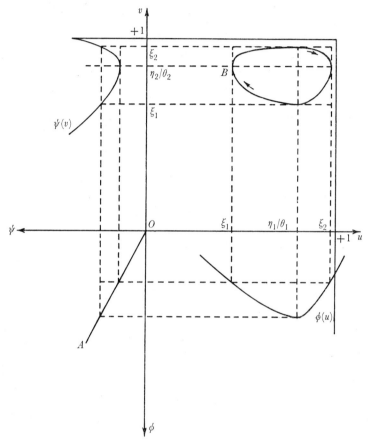

Fig. 3.

point u indicates the distribution of income, workers' share to the left, capitalists' to the right. The capitalists' share, multiplied by a constant, $1/\sigma$, gives us the profit rate and the rate of growth in output, $\dot{q}/q$. When profit is greatest, $u = \xi_1$, employment is average, $v = \eta_2\theta_2$, and the high growth rate pushes employment to its maximum ξ_2 which squeezes the profit rate to its average value η_1/θ_1. The deceleration in growth lowers employment (relative) to its average value again, where profit and growth are again at their nadir ξ_2. This low growth rate leads to a fall in output and employment to well below full employment, thus restoring profitability to its average value because productivity is now rising faster than wage rates. This is, I believe, essentially what Marx meant by the contradiction of capitalism and its transitory resolution in booms and slumps. It is, however, un-Marxian in asserting that profitability is restored not (necessarily) by a fall in real wages but rather by their failing to rise with productivity. Real wages must fall in relation to productivity; they may fall absolutely as well, depending on the severity of the cycle. The improved profitability carries the seed of its own destruction by engendering a too vigorous expansion of output and employment, thus destroying the reserve army of labour and strengthening labour's bargaining power. This inherent conflict and complementarity of workers and capitalists is typical of symbiosis.

An undisturbed system has constant average values η_1/θ_1 for u and η_2/θ_2 for v, hence a constant long-run average distribution of income and degree of unemployment. Much more remarkable is the fact that a *disturbed* system still has the same constant long-run values. The time averages of u and of v are independent of initial conditions. We can see this from the fact that a rotation of A (an outside change) will only make the curve B larger or smaller but will not alter its central point. Therefore continual shocks will alter the shape of the cycle but not the long-run average values. Output and employment both will show alternating rates of growth. Whether they actually decrease or merely rise less rapidly will depend on the severity of the cycle. For a mild cycle the growth rate may decrease but never become negative, in other cases there may be a sharp fall. However, the increases must predominate over the decreases, since the time average of $1 - u$ is positive and hence so also is that of $\dot{q}/q$. Likewise employment grows in the long-run at the same rate as labour supply, since the time average of v is constant. Similarly the equality of the growth rate in wages to that in productivity follows from the constancy of u. By contrast the profit rate is equal to $1 - u$ and therefore tends to constancy. We may look at this as standing Ricardo (and Marx) on his head. Progress first accrues as profits but profits lead to expansion and expansion forces wages up and profits down. Therefore we have a Malthusian Iron Law of Profits. This is because of the tendency of capital, though not capitalists, to breed excessively. By contrast labour is something of a rent good since the supply, though variable, does not seem to be a function of wages. Hence it is the sole ultimate beneficiary from technical progress. By now there would, I suppose, be considerable agreement that what happened in history is: wage rates went up; profit rates stayed down. It is to the explanation of this that the present paper is addressed.

THE APPLICATION OF
MARX'S MODEL OF EXPANDED
REPRODUCTION TO TRADE
CYCLE THEORY

PÉTER ERDÖS

In contemplating the unexpected opportunity of discussing some of the basic ideas of Marxist theoretical research, in a symposium addressed to both Marxist economists in socialist countries and to economists of differing tradition elsewhere, I have become aware of the great difficulty of the task. This is not primarily due to the fact that we often think in categories which frequently require laborious translation to become comprehensible to those in our profession who are not specialized in the matter. It is rather that economic ideas which have long ago become commonplace in one camp, in the other camp remain totally unknown; or else, and no less frequently, are known but wholly rejected. This is the fate even of true insights if they happen to have been derived with the help of emotionally pregnant or ideologically coloured arguments, or if they in turn gave rise to arguments which the other camp simply could not accept.

In this article I want to sketch the starting point of the analysis of certain elements of a trade cycle theory (*Konjunkturlehre*) which would lead ultimately to a theory of the cyclical crises proper. This will be done with the help of models derived from the Marxist schema of the expanded reproduction of the social product. Marxist economists possess a theory of economic crisis. Put more accurately, the vast majority of economists in the socialist countries accept today a particular theory of economic crisis which was developed after Marx, in particular by Soviet scholars. Other Marxists, some of them in the capitalist countries, have also developed several variations of the theory of crisis which do not, however, agree with the former in all respects. A Marxist theory of irregular fluctuations of economic activity does not really exist at all.

As regards the first of the two sorts of difficulty which I mentioned to begin with, I am fortunate in that the content and the meaning of this Marxist schema has recently been interpreted by no less, and no less suitable, an economist than Mrs Joan Robinson.† But one of the purposes

† In her introduction to the English translation of Rosa Luxemburg's *The Accumulation of Capital* (London, 1951).

of the study which I want to outline in its essentials is to apply the tools of Marxist political economy to problems which J. M. Keynes posed in his *Treatise on Money* and in his *General Theory*. He analysed them by the methods of what he calls classical economics, while we, by our means, hope to obtain more appropriate answers. Others will have to judge the final result of this attempt, which is not as yet complete. But no one will be surprised to find that the results of this approach, in so far as they are already available, though far from identical with those derived by Keynes nevertheless strike the Western-trained economist as quite familiar. This will not prevent one or the other economist, for instance in Hungary, finding them novel. Hence I must ask the indulgence of both groups of possible readers: one will have to excuse the undue prolixity of my explanations, while the others must forgive the unjustifiable brevity.

Thanks to Mrs Robinson, I may deal only briefly with my main analytical tool. In its initial form it is all but identical with Marx's schema of expanded reproduction. Production is divided between two departments, namely Department I which produces the means of production, capital equipment and raw materials, and Department II which produces consumption goods. We may write:

$$\text{I.} = c_1 + v_1 + s_1,$$

$$\text{II.} = c_2 + v_2 + s_2$$

(where I conform to English usage by writing s for the otherwise accepted symbol m). v represents the variable capital in the form of the 'annual' wages fund; c, constant capital, represents the contribution of raw materials and capital equipment to the year's product, including also the cost of maintaining the physical stock of capital at the initial level. Finally, in definition, s represents the surplus value. This concept should be well known in the Western world if only because Marx equated it with the exploitation of workers and thus caused many economists—Menger, J. B. Clark and others—to attempt to show that in the sense defined by Marx it did not exist. But to avoid the overtones of this concept I should again like to accept Mrs Robinson's interpretation: the surplus s is the annual sum of rent, interest and net profit. Hence $v + s$ represents the annual national income.

The sum $I + II$ is known in Marxist terminology as the social product. The reader should remember that this is in no sense identical with the Gross National Product (GNP) of the Americans, nor with that part of it which measures the 'Income originated in Business' though it is nearer to the latter than to the former. The chief difference lies in the fact that the GNP represents final products while our social product includes, in

c, all kinds of raw materials and intermediate products. With a little simplification it is best to think of the social product as including all things produced which were sold in the period. The social product thus includes a certain measure of duplication. National income is $v+s$, not $c+v+s$. Department II makes only goods ready for consumption, 'first-order goods' in Menger's terminology; goods of remoter order are produced in Department I.

Mrs Robinson is completely right in saying that in this model the capital stock exists only behind the scenes. In the account of accumulation, the stock of capital and its increment are equated with the consumption of capital in the following year. This is only consistent with the notion that the entire capital gets used up and replaced once a year. That, she says, is a cumbersome rather than a convenient simplification; but it is merely a simplification and does not invalidate the analysis of Rosa Luxemburg. I agree in the main, and in this note I too will use this simplification, believing that it cannot invalidate the following analysis. Were I to analyse in this article the mechanism of cyclical crises, the simplification would have to be abandoned. But having done this elsewhere, and knowing what mathematical complications ensue I will not attempt it here.

A further problem is that of the unit of accounting. Marx himself expresses all relevant magnitudes in terms of labour hours. One may think instead, for example, in terms of average prices. But this would require an assumption about the nature of these average prices. In his arithmetic examples, Marx maintains a constant ratio of s to v in both Departments even though the ratio of constant to variable capital in the two Departments is not always assumed the same. Mrs Robinson considers this as an obvious mistake since the two Departments must trade with each other not on the basis of values but at market prices. Mrs Robinson considers this an interesting mistake inasmuch as it shows that in unguarded moments Marx forgets that prices cannot be taken as proportional to values unless capital has the same organic composition in all branches of industry.

At this point I find myself somewhat embarrassed by another brilliant article by Mrs Robinson from which I learn that no true Marxist ever can or must acknowledge that Marx had unguarded moments. And yet I have to say that in this instance there can hardly be a question of a mistake. It is generally known that Marx developed his concepts step by step, following out historical-logical trains of thought. In the first two volumes of *Capital* he assumes always and without exception that the exchange of commodities is proportional to values rather than to so-called prices of production. In the first two volumes, the rate of surplus s/v is the same for each kind of commodity. Only in the third volume does he find that this is not at all what happens under capitalism: under that system it is the rates of profit rather than the ratios s/v which are equal. (As regards Marx's habit of writing the rate of profit as $s/(c+v)$ I must agree with Mrs Robinson that it is rather unfortunate.) The problem of the reproduction of total capital is, however, treated in the second volume.

In arithmetic illustrations of the laws of reproduction Marxists persisted even after the publication of volume III in setting the s/v ratio equal in both Departments. This is no more than a further simplification. In the first place, the conversion of the schema of reproduction from the value base to the base of production prices demands even in the case of only two Departments a system of several equations of the form

$$y + axy + bx + c = 0.$$

Their numerical solution is rather cumbersome. Secondly, such a conversion is always possible for n Departments, as was first proved mathematically by the Hungarian economist Andreas Brody. Thirdly, while such a conversion changes the numbers it fails totally to affect the principal relationships which arise from the model. In brief, this is another assumption which is justified on the grounds that it simplifies remarkably without distorting any essential feature.

Finally, a comment on the model. Mrs Robinson has said of Rosa Luxemburg that she deliberately took v to represent that part of capital which is advanced as wages before the revenue from the sale of produced commodities is received. While it is true that some Marxists might object to this interpretation I accept it as being in fact an unavoidable logical implication of the model. The model divides into fixed periods, called years, what is in reality a continuous process of production. For the purpose of the following analysis I would merely suggest, in this context, that successive years should not be understood as real years. The different products are not on the whole sold immediately to the last buyers but rather remain unsold during a certain period—say, on average, one quarter—in the stocks of wholesalers and retailers. My own suggestion, pointing again to a crude simplification, is to regard this medium period as equal to a year. This implies the following consideration. In the first 'year' workers received altogether a sum of wages equal to v. This is the wages-cost of the corresponding volume of commodities. The commodities, however, are sold in the second 'year'. Production will generally have been expanded in the meantime. The sum of wages paid in the second year will accordingly not equal v but exceed it at, say, $v + s_v$. It follows that while the wage costs of a volume of commodities amount to v, the consumption demand of workers for these commodities at the time of their sale will amount to $v + s_v$.

Next, the equilibrium conditions of the model. Mrs Robinson explains the case of simple reproduction and states

$$\text{I.} \quad c_1 + v_1 + s_1 = c_1 + c_2;$$

$$\text{II.} \quad c_2 + v_2 + s_2 = v_1 + v_2 + s_1 + s_2;$$

and therefore $v_1 + s_1 = c_2$.

In the case of expanded reproduction one must write $s = s_k + s_c + s_v$, where s_k represents the personal consumption of capitalists, s_c the part of the surplus which is accumulated in the shape of constant capital and s_v the wages of the additional workers.

The equilibrium conditions of this expanded model were first put in a quasi-mathematical form by N. Bucharin, as follows:

It is easily seen that simple reproduction now appears as a limiting case of expanded reproduction. The latter may be written as

$$\text{I.} \quad c_1 + v_1 + s_{k1} + s_{c1} + s_{v1} = c_1 + c_2 + s_{c1} + s_{c2}$$

$$\text{II.} \quad c_2 + v_2 + s_{k2} + s_{c2} + s_{v2} = v_1 + v_2 + s_{k1} + s_{k2} + s_{v1} + s_{v2}$$

and hence $\qquad v_1 + s_{k1} + s_{v1} = c_2 + s_{c2}.$

This last equation represents the basic equilibrium condition of expanded reproduction. Note that it is an equilibrium condition. It is assumed that the equality $s = s_k + s_c + s_v$ applies to each Department separately. In no way does the model imply that this must hold also in the absence of full equilibrium.

In contemporary Marxist literature we find the following comment on this matter. Certain economists advanced the theory that pure capitalism, a system comprising capitalist and wage-labour only, would be unable to sell, or 'realize' the entire social product. Thus, for instance, Malthus on the one hand and certain petty-bourgeois critics of classical political economy on the other hand. But Marx proved that capitalism was in theory able to realize the social product: in equilibrium the social product can be sold, or realized, if the equality $v_1 + s_{k1} + s_{v1} = c_2 + s_{c2}$ is maintained. Under capitalism, however, this necessary equality cannot be maintained continuously but, at best, only on the average of a long period. Hence one cannot escape disruptions of equilibrium, sales troubles and also crises. This is taken to be the true significance of Marx's analysis of expanded reproduction.

I believe that current Marxist literature unduly neglects Marx's theory of reproduction and the schema pertaining to it. During the first two decades of this century much interest focussed on this question. Certain economists attempted to turn Marx's schema into a kind of growth theory in order to prove that capitalism would always be capable of continuing expanded reproduction without any limit. Best known amongst them is Tugan-Baranowsky who went so far as to assert that a system of pure capitalism would be capable of surviving even if the working class were to shrink down to a single worker, 'operating an immense mass of machines' to make further machines.† On the other hand there were Marxists who employed the same scheme in attempts to prove that pure capitalism—that is capitalism without third persons—was automatically doomed to collapse for its inability to realize the whole national product. Rosa Luxemburg is the best known amongst them. Many economists participated in the heated debate which followed. Among them Otto Bauer who opposed Rosa Luxemburg and who introduced into his analysis the very feature that Mrs Robinson finds lacking in Rosa Luxemburg, namely the possibility of accumulating a part of the surplus outside the Department in which it is produced. Rosa Luxemburg was opposed by N. Bucharin in whose arguments algebraic formulae take the place of concrete numbers. Fritz Sternberg, whose work *Der Imperialismus* appeared in Berlin in 1926 was one of the last and best known theorists of collapse. Many further authors might be named.

So far as my knowledge extends, all these authors have one thing in common. They all take the rate of surplus as a given initial magnitude. There are amongst them those who assume the ratio s/v to have the same value in successive years. Others, regarding this as illicit, consider the rate s/v as continuously growing in consequence of technical progress but yet feel free to allot to it a value which, though subject to this continuous increase, is otherwise chosen at will and independently of the composition of the social product.

Mrs Robinson rightly points out that the conjunction of these assumptions causes the model to be overdetermined. The meaning of this we may approximate by assuming that the first Department is somehow given to us in all its parts. We therefore take each of the following magnitudes as fixed and given (in terms of, say, average prices).

$$\text{I} = c_1 + v_1 + s_{k1} + s_{c1} + s_{v1}.$$

† *Theoretische Grundlagen des Marxismus* (Leipzig, 1905) p. 230.

Let us imagine also that the ratio $(s_k + s_c + s_v)/v$ remains constant in both Departments throughout all succeeding years (or, alternatively, that it varies in an initially determined proportion); that the consumption of capitalists, s_{k1} and s_{k2} is subject to a certain regularity (for example, as unique functions of s_1 and s_2); that s_c/s_v is equal (or else varies in an initially determined manner) and assume, finally, that each accumulates only within its own Department. Now it is true that one may find an infinity of possible second Departments which would be in equilibrium with the given first Department, *in the given year*. But, in the normal case, the state of equilibrium is bound to disappear already in the following year. Consider this second year: if production starts in Department I with a constant capital of $c_1 + s_{c1}$ and variable capital of $v_1 + s_{v1}$; if one then obtains s_1, the rate of surplus remaining what it was in the first year (or as initially given according to some rule); if s_1 is thereupon reduced by an arbitrarily determined amount s_k, to be consumed by the capitalists; if the 'saved' residue is thereafter split up into two parts, s_{c1} and s_{v1}, in proportion to the composition of capital; if all this is finally repeated in Department II, it will follow in the normal case that the resulting sum $v_1 + s_{k1} + s_{v1}$ relating to this second year will not equal $c_2 + s_{c2}$.

As against this it can be proved that for any arbitrarily given Department I there exists a unique Department II of fully determined internal relations for which equilibrium can be maintained from year to year while satisfying the stated conditions. This can be achieved, for instance, by choosing s_k as any linear function of s. It obviously remains an exceptional case.

Marx did not always work with such specially selected numbers. In one of his arithmetic examples it was assumed that the capitalists in Department I regularly consume one half of their surplus. To maintain equilibrium in the following years he had to adjust consumption in Department II. It turned out that consumption in Department II declined from year 1 to year 2, but increased in Department I. Not a very convincing solution since it is hard to think of reasons for this variation in personal consumption. The assumption was, of course, necessary since without a reduction in the consumption of Department II, 'savings' would have been inadequate to buy and accumulate the surplus of producers' goods which was forthcoming from Department I.

The case where $v_1 + s_{k1} + s_{v1}$ exceeds $c_2 + s_{c2}$ has been unduly neglected in Marxist literature. Because of this neglect one commonly meets the view that in this case a part of the means of production remains unsaleable or can only be sold at lowered prices, 'at less than their value'. This would be a case of 'overproduction'. But this view rests on a tacit assumption regarding the rate of surplus. This is taken as strictly equal to the initially assumed rate—to the average rate in our case or to whatever other rate was settled on. For the short period it is hardly possible to justify this procedure. It is at this very point that I see the possibility of developing the Marxian theory of reproduction into a kind of trade cycle theory.

In the first place, it appears that the accepted view errs in assuming that the proportions of the two Departments will determine whether or not the social product can be wholly realized according to the rules of the Marxian model, that is, at prices which are proportional to the values or the average prices. For any given social product, trade between the two departments may in fact balance. An arithmetic example will illustrate the point. Let

$$
\begin{aligned}
\text{I} &= 2000 & \text{II} &= 1300 \\
c_1 &= 1000 & c_2 &= 500 \\
s_{k1} &= 200 & s_{k2} &= 40
\end{aligned}
$$

and assume also a rate of surplus of 100 per cent. If the composition of capital stays constant, the following schema results:

$$2000 \ \text{I} \ = \ 1000c_1 + 500v_1 + 500s_1;$$
$$s_1 = 200s_{k1} + 200s_{c1} + 100s_{v1}.$$
$$1300 \ \text{II} \ = \ 500c_2 + 400v_2 + 400s_2;$$
$$s_2 = 40s_{k2} + 200s_{c2} + 160s_{v2}.$$

Hence $\quad v_1 + s_{k1} + s_{v1} = 800 \quad$ and $\quad c_2 + s_{c2} = 700.$

It may seem as though there exists an excess of means of production, equal in value to $800 - 700 = 100$, which cannot be sold or realized.

But the same quantity of production can equally well be accounted for in the following schema, remembering only that $v_1' + s_1' = v_1 + s_1$, and $v_2' + s_2' = v_2 + s_2$.

$$2000 \ \text{I} \ = \ 1000c_1 + 433 \cdot 28v_1' + 566 \cdot 72s_1';$$
$$s_1 = 200s_{k1} + 255 \cdot 86s_{c1}' + 110 \cdot 86s_{v1}'.$$
$$1300 \ \text{II} \ = \ 500c_2 + 346 \cdot 62v_2' + 453 \cdot 38s_2';$$
$$s_2 = 40s_{k2} + 244 \cdot 14s_{c2}' + 169 \cdot 24s_{v2}'.$$

In this case, $\quad v_1 + s_{k1} + s_{v1} = c_2 + s_{c2} = 744 \cdot 14.$

It appears that the entire product can be realized at prices which are proportional to the average prices (or to the values in the sense used by Marx).

The trick which we performed on an arbitrarily selected arithmetic example, can be repeated for every conceivable social product. The numbers in the second example result quite simply from the following simultaneous equations:

$$s_1' = s_{k1} + s_{c1}' + s_{v1}'; \quad s_2' = s_{k2} + s_{c2}' + s_{v2}';$$

$$v_1' + s_1' = v_1 + s_1; \quad v_2' + s_2' = v_2 + s_2;$$

$$v_1' + s_{v1}' + v_2' + s_{v2}' = \text{II} - [s_{k1} + s_{k2}];$$

$$c_1 s_{v1}' = v_1' s_{c1}'; \quad c_2 s_{v2}' = v_2' s_{c2}'; \quad v_2 v_1' = v_1 v_2'.$$

The further necessary equation $v_2 s_1' = v_1 s_2'$ is already implied in the system. Let

$$v_1' + s_{v1}' = k; \quad v_2' + s_{v2}' = 1;$$

$$c_1 + s_{c1} = m; \quad c_2 + s_{c2} = n;$$

$$\frac{v_1 c_2}{c_1 v_2} = a + 1;$$

$$\frac{\text{I} - s_{k1}}{\text{I} - (s_{k1} + s_{k2})} = q_1; \quad \frac{\text{II} - s_{k2}}{\text{II} - (s_{k1} + s_{k2})} = q_2$$

and
$$k = (x - 1)l, \quad \text{where} \quad x > 1.$$
We then find for x

$$q_2 x^2 - [q_1 + q_2 + a(q_1 - 1)]x - a = 0.$$

Writing $f(x)$ for the left-hand side, we get

$$f(\pm \infty) > 0; \quad f(1) = -q_1(a + 1) < 0.$$

This means that in the range of $x > 1$ the equation has precisely one root. Returning now to the original unknowns of our system of equations, it is easily seen that one will obtain for them values which are unique, real and economically meaningful.

Secondly, the rate of surplus in my first example was 100 per cent, but in my second example I put it at 130·8 per cent. This was necessary because the assumption of an average rate of surplus of 100 per cent in the first example left Department I with an apparent excess of produced means of production $(v_1 + s_{k1} + s_{v1})$ which seemed greater than the maximum possible 'savings' plus replacement requirements in Department II $(c_2 + s_{c2})$. But in fact it does not follow that this excess of means of production would be unsaleable in principle. The opposite is true. Since workers in a capitalist society do not buy means of production, this residue of means of production is basically nothing else but additional surplus value for the actual accumulation of which a further element of surplus value in the form of s_v will be required. Unless the personal consumption of capitalists declines, the rate of surplus must rise if all produced means of production are to be accumulated. Savings may accordingly increase as well. While nobody should be surprised by this conclusion, it has not so far been derived from Marx's schemas.

There follows a further conclusion. Let the sum $II = c_2 + v_2 + s_2$ be given in terms of average prices. v_2 gives the wages of the required workers reckoned at average nominal wage per head; similarly for v_1, s_{v1} and s_{v2}. Let p_{II} stand for the fraction II_p / II, where II_p represents *actual* prices times quantities of the produced means of production, as distinct from II which represents average prices times quantities. It follows that

$$p_{II} = \frac{v_1 + v_2 + s_{v1} + s_{v2} - Z_a}{II - (s_{k1} + s_{k2}) - L},$$

where Z_a represents the possible savings of workers and L stands for the increment in the inventories of consumption goods. We may neglect these two magnitudes and approximate by writing:

$$p_{II} = \frac{v_1 + v_2 + s_{v1} + s_{v2}}{II - (s_{k1} + s_{k2})}.$$

s_{v1} and s_{v2} appear in this formula because we decided earlier on that commodities will only be sold after the lapse of a certain period. The reader will observe a remote resemblance between this formula and the Fundamental Equations of Keynes' *Treatise on Money*.

If one works Marx's schema on the assumption of an average rate of surplus and if the condition

$$v_1 + s_{k1} + s_{v1} = c_2 + s_{c2}$$

fails to be satisfied, one may write

$$v_1 + s_{k1} + s_{v1} - c_2 - s_{c2} = X.$$

In our first arithmetical example, X was a positive magnitude. Since

$$v_1 + s_{v1} = c_2 + s_{c2} - s_{k1} + X$$

one obtains

$$p_{II} = \frac{c_2 + v_2 + s_{c2} + s_{v2} + X - s_{k1}}{II - (s_{k1} + s_{k2})}$$

$$= \frac{II - (s_{k1} + s_{k2}) + X}{II - (s_{k1} + s_{k2})}$$

$$= 1 + \frac{X}{II - (s_{k1} + s_{k2})}$$

This means that the price level of consumption goods will be above or below its average value (nominal wage per employee remaining constant) according to whether the value of X is positive or negative.

From this, it seems to follow as a fourth conclusion that a schema of the social product which is based on the assumption of an average rate of surplus may serve as an indicator of the state of trade. If the calculation results in a positive X the indication is that both the rate of surplus and the price level of consumption goods will rise above the average. This points to a rise in the prices of capital goods. If X is negative, the opposite is implied.

I do not believe that this conclusion can be rejected on the grounds that I employ ex-post magnitudes which can at best help to establish what has already happened. Consider three successive time periods 1, 2, 3 and assume that with the average rate of surplus expanded reproduction is in equilibrium in period 1. This is equivalent to assuming that period 2 has available to it the capital taken from the schema for period 1, increased by s_c and s_v, and that the goods produced in period 1 will be sold in period 2 at their average prices. But if a constant rate of surplus is postulated, quite exceptional circumstances are needed to bring about equilibrium in the system of period 2 without a positive or negative value for X. Assume therefore that X is positive. This is the situation of which I maintain that it indicates a state of activity higher than average. So far we have no reason to expect that capitalists will accelerate accumulation, the available excess of means of production notwithstanding. All that is probable is that they will continue to plan accumulation at something like the average pace. (We postulate a compulsion to accumulate: capitalists must accumulate unless there are reasons to the contrary. Competition compels this behaviour.) This accumulation will be performed in period 3. But the equation which we derived for p_{II} tells us that the prices of consumption goods will shoot up already when accumulation still proceeds at the average rate. The capitalists will therefore recognize the rising tendency of prices, and this is presumably going to lead to a revision of their plans so as to speed up accumulation. The process leads to further rises in prices. Optimism justifies itself and the improvement of trade continues for the time being. In the opposite case the process would occur in the opposite direction.

Against this it might be objected that the state of production of *fixed* capital might give rise to opposing tendencies. In such circumstances it might well be possible that a rise in prices would fail to stimulate accelerated accumulation. The objection may be justified. The system that we have presented in its simplest form does not comprise any fixed capital. But it is capable of expansion and may be so developed as to take account of this circumstance. This would lead us into the field of the theory of the cyclical crises proper and would therefore take me outside the limits of this article.

Instead I should like to sketch briefly a further train of reasoning that relates to the long period. First of all an introductory comment. The model which we described fully confirmed Keynes' parable of the widow's cruse. If capitalists as a group decided to consume more, the increase reckoned at constant prices is added automatically to their profits. This is quite clear because their consumption is surplus value by definition. Reckoned in actual prices, this profit would be even greater, all else being held constant: the formula for p_{II} has capitalists' consumption $(s_{k1} + s_{k2})$ in its numerator and prices must accordingly rise. Let us now turn to the argument.

Let us imagine an economy containing only capitalists and productive wage labour. If steady growth is postulated for this economy, the only way of preventing the tendency of the rate of profit to fall is through the accumulation of a rising share of the national income. This is so because we cannot realistically expect the personal consumption of capitalists to keep pace with the growth in the production of consumption goods. National income is made up of $v + s_k + s_c + s_v$. Since s_k must become relatively smaller, $s_c + s_v$ have to grow relatively because otherwise the rate of surplus $(s_k + s_c + s_v)/v$ would decline and this decline would reduce the rate of profit even with a constant organic composition of capital (c/v).

As a matter of experience, however, the rate of private accumulation in the developed capitalist countries shows no tendency to accelerate. This, combined with the capital-saving bias of modern technology, led J. M. Gillman[†] to the conclusion that the excessively large social surplus of the mature capitalist economies can only be disposed of through high unproductive expenditures. His social surplus is surplus value less capitalists' consumption. It seems to me that this view contains the same error which we attributed earlier on to most Marxist authors: like them, Mr Gillman tries to fix the level of surplus independently of the whole system. He seems to suppose that the social surplus must be large whenever a capitalist economy is a mature one.

I would argue the opposite. Capitalists, in a mature capitalist country, cannot possibly consume the entire product. For reasons that come easily to mind private accumulation is rather limited. If surplus or profit were really to consist of s_k, s_c and s_v, profits would have to be rather low unless unproductive activities were being carried on. Whether capitalists increase consumption or the state taxes enterprise and transfers the revenue directly or indirectly to unproductively employed workers and salaried employees who then spend the money on consumption, the effect will be the same and the widow's cruse will have worked the miracle. The surplus itself (or the Social Surplus) is raised in the process. Profits are raised and this is essential wherever profits form the stimulus to produce. All this holds only for profits gross of tax, but this fact does not vitiate the ar-

† In his new book *Prosperity in Crisis* (New York, 1965).

gument. A variety of multiplier-effects will be at work. But even without those, the course of action that we have described contributes significantly to Mr Gillman's 'capitalist viability'. One need think only of the multiplicity of small enterprises which have in any case to make do with low profits and whose tax burden will be small under a progressive tax system. Except for the generally high level of taxes which acts to raise the rate of profit gross of tax, many of them would be working at a net loss. But whether one accepts this unconditionally as an argument for the usefulness of unproductive employment and its finance from taxation must depend on whether one accepts that capitalism will survive indefinitely.

ON THE TENDENCY FOR THE
RATE OF PROFIT TO FALL

A. A. KONÜS

I. A MISUNDERSTANDING ABOUT CONSTANT CAPITAL, C.

The tendency of the rate of profit to fall is admitted by many economists, irrespective of their ideology. 'Orthodox economic theory also contains a law of falling profits' writes Marx's critic—Professor Joan Robinson.† In the labour theory of value it is simply a problem of the comparative increase of the organic composition of advanced capital and of the rate of surplus value. There is therefore no need to consider the tendency of the rate of profit to fall as a prediction. Maurice Dobb stresses this in particular, whenever he discusses Marx's views on the problem: 'But it has to be remembered that in speaking of the "tendency for the rate of profit to fall" he spoke of this as no more than a *tendency* to which there were a number of "counteracting tendencies" which he explicity stressed in detail. To put it in a nutshell, the reason he saw for this tendency was that technical progress would tend to raise the ratio of "stored-up labour" (plant and structures) to "living labour" in production; and two among the counteracting tendencies he mentioned were the simultaneous effect of technical progress in cheapening the production of machinery etc. itself, and in raising the amount of surplus-value produced by each worker in a given time as a result of raised productivity.'‡

These remarks by Dobb solve the problem completely. None the less it can be seen from the literature that a misunderstanding persists. This originates in the vague notion about the content of the 'organic composition of capital' and the 'rate of profit'. Joan Robinson recognizes this in the first pages of her *Essay*: 'Marx conducts his argument in terms of three ratios: s/v, the *rate of exploitation*; c/v, the *organic composition of capital*; and $s/(c+v)$, the *rate of profit*.' ('...the total product for any period, say a year, is then represented by $c+v+s$'.)

'The rate of exploitation is unambiguous. The other two ratios, c/v and $s/(c+v)$, involve some confusion. Both the organic composition of capital and the rate of profit are connected with the stock of capital employed, not with the depreciation of capital...We can avoid ambiguity, without falsifying Marx's meaning, if we use the symbols c, v and

† Joan Robinson, *An Essay on Marxian Economics* (London, 1949), p. 36.
‡ Maurice Dobb, *Capitalism Yesterday and Today* (London, 1958), p. 38.

[72]

s only for rates per unit of time of depreciation and raw material cost, wages and profit, and speak of the organic composition of capital, not as c/v, but as capital per man employed'.[†]

Although the method used by Professor Robinson is very popular, it departs from the mathematics of Marx, i.e. from the ratios mentioned above, since the constant capital c is given two different meanings. This weakens the whole of her *Essay* and leads to the astonishing assertion 'that no point of substance in Marx's argument depends upon the labour theory of value'.[‡]

The problem is not an easy one. Paul Sweezy has also commented on it He writes: '...the formula $s/(c+v)$, strictly speaking, shows the rate of profit on the capital actually used up in producing a given commodity. In practice the capitalist usually calculates the rate of profit on his total investment for a given period of time, say a year. But total investment is generally not the same as capital used up during a year since the turnover time of different elements of total investment varies widely...In order to simplify the theoretical exposition, and to bring the rate of profit formula into conformity with the usual concept of an annual rate of profit, Marx makes the assumption that all capital has an identical turnover period of one year'. And in contrast to Professor Robinson, Sweezy uses this method in his argument: '...in order to restrict the scope of our discussion and to focus attention on the essential elements of the theory, we shall retain the assumption given above throughout the present work'.[§]

This ambiguity compels Professor Joseph Gillman (who subjected the theory of the tendency for the rate of profit to fall to statistical tests) to use simultaneously both Joan Robinson's method (in which c includes all fixed capital) and Sweezy's (c includes only depreciation). He notes: '...the ratio of surplus-value extracted in a given period to the capital used up in that period provides us with only an elementary definition of the rate of profit. Normally, the rate of profit is figured on the basis of the invested capital...To simplify his argument Marx assumed an average annual turnover of the capitals of one'.[||]

Further on Gillman explains his approach to the ratios c/v (organic composition of capital) and $s/(c+v)$ (rate of profit):

'...all these ratios are here calculated on the basis of capital consumed. This we shall call the "flow" basis. Subsequently we recalculate them on the basis of the invested capital. That we shall call the "stock" basis'.

'...In our empirical test of the law we use both the flow and the stock bases for whatever light each may yield'.[¶]

† Robinson, *op. cit.*, pp. 6, 7.　　‡ Robinson, *op. cit.*, p. 22.
§ Paul M. Sweezy, *The Theory of Capitalist Development* (Oxford, 1942), pp. 67–8.
|| Joseph M. Gillman, *The Falling Rate of Profit. Marx's Law and its Significance to Twentieth-Century Capitalism* (London, 1956), p. 17.　　¶ Gillman, *op. cit.* pp. 18 and 35.

2. THE RENTS PAID FOR THE USE OF DURABLE CAPITAL GOODS AS THE REPLACEMENT OF THEIR VALUES

The opinions adduced, especially those of Gillman, show that the problem of calculating the rate of profit and, correspondingly, the organic composition of capital correctly and indisputably has not yet been solved.

It is all the more incomprehensible why this problem is ignored by Professor Nobuo Okisio whose purpose is to 'reformulate some Marxian theorems in mathematical terms, hoping thereby to clarify Marxian doctrines for those who are confused by the rather obscure expression of Marx'.[†] In an article on the rate of profit Okisio gives his point of view.[‡]

'The rate of profit $s/(c+v)$ cannot exceed the inverse of the organic composition of production, namely

$$\frac{s}{c+v} \leqslant \frac{v+s}{c}.$$

'...This unquestionable relation demonstrates that the inverse of the organic composition of production is an upper limit of the rate of profit.

'...Therefore, however high the rate of surplus value may become, the rate of profit cannot exceed the upper limit, which itself decreases as time passes by...The above reasoning seems to be logically sound. Unfortunately this appearance is misleading...

'...Marx calculated the general rate of profit as aggregate surplus value divided by aggregate capital in terms of value, that is $s/(c+v)$. But this procedure is not correct. The general rate of profit, ρ, is determined by the following equations:'

$$p_i = (1+\rho)(\Sigma a_{ij} p_j + \tau_i W),$$
$$W = \Sigma b_i p_i.$$

In these equations Okisio uses the notation:

p_i = the price of a unit of the ith commodity;

a_{ij} = the amount of the jth commodity necessary to produce a unit of the ith commodity;

τ_i = The amount of labour directly needed to produce a unit of the ith commodity;

W = the money wage rate;

and $(b_1, b_2, \ldots, b_i, \ldots, b_m)$ = the basket of consumption goods a labourer receives for a unit of labour.

[†] Nobuo Okisio, 'A Mathematical Note on Marxian Theorems', *Weltwirtschaftliches Archiv*. Bd. 91, H. 2. 1963, p. 287.

[‡] Nobuo Okisio, 'Technical Changes and the Rate of Profit', *Kobe University Economic Review* 7, 1961, pp. 89, 90.

It is impossible to judge how far Okisio's conclusion is correct because it is not clear from these two articles of 1961 and 1963 how he deals with the problem of fixed capital. Only in his earlier paper of 1955 does he indicate his position: 'As to fixed capital; the fixed capital being huge in highly developed capitalistic production, we must consider the degree of utilisation of machines and equipment in order to tell the amount of these necessary to produce one unit of output. So when we define a_{ij}, we assume the economically normal degree of utilisation. And in the first stage of our argument, we neglect the existence of fixed capital.'[†]

This last little remark invalidates the argument in all the papers by Okisio which we have quoted, despite his excellent mathematics. Fixed capital is the essential feature of production and it is inadmissible to ignore it.

Professor Okisio defines a_{ij} as 'the amount of the jth commodity necessary to produce a unit of the ith commodity'. To produce a quantity of textiles, for example, it is necessary to have real weaving looms at one's disposal for the given period of time, and not 'the economically normal degree of utilisation'.

Consequently a_{ij} must be the quantity of capital goods j (in this example—the number of weaving looms) that are required to produce a unit of commodity i in the given period of time. Then the price p_i will be the rent paid for the use of a unit of the durable capital goods in that period of time.

Marx envisaged this form of advanced capital when calculating the constant part of the value of yarn in Chapter VII of vol. 1 of *Capital*: 'The rent of the factory is £300, or £6 per week'.

In *The Housing Question*, Engels contended that in general the rent for durable goods is the replacement of their value: 'As is known, the sale of a commodity consists in the fact that its owner relinquishes its use value and puts its exchange value into his pocket. The use values of commodities differ from one another amongst other things in the varying periods of time required for their consumption. A loaf of bread is consumed in a day, a pair of trousers will be worn out in a year, and a house, if you like, in a hundred years. Hence, in the case of commodities with a long period of wear, the possibility arises of selling their use value piece-meal and each time for a definite period, that is to say, to *let it* out. The piecemeal sale therefore realises the exchange value only gradually.'[‡]

Finally, at the present time Professor Michio Morishima has based one of his models on a similar idea: '...capital goods are not subject to purchase and sale, only their services being traded on the market.'[§]

[†] Nobuo Okisio, 'Monopoly and the Rates of Profit', *Kobe University Economic Review* **1**, 1955, p. 74.   [‡] F. Engels, *The Housing Question* (London, 1935), pp. 84–5.
[§] Michio Morishima, *Equilibrium, Stability and Growth* (Oxford, 1964), p. vii.

3. PRICES AND LABOUR COSTS WHEN THE STATE OF
THE ECONOMY IS OPTIMAL

There have been many statements in economic literature to the effect that an optimal state of the economy requires that prices of consumer goods should be proportional to their 'values', i.e. to the amounts of labour necessary to produce them.†

Among the comments on these statements‡ one common criticism which should be noted is that these statements would be correct if 'the average labour cost per unit of production coincided with the marginal labour cost'.§

The purpose of the present section is to prove that at an optimal state of the economy (in the sense of the maximum utility of a basket of commodities maintaining a given amount of labour) the average labour costs of the commodities need not be equal to the marginal labour costs (and consequently to prices), but only proportional to them.

Like any other economic model, the model under discussion requires a considerable degree of abstraction.

We examine the commodities which are the consumption goods of the workers. Such is the nature of political economy. As long ago as at the beginning of the last century Ricardo proved that 'in all countries, and all times, profits depend on the quantity of labour requisite to provide necessaries for the labourers, on that land or with that capital which yields no rent'.‖

L. v. Bortkiewicz has corroborated this statement of Ricardo mathematically: 'Equation (30) indicates that the rate of profit depends *only* on those amounts of labour and those turnover periods which concern the production and distribution of the goods forming the real wage rate. This theoretical result agrees entirely with Ricardo's thesis that the rate of profit cannot possibly be affected by the conditions of production of those goods which do not enter into real wages.'¶

It is assumed that accumulation (savings) will not have a place in the

---

† N. Stolarof, *Démonstration analytique de la formule économique: 'Les degrés finals de l'utilité (des produits librement créés) sont proportionnels à la valeur du travail* (Kiev, 1902); Leif Johansen, 'Forenklet velferdsteoretisk modell for en sozialistisk økonomi', *Nationaløkonomisk tidsskrift*, 1955, H. 3–4; A. A. Konüs, 'Teoreticheskie voprosy cen i potreblenya', *Voprosy economiki, planirovanya i statistiki*. (Moscow, 1957). ('Theoretical problems concerning prices and consumption', *Problems of economics, planning and statistics*.)

‡ Eberhard M. Fels in *Journal of the American Statistical Association*, vol. 54, no. 285, 1959; Robert W. Campbell in *Slavonic Review*, vol. xx, no. 3, 1961; J. M. Montias in *Econometrica*, vol. 29, no. 3, 1961.

§ A. L. Lur'ye in *Ekonomika i matematcheskiye metody* (*Economics and Mathematical Methods*), vol. ii, no. 1, 1966, p. 24.

‖ *The Works and Correspondence of David Ricardo* (London, 1952), vol. i, p. 126.

¶ L. v. Bortkiewicz, 'Value and price in the Marxian System', *International Economic Papers*, no. 2, 1952, p. 32.

budget of a worker's family. Consequently such 'commodities' as unique works of art, cancelled postage stamps, etc. are eliminated; durable goods such as furniture, refrigerators, etc., are hired but not purchased.

For the sake of simplicity it is assumed that labour is homogeneous, all workers get the same wage, and that the form of the utility function is the same for all workers' families.

With these assumptions one can determine for each commodity the amount of labour necessary to produce it. This amount of labour v_i is assumed to be a function of the quantity X_i of the commodity i ($i = 1, \ldots, m$, where m is the number of commodities, or specially formed groups of commodities):

$$v_i = v_i(X_i) \quad (i = 1, \ldots, m). \tag{1}$$

At the given prices $a_1, \ldots, a_m$ and money income L (= total expenditure of the consumer) the consumer (the worker's family) selects the quantities to be consumed in such a way that the ordinal utility function $\Phi(X_1, \ldots, X_m)$ should be a maximum, i.e. with

$$L = a_1 X_1 + \ldots + a_m X_m, \tag{2}$$

$$\Phi(X_1, \ldots, X_m) = \max. \tag{3}$$

It is assumed that there is no relationship other than (2) between $a_1, \ldots, a_m$ and L. For example, there are no monopolistic prices.

As is known, it follows from (2) and (3) that

$$\frac{\partial \Phi / \partial X_1}{a_1} = \ldots = \frac{\partial \Phi / \partial X_m}{a_m} = \lambda, \tag{4}$$

where λ is the Lagrange multiplier.

There is a given quantity of labour V that is allocated to the reproduction of the consumed goods $X_1, \ldots, X_m$:

$$V = v_1(X_1) + \ldots + v_m(X_m) = \text{const.} \tag{5}$$

It is assumed that there is no relationship other than (5) between $X_1, \ldots, X_m$.

The 'optimal state of the country' is assumed to be such that the utility function $\Phi(X_1, \ldots, X_m)$ will be a maximum not only for condition (2) but also for condition (5).

It follows from (3) and (5) that:

$$\frac{\partial \Phi / \partial X_1}{\partial V_1 / \partial X_1} = \ldots = \frac{\partial \Phi / \partial X_m}{\partial V_m / \partial X_m} = \frac{1}{\mu}, \tag{6}$$

where $1/\mu$ is the Lagrange multiplier.

If the systems of equations (4) and (6) are consistent, then

$$\frac{\partial V_1 / \partial X_1}{a_1} = \ldots = \frac{\partial V_m / \partial X_m}{a_m} = \lambda \mu. \tag{7}$$

Multiplying the numerator and the denominator of each of the ratios by X_i ($i = 1, \ldots, m$) and summing them we have:

$$\frac{(\partial V_1/\partial X_1)X_1 + \ldots + (\partial V_m/\partial X_m)\, X_m}{a_1 X_1 + \ldots + a_m X_m} = \lambda\mu.$$

Or, using (2): $\quad L = \dfrac{(\partial V_1/\partial X_1)}{\lambda\mu} X_1 + \ldots + \dfrac{(\partial V_m/\partial X_m)}{\lambda\mu} X_m.$ (8)

The money income L can be defined in a given ratio to the total amount of the labour V contained in the consumed commodities, i.e.

$$L = \eta[v_1(X_1) + \ldots + v_m(X_m)],$$

where η is constant.

The substitution of this expression in (8) gives

$$V_1(X_1) + \ldots + V_m(X_m) = \frac{(\partial V_1/\partial X_1)}{\lambda\mu\eta} X_1 + \ldots + \frac{(\partial V_m/\partial X_m)}{\lambda\mu\eta} X_m$$

Let us make the assumption that the utility function (3) has the form:

$$\Phi = f_1(X_1) + \ldots + f_m(X_m)$$

and that the marginal labour cost of the adopted money unit is constant whatever the form of the utility functions $f_1(X_1)$ may be. In this case[†] the factor $\lambda\mu\eta$ does not depend on $X_1, \ldots, X_m$. We have assumed (5) is the only relationship between $X_1, \ldots, X_m$. Furthermore $V_i(0) = 0$.

We can take:

$$V_i(X_i) = \frac{(\partial V_i/\partial X_i)}{\lambda\mu\eta} X_i \quad (i = 1, \ldots, m).$$

Hence we get $\quad \dfrac{\partial V_i}{\partial X_i} = \lambda\mu\eta \dfrac{V_i(X_i)}{X_i} \quad (i = 1, \ldots, m),$

i.e. the marginal labour costs $\partial V_i/\partial X_i$ are proportional to the average labour costs $[V_i(X_i)/X_i]$. Consequently, in accordance with (7), the prices $(a_1, \ldots, a_m)$ are proportional to the average labour costs. The function $V_i(X_i)$ takes the form $V_i = b_i X_i{}^q$ where b_i and q are constants.

It is to be noted that there are two limitations arising from the assumptions we have made.

First, it is impossible to determine the amount of labour in commodities in joint production, for example, grain and straw. It is only possible to compare the sum of their prices with the total amount of labour necessary to produce them. The prices of grain and straw taken separately are determined by their marginal utilities. This is the case of the famous example of Böhm–Bawerk about the prices of new and matured wine. The labour on the vineyard is used to produce the new and the matured

---

† Cf. R. Frisch, *New Methods of Measuring Marginal Utility*, (Tübingen, 1932).

wine together. The prices of these kinds of wine are proportional to their marginal utilities.

Secondly, the prices of the commodities satisfying the same needs, for example, coal and oil, are not mutually independent. It is only the sum of the prices of the oil and coal which must be compared with the total amount of the labour spent on the production of fuel. It is here that the phenomenon of differential rent arises.

This solution of the principle problem of the labour theory of value is distrusted because its consequences are at first glance unusual.

If the total sum of the rental payments for the services of durable capital goods, according to Engels, equals their value, then the prices at which the durable goods are sold after their manufacture are below their value.

It is in this way that Marx explains the source of commercial profit in chapter XVII of the third volume of *Capital*: 'Or, looking upon the matter from the point of view of the total commodity-capital, the prices at which the class of industrial capitalists sell are lower than the values of commodities.'†

Consequently the source of the profit of the owners of buildings and machinery is in the surplus labour expended during their production (the conditions of reproduction are implied).

The main thing is that the exchange value of a commodity is realized not in its sale but in the realization of its use value, i.e. in its final consumption.

The idea of the value of consumer goods as a starting-point for the prices of the means of production is not only Menger's: 'The value of goods of lower order cannot, therefore, be determined by the value of goods of higher order that were employed in their production. On the contrary, it is evident that the value of goods of higher order is always and without exception determined by the prospective value of the goods of lower order in whose production they serve.'‡

This idea can also be discovered in Marx: 'The selling price of the merchant, then, stands above his purchase price, not because the former stands above the total value, but because the purchase price stands below this value.'§

Finally, in the early fifties the authors' collective of the USSR Academy of Sciences openly accepted Menger's point of view: 'The law of value influences the production of means of production through consumer goods, which are needed to replace the expenditure of labour power.'‖

† Marx, *Capital*, vol. III, p. 336.
‡ Karl Menger, *Principles of Economics* (Glencoe, Illinois, 1950), pp. 149–50.
§ Marx, *op. cit.* p. 337.
‖ Politichskaya Ekonomia, (Moscow, 1954) (*Political Economy*, London, 1957, p. 594.)

It will be recalled that Ricardo, in his letter to McCulloch of 18 December 1819, attached great importance to the demonstration of this 'law of value': 'I am more convinced than ever that the great regulator of value is the quantity of labour required to produce the commodity valued. There are many modifications which must be admitted into this doctrine, from the circumstance of the unequal times that commodities require to be brought to market, but this does not invalidate the doctrine itself. I am not satisfied with the explanation which I have given of the principles which regulate value. I wish a more able pen would undertake it—the fault is not in the inadequacy of the doctrine to account for all difficulties but in the inadequacy of him who has attempted to explain it'†

It is the duty of every econometrician to accept this challenge of Ricardo.

The combination of the labour theory of value and econometrics, although it is founded on the theory of marginal utility, is necessary for the development of political economy.‡ As far back in the 'twenties the opinion was expressed in the Soviet economic literature that the theory of marginal utility is a negation (in the philosophical sense) of the labour theory of value—i.e. the former is a necessary stage in the development of the labour theory of value.

4. THE ORGANIC COMPOSITION OF CAPITAL

In the chapter 'Rate and Mass of Surplus Value' of Vol. 1 of *Capital* Marx formulated the following 'third law' of surplus value: 'The masses of value and of surplus-value produced by different capitals—the value of the labour-power being given and its degree of exploitation being equal—vary directly as the amounts of the variable constituents of these capitals, i.e., as their constituents transformed into living labour-power.'

Then Marx goes on: 'This law clearly contradicts all experience based on appearance. Everyone knows that a cotton spinner, who, reckoning the percentage on the whole of his applied capital, employs much constant and little variable capital, does not, on account of this, pocket less profit or surplus-value than a baker, who relatively sets in motion much variable and little constant capital. For the solution of this apparent contradiction, many intermediate terms are as yet wanted, as from the standpoint of elementary algebra many intermediate terms are wanted to understand that $0/0$ may represent an actual magnitude.'§

† *The Works and Correspondence of David Ricardo*, vol. VIII, p. 142.
‡ Leif Johansen, 'Labour Theory of Value and Marginal Utilities', *Economics of Planning*, vol. 3, no. 2, 1963.
§ Marx, *Capital*, vol. 1, p. 335.

Since the advanced constant capital c includes only rents paid for the use of durable capital goods the 'contradiction' in the example given by Marx is indeed 'apparent': statistics show that the constant part c of the advanced capital $(c+v)$ of 'a baker' included in the value $(= c+v+s)$ is relatively not less than that of 'a cotton spinner'.

The observed variation in organic composition of the advanced capital (i.e. of cost-price) is engendered by the different periods of its circulation (including for the durable goods produced also the period of their consumption) and by the presence of differential rent. This means that the condition for a common annual rate of profit does not require obligatory deviations of prices from their value equivalents.

Let n be the rate of turnover of the advanced capital per year, ρ the rate of profit and r the differential rent. If the value of a commodity coincides with its price we have the equation:

$$c+v+s = (c+v)\left(1+\frac{\rho}{n}\right)+r \qquad (9)$$

which after simple manipulation, gives

$$\frac{c}{v} = \frac{n(s/v - r/v)}{\rho} - 1. \qquad (10)$$

(It will be recalled that the rate of turnover of the advanced capital must be calculated taking into account the period of the consumption of the durable commodities produced.)

The ratio s/v (the rate of surplus value) is determined by the formula:

$$\frac{s}{v} = \frac{\text{The length of the working day in hours}}{\substack{\text{The number of hours of labour contained in the} \\ \text{commodities comprising the daily wage}}} - 1. \qquad (11)$$

The demoninator in this formula can be roughly determined by an input–output table.

The rate of surplus value s/v has a tendency towards equalization in different industries. (It is to be noted that this applies also in socialist countries.)

It is impossible to understand why econometricians ignore formula (11). It should be recalled that Marx's priority in this problem was disputed by Rodbertus, an economist with a very different ideology: 'I have shown where the capitalists surplus value arises in my 3rd Social Letter; essentially in the same way as Marx, but only more clearly and briefly.'†

† *Briefe und Socialpolitische Aufsätze von Rodbertus Yagetsow*, herausgegeben von R. Meyer. Bd. 1 (1884), p. 111.

Equation (10) corresponds to the facts as they appear in the statistical data of capitalist countries:

the greater the ratio r/v (differential rent in the industry to wages) the lower is the organic composition of the advanced capital;

the greater the annual rate of turnover of advanced capital, the higher is its organic composition.

By making appropriate assumptions (there is no differential rent, the circulating period of advanced capital is the same, the prices are considered as independent variables) one can prove that if the production methods are chosen so as to minimize the cost of production and the rates of profit are the same in different industries, then the organic composition of advanced capital must be the same in every industry.[†]

This conclusion is based on the conception that the organic composition of advanced capital does not depend on its technical composition but is affected by economic considerations, in the same way as the production function is not a purely engineering concept.[‡]

5. COST CRITERION AND THE RATE OF PROFIT

We can now return to the problem of the tendency of the rate of profit to fall. As Professor Okisio points out '...capitalists choose a new production technique, above all, according to cost criterion. Even if there were techniques which increase productivity of labour greatly, they could not be introduced by capitalists, unless they reduce the cost of production'.[§]

This problem is solved by careful examination of the expression of the rate of profit:

$$\rho = \frac{s-r}{c+v}. \tag{12}$$

The equations suggested by Professor Okisio to determine the rate of profit (see p. 74 above) assume a differing composition of capital in different branches of production (provided the period of its turnover is the same). As L. v. Bortkiewicz has proved,[‖] this assumption involves

[†] A. A. Konüs, Notes to article by L. Johansen 'Labour Theory of Value and Marginal Utilities' in *Economics of Planning*, vol. 3, no. 2, 1963. *Economics of Planning*, vol. 4, no. 3, 1964.

[‡] Cf. R. Dorfman, P. A. Samuelson and R. M. Solow, *Linear Programming and Economic Analysis* (New York, 1958): '...the technologists do not take responsibility for the production function...They regard the production function as an economists concept, and as a matter of history nearly all the production functions that have actually been derived are the work of economists rather than of engineers'.

[§] Okisio, *Technical Changes and the Rate of Profit*, p. 91.

[‖] L. v. Bortkiewicz, 'Zur Berichtigung der Grundlegenden theoretischen Konstruktion von Marx im dritten Band des Kapital', *Jahrbücher für National Ökonomie und Statistik*. III Folge, 34 Bd. (Jena, 1907).

the rejection of the labour theory of value, since, if the sum of the prices equals the sum of the values the sum of the profits will not equal the sum of the surplus values.

Expression (12) is here applied to the aggregate of the commodities which are the consumption goods of the workers (the constant capital c including the rents paid for the use of durable capital goods). It was shown in § 3 that the prices of the especially formed groups of these commodities are proportional to the amount of labour necessary to produce them, and therefore the expression (12) must be considered true.

First of all expression (12) shows that an increase in differential rent, *ceteris paribus*, reduces the rate of profit.

Let us take the case when differential rent r is zero and suppose that the constant capital c increases. The cost criterion for the given output consists in the fact that an increase in c must be accompanied by a decrease in the sum $(c+v)$. The rate of profit will fall if the increase of surplus value s is relatively less than the increase in the advanced capital $(c+v)$, i.e. the cost of production. That takes place when the reduction in the number of workers is comparatively greater than the corresponding increase in the rate of surplus value (i.e. the productivity of labour). Otherwise the rate of profit will rise. None the less there is an upper limit to this increase, as can be seen from Okisio's inequality (see p. 74), if it is applied to the aggregate of commodities which are the consumption goods of the workers.

Thus the tendency for the rate of profit to fall and the counteracting tendencies which are always emphasized by Maurice Dobb are substantiated in detail by the analysis of the fundamental formulae of the labour theory of value.

PART II

PLANNING AND THE MARKET

THE CURVE OF PRODUCTION AND THE EVALUATION OF THE EFFICIENCY OF INVESTMENT IN A SOCIALIST ECONOMY

MICHAL KALECKI

I. CHOICE OF TECHNIQUE

An increment of the national income of a given volume and structure in terms of final products, resulting from new investment, may be achieved by a variety of techniques. Each of the variants will involve a different outlay on investment I and a different amount of labour force R in-

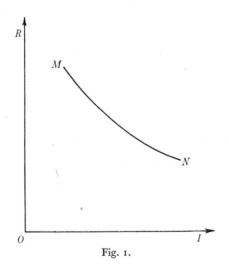

Fig. 1.

dispensable to run the newly created productive capacities. As the increment of the national income consists of many final products and each of them may usually be produced by different methods, a great number of variants comes into the picture. If we denote by N the number of groups embracing kindred products (we shall call them below commodity groups) and if for each only two variants are considered, there will be altogether 2^N variants of producing a given increment of the national income.

[87]

If one of the variants involves a greater investment outlay than another, while the labour force is the same or greater, this variant is absolutely ineffective. The same applies to a variant for which the labour force is greater and the investment outlay no less than in another case. We shall discard all the absolutely ineffective variants and shall consider only those in which a greater investment outlay is associated with a lesser labour force or *vice versa*.

Let us represent all these variants by a diagram, on which we plot the aggregate investment outlay I on the abscissa—and the labour force R associated with it on the ordinate axis (see fig. 1). To each of the variants there corresponds a point in the plane I, R. It follows from the above that the downward sloping curve MN corresponds to the set of acceptable variants. Indeed, to each I there corresponds only one value of R, namely that of a variant where the investment outlay I is associated with the least labour force. Moreover, the curve is downward sloping because greater investment outlays are associated with lesser labour force. The line MN is called the curve of production.

2. THE APPROPRIATE CRITERION

This concept is clearly based on the assumption of a uniform labour force and of an equal life-span for all types of equipment, since only in such a case can a given variant be fully characterized by the investment outlay and the labour force associated with it. We shall deal in the final part of this paper with the problems arising when these simplifications are discarded. But even taking these assumptions for granted this approach to the curve of production may raise some reservations. Indeed, the central planning authorities are obviously unable to consider the enormous number of possible variants of producing an increment of the national income in order to eliminate those which are absolutely ineffective. Thus the curve of production appears to be purely theoretical in character since its points are not necessarily realized in practice (i.e. it is not excluded that an absolutely ineffective variant may be selected). We shall show, however, that this problem does not arise if the evaluation of efficiency of investment for any commodity group is based on the criterion

$$\frac{i}{T} + k = \text{minim.}$$

where i is the investment outlay integrated over all stages of production, k the integrated current costs (exclusive of depreciation) and T the so-called recoupment period. Indeed, we shall prove that to a given T there corresponds a point situated on the curve of production. It should be pointed out that, on the assumption of a uniform labour force and an equal life-span for all types of equipment, the simple condition

$$\frac{i}{T} + k = \text{minim.} \tag{1}$$

is an appropriate criterion for the choice of variants.

We shall assume that in the case where the 'joint investment and labour outlay' $(i/T) + k$ is equal for two variants the less capital intensive one is chosen, i.e. that with a smaller i.

We denote by i_w and k_w the investment outlay and the costs of the variant of production selected for a given commodity group and by i and k these characteristics of any variant for this group. We have then

$$\frac{i_w}{T} + k_w \leqslant \frac{i}{T} + k.$$

By adding these equations for the economy as a whole we obtain

$$\Sigma \left(\frac{i_w}{T} + k_w \right) \leqslant \Sigma \left(\frac{i}{T} + k \right)$$

$$\frac{1}{T} \Sigma i_w + \Sigma k_w \leqslant \frac{1}{T} \Sigma i + \Sigma k. \tag{2}$$

Σi_w and Σk_w, however, are nothing else but the aggregate investment outlay I_w and the aggregate costs K_w required for a given increment of the national income by the adopted methods while Σi and Σk are the aggregate values I and K for any 'aggregate variant'. We have thus:

$$\frac{I_w}{T} + K_w \leqslant \frac{I}{T} + K \tag{3}$$

It follows directly that the point I_w, K_w cannot correspond to an absolutely ineffective variant. Indeed, if I_w were, for instance, greater than I' of a certain other variant, and K_w would not be less than K', we could write

$$\frac{I'}{T} + K' < \frac{I_w}{T} + K_w$$

which would contradict the inequality (3).

Let us denote now the hourly wage by g. To the aggregate costs K_w there corresponds a labour force $R_w = K_w/g$. It follows from the above that the point I_w, R_w is situated on the curve of production, because the latter represents all the 'effective' variants of producing a given increment of the national income (i.e. all variants which are not absolutely ineffective).

I_w, R_w is a point on the curve of production corresponding to a given period of recoupment T; it will be noticed that the greater T is, the farther to the right on the curve of production the corresponding point I_w, R_w is situated—because a higher recoupment period 'lets in' the more capital intensive and less labour intensive variants for particular commodity groups. However, we shall not be satisfied with this rather intuitive argument, but shall prove the theorem rigorously; at the same time we shall demonstrate that the curve of production is concave (as in fig. 1).

3. THE CURVE OF PRODUCTION

Let us start with a diagrammatic representation of the variants of production of a given commodity group, plotting the investment outlays i on the abscissa—and the current costs k on the ordinate axis.

If the recoupment period is T, it will be noticed that the best variant is determined by the point through which passes the lowest of the straight lines of a slope $-i/T$. Indeed, the equation for the straight line of such a slope is:

$$k = -\frac{i}{T} + b,$$

where b is the distance of the point of intersection of this straight line with the ordinate axis from the zero point. Thus

$$\frac{i}{T} + k = b$$

and the condition for the best variant is

$$\frac{i}{T} + k = b_{\text{minim.}}$$

It follows directly that there must be chosen such a point i, k through which passes a straight line with the least b. It follows, moreover, that at no T does the point C come into consideration and we are left only with A, B, and D situated on the lower concave boundary to choose from. Let us denote now the recoupment periods corresponding to the slopes AB and BD by T_{AB} and T_{BD}. If $T = T_{AB}$, we shall choose the variant A; indeed for the variants A and B the value of the expression $(i/T) + k$ is the same and according to our rule we choose then the less capital intensive variant. If $T_{AB} < T \leqslant T_{BD}$ we choose the variant B (the case represented in fig. 2). Finally, when $T > T_{BD}$, the variant D will prove the best. In other words, when increasing the recoupment period T we pass the level T_{AB}, we shift from the variant A to a more capital intensive and a less labour intensive variant B. (If we pass the value T_{BD} we shift correspondingly from the variant B to the variant D.)

Let us consider now all the commodity groups, for which we may draw diagrams analogous to fig. 2. Let us derive from each diagram the recoupment periods T corresponding to the segments of the lower concave boundary such as T_{AB} and T_{BD}. Let us range all these recoupment periods according to their length; we shall obtain an increasing sequence $T_1, T_2, \ldots, T_j, T_{j+1}, \ldots, T_m$. It should be noted that T_j may correspond to a number of commodity groups and that T_{j+1} may obviously correspond to other commodity groups than T_j.

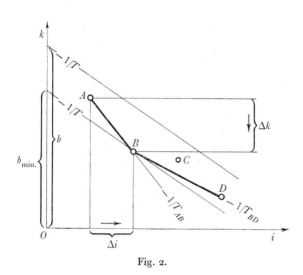

Fig. 2.

Let us imagine that a recoupment period T_j has been adopted to which corresponds the point I_j, R_j on the curve of production and that next we pass from T_j to T_{j+1}. Then for the commodity groups, to which corresponds T_j this level of the recoupment period will be passed (for instance T_{AB} in fig. 2) and, according to the above, a shift will occur for these commodity groups to the more capital—and less labour intensive variants (for instance from variant A to variant B). As a result the value of the investment outlay in the economy as a whole will increase as well from I_j to the higher level I_{j+1}, and the labour force required will fall from R_j to R_{j+1}. Therefore the point I_{j+1}, R_{j+1} on the curve of production corresponding to T_{j+1}, will be situated to the right of and below the point I_j, R_j which corresponds to T_j (see fig. 3).

Nor is that all. Indeed T_j corresponds to a side of the lower boundary of the set of points representing the variants on one or more diagrams relating to the particular commodity groups (for instance AB in fig. 2). When T_j is passed a shift occurs from the beginning of that sid· to its end (e.g. from A to B). Thus the respective increases in current costs Δk and investment Δi bear the relation $-I/T_j$ (e.g. the relation $-I/T_{AB}$)

i.e.
$$\Delta k = -\frac{\text{I}}{T_j}\Delta i. \tag{4}$$

Since just these increases constitute the increments of the aggregate investment outlay and of the aggregate costs, we obtain:

$$K_{j+1} - K_j = -\frac{\text{I}}{T_j}(I_{j+1} - I_j), \tag{5}$$

and thus
$$R_{j+1} - R_j = -\frac{\text{I}}{gT_j}(I_{j+1} - I_j).$$

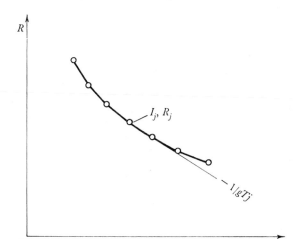

Fig. 3.

It follows directly that the straight line connecting the subsequent points I_j, R_j and I_{j+1}, R_{j+1} situated on the curve of production has a slope $-\text{I}/(gT_j)$. In other words the segment starting from the point I_j, R_j has the slope $-\text{I}/(gT_j)$ (fig. 3). Consequently, the greater the recoupment period T_j, the more to the right is situated the corresponding point I_i, R_i —which was already proved above—and the smaller the slope of the segment starting from this point. This means, however, that the line represented in fig. 3 is concave.

If the points I_j, R_j are sufficiently close to each other, this line approaches the curve of production and the slopes of its sides—those of the tangents at these points. The tangent of the curve of production at the point I, R is consequently equal to $-\text{I}/gT$ and thus it is easy to read from the diagram the recoupment period corresponding to a given point.

Because I increases together with T, the curve of production is concave (fig. 4).

On the basis of the curve of production it is possible to determine the recoupment period corresponding to the assumed increment of the national income and to the labour force R_1 available for this purpose. Let us draw a curve of production for the assumed increase of the national income and let us find on it the point with the ordinate R_1; then the abscissa I_1 yields the value of the investment outlay required and the slope of the tangent at the point I_1, R_1—the recoupment period T_1 which must be applied in the evaluation of efficiency of investment for realizing the variant which corresponds to the point I_1, R_1, and thus for securing equilibrium in the balance of the labour force.

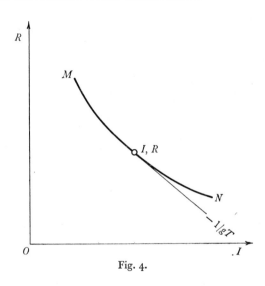

Fig. 4.

4. THE EFFECT OF TECHNICAL PROGRESS

The above discussion is of some importance for the theory of growth because the curve of production is an essential element in the analysis of technical progress. The curve of production represents the set of 'effective' variants of producing an increment of the national income which are based on the technical knowledge at a given time. A change in this knowledge, i.e. technical progress, may be represented by a downward shift of the curve of production. Thus a reduction of labour which is required to produce a given set of goods takes place, i.e. an increase in the productivity of labour, which is not 'paid for' by an increase in capital intensity. This process is represented in fig. 5, where MB is the curve of production at time t and $M'B'$—at time $t+1$. With an unchanged investment out-

lay OA (valued at constant prices) the labour force required for producing
a given increment of the national income declines from AB to AB', and
the productivity of labour increases, of course, in the inverse proportion.

The slope of the tangent at point B' will in general be different from
that at point B. Indeed, with an unchanged wage rate g to a given I there
corresponds in general a recoupment period which is different at time
$t+1$ from that at time t: as a result of the technical progress the variants
for the particular commodity groups are transformed in the direction of
the reduction of current costs associated with a given investment valued
at constant prices; this reduction, however, varies considerably from

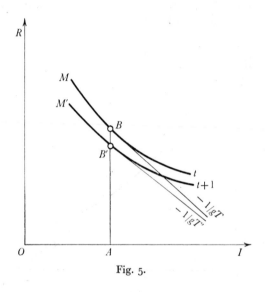

Fig. 5.

asset to asset. In the case presented in fig. 5, where all the ordinates of the
curve of production decline in the same proportion (i.e. when productivity of labour shows an equal rate of increase for all the values of I), the
slope of the tangent at point B' is reduced as compared with the slope of
the tangent at point B in the relation AB'/AB; it follows directly that the
recoupment period increases in this case in the same proportion as the
productivity of labour.

In order to be able to present the technical progress, as above, it is
essential to make sure that to a point on the curve of production there
corresponds a real situation. As was pointed out, it cannot be assumed
that the variant corresponding to this point is realized by central planning authorities discarding the absolutely ineffective variants. As has
been shown, this point is realized by the evaluation of efficiency of investment at the lower echelons of economic management.

In accordance with our assumptions we have postulated so far a rather simplified method of this evaluation. Let us inquire now what is the position when these simplifications are discarded and the methods of evaluation of the efficiency of investment which are actually applied in socialist countries are taken into consideration.

5. THE COMPOSITION OF THE LABOUR FORCE

First of all the assumption that the employment is proportionate to the wage bill must be abolished. Indeed a shift from one production variant to another may involve a change in the proportion of better paid employees and as a result the average earnings may change. Therefore the above argument applies, strictly speaking, only when the outlay of labour is measured by the ratio when $\Sigma k/g$—where g is the hourly wage of unskilled labour—rather than in man-hours. Thus instead of the labour force we should consider its equivalent in terms of unskilled labour calculated on the basis of wage relations. If when moving along the curve of production the average wage does not change significantly— which is quite likely within a limited range of I—the preceding discussion would apply approximately to the curve of production based on the number of man-hours.

The question may arise here, how should the quantity of labour be measured in the theory of growth: in actual man-hours or rather by the equivalent in man-hours of unskilled labour? The answer to this question is by no means simple and is outside the framework of this paper.

6. DIFFERENTIATED RECOUPMENT PERIODS

What will be the repercussions of the application of different recoupment periods for various commodity groups, as is the case for example in evaluation of the efficiency of investment in the Soviet Union. Let us assume that these recoupment periods bear a constant relation to each other, so that the recoupment period of the commodity group s may be represented as T/a_s, where a_s is a constant coefficient. As a result all recoupment periods change proportionately to T. The formula for evaluation of the efficiency of investment for the commodity s may be now written as follows:

$$\frac{1}{T}a_s I + k = \text{minim.} \tag{6}$$

From the course of our argument it follows directly that it would fully apply to a curve of production obtained by plotting on the abscissa axis the $\Sigma a_s i$ rather than $\Sigma i = I$. (This will be the sum of investment outlays weighted by coefficients a_s.) In general the curve of production obtained in this way will not be equivalent to the production curve constructed on the assumption of the same T for all commodity groups, when it is $\Sigma i = I$ that we plot on the abscissa axis. The variant of producing a given increment of the national income discarded as absolutely ineffective in one system, may be accepted in another.

There is nothing strange about this. Indeed the system of differentiated recoupment periods aims at fostering the capital intensity in certain industries. Therefore whereas to a given aggregate cost $K = \Sigma k$ there corresponds in the system of one recoupment period for all commodity groups the least aggregate investment outlay $I = \Sigma i$—what is minimized in the system presently considered is the sum in which the investment in 'privileged' industries is more heavily weighted.

There arises the difficulty, however, that from the point of view of the theory of growth the sum $\Sigma a_s i$ is not a suitable variable, the actual investment outlays $I = \Sigma i$ being in the centre of discussion. This difficulty may be overcome by modifying the concept of the curve of production related, as previously, to the investment outlays I and the labour force R. The point I_j, R_j of this curve is now determined simply as that variant of producing a given increment of the national income which is obtained by the evaluation of efficiency of investment based on recoupment periods differentiated for particular commodity groups T/a_s for $T = T_j$. The fact that the investment outlay I_j will not now be necessarily the lowest of those associated with R_j does not interfere with the suitability of such a curve of production for the theory of growth. It is only important to check whether such a curve is downward sloping, because this *is* essential in the analysis of technical progress. We shall prove that this is the case.

When T is increased from T_j to T_{j+1} a shift to a more capital- and less labour-intensive variant takes place for one or more commodity groups. As a result the aggregate investment outlay increases from I_j to I_{j+1}, and the labour force decreases from R to R_{j+1}, i.e. the curve of production is downward sloping here as well. However it is impossible to prove in this case that the curve is concave. Indeed, formula (4) will now read as follows:

$$\Delta k = - \frac{a_s}{T_j} \Delta i. \tag{7}$$

Therefore the slope of the production curve $(R_{j+1} - R_j)/(I_{j+1} - I_j)$ is influenced not only by the magnitude of T_j, but also by the coefficients a_s of those commodity groups where a shift to a higher capital intensity occurred, when I increased from T_j to T_{j+1}. Since in the course of the further increase in T the shifts in the variants of other commodity groups with different coefficients a_s will be relevant, it is impossible to prove that the slope of the segment starting from I_j, R_j will decrease along with T.

It is not certain, therefore, whether in this case the curve of production is concave. This however is not essential for the analysis of technical progress in the theory of growth.

7. LENGTH OF LIFE OF THE EQUIPMENT

We shall now consider the problem of different life-spans of various types of equipment. Let us start with the case where in evaluation of the efficiency of investment this is accounted for by differentiating the recoupment period T according to different rates of depreciation. (For instance, if the life-span amounts to 20 years for one asset and to 40 years for another and for the first asset $T = 6$ years and thus $1/T = 0.167$ —then for the second asset we shall have $1/T = 0.167 - 0.050 + 0.025$ $= 0.142$, and thus T' amounts to about 7 years; it should be recalled that according to our assumption depreciation is *not* included in the current costs.)

This case is thus similar to the previously considered differentiation of the recoupment period between industries; and as in the other case the curve of production must be constructed on the basis of variants which are realized through the practice of evaluation of the efficiency of investment. Again to a given labour force R there will not correspond on this curve the least investment outlay, because apart from the capital and labour intensity of an asset its durability is taken into consideration as well.

As regards the proof that the curve of production is downward sloping, the position is more complicated here than for the differentiation of the recoupment period between industries; there exists a theoretical possibility in this case that for a particular commodity group the more capital and more labour intensive variant may prove 'better' because its much lower rate of depreciation would outbalance its higher capital and labour intensity. This is, however, unlikely. In practice more capital intensive assets which are at the same time more durable require as a rule less labour. It may reasonably be assumed that when as a result of the increase in the recoupment period the more capital intensive variants are 'let in' they are at the same time less labour intensive. As a result the aggregate investment outlay of investment I increases with T and the aggregate labour force declines or the curve of production is downward sloping.

However—just as in the case of recoupment period differentiated between industries—it cannot be assumed that the curve of production is concave. For the relation of the decline in the labour force R to the increase in the investment outlays I accompanying the rise in the recoupment period is influenced by the depreciation rates of these variants of particular commodity groups between which occurs a shift in the direction of greater capital and lesser labour intensity.

In Soviet practice the two cases considered last overlap because the recoupment period is differentiated between industries and reflects the differences in depreciation rates. (In fact depreciation is included in current costs, but this amounts to the same as allowing for the difference in depreciation rates in the length of the recoupment period, since depreciation is proportionate—at a given depreciation rate—to the investment outlay.)

8. THE NEW POLISH APPROACH

In the Polish methodology of evaluation of the efficiency of investment the recoupment period is not differentiated between industries, but up to 1960 the difference in the rates of depreciation was taken care of in the way described above. In the new methodology the approach to the problem of different life-spans is more complicated. We shall give here a general outline of this approach, with an emphasis on the points which are relevant to the problem of the curve of production.

The new approach based on a theoretical inquiry consists of allowing for the life-span of equipment through multiplying the investment outlays i and the current costs k by coefficients $f(n)$ and $\phi(n)$ which are definite functions of n; thus 'joint investment and labour outlay' of a variant with a life-span n can be written as follows:

$$\frac{i \cdot f(n)}{T} + k \cdot \phi(n).$$

It must be added that f is a decreasing function, and ϕ an increasing one and that the above expression reaches its minimum at a certain value n. The value—depending on i and k—is thus the optimum life-span $n_{opt.}$. It is this life-span that is accepted for evaluation of the efficiency of investment rather than that corresponding to a conventional norm of depreciation for a given type of equipment. Thus the 'joint investment and labour outlay' for a given variant is finally:

$$\frac{i \cdot f(n_{opt.})}{T} + k \cdot \phi(n_{opt.}).$$

We thus have by definition the inequality:

$$\frac{i \cdot f(n_{opt.})}{T} + k \cdot \phi(n_{opt.}) \leqslant \frac{i \cdot f(n)}{T} + k \cdot \phi(n), \tag{8}$$

where n is any life-span of the equipment considered.

Let us turn to our curve of production. We construct it, as in the cases previously discussed, on the basis of the variants i, k, selected for particular commodity groups by minimizing the 'joint investment and labour outlays'

$$\frac{i.f(n_{\text{opt.}})}{T} + k.\phi(n_{\text{opt.}}).$$

It has now to be proved that the curve of production is downward sloping. It appears that in this case no additional assumption is necessary, as contrasted with the previous approach to the influence of different life-spans of equipment. Indeed it may be proved here that a more capital intensive and no less labour intensive variant is 'worse' for any recoupment period T.

Let us denote the investment outlays and the cost of a variant for some commodity group by i and k, and for a more capital intensive variant by i' and k'. Let us further denote the optimum life-span of equipment for the first variant by $n_{\text{opt.}}$ and for the second one by $n'_{\text{opt.}}$. Let us assume that although $i' > i$, we have $k' \geqslant k$. We can thus write   *119320*

$$\frac{i.f(n'_{\text{opt.}})}{T} + k.\phi(n'_{\text{opt.}}) < \frac{i'.f(n'_{\text{opt.}})}{T} + k'.\phi(n'_{\text{opt.}}),$$

(i.e. the first variant is 'better' if for both variants we apply the life-span of the second asset). We have next, according to formula (8):

$$\frac{i.f(n_{\text{opt.}})}{T} + k.\phi(n_{\text{opt.}}) \leqslant \frac{i.f(n'_{\text{opt.}})}{T} + k.\phi(n'_{\text{opt.}}),$$

(i.e. it is better to use the first asset for $n_{\text{opt.}}$ years than for $n'_{\text{opt.}}$ years). But from these two inequalities it follows:

$$\frac{i.f(n_{\text{opt.}})}{T} + k.\phi(n_{\text{opt.}}) < \frac{i'.f(n'_{\text{opt.}})}{T} + k'.\phi(n'_{\text{opt.}})$$

and thus the first variant is 'better' than the second for any value of T.

Therefore the more capital intensive variants for particular commodity groups which are 'let in' as a result of the increase in T are less labour intensive; thus the increase of the aggregate investment outlay will be accompanied by a reduction of the labour force associated with it, i.e. the curve of production is downward sloping. However, in this case, as in that previously considered, it cannot be maintained that the curve is concave.

9. CONCLUSIONS

To summarize: the evaluation of the efficiency of investment practised in socialist countries determines, given the level of the recoupment period (or periods), the investment outlays I and the labour force R required for producing a given increment of the national income. When the recoupment period is raised the investment outlays increase, and the labour requirements decline. Consequently the set of points I, R represents a downward sloping curve, which we call the curve of production. If the same recoupment period T for all industries is accepted, the differences in the life-span of equipment are disregarded and the labour force is measured by the aggregate costs divided by the hourly wage g for unskilled labour—then the curve of production exhibits in addition the following characteristics: (a) to a given labour force R there corresponds the least investment outlay, (b) the curve is concave, and (c) the slope of the tangent in its point I, R—corresponding to the recoupment period T, is equal to $-i/gT$. The differentiation of the recoupment periods between industries, as well as allowing for the differences in the life-spans of equipment, deprives the curve of production of these characteristics because they introduce in the evaluation of variants new variables in addition to the investment and labour outlays. It is probable, however, that the actual curves of production can be fairly well approximated by curves possessing the characteristics (a) and (b).

A MODEL FOR THE
PLANNING OF PRICES†

O. KÝN, B. SEKERKA, L. HEJL

I. INTRODUCTION

The interest of economists has recently concentrated a great deal on the problem of prices. Under conditions of a centralized system of management of the economy it was not correct to identify the planning of prices with centralized administrative price fixing of all products. Since no adequate method of planning prices existed and since it was practically impossible to make available to the centre the huge amount of information (as well as to process such information at the centre) necessary for the fixing of prices for all products, all the centre could do was adjust prices from time to time on an 'ex post' principle. Under such conditions it was only natural that after some time the system of prices prevailing in the economy became so deformed that it almost ceased to fulfil any rational economic function.

This deformation of the price system has at present two important negative consequences for the Czechoslovak national economy: (*a*) the basic criterion for evaluating the efficiency of the economic process has been deformed, which means that under the old price system it is impossible to make rational economic decisions either at the centralized or at the decentralized level; (*b*) with the price system in operation until now, existing prices are at such variance with equilibrium market prices that it is very difficult to renew quickly the functioning of a market mechanism.

Thus the task of rationalizing the price system has become one of the basic conditions for a better functioning of the socialist economy as a whole. During the last few years this problem has, to an increasing extent, become the focus of interest among economists in the socialist countries. This was apparent in the discussions concerning the functioning of the law of value and the role of the market mechanism under conditions of socialism, as well as in the discussions concerning the so called 'rational price-formula.'

This paper aims at following up the discussions about a rational price-

† We should like to thank Martin Černý for valuable criticism of the mathematical apparatus and F. Nevařil, St. Kysilka and J. Mrenica who cooperated with us in the practical calculations.

formula, and especially the work of Belkin, Nemchinov, Novozhilov, Korać, Csikos-Nagy, Ganczer and Racz.†

We have tried to generalize individual price formulae (or types of prices) and project them into a more general price theory. We have also, by way of experiment, made calculations of basic price types on empirical data from the Czechoslovak economy for the year 1962. On the basis of a theoretical analysis of the individual types of prices we have tried to sketch the method by which a model of price planning might be used.

The mathematical and economic apparatus used in this paper is simple and is based on economic models of the Leontief type. More sophisticated optimalization models exist today, which can give an optimal price system as their solution. But these optimalization models still present a number of unsolved problems and also the information necessary for their use is not available and so makes them impossible to use for the practical planning of prices in the near future. In this paper we do not claim to have found the best price system, but we think that the suggested method can be used under present conditions to find a price system that will at least be more rational than the present one. The practical use of this price model has been tried out by experimental price calculations (see Hejl, Kýn, Sekerka),‡ by use in the preparations for a general reform of wholesale prices which came into effect in Czechoslovakia on 1 January 1967, and also in a forecast of price development until 1970 which was made by the State Commission for Finance, Prices and Wages at the beginning of 1966.

One more point must be made about the relationship of this model to the functioning of the market mechanism. Some authors believe that mathematical methods and the use of computers will enable such exact calculations of prices of all important products as to make it possible to set these prices centrally as binding for all enterprises. We do not share this opinion. The statistical information necessary for price calculations is never sufficiently perfect, nor does it reach the centre quickly enough, to make it possible to consider the calculated prices as entirely adequate to the momentary state of the economy. Even if the largest computer available were used, it would not be possible or efficient to calculate millions of prices of various concrete products. We therefore think the importance of price calculations lies especially in the fact that they yield

† V. D. Belkin, *Tseny yedinnogo urovnya i ekonomicheskiye izmereniya na ikh osnove* (Moscow, 1963); V. S. Nemchinov, 'Osnovnye kontury modeli planovogo tsenoobrazovaniya, *Voprosy ekonomiki*, 12/1963; V. V. Novozhilov, *Zakon stoimosti i planovoye tsenoobrazovaniye*, (Leningrad, 1965); M. Korać, 'Osnovni teorijski problemi analize ekonomskog položaja privrednih grupacija', *Ekonomist* (Beograd), **4**, 1964; B. Csikos-Nagy, S. Ganczer, J. Rácz, 'Az elsö termékrend szerü ármodell', *Közoazdasagi Szemle*, 1/1964.

‡ L. Hejl, O. Kýn, B. Sekerka, 'Experimentální propočty typu ceny', *Plánované hospo-dářství*, 11/1965.

information on how basic, macroeconomic price relations should develop—in other words how the relations between aggregate price levels of individual industries should develop. Such information can then help planning institutions to better planning and enable institutions concerned with day-to-day management to use those indirect methods of influencing the economic process which will lead to such development that current prices, formed by the market, become as close as possible to planned prices. Such a concept of the planning of prices with the help of mathematical models and computers does not presuppose an elimination of the market mechanism, but, on the contrary, presupposes its existence. The planned price should at the same time be an equilibrium market price, with current market price moving according to momentary supply and demand.

2. THE BASIC EQUATIONS

We shall use a model of the national economy of the Leontief type with n sectors. Output is priced by three different systems of prices. In accordance with the terminology generally in use we shall distinguish the following:

(a) A system of *wholesale prices*, which serves in the exchange of products between socialist enterprises. Everything produced receives a wholesale price.

(b) A system of *retail prices*, which serves in the exchange between retail trade enterprises and the consumer. Only the vector of personal consumption from the second quadrant of the input–output table is priced in this way.

(c) A system of *foreign prices* which are paid for imported goods bought abroad, or for which our exported goods are sold on foreign markets. This system is used to price only the import and export vectors of the second quadrant of the input–output table.

Our model will have only one (wholesale) pricing both for elements of the input–output matrix (i.e. the first quadrant) and for vectors of social consumption and investment (in the second quadrant). The vectors of personal consumption will have double pricing (in wholesale as well as retail prices)† and the vector of imports and exports will be priced in wholesale prices and foreign prices (there may be several systems of foreign prices).

---

† Such a division is only roughly in accord with what is actually used: some elements of the first quadrant, or of the vector of social consumption and investment, are also priced in retail prices. The vector of personal consumption includes also consumption in kind. But these deviations are, from a practical point of view, unimportant and to keep our model as simple as possible we shall leave them out.

Let us introduce the following relations:

$p = (p_1, p_2, \ldots, p_n)$ is the vector of wholesale prices;[†]

$q' = (q_1\, q_2 \ldots, q_n)$ is the vector of total output in physical units;

$x = (x_1, x_2, \ldots, x_n)$ is the vector of total production priced in wholesale prices.

All three vectors are connected in the following relationship:

$$p = x\hat{q}^{-1}, \tag{1}$$

where $\hat{q}$ is a diagonal matrix formed from the q vector.[‡]

A Leontief model in which the output of all sectors would be expressed directly in physical units would have to contain so many sectors that calculation would become very difficult. For practical reasons therefore the output of at least several sectors (which produce non-homogeneous products) will be expressed in the 'value of production' and not directly in physical units.

The price model we shall describe can be used for the solution of two problems:

Problem No. 1 Finding prices for a given structure of output in physical units.
Problem No. 2 Finding indices of the transformation from the old price system to the new, if the structure of output in the old prices is known.[§]

For the sake of simplicity and explicitness we shall in this paper use the terminology of problem 1; but the same model could serve to solve problem 2, if the expressions already introduced are given the following economic interpretation: q is the vector of total output expressed in old prices; x is the vector of total output in new prices.

From the relationship given in equation (1) it is evident that p is in this case the vector of indices expressing the transformation from the old price system to the new. A similar interpretation could then also be given to the other expressions used. Since both models are otherwise completely similar, we may limit ourselves to the terminology of problem 1.

Let Q be the input–output matrix expressed in physical units and containing the means for simple renewal of productive capacities (amortization). This matrix can then be defined in the same way as is done by Oscar Lange.[‖]

[†] Column vectors will be represented by the symbol '.
[‡] In this paper we shall always use the symbol ∧ to designate a diagonal matrix.
[§] This is in essence the so-called 'inverse transformation problem' of Morishima and Seton. (See M. Morishima, F. Seton, 'Aggregation in Leontief Matrices and the Labour Theory of Value', *Econometrica*, 1961.)
[‖] Oskar Lange, *Teoria reprodukcji i akumulacji* (Warsaw, 1961).

Let B be the matrix of output coefficients defined by the following relationship:

$$B = \hat{q}^{-1}Q. \tag{2}$$

Let V be the vector of wages whose elements signify the total volume of wages paid out in the given sector during a unit of time.

Let Z be the vector of profits, whose elements express the total volume of profits made by the given sector during a unit of time.

If the 'dual balance equation' of the Leontief type model (column sums)

$$x = xB + V + Z \tag{3}$$

is multiplied from the right by the matrix $\hat{q}^{-1}$ and the following definitions are used:

$A = Q\hat{q}^{-1}$ is the matrix of input coefficients,

$v = V\hat{q}^{-1}$ is the vector of wage cost coefficients,

$z = Z\hat{q}^{-1}$ is the vector of coefficients, expressing the amount of profit in units of output,

then we obtain the following *basic equation of the price model*:

$$p = pA + v + z, \tag{4}$$

This equation expresses the dependence of wholesale prices on material costs, wage costs and profits.

We shall further suppose, that retail prices differ from wholesale prices only because of an indirect tax (turnover tax). The trade margin may be considered as the costs and profits of the trade sector.

Let us then write:

π as the vector of retail prices;

d as the vector of turnover taxes per physical unit of output.†

The relation between the system of wholesale and retail prices is then given by the following equation:

$$\pi = p + d. \tag{5}$$

Let us further introduce δ as a vector of turnover tax rates, which is defined as

$$\delta = d\hat{p}^{-1}. \tag{6}$$

The relation between the system of wholesale and retail prices may then be expressed in the following way:

$$\pi = p(I + \hat{\delta}). \tag{7}$$

We shall distinguish two different cases: (a) a system where the turnover tax rate is differentiated, and (b) a system where the turnover tax rate is uniform.

† In case of subsidies some elements of the vector will be negative.

For the first case it will prove useful to introduce an average rate of turnover tax expressed as $\bar{\delta}$, which is defined by the following equation:

$$\bar{\delta} = \frac{p\hat{\delta}q_s'}{pq_s'},\qquad (6\text{a})$$

where q_s is the vector of personal consumption in physical units.

In the second case the numbers expressing the turnover tax rate are the same for all sectors of the economy and are equal to the average rate. For conventional reasons we shall in this case also use the symbol $\bar{\delta}$ to designate the number expressing this uniform turnover tax rate.

In a system with a uniform rate of turnover tax it is possible to simplify (7) to the following:

$$\pi = p(1 + \bar{\delta}).\qquad (7\text{a})$$

We shall now turn to the problem of distinguishing (a) price relations and (b) price levels under different price systems. By price relations we understand the relations pi/pj $(i, j = 1, 2, \ldots, n)$. It is evident that these price relations do not change if we multiply the price vector by a scalar.

Therefore we shall say that price vectors p and p^* for which

$$p = \lambda p^*$$

holds true (λ is a number), express the same price relations and the same price level if $\lambda = 1$, and a different price level if $\lambda \neq 1$. The number $|1 - \lambda|$ then signifies the 'distance' between price levels. The relationship of price levels of two price vectors of different relations can be measured only by a weighted average

$$\bar{\lambda} = \frac{pw'}{p^*w'},\qquad (8)$$

where w is the vector of weights. This can be a vector of total output, final output, personal consumption, etc. It is quite clear that the distance between price levels of the same price vectors can be different if we choose different weights.

We shall call a system in which the level of wholesale and retail prices are different *a two-level system of prices*, and a system in which the level of wholesale prices is equal to the level of retail prices a *one-level system of prices*.

Since retail prices only pertain to personal consumption, the only way we can measure the relationship between the levels of wholesale and retail prices is to use the vector of personal consumption q_s as a vector of weights. We shall use $\bar{\lambda}$ for expressing the relationship between the levels of wholesale prices and retail prices. (Let us write $\bar{\lambda} = \pi q_s'/p q_s'$.)

In a *one-level price system* $\bar{\lambda} = 1$, or, to put it differently, $pq'_s = \pi q'_s$. This at the same time means that the total revenue from turnover taxes for the economy as a whole is equal to zero and that $\bar{\delta} = 0$. In the case of a uniform rate of turnover taxes $p = \pi$ must hold true, and the systems of wholesale and retail prices are identical, being identical not only in their levels, but also in their relations.

For a *two-level price system* it is true that $\lambda \neq 1$. For practical purposes the only relevant case is the one where the level of wholesale prices is lower than the level of retail prices, or to put it differently $pq'_s < \pi q'_s$. In such a case $\bar{\delta} > 0$. The average turnover tax rate in such a case determines the distance between the levels of wholesale and retail prices.

In the case of a uniform rate of turnover tax, the vectors p and π differ only in their levels but contain the same price relations. (This implies $\lambda = 1 + \bar{\delta}$).

We can now sum up several aggregate relationships in the national economy: Let

$P = pq'$ be the volume of the gross social product priced in wholesale prices;

$\Pi = p(q' - q'_s) + \pi q'_s$ be the volume of the gross social product in which all components, with the exception of personal consumption, are priced in wholesale prices and personal consumption is priced in retail prices;

$D = dq'_s$ is the total volume of the turnover tax.

From this the following equation holds true:

$$\Pi = P + D. \tag{9}$$

The volume of national income Y is equal to the gross social product after material costs have been subtracted

$$Y = \Pi - pAq'. \tag{10}$$

The national income can then be understood as composed of three basic components: wages, profits and turnover tax

$$Y = vq' + zq' + dq'_s. \tag{11}$$

In the case of a one-level system of prices the whole national income is composed of wages and profits: in a two-level price system only part of the national income is realised through wholesale prices and the rest is realized by the turnover tax.

3. ALTERNATIVE PRICE FORMULAE

We may now attempt to formulate equations for different types of prices. Let us suppose that the following indicators of the economic system are given:

the A matrix of input coefficients expressed in physical units;

the K matrix of capital-output coefficients expressed in physical units; element k_{ij} of this matrix expresses the stock of capital of i-kind necessary for the production of a unit of output in the j-sector during a given unit of time;

the l vector of labour; l_j is the volume (number of man-hours) of labour necessary for the production of a j-kind unit of output.

If we know the ω vector of average wages in the sectors (which is supposed to be constant) we can also express the labour coefficients by the vector of coefficients of wage costs

$$v = l\hat{\omega}. \tag{12}$$

We are looking for a 'rational price formula', which would assign some price system to the technological characteristics of the economic system designated by A, K, and v.

We shall investigate primarily one class of formula, which sets prices in such a way that they cover material cost and distribute income in some uniform manner into all prices. Income may be distributed according to the following principles:

(a) in proportion to material costs;

(b) in proportion to wage costs;

(c) in proportion to stock of capital.

From the class of formula mentioned above, we are interested mainly in those which cover not only material, but also wage costs, and distribute profit instead of income according to certain principles.

The coefficients according to which profits are distributed into prices by the various principles mentioned above may in principle differ in various sectors of the economy. But insofar as there do not exist serious factual reasons for setting differentiated coefficients, it seems much more reasonable to set uniform coefficients as a point of departure. Ricardo, Marx, Walras, Dmitriyev, von Neumann, Morishima, and Sraffa,[†] whose work the theory of price types directly follows, in most cases presupposed uniform coefficients.

[†] V. K. Dmitriyev, *Ekonomicheskiye ocherk*: (Moscow, 1904); John von Neumann, 'A Model of General Economic Equilibrium', *Review of Economic Studies*, XIII (1945–46); M. Morishima, F. Seton, 'Aggregation in Leontief Matrices and the Labour Theory of Value', *Econometrica*, 1961; M. Morishima, *Equilibrium Stability and Growth* (Oxford, 1964); P. Sraffa, *Production of Commodities by Means of Commodities* (Cambridge, 1963).

Let us first derive a general formula, a so-called *three-channel price* in which profits are distributed according to all three principles at the same time, i.e. by the following three channels:

(1) In the first channel profits are distributed proportionally to material costs

$$z_1 = \nu pA. \tag{13}$$

(2) In the second channel profits are distributed proportionally to wage costs,

$$z_2 = \mu v. \tag{14}$$

(3) In the third channel profits are distributed proportionally to capital stock

$$z_3 = \rho pK. \tag{15}$$

The sum of all three channels gives us total of profits, present in wholesale prices:

$$z = z_1 + z_2 + z_3. \tag{16}$$

ν, μ, ρ are the parameters of the model. We assume $\nu \geqslant 0$, $\rho \geqslant 0$. If $\mu = -1$, then the whole income is distributed through channels 13 and 15, i.e. $z_1 + z_3 = v + z$. We assume $\mu \geqslant -1$ but it should be realized that if $-1 \leqslant \mu < 0$ there is no guarantee that prices will cover wage costs.

Setting (13), (14), (15) and (16) into (4) we obtain:

$$p = (1+\nu)pA + (1+\mu)v + \rho pK. \tag{17}$$

The solution for p gives us the following general formula for a three-channel price:

$$p = (1+\mu)v[I - (1+\nu)A]^{-1}\{I - \rho K[I - (1+\nu)A]^{-1}\}^{-1}. \tag{18}$$

This formula expresses the dependence of wholesale prices on the technological characteristics of the economic system A, K and v, and on the three parameters ν, μ and ρ. If we also take into consideration that in order to find a system of retail prices we must also know the vector of the turnover tax rate δ, we can briefly describe the whole price system in the following way:

$$\begin{matrix} p = F(A, K, v, \nu, \mu, \rho), \\ \pi = G(A, K, v, \nu, \mu, \rho, \delta). \end{matrix} \tag{19}$$

By choosing parameters ν, μ, ρ and δ we can then make the price system a definite one, or in other words for a given A, K and v we can choose specific price relations and levels.

The formula for a three-channel price (18) is a general formula, which includes special cases of simpler types of prices—so called two-channel prices, as well as elementary types of prices such as value price, production price, income price and cost price.

Formula (18) looks complicated, but its composition is advantageous from the point of view of economic interpretation. This economic interpretation is especially evident if we choose $\nu = 0$. In such a case we see that besides the parameters, prices depend only on two factors:

$v(I-A)^{-1}$ the vector of full wage costs coefficients,

$K(I-A)^{-1}$ the matrix of full capital-output coefficients.

The parameters μ and ρ are specific kinds of 'weights' by which full wage cost and full capital-output ratios enter into the setting of a price.

If we investigate the possibility of $\nu \neq 0$, we then come to the conclusion that the parameter ν does nothing more than change the weight by which direct material costs A influence full wage costs and full capital-output ratios.

From equation (18) we see that the parameter μ influences only the level of prices, but not their relations, while parameters ν and ρ influence both the level of prices and price relations.

If in equation (18) we make any of the parameters equal to zero, we obtain a so called *two-channel price*. There exist three possible types of two-channel prices. We shall investigate especially the following two types:

By an N-two-channel price,† we mean a price which keeps the channel proportionate to material costs and the channel proportionate to wage costs. Putting $\rho = 0$, in (18) we obtain the following formula:

$$p = (1+\mu)v[I-(1+\nu)A]^{-1}. \tag{20}$$

By an F-two-channel price† we mean a price which keeps the channel proportionate to wage costs and the channel proportionate to capital. Putting $\nu = 0$ we obtain the following:

$$p = (1+\mu)v(I-A)^{-1}[I-\rho K(I-A)^{-1}]^{-1}. \tag{21}$$

From equations (20) and (21) it is evident that in both types of two-channel price there can exist different price relations and price levels for the same technological circumstances, depending on how we choose the various parameters. In an *N*-two-channel price, price relations will depend wholly on v, A and the parameter ν. At the same time price relations are in effect equal to the relations between hypothetical full wage costs, which would exist if technological consumption in all sectors was $(1+\nu)$ times larger than it is in reality.

On the other hand the relations between *F*-two-channel prices depend on v, A, and K. In this type of price two elements are evident: full wage costs and the full capital-output ratios. The parameter ρ gives the weight, by which the full capital-output ratios influence prices.

† Costs in Czech: 'náklady' (N); Capital in Czech: 'fondy' (F).

In both types of two-channel price the parameter μ influences only the level of prices and not price relations. Each of the two-channel price formulae contains, as special cases, 'elementary' types of prices.

If, in formula (20), for an N-two-channel price we put

(1) $\nu = 0$, we obtain a *value price* (in the labour theory of value sense of the word), in which profits are distributed only by one channel, proportionally to wage costs. The formula for a value price reads as follows:

$$p = (1 + \mu)v(I - A)^{-1}. \tag{22}$$

In a one-level price system the number μ has an evident economic interpretation—it expresses the rate of surplus value.

(2) Similarly if we put $\mu = \nu$, we obtain a so-called *cost price*, in which profits are distributed in proportion to total costs (the sum of material and wage costs). The formula for a cost price reads as follows:

$$p = (1 + \nu)v[I - (1 + \nu)A]^{-1}. \tag{23}$$

The number ν in this case expresses a uniform rate of rentability i.e. the ratio of profits to total costs.

(3) If we distribute total income $(v + z)$ into prices in proportion to material costs, we obtain a type of price, which we shall call an *N-income price*. Take (17) and put $\mu = -1$ and $\rho = 0$. This is a formula for N-income price, from which we can obtain

$$p[I - (1 + \nu)A] = 0. \tag{24}$$

The number ν in this case evidently expresses a uniform rate of income in relation to material costs. An N-income price also means that the relative share of income in all prices is the same. From formulae (22), (23), and (24) it is evident that: (*a*) the relations between value prices are determined only by the relations between full wage costs, (*b*) the relations between cost prices are equal to relations between value prices which would exist if direct consumption of material were $(1 + \nu)$ times higher than it is in reality, and (*c*) the relations between N-income prices depend only on the properties of the A matrix.

With value prices the parameter μ has no influence on price relations, which means that the value price formula gives us the same price relations whatever the price level is. This does not hold true for the cost price, where it is evident that the size of parameter ν influences the price level as well as the relations between prices. We assume that parameter ν in a cost-price formula can be arbitrarily chosen, provided $\nu \geqslant 0$.

With N-income prices the situation is somewhat different. Here the parameter ν cannot be set arbitrarily. The condition for the existence of a non-zero p vector, according to equation (24), is the following:

$$|I - (1 + \nu)A| = 0.$$

It is evident that $1/(1+\nu)$ is the characteristic root of the A' matrix and p' is the corresponding characteristic vector. Since A' is non-negative and non-zero matrix, there exists a non-negative characteristic vector p', which corresponds to a positive, real, characteristic root with maximum absolute value.† Since from the economic point of view a solution giving negative prices has no meaning, we can come to the conclusion that price relations are given by equation (24). But this equation does not give us the level of prices, which may be set arbitrarily, or rather derived from the $(n+1)$st condition.

N-income prices have some surprising features, from the point of view of their economic interpretation: their relations depend only on the properties of the A matrix, and are the same, regardless of the vector of total output q; the rate of income ν is given independently of the manner in which the national income is distributed between income realized by the enterprises and income realized through the turnover tax.

Let us recall that from the theory of Leontief type models we know that the maximum characteristic root of an A matrix has one more interesting economic interpretation: it expresses the 'productivity' of the system characterized by matrix A. If this characteristic root is equal to 1 (as is the case in a closed model $Aq' = q'$), this means that total output is equal to input. The smaller the characteristic root is, the more productive is the system, the greater is its net efficiency or final output. We thus come to the conclusion, that the number ν in a system of income prices expresses a certain 'average' productivity of the economic system or the average relative surplus of final output over material input.

From formula (21), for an F-two-channel price we can deduce three elementary types of prices:

(1) If we write $\rho = 0$ we obtain a *value type price*

$$p = (1+\mu)v(I-A)^{-1}. \tag{25}$$

(2) If we write $\mu = 0$, we obtain a so-called *production price* (in the sense of the term used in the third volume of Marx's *Das Kapital*), where profits are distributed on the basis of a uniform rate of profit in relation to capital:

$$p = v(I-A)^{-1}[I-\rho K(I-A)^{-1}]^{-1}. \tag{26}$$

In a production price then the ρ parameter expresses an average rate of profit.

(3) If we write $\mu = -1$, we obtain a so-called F-income price, which can be determined by the following equation:

$$p[I-\rho K(I-A)^{-1}] = 0 \tag{27}$$

† See G. Debreu and I. N. Herstein 'Non-negative Square Matrices', *Econometrica*, vol. 21, 1953.

The number ρ in this case expresses a uniform rate of income in relation to capital.

We have already mentioned the properties of a value price. Let us note that value price represents an extreme case of an N-two-channel price, as well as an F-two-channel price. Value price thus forms a sort of bridge between N- and F-two-channel prices. Income prices form extreme cases at the other end.

It is evident from what has been said that the relations between F-income prices are independent of wage costs and are given by the full capital-output ratios. Production prices are then a sort of 'mix' of relations between value prices and relations between income prices. The weight of the influence of the full capital-output ratios on the relations between production prices depends on the size of parameter ρ. Let us further note that for the same ρ the relations between production prices and the relations between F-two-channel prices are the same. If the same ρ is given, then from the point of view of price relations there is no important difference between a production price and an F-two-channel price. There is of course a difference, in that for $\mu > 0$, the size of ρ in a two-channel price cannot achieve the maximum possible size of ρ in the production price, if the level of wholesale prices is not to be above the level of retail prices.

With the F-income price we may again note that $1/\rho$ is the characteristic root of a matrix of full capital-output ratios $[K(I-A)^{-1}]'$. The number ρ here expresses the average 'productivity' or efficiency of capital and is independent of the q vector, and of the proportion in which the national income is distributed between the income of enterprises and turnover taxes.

4. THE RELATIONSHIP BETWEEN WAGES AND PRICES

Our discussion up to this point has usually presupposed that the vector of average wages ω is given so that we have been able to consider the vector of wage costs as a technological characteristic of the need for labour for a given output. Since price calculations are only looking for new prices to a given physical structure of output, our model must also define the relation between the wage level and the level of retail prices in such a way that the real final distribution of output between personal consumption on the one hand and social consumption and investment on the other, is not influenced.

It is possible to define this relation in two ways: (1) so that during calculation the level of wage-rates and the level of retail prices do not change; (2) so that during calculation we make sure that the level of wage rates moves in accordance with changes in the level of retail prices and thus average real wages remain constant.

In this paper we have chosen the first alternative. In all of the formulae (with the exception of income prices) mentioned in part 3, wage cost has been of a given and unchanging magnitude.

From this, then, stems the demand for the level of new (calculated) retail prices to be the same as the level of old retail prices.

If we now return to the formulation of equation (19) which sets a price system we see that we have:

n equations for wholesale prices, n equations for retail prices and one condition (keeping the level of retail prices constant), we have then $2n + 1$ equations;

n unknown wholesale prices, n unknown retail prices, n unknown turnover tax rates and three unknown parameters μ, ν, ρ. We have then $3n + 3$ unknowns.

This means that it is possible to set all the turnover tax rates and two parameters arbitrarily; the size of the third parameter will be the result of the solution of the system of equations.

We may simplify our calculations by choosing a price system with a uniform turnover tax rate; in such a case the number of degrees of freedom is reduced to three. Of the four parameters ν, μ, ρ and $\bar{\delta}$ we may set three and calculate the fourth from the system of equations. If, for instance, we arbitrarily set μ, ν, and ρ, then the size of $\bar{\delta}$ or the distance between the levels of wholesale and retail prices is also given.

From an economic point of view the case where $\bar{\delta}$ and two of the remaining parameters are set, is of special interest. Choice of $\bar{\delta}$ will designate the distance between the level of wholesale and retail prices and the choice of two parameters gives us the type of price.

We shall investigate only the case where $\bar{\delta} = 0$ (i.e. a one-level price system), without a differentiated turnover tax rate. In such a case $p = \pi$ and the number of unknowns and equations can be lower by n.

Let us write

x_s for the vector of personal consumption priced by the old retail prices.

q_s for the vector of personal consumption in the old wholesale prices.†

$j = (1, 1, \ldots, 1)$ is the n-dimensional vector of unities.

p will in this case represent the vector of transformation indices from the old wholesale prices to the new ones.

The wish to keep the level of retail prices (under conditions of having a single-level system) can be formulated in the following:

$$pq_s' = jx_s' = (1 + \bar{\delta})jq_s \tag{28}$$

† We want the new system to be of the single-level type, whereas the old system may be a double-level one, with a differentiated turnover tax rate.

Relation (28) forms the $(n+1)$st equation of the price model. It will prove advantageous to adjust it in the following manner:

$$pb' = 1, \tag{29}$$

where
$$b' = \frac{b*'}{1+\bar{\delta}} \quad \text{and} \quad b*' = \frac{q'_s}{jq'_s} \tag{30}$$

$\bar{\delta}$ being here the average turnover tax rate in the old price system.

The $b*$ vector has an evident economic interpretation, since it expresses the relative shares of outputs of individual sectors in total personal consumption (in the old wholesale prices). Vector b keeps relations of $b*$ but has a different level. The difference between the levels of b and $b*$ is due to the necessity of keeping balance between retail prices and wages.

We shall now demonstrate the solution of a model with $(n+1)$st condition on the example of the basic types of prices. Let us return to equation (17) (where we presuppose $\pi = p$), and let us choose:

(1) $v = 0$, $\rho = 0$. By this we have chosen the *value type* of price. Keeping the $(n+1)$st condition in mind it must now hold true that:

$$p = pA + (1+\mu)v, \quad pb' = 1. \tag{31}$$

From (31) we may derive: $p = pA + pb'v(1+\mu)$, and further

$$p[I - (1+\mu)b'v(I-A)^{-1}] = 0. \tag{32}$$

It is now evident that $1/(1+\mu)$ is the characteristic root of the $[b'v(I-A)^{-1}]'$ matrix. The coefficients, which form the $b'v$ matrix, have the following economic meaning: they express the deliveries (in old wholesale prices) of i-kind products for the consumption of workers in the j-sectors which is necessary for a unit of production. Here we are presupposing that the structure of consumption by workers is the same in all sectors. This $b'v$ matrix is somewhat similar to the matrix of technological input coefficients A which also expresses the necessary consumption of i-kind products for the production of a unit of j-kind of output. This does not however pertain to the direct consumption of these products in the technological process, but to consumption, which reproduces the labour used up in production. The $b'v(I-A)^{-1}$ matrix can thus be interpreted as the matrix of complex workers' consumption. The rate of surplus value μ is then the function of the characteristic root of this matrix, in a system of value prices.

To obtain μ it is possible to find a simple method of calculation. From (31) it follows that:

$$\frac{1}{1+\mu} = v(I-A)^{-1}b'. \tag{33}$$

(2) $v = 0$, $\mu = 0$. By this we have chosen a *production type* of price›
whose equation with the $(n+1)$st condition may be written as follows:

$$p = pA + v + \rho p K, \quad pb' = 1. \tag{34}$$

and thus
$$p = pA + pb'v + \rho p K. \tag{35}$$

Let us introduce the matrix $A^* = A + b'v$, which we shall call an augmented matrix of productive consumption according to Morishima. We
can now write equation (35) in the following manner:

$$p[I - \rho K (I - A^*)^{-1}] = 0, \tag{36}$$

where $1/\rho$ is the characteristic root of matrix $[K(I-A^*)^{-1}]'$.

(3) $\mu = v$, $\rho = 0$. By this we have chosen a *cost type* of price whose
equation, taking the $(n+1)$st condition into account, is the following:

$$p = (1+v)pA + (1+v)v, \quad pb' = 1; \tag{37}$$

from which it follows that

$$p = (1+v)p(A+b'v)$$

and thus
$$p[I - (1+v)A^*] = 0. \tag{38}$$

In a system of cost prices $1/(1+v)$ is the characteristic root of matrix
$(A^*)'$.

From the point of view of economic interpretation it is interesting to
compare equations (36) and (38) with equations (27) and (24). We see
some similarity between cost price and N-income price on the one hand
and between production price and F-income price on the other. The only
difference between them is that in income prices we have a pure A
matrix, while in the cost and production prices an augmented matrix
$A^* = A + b'v$ appears.

5. SOME PRACTICAL CALCULATIONS
BASED ON THE MODEL

In conclusion we would like to make a few points concerning the practical
use of price models.

During 1964 and 1965 *experimental calculations* of various types of
prices were made with the help of models. These calculations were based
on an input–output table of the Czechoslovak republic expressed in
terms of value for the year 1962, aggregated for 48 sectors. The information about capital assets was taken from normal statistical sources, which
are however grouped according to organizational principles and not
according to pure sectors. In calculating various types of prices the data
on capital assets were in some cases based on original costs and in others
on current replacement costs.

The experimental calculations were carried out only for a single-level price system without a differentiated turnover tax rate. As the $(n+1)$st condition the constant level of retail prices was taken. The following basic types of prices were calculated:

(1) the value type;

(2) the cost type;

(3) the production type;

(4) the F-income type;

(5) the F-two-channel type in the following alternatives: $(a)\ \rho = 6$, $(b)\ \rho = 12$, $(c)\ \rho = 18$, $(d)\ \rho = 24$ per cent.

The aims of these experimental calculations may be summed up as follows: (a) to prepare and test methods of practical calculations by price models, (b) to demonstrate the relations between individual types of prices, especially in relation to existing prices, under conditions which existed in Czechoslovakia in 1962. Such data can help to achieve a better knowledge of the economic situation and at the same time help to form a realistic basis for discussions about which type of price is most advantageous.

The results of calculations for 48 sectors and various types of price have been published.[†] The price indices for the four basic types of prices are given in Table 1. The list of vectors for which the indices were computed is listed on p. 119.

The values of the parameters for the individual types of prices are shown in Table 2. (The numbers describing the types correspond to the list of price types above).

Statistical indicators which aim to describe macroeconomic aggregates or the shares of individual sectors in the total depend to a great extent on the price system used to evaluate output. The price system in effect until now distorted a number of these indicators. Experimental calculations make it possible to find out what these indicators might be given various types of one-level prices.

During the phase of development which followed, the price calculations were used by the State Planning Commission to accelerate the work being done in preparation for *a general reform of wholesale prices*, which came into effect on 1 January 1967. By the methods in use until now the preparations for a general reform of wholesale prices took from three to four years. By using price models and computers it was possible to shorten the duration of the preparations to one and a half years.

† Hejl, Kýn, Sekerka, 'Experimentální propočty typu ceny', and 'Vlastnosti dvoukanálové ceny', *Ekonomický časopis SAV*, 6/1966.

Table 1

	Cost price	Value price	Production price†	Income price
1	94·6	99·5	167·9	215·8
2	143·3	175·8	177·2	167·3
3	96·2	100·4	168·8	261·1
4	161·4	161·3	227·4	274·4
5	118·0	113·6	181·0	230·3
6	149·3	166·6	208·3	245·4
7	197·8	224·9	354·6	518·7
8	146·2	146·3	185·1	218·2
9	148·1	122·4	156·5	186·0
10	118·7	117·4	141·9	163·6
11	106·5	101·0	129·0	183·1
12	124·9	123·7	143·3	169·3
13	89·6	91·4	98·4	102·5
14	104·9	117·6	110·6	105·4
15	99·8	102·1	99·6	98·9
16	105·6	110·8	114·1	120·4
17	113·5	124·3	109·8	97·0
18	96·7	114·6	102·7	94·8
19	130·6	138·1	139·4	138·7
20	117·8	128·6	108·7	90·1
21	129·3	134·7	122·4	111·1
22	112·4	137·3	122·9	108·8
23	103·7	131·7	142·8	146·5
24	113·4	135·5	123·4	104·6
25	109·6	127·6	108·7	88·2
26	106·7	130·0	116·2	102·2
27	93·9	105·5	94·1	83·0
28	123·6	135·7	153·3	163·0
29	123·6	143·1	148·2	147·2
30	228·8	210·8	213·1	216·3
31	223·1	198·0	197·9	198·9
32	126·1	108·7	112·1	115·3
33	181·3	174·9	208·7	234·5
34	135·5	132·6	155·5	174·5
35	149·4	140·4	135·7	150·0
36	228·6	207·6	204·7	202·7
37	162·7	147·3	151·0	153·0
38	138·2	141·8	162·0	175·9
39	140·9	139·3	149·9	158·3
40	150·8	152·7	152·3	148·6
41	108·5	128·6	104·1	80·6
42	157·0	174·9	173·9	175·4
43	120·6	171·7	161·5	137·5
44	96·5	119·4	157·5	181·7
45	101·1	138·5	134·6	121·8
46	43·7	60·5	89·9	248·1
47	81·0	119·1	117·0	114·7
48	74·1	104·5	144·9	258·9

† Capital assets in purchase prices.

Industry branches scheme used for the verification of rational price types

1 Electric-power and heat production
2 Coal mining and processing
3 Oil and natural gas drilling
4 Coke production
5 Gas production
6 Iron and manganese ore production
7 Non-iron metals, garnets, graphite and chemical raw-materials production
8 Ferrous metallurgy
9 Non-ferrous metallurgy
10 Chemicals (including plastics)
11 Oil and tar products
12 Rubber and asbestos products
13 Pharmaceutics
14 Engineering
15 Electrotechnical industry
16 Means of transportation
17 Metal consumer goods
18 Precision mechanics
19 Textiles
20 Clothing
21 Leather, footwear and fur industry
22 Glass industry
23 Porcelain and ceramics
24 Wood processing, carpentry and joinery
25 Furniture production
26 Wood consumer goods and matches
27 Printing industry
28 Paper and cellulose
29 Building materials
30 Dairy industry
31 Meat, poultry and fish
32 Fats, edible oils, soap, cosmetics and 'other food processing'
33 Sugar production
34 Spirit, liquors, wine, yeast, vinegar and starch
35 Fruit and vegetable processing
36 Flour, paste products, bakery and fodder industry
37 Confectionary and durable pastry
38 Brewery and malt production
39 Tobacco
40 Other industrial production, mineral spring and salt production
41 Construction
42 Agriculture
43 Forestry
44 Transport
45 Communications
46 Materials-distribution services
47 Internal trade
48 Agricultural products procurement

Table 2

	2	1	5a	5b	5c	3	5d	4
μ	0·24	1·14	0·82	0·51	0·21	0	−0·1	−1
ν	0·24	0	0	0	0	0	0	0
ρ	0	0	0·06	0·12	0·18	0·22	0·24	0·44
$\bar{\delta}$	0	0	0	0	0	0	0	0

The input–output table for 1962 was used as basic data for the calculations connected with the general reform of wholesale prices, but the figures were recalculated into 1964 prices and into the volume of output planned for 1966.

Table 3. *Some macroeconomic indicators priced by various types of prices*

	Value price	Cost price	Production price	F-income price	1962 prices
Social product (in billions of crowns)	471	448	493	503	397
National income (in billions of crowns)	183	173	174	164	178
Share of material costs in social product	0·61	0·61	0·65	0·67	0·55
Rate of surplus value	1·35	1·22	1·23	1·10	1·29
Rate of accumulation†	0·222	0·201	0·196	0·170	0·184
The relation between sector I and II	2·30	2·24	2·54	2·71	1·73

† Share of net investment in national income.

The procedure in making use of the price model during the general reform can be summarized as follows:

(*a*) A preliminary *F*-two-channel type of price was chosen, keeping a double price level.

(*b*) Calculations for several sizes of μ and ρ were made.

(*c*) On the basis of an analysis of the results and the situation in the national economy the following values were chosen for the reform: $\mu = 0·22$, $\rho = 0·06$.

(*d*) For these parameters, price indices on the basis of a table of 92 sectors were calculated. These indices were directly used to reprice capital stock and depreciation.

(*e*) On the basis of a special investigation, data were obtained which made it possible to compute approximate price indices for 24 thousand groups of output.

(*f*) By means of these indices, prices in the above mentioned group were recalculated.

A forecast of the development of prices until 1970 was made by the State Commission for Finance, Prices and Wages, during the first months of 1966, with the help of the price model.

Essentially the forecast of price development builds on changes in the cost factors influencing the prices. The resulting price vectors, which were obtained with the help of the model for the year 1970, can be interpreted only as a price base, while real prices can deviate from this base as the result of disequilibrium between supply and demand. It would have been useful to take the influence of supply and demand into account when making a forecast of prices, but sufficient data were not available. In any case, when a forecast for a period of five years is being made it is possible to anticipate that changes in productive capacities and in international trade will be of such magnitude as to balance out the mutual effects of supply and demand.

For the calculations concerned with making the forecast of price development we divided the vector of wage-cost coefficients v, according to (12), into two elements: the vector of coefficients of the direct need for labour l and the vector of wage rates ω.

For calculation of the vectors of wholesale and retail prices for 1970 it was necessary to presume the following data (for 1970): matrices A and K, vectors l and ω and parameters μ, ν, ρ, and the δ vector.

These data can roughly be divided into two groups:

(a) Data which from the point of view of the central body are exogenous, or given from the outside. This is particularly true of A, K and l. Changes in technological coefficients, capital-output coefficients and the direct need for labour depend on changes in technology and are thus not the direct result of economic policy and decision-making. However, in the further development of the model, the possibility of various alternatives in technology, which do depend on centralized decision-making, could perhaps be taken into consideration.

(b) Data which depend on the economic policy of the centre. This is especially the planned vector of wage rates ω and the parameters on which the type of price system depends: μ, ν, ρ and δ.

The forecast of the development of prices was made in several variants. Several alternative vectors for the year 1970 were calculated, based on different data. This was done for two reasons: (1) for the exogenous factors it is impossible to make exact forecasts of their size; (2) the second type of factor cannot be forecast precisely just because it can be influenced by centralized decision making.

In calculating our forecast we chose three different possibilities of how the exogenous factors can develop, from the best to the worst. Besides the extreme points a middle point was also chosen and we thus obtained three sets of possible exogenous factors:

$(A, K, l)_C$ for the best economic conditions,

$(A, K, l)_B$ for average conditions,

$(A, K, l)_D$ for the worst conditions.

For the vector of planned wage rates two alternatives were chosen:

a *basic alternative* according to which average money wages will be increased by approximately 7 per cent till 1970.

a so-called *higher level alternative*, according to which average money wages will grow by 13 per cent during the same period.

The parameters μ, ν, ρ and δ were also chosen in several alternatives. In all cases $\nu = 0$. The so-called basic alternative is calculated with a two-

Table 4 (part 1). *Price indices development forecast*

Sector	A_z	B	C	D
01	114·7	105·1	114·0	99·1
02	122·4	115·4	127·7	108·3
03	112·4	93·1	107·5	81·9
04	126·0	117·7	127·7	105·6
05	130·0	117·3	133·4	104·9
06	189·1	139·3	154·7	126·2
07	120·2	106·4	115·5	99·0
08	111·3	99·9	115·2	88·0
09	122·2	103·0	113·2	95·6
10	132·7	117·5	127·8	109·7
11	120·4	90·3	100·6	82·9
12	114·0	103·8	113·7	96·8
13	112·8	93·8	101·9	87·8
14	115·4	98·4	105·7	91·1
15	114·3	98·5	107·9	90·3
16	119·4	101·5	113·2	94·8
17	115·3	98·0	106·6	90·9
18	122·5	105·9	115·5	98·3
19	121·1	121·2	131·6	111·8
20	120·0	116·5	124·7	108·8
21	104·9	98·9	106·4	92·5
22	122·6	112·2	121·5	106·7
23	125·4	114·8	121·0	110·8
24	111·0	104·5	109·9	100·7
25	112·9	101·1	107·0	96·1
26	111·2	104·9	110·9	99·4
27	107·7	98·6	103·7	92·7
28	127·5	118·4	127·1	112·3
29	125·8	110·4	118·8	104·2
30	113·9	122·5	127·8	116·9
31	114·0	112·9	122·7	105·8
32	121·6	117·2	127·5	107·5
33	118·4	124·6	132·0	117·1
34	120·3	119·5	128·3	109·1
35	120·5	121·3	132·2	113·5
36	106·0	106·6	114·2	100·9
37	116·0	113·3	122·6	107·2
38	109·6	112·9	120·6	107·9
39	136·7	139·4	152·6	127·4
40	148·5	137·8	149·2	127·1
41	117·7	107·8	113·5	106·3
42	108·4	105·2	110·2	102·9
43	113·2	114·4	117·8	112·1
44	116·6	108·7	112·0	104·7
45	99·4	92·3	95·6	84·3
46	113·6	107·9	115·3	103·9
47	96·5	93·0	97·7	89·2
48	117·7	109·0	121·1	98·9
49	92·8	86·7	90·8	82·8

Table 4 (part 2). *Price indices development forecast*

Sector	$A_{\xi d}$	E	F	G	H
01	135·0	143·7	128·1	120·4	126·8
02	150·9	141·5	141·0	139·8	146·9
03	136·6	116·9	132·6	111·5	117·9
04	147·5	149·0	139·9	134·9	141·1
05	154·4	155·5	142·4	135·7	143·2
06	233·4	174·9	173·3	171·4	180·6
07	142·6	133·0	127·1	123·8	129·4
08	132·9	130·0	121·5	117·2	123·4
09	147·3	132·9	125·8	122·1	128·6
10	162·1	147·7	143·7	141·2	149·6
11	146·2	112·2	109·5	107·7	113·2
12	139·9	128·5	126·5	125·0	132·7
13	136·3	120·1	114·0	110·8	115·7
14	142·1	120·0	120·2	119·6	125·6
15	141·0	119·7	120·3	119·9	125·3
16	146·8	122·9	123·3	122·9	129·0
17	142·7	116·3	119·1	119·6	125·9
18	151·9	127·1	129·7	130·1	136·7
19	150·8	148·9	148·8	148·0	155·6
20	152·5	136·4	143·5	145·7	153·3
21	131·5	116·9	119·9	120·6	126·8
22	154·9	133·7	138·1	139·1	150·8
23	156·1	139·9	140·6	139·9	145·0
24	139·9	122·8	128·6	130·3	143·1
25	143·3	117·2	124·1	126·4	134·5
26	138·9	126·5	128·4	128·4	136·3
27	133·1	114·4	119·0	120·3	128·0
28	156·5	149·3	145·2	142·6	153·3
29	155·0	133·6	134·4	134·0	140·5
30	136·6	160·9	148·7	143·2	145·3
31	136·6	148·8	137·1	131·9	134·3
32	146·3	148·8	141·7	138·1	143·8
33	142·8	162·1	151·5	146·6	151·0
34	143·6	155·1	144·2	139·2	144·0
35	145·4	164·7	147·5	140·5	145·4
36	127·5	138·6	129·4	125·3	128·1
37	141·5	143·3	138·2	135·5	140·3
38	131·1	149·9	137·2	131·4	135·4
39	163·1	183·7	169·7	163·6	170·1
40	162·4	192·4	160·8	146·2	151·0
41	147·8	123·0	130·9	133·5	140·1
42	129·5	139·2	127·5	122·4	124·1
43	143·3	132·5	140·7	143·3	162·6
44	151·2	132·9	137·5	138·7	146·0
45	135·0	118·1	122·1	123·0	128·8
46	139·4	129·6	130·7	130·3	137·2
47	122·2	103·8	113·2	116·5	121·5
48	143·3	132·2	131·5	130·4	137·0
49	112·8	107·2	104·3	102·5	107·3

Note: Several classification changes were made in the aggregation of sectors. This is the reason why the numbering of sectors in this table does not correspond to the sectors of Table 1.

level system of prices, μ and ρ are chosen so as to correspond to the general reform of wholesale prices. Several alternatives of single-level price system with various relations between parameters μ and ρ were also calculated.

Table 4 gives the vectors of wholesale prices for 49 sectors in nine alternatives marked as A_z, B, C, D, $A_{čd}$, E, F, G, H. All indices express the changes which take place in wholesale prices in comparison to the prices in effect in 1965. Alternative A_z is calculated for conditions in 1966 and is in accord with the general reform of wholesale prices. Alternative $A_{čd}$ is also calculated for 1966 and presupposes doing away with the double level system of prices. All the other alternatives are forecasts for 1970.

The list of parameters for individual alternatives is presented in Table 5.

Table 5

	A_z	B	C	D	$A_{čd}$	E	F	G	H
A, K, l	66	aver.	worst	best	66	aver.	aver.	aver.	aver.
ω	66	basic	basic	basic	66	basic	basic	basic	higher
μ	0·22	0·22	0·22	0·22	0·68	0·22	0·54	0·67	0·67
ρ	0·06	0·06	0·06	0·06	0·04	0·117	0·06	0·036	0·036

On the basis of the forecast of the development of wholesale prices several subalternatives were later calculated for retail prices on the basis of various forecasts concerning the turnover tax rate.

The aim of the forecast was to gain information about possible changes in price-relations and price-levels up to the year 1970 and to demonstrate to what extent these changes depend on changes in technology and to what extent they depend on economic policy. These calculations make it possible to choose a certain strategy of price policy, which is best for given conditions. At the same time a forecast of the development of prices may contribute to improving centralized as well as decentralized planning and economic decision-making, since it makes it possible to calculate the efficiency of various types of production and investment on the basis of future prices.

SOME SUGGESTIONS ON A MODERN THEORY OF THE OPTIMUM REGIME

JAN TINBERGEN

I. INTRODUCTION

Ever since its birth economic science has been used to find out what economic order or regime leads to the maximum well-being of a nation or a wider community. For a long time, economists have defended the idea that a system of free enterprise and free-competition markets represents the optimum regime. Those who intuitively doubted this threw away economic theory instead of amending it. With the recent changes in Western and Eastern (I mean, communist-ruled) countries it becomes increasingly interesting to modernize economic theory and to try again. Much of Maurice Dobb's work can be interpreted in this way.

In this essay in his honour I propose to pursue further some attempts I undertook, along different lines, to attain a similar aim.† These attempts were of modest quality only, as I am afraid this new one will be. Economists endowed with more mathematical talents are needed for this purpose; my hope is that I may stimulate some of them to reinforce this approach.

In my previous articles I made an attempt to reformulate welfare economics with a view to developing the theory of the optimum regime. Indeed, in essence, welfare economics constitutes such a theory, but it was given a very abstract form and few authors tried to interpret its results in modern political terms or to introduce more specific assumptions so as to illustrate the implications in plain language.

It seems to me that a large field is still awaiting further exploration and that recent experiences in the Eastern and the Western world justify a further modernization of the tools of analysis of welfare economics.

---

† J. Tinbergen, *Selected Papers* (Amsterdam, 1959); 'The Significance of Welfare Economics for Socialism', in: *On Political Economy and Econometrics, Essays in Honour of Oskar Lange* (Warsaw, 1964); 'Welfare Economics and Management of Public Enterprises', *Annals of Public and Co-operative Economy*, XXXV (1964), p. 99.

2. NEW ELEMENTS

I am not going to discuss all the elements which should be added to my previous analyses in order to meet their obvious shortcomings since some work is already under way which should not be duplicated. In this essay I want to concentrate on three elements not yet given sufficient attention but, I believe, of particular relevance for an East–West discussion on the optimum regime. They will be enumerated in this section, but the way they are going to be handled will only be clear—if at all—in the later sections.

(*a*) First I want to consider one particular form of dynamic analysis needed in order to deal with the existence of *time lags*, especially in production functions at the basis of the cobweb theorem and similar theorems on some unstable markets. The institutions required for the stabilization of such markets may serve as an illustration of elements of an optimum regime which admit of a rather simple treatment.

(*b*) Secondly I propose to elaborate on the changed position, comparing to-day's world with Adam Smith's or Pareto's, of the element of *information*. I am inclined to say that information was treated as a free commodity in the past. Perhaps this can be motivated by pointing out that in the optimum regimes as seen by these authors information could be taken, by most producers and consumers, 'from nearby': either from their own enterprise or household, or from the markets they were in close contact with. Other institutions were not needed, moreover. Some of the institutions required by an optimum regime under modern production laws must obtain their information over longer distances: from other institutions farther away, or from greater areas as a consequence of decreasing transportation costs. This is partly due to the greater importance of external effects in modern production processes or from a higher degree of indivisibility of equipment. The explicit consideration of long lags, already suggested under (*a*), will reinforce this necessity to obtain information further separated. The higher rate of technical progress provides a final argument.

Information as understood here will be of two types at least: factual information and information on possibilities (technologies), springing from research of an intensive character. For the latter type of information, duplication may mean waste and should be avoided as much as possible—which creates a need for even more information.

(*c*) The third new element to which I propose to give some thought may be labelled *decision making*, another eye-catcher in to-day's world. In a way it is not new to welfare economics or even to economics generally; but our interest to-day, especially in East–West discussions, is focussing in particular on the question, by what institutions some types of decision should be made.

3. CONCEPTS NEEDED IN THE ANALYSIS

In any piece of scientific analysis it is desirable that the various categories of concepts (for the mathematician often identical to categories of variables) are defined as clearly as possible. For a rather complicated subject such as ours this is all the more necessary. It was one of the points of my former studies that often the essence of the problem welfare economics tries to solve is hardly mentioned.

For the setting of the problem we need at least: (a) the concept of *welfare*, either individual or group (national or world) welfare; (b) the phenomena making for welfare, entering as 'arguments' (in the mathematical sense) into welfare functions: these will be *quantities of goods* consumed, and of *efforts* made, also their distribution over individuals; (c) a number of constraints, limiting the possibilities to increase wellbeing: above all, *production laws*, characterized by technical coefficients. We should add here the *costs of some institutions*—although unknowns of the problem—which may together constitute the optimum order and among these costs the costs of the information needed by these institutions for their operation.

The problem of the optimum order may then be formulated to find the set of institutions which together make for a maximum of welfare, taking into account the constraints.

For its solution we may use various methods, which may introduce further concepts. A traditional approach still of considerable power is the use of (d) *Lagrangian multipliers*, which may later appear to be identical with prices. A more modern instrument is that of mathematical programming, with the well-known drawback that it cannot easily be applied in a general way, but mostly for given numerical problems. Parametric programming, however, opens up some roads to more general insights. In the dual problem to any linear programming problem prices may again turn up, very similar to the role of Lagrangian multipliers.

The optimum found must then be interpreted to represent (e) a *set of institutions*, each of them characterized by their behaviour or directives for the use of (f) the *instruments of policy* or *action parameters* at their disposal. Sometimes these instruments may indeed be prices, appearing as Lagrangian multipliers; for instance, if the institution of the free enterprise shows up in the set. Sometimes these instruments are more complicated functions of the coefficients in the welfare functions and the production or cost functions; this may be the case for some types of *taxes*, appearing as instruments of the state as an institution.

The *direct* interpretation of the optimum in terms of a set of institutions may not be possible. In those cases we can only use an *indirect* method, consisting of considering a number of alternative orders (i.e.

sets of institutions) and finding out which of these is conducive to the highest welfare. In a previous study I expressed the view that the direct method can only be followed if the institutions—which are not given in advance—do not show costs. I now believe that in a number of cases we can also follow the direct method when the institutions show costs. The way to arrive at a solution consists of introducing, as unknown parameters, the *frequencies* of a number of alternative institutions, each characterized by their constraints, and treating these parameters in the same way as the other unknowns, such as the arguments of the welfare function, that is, putting equal to zero the partial derivative of the welfare function plus the terms corresponding with the constraints (each multiplied by a Lagrangian multiplier).

4. THE CENTRAL QUESTIONS TO BE ANSWERED

In the interpretation of the optimum—whether found by the direct or by the indirect (second-best) method—some questions are of particular relevance. They may therefore be mentioned explicitly.

(*a*) To begin with, we may repeat that the main question is what *set of institutions* makes for a maximum of welfare. In a previous study I suggested, and illustrated this suggestion by examples, that public enterprises and a tax-levying state should exist alongside with private enterprises, thus constituting a mixed economy. I also suggested that public enterprises would be needed in sectors of production showing either external effects or indivisibilities or both. I repeated the well-known proposition that taxes should be of the lump-sum type and gave examples of the parameters on which they should depend. I summed up some decisions which must be taken by the state and included the decision on the volume of investment. I now repeat these examples only to clarify the concept of a set of institutions.

(*b*) A second main question to be answered is what *decisions* have to be taken by *what institutions*. The illustration of the previous question already contains examples of this type of answer also: the level of investment for the economy as a whole should be a decision of the state (as a representative of the community) rather than of the individual investors. The question about decisions is particularly relevant if we consider a community subdivided into smaller communities, even at different levels. In ordinary language, we may have to have authorities at the local, the provincial, the national, the continental and the world level and some of the community's instruments may have to be handled by the lower, but others by the higher levels of authority. In still other terms it is the topical question of what degree of decentralization is optimal, both in production and in administration.

(*c*) A third question, completely disregarded in previous welfare-economic studies, but repeatedly posed by other analyses is, what *flows of information* are needed for the decision-making processes characterizing the optimum? These flows must be specified in considerable detail, not only as a quantitative concept, but qualitatively, by stating the subject on which information is to be supplied, the time at which, and the origin as well as the destination of such information. Finally, the cost of such information must be ascertained and play its part in the determination of the welfare level.

5. SOME TENTATIVE CONCLUSIONS

This essay is only to make some suggestions; it is not a full treatment of any specified problem but it draws partly on past studies by the author and partly on studies undertaken, but not yet finished, by him, in co-operation with J. Pronk. Some of the past studies have not been published so far, since they must be integrated into a wider frame. In this final section of the present essay a number of conclusions reached in partial studies will be mentioned. By partial studies I mean studies referring to highly simplified models showing a few features only. The conclusions are tentative in the sense that they may not apply to a more general model in which many of these features are assumed to exist simultaneously.

(*a*) The direct method of finding a set of institutions yielding the maximum of welfare can only be applied in some cases. Among these are a few which nevertheless throw an interesting light on our problem and may be relevant in an East–West dialogue. The condition to be fulfilled for the direct method to apply is that we can find a set of institutions whose joint conduct can be described by the same set of equations as found from the maximization of welfare under the constraints assumed. Thus, in the absence of externalities and indivisibilities, a set of free enterprises acting in free competition plus an administration imposing lump-sum taxes of a particular type, without making costs, will act according to a set of equations coinciding with the optimum conditions of welfare—provided the welfare function itself is of some simple type. This is a result as close to Pareto as can possibly be attained; but even this *contains the lump-sum tax* as an element.

(*b*) By the introduction of *externalities* the set of free enterprises with a lump-sum tax administration will no longer fulfil the conditions of the optimum. The externalities require some *integration* or *centralization* of production decisions. In the well-known simple example of externalities presented by J. E. Meade, where mutual externalities exist between the two industries producing apples and honey, it is sufficient that these two be integrated. Whenever the externalities are widespread, as in the case of education or the maintenance of roads, practically a decision-making process of the community at large, that is, of the government will be needed in order to meet the optimum conditions.

By the introduction of *indivisibilities* (and hence marginal costs below average costs) a situation is created where it can at least be concluded that the normal free enterprise will not take the decisions required for the optimum, namely marginal-cost pricing, except by the introduction of a two-part pricing system. I tried to argue elsewhere† that a joint administration of income taxes and such two-part price sales may be an efficient institution to take care of this portion of the operation of an optimum order.

(*c*) Methodologically the direct method may have to be abandoned whenever the operation of some institutions implies *costs*. As long as the set of institutions is unknown, how can we take care of the costs in the social welfare function? As observed already, I think this difficulty can be overcome, at least in a few simple cases, by the introduction, among the unknowns of the optimum problem, of the frequencies of alternative institutions. The method is similar to the one I used in the solution of some simple optimum problems on the spatial dispersion of economic activities.‡ We must also be aware that in the presentation of the optimum welfare problem now under discussion some institutions are *a priori* assumed to exist, namely, production units of a given size, with given production functions. We may have to treat this element in a similar way, namely by introducing the frequencies of each of the alternative unit size groups as unknowns into our problem and then apply the Lagrange multiplier method.

(*d*) If a number of different decisions have to be taken, some of them at the production unit level, others at 'higher' levels it becomes interesting to distinguish between the various 'higher' levels and to introduce some *system of levels*. This then comes to introducing spaces of different order, such as the locality, the province, the state, the continent or the world, as announced.

A rule which will then roughly correspond to the optimum set of decision-making levels is probably that decisions should be taken at a level high enough to make external effects of such decisions negligible; that is, make the influence on well-being of areas outside the one whose authorities take the decisions negligible.§ This is equivalent to saying that the various instruments of economic policy (which are the action

---

† Tinbergen, *op. cit.*

‡ Tinbergen, 'Sur un modèle de la dispersion géographique de l'activité économique', *Revue d'économique politique*, janv/févr. 1964.

§ Tinbergen, *Economic Policy: Principles and Design* (Amsterdam, 1956, 1964).

parameters of the higher levels—taxes, investments and so on) each have their own optimum level. For some of these this will be the world level or anything comparable to it.

(*e*) Among the costs of some institutions those connected with the necessary *flows of information* may rank high. This is particularly true for such institutions as planning offices, if planning of a large number of details is their task and if such information has to come over long 'distances'. The word 'distances' stands for the length of the chain of other institutions over which the information has to be supplied. Thus, in the Eastern economic systems, information about the assortment of goods to be produced often comes in a roundabout way, for instance, from consumer behaviour, passing through statistical inquiries, the central planning agencies and lower planning agencies down to the producing factory. The recent experiments in the Soviet clothing industry where information about the assortment is now directly obtained from the department stores represents an attempt to reduce such information costs.

(*f*) In some cases where the production laws assumed by Pareto do not apply and hence free enterprise does not necessarily guarantee that an optimum be attained, such an optimum may nevertheless be reached if only some *specific type of information* be made available to private entrepreneurs. The simplest case conceivable to illustrate this state of affairs is the situation to which the cobweb theorem applies. It is characteristic for that situation that production takes time; as a consequence, and in the absence of the type of information to be specified, the well-known cycles in prices and production occur which are the simplest example of an important class of 'commodity problems'. Such cycles represent a deviation from the optimum of welfare; welfare will be considered higher by most individuals involved if prices and production move along their trend. Such a trend movement can be approximately obtained if all potential suppliers are informed, at the moment of the *beginning of each production process*, about the *production started* by all other suppliers. This enables them to estimate the price to be expected at the end of the production process instead of only knowing the price prevailing at the beginning of the process. This type of information may be considered as a rudimentary form of planning and under some conditions will suffice to eliminate the cycles. Whether in this extremely simplified case this institution of a centre collecting and distributing information, together with the production units, will indeed represent the optimum order still depends on (i) the gain in well-being due to the elimination of the cycles, and (ii) the costs of the information centre. If (i) surpasses (ii) the information centre should be added to the production units. If (ii) surpasses (i) it should not. The gain from stabilization mentioned under (i) depends on the shape of the marginal utility curve of the commodity considered and the amplitude of the cycles and may also depend on the cost curve of the production units. This case represents a prototype of a large class of possibly and probably much more complicated cases where in a similar way flows of information may have to enter the picture and where analyses of this kind will be needed to spot the optimum. The number of alternative solutions generally will be larger than only two. Even in the simple cobweb case one can imagine other solutions, for instance the presence of an imperative planning centre which imposes a production programme on each of the production units.

(g) One of the deviations of a free society from the optimum of welfare may be due to a preference of entrepreneurs for independence leading to too small production units. The disadvantages to the rest of the economy may well surpass the psychological advantages to the entrepreneurs concerned. A conceivable very simple institution which may help to approach the optimum is an agency issuing licences for some types of production units, provided its costs are less than the net advantage of having larger units. The licences should only be issued for optimal-size units.

(h) Among the decisions which cannot be left to single enterprises or production units are those regarding the investments to be made in units with indivisibilities of considerable size. While these units can be left to private operators only if a two-part price system is applied (and while even then it is doubtful whether or not public ownership would be simpler), their investment decisions can only be based on the rather arbitrary choices they make concerning the fixed amount in the two-part rates. The only guarantee for an optimal investment policy in such units can be obtained by central planning of their capacities.

(i) An optimum regime will also have to make decisions on the rate of growth of the economy, implying a choice about its rate of savings. This latter choice is one showing external effects since not only the interests of those who save are involved but also the interests of all workers: their productivity and hence income will also depend on the stock of capital of the economy. If a rather high rate of growth is desired—and there are indications that it may be so—savings must also be relatively high. This does not imply the desirability of an uneven income distribution; savings need not be made by private consumers or enterprises only. They can also be made by the government. There is no rigid link therefore between the choice of a high rate of growth and the choice of an equitable income distribution, whatever the meaning given to this latter phrase.

SOCIALIST MARKET
RELATIONS AND PLANNING†

OTA ŠIK

My aim in this article is to summarize some of the theoretical aspects underlying the interrelation between socialist planning and market relations. First, we need to understand why commodity production is still necessary under socialism, what socialist commodity production has in common with its pre-socialist opposite numbers, what is their mutual basis and at what points they diverge. I shall try to confront the theoretical definition of features peculiar to socialist commodity production with the views hitherto current, especially among Marxist economists in the socialist countries under the influence of Stalin's interpretation. I shall also refer briefly, more in the way of marginal notes, to the relevance of these theoretical views to the new system of planning and management in Czechoslovakia.

I. THE SIGNIFICANCE OF COMMODITY PRODUCTION

The question of what socialist and private commodity production have in common and in what respect they differ, that is where their special features lie, cannot be answered by superficial descriptions; deeper analysis is necessary. We cannot be satisfied with some of the views advanced hitherto, which try to reduce the differences between the two forms to the existence of private ownership as the basis on the one hand and socialist ownership on the other. Such an answer simply substitutes an abstract concept for what is to be explained. Moreover, those who apply the category of ownership in this way usually interpret it as a volitional or legal category. They label types of ownership according to 'who decides about the utilization of means of production, about production etc.'

A deciding, directing agent exists, however, in many forms and types of ownership. Differences emerge when we examine the divergent interests, aims and the like with which the deciding or directing agent is concerned. Putting the question in this way we see that the volitional or legal aspects will not take us far and that we shall have to probe deeper into economic relations. Once we pose the questions in whose interests

† Abridged from a book *The Plan and the Market Under Socialism.*

decisions are made, what the maker of them wants, how his interests as
the directing agent relate to the interests of the actual producers, and so
on, we have to analyse economic relationships and the position of these
agents in this context. Only on this basis can we define the specific role
of the given agent and his part in the process of appropriation. Thus we
have to answer the question of the comparative status of both managers
and operators engaged in expropriating nature, for example in a socialist
economy as distinct from a capitalist economy. Naturally the answer
cannot be found in a superficial assertion that decisions are taken here
by one or there by another agent. A full analysis and comparison has to
be made of the methods by which, under two social systems, people
appropriate nature, taking into account aspects of their volitional (possibly legal and political) relationships, but concentrating on production
relations.

He who owns, appropriates, and to own all the time, he must appropriate all the time. For his method of appropriation to differ from other
methods, he must have not only different rights, but above all a different
economic status. In short, appropriation does not signify gaining something by a transient, chance legal or illegal act, but to gain something
permanently through the agency of certain economic relations of relatively long duration in the historical sense, within which relations those
who gain have a certain constantly regenerating economic standing. And
while specific economic relationships always assert themselves through
specific legal forms of action, the particular nature of these economic relationships must be analysed before we can understand their legal aspect.

Consequently, if we want to demonstrate the similarities and dis-
parities of private and socialist commodity production, we cannot content
ourselves with looking at their volitional or legal forms; it is necessary to
recapitulate the salient features and the causes of private commodity
production and then compare them with the corresponding aspects of
socialist commodity production.

2. PRIVATE COMMODITY PRODUCTION

Private commodity production, as a certain type of commodity production of long duration, made its appearance in history in two forms. First,
as simple commodity production, and secondly in its capitalist form. We
will examine first the general features of this type, in other words, what
simple and capitalist commodity production have in common.

In both these economic forms analysis shows the existence of separate,
relatively independent producers partially linked by ties originating in
the spontaneous social division of labour. Their labour is not purposefully
expended as a component of social labour. They have no exact informa-

tion about each other, about the amount and nature of all work, about the quantities of products and their use values nor about the requirements of all producers and so on. No producer turns out all the use values he needs (neither means of production, nor consumer articles) for himself. Nevertheless, people can live, consume and produce for the sole reason that they are producing for each other.

While in their immediate relationships they are working as independent, private producers, they are in fact producing for society and are dependent on society. In this sense their labour is social, but only on the market do they discover, according to sales and the prices realized, whether it was socially necessary. We therefore refer to this as *indirect* social labour.

Conditions are such that labour is not the prime desire of man: no one works for the mere sake of working and no one is willing to give his labour free for his fellowmen. In addition, this takes place under conditions of a relative insufficiency of articles of consumption for the majority. Hence the everlasting struggle to acquire more things, at the very least as many articles of consumption as other people are able to possess.

Articles of consumption are, however, the fruits of labour (both embodied and living). People are no longer able to produce all their material wants. They must, therefore, get the articles they need for their own use, and the means of production they need, by exchange. People are willing to expend their labour for others or to produce use values for others solely on the condition that they will receive in exchange the things they require. They can get use values from others only to the amount to which the socially necessary labour expended on their production corresponds to the socially necessary amount of labour which they themselves expended on the production of use values for others.

If we express the socially necessary amount of labour expended in producing commodities of given use values as value, we can then briefly define the law underlying this exchange as follows: *each receives on an average from other producers of commodities certain use values solely to the value to which he himself has produced commodities for others*. This is a very general statement of the law of value, that is, the basis of commodity production.

There is, of course, a dialectical link between value and use value which assumes a definite form in exchange ratios or prices (in money exchange). I am not particularly concerned here, however, with the interaction of value and use value in price formation, or with the market mechanism through which the law of value is able to assert itself under conditions of private commodity production. I merely wish to recall the cardinal features and causes of the existence of private commodity production in order to bring out later the broad aspects of the common basis of private and socialist commodity production.

What are the distinguishing features of simple private commodity production and capitalist commodity production? Above all simple commodity production is carried on with a very slight degree of co-operation. To be more exact one should refer to independent and separate individual producers, who engage in certain types of production only as a result of the fundamental growth of social division of labour. However, these individuals have never actually worked in complete isolation, for at least members of their families co-operated. In this sense one can speak of partial co-operation at this stage, too.

These craft groups at first produced their own means of production. By degrees, however, even at this primitive initial stage, social division of labour advanced so far that craftsmen stopped making their means of production themselves and began to obtain them, as well as articles of consumption, in exchange for their own commodities. In this way there emerged both the specialized production of means of production and their spontaneous distribution among production branches through commodity exchange.

Naturally, as these economic relations spread spontaneously, they began to take on the appropriate forms of group, volitional and legal relations. The separate, independent producers became interested in winning for as little of their own labour as possible the maximum of use values from others. Their goal, in short, was to amass the greatest amount of use values and to this end they directed all their volitional actions. These interests and this goal governed their decision in using their means of production, what they produced and sold, and their purchases of new means of production etc.

The aims and interests of private producers were bound to be at variance, and the mutual contradictions could only be resolved by conflict. It was a lasting contradiction in which necessity was enforced through rivalry. Nevertheless, this spontaneous economic struggle called for certain rules, some agreement and regulation of its course in the interests of all concerned. The common interest demanded a general adjustment of the processes of private production and the exchange of goods. Thus the spontaneous growth of commodity relations gave rise to a set of rules by which they were regulated, and these rules, being upheld and enforced by power, were legal rules.

With the emergence of laws corresponding to private commodity production, the standing of the private producer, and his relations with other producers, is no longer purely economic and he no longer enforces his own will alone in an elemental way. He becomes legally recognized as a private producer with the right to decide about his production, the use of his means of production and the disposal of his goods. Ceasing to be merely an economically separate independent appropriator of nature relying on his own labour and commodity exchange, he becomes a private appropriator of both means of production and articles of consumption who, as the owner of these things, is on all occasions protected by law.

However, while he consumes the articles of consumption, the means of production enables him to keep on producing, to enter repeatedly into exchange relations with others and thereby to continue appropriating, that is, renewing his standing as a private owner. In this sense private ownership (appropriation) of the means of production, realized through commodity exchange, is the basis for the reproduction of private commodity relations over a relatively long period of history.

The feature distinguishing capitalist commodity production from the simple form is, of course, the existence of large-scale working co-operation. These groups, in which a number of producers are always associated, originated primarily by commodity exchange leading to the accumulation of considerable quantities of means of production in the hands of individuals.

On the other hand, there appeared a mass of people deprived of both means of production and articles of consumption; consequently, a section acquired the ability to purchase for their products not only articles of consumption and means of production, but also the labour power of the expropriated. They could bring these people together with the means of production they had bought, and supervise them. Then, at first by simple co-operation, later by the growing division of labour (within the co-operation), they were in a position to carry out highly productive large-scale production.

This technically and economically more productive and progressive capitalist large-scale production demanded adaptation of the legal superstructure, which in turn codified and stimulated the growth of this large-scale production. The opportunity for individuals to buy the labour power of others (alongside the earlier right to dispose of the fruits of their own labour) gained legal sanction. They could sell the products as their own and realize their value (still fixed by the amount of socially necessary labour). Moreover, by paying solely for the value of the workers' labour power, they could appropriate the value created over and above this value, i.e. surplus value.

Why do I repeat these more or less well-known things? Chiefly because some economists, while acknowledging the importance of so-called Marxist historico-logical methods, still fail to grasp the real, deep, underlying causes of the existence of commodity production. They alledge, mistakenly, that Marx derived commodity production from the existence of private ownership, and they fail to appreciate the economic meaning of the category 'private labour' and its relation to the category 'social labour'. Moreover, they cannot conceive of private ownership as anything other than 'the right of individuals to dispose of certain things and to decide about them', nor do they see that this right has always been a reflex of economic development, though being relatively independent and reacting back on the economy. They do not see that the origin and existence of a form of commodity production cannot be explained by the existence of this or that specific system of law. On the contrary, commodity production must always be interpeted as belonging to a given system of appropriation (manifested at every moment of observation in the shape of a definite, seemingly rigid, legally established form of ownership), which is linked with a certain inner contradiction in social labour and with a given level of the forces of production.

While commodity production, both simple and capitalist, possesses the special features which I have tried to recapitulate, the common basis, which has its common causes can be summarized as follows: production is carried on by separate, independent producers linked by certain ties, but producing without direct reliance on each other specific goods (within the social division of labour) for a relatively unknown social consumption. There is, therefore, a contradiction between private and social labour. Products are produced as commodities, that is exchanged on the basis of value, because they are produced under conditions where labour is not yet man's prime want. A producer of one type of product (forced to rely on other products) can obtain use values from other producers only by equivalent exchange of a socially necessary amount of labour, i.e. the value of commodities. Because their work makes people mutually dependent—though work is for each merely the essential condition for gaining as much use value as he can from others, because no one is willing to work unpaid for his fellows, labour becomes the underlying regulator of the quantitative relations in which use values are exchanged.

Naturally this ultimate common basis manifests itself in special features of the two distinct types of private commodity production, without, however, the deep-lying, hidden substance being negated. In simple commodity production, the producer sells his own goods, and his immediate incentive to produce and sell is the urge to acquire use values for his reproduction (personal and production consumption). In capitalist commodity production, on the other hand, the seller of commodities (legal owner) is not the immediate producer and his incentive is no longer the mere acquisition of use values from others, but the very process of expanding value (constantly adding to the surplus value). From these specific features stems the necessity to transform value to the capitalist price of production, which does not, however, cancel the substance of the law of value. Obtaining use values from others for personal consumption and for extended reproduction remains the fundamental condition for the growth of commodity production (i.e. its deepest, hidden substance) although its specific motive is provided by the process of acquiring surplus value.

Many economists, however, tend to lose altogether the most fundamental substance and cause of commodity production beneath this specific form, which prevents them from grasping the need for commodity production under socialism.

3. LABOUR UNDER SOCIALISM

Enough has perhaps been said to show why commodity production continues under socialism. In analysing the most fundamental and general causes of all its types, we can, if we leave aside the specific features of the capitalist and simple forms, and indeed exclude the peculiarities of the private type, arrive at the common nature of private and socialist commodity production. While less significant features distinguish the capitalist from the simple form of commodity production, the differences between the private and socialist types are more substantial. However, before taking a closer look at these distinctive features, let us recapitulate what they have in common and what, therefore, justifies us in speaking of socialist production as a type of commodity production.

Under socialism, too, with its highly developed social division of labour, there is *production of specific products in separate, relatively independently producing and deciding groups* in which people are associated to produce for each other and to meet social needs, *to cover the consumption of all members of the socialist society*. Nevertheless, *labour cannot yet be man's prime want*.

And so a state of affairs in which the majority of people lack a vital interest in work still prevails. At the socialist stage of development *labour is still relatively onerous* (long hours) *and intensive*. There is a *relative lack of variety*, work is monotonous and, for most people, offers little creative scope. There is still a *fairly rigid division of labour*, binding the majority to *one occupation for life*. Consequently, as a general rule people expend their labour for others primarily because *labour is the condition for acquiring from others the use values needed for themselves*.

In my opinion, errors in theory have been made in the past on this question. The fact that the attitude to work changes with the ending of capitalist exploitation has often been equated with the birth of a communist attitude to labour. Of course, the fact that the surplus product is no longer appropriated by capitalists and that its distribution and utilization are decided by public bodies plays a part in encouraging a new attitude among a majority. But even this change has not been adequately studied. The very simplified general conclusions drawn so far have not been founded on detailed psychological and sociological research, and have been strongly coloured by subjective ideas and wishful thinking. Little attention has been devoted to *how this economic change has penetrated into people's consciousness* and what is its *real impact on their thinking, feelings and actions.*

I believe, for example, that in the early post-revolutionary period the change penetrated people's consciousness primarily through its most apparent, outward manifestations, such as the removal of the capitalists and their aides from the factories, changes in management with a rapid rise in the numbers of leading people *coming straight from the working class.* The rapid abolition of such evils as *pauperism*, unemployment, fear of old-age, sickness etc., all helped to inspire the initial enthusiasm. But it by no means signifies that labour has become *Communist labour in the sense Marx spoke of it.*

Work is not done for its own sake. Marx always spoke of Communist labour as an activity which would be highly interesting, thought-inspiring, a constant source of fantasy, initiative and desire for new things. It must be an activity the accomplishment and results of which give people the greatest measure of satisfaction—as is the case today with a few occupations, for example, the work of some scientists, artists, etc. Such work is still exceptional.

This, of course, does not mean—as an oversimplified view sometimes asserts—that people are by nature lazy and that they would never work if they did not have to. But if everyone could choose their work according to taste, they would undoubtedly want to do something creative, they would want a change from time to time, and they would not overwork themselves. They would definitely not find satisfaction in standing eight hours a day, day in day out, at the same machine, with the same monotonous movements.

Here we should distinguish between work under socialism *done with a sense of social awareness*, perhaps with a degree of *enthusiasm, and creative work, done primarily for its own sake.* While there is a certain intermingling which will grow, it would be making a mistake—and to some extent we have done so—if we failed to see these technical, economic and other socially-conditioned differences in the nature of work as being significant differences between the two stages of Communist society. The first mentioned attitude can exist at the socialist stage without the second when the majority do not work for work's sake, for personal satisfaction, which does not exclude the possibility that they may perform it in a conscious way, and some of them with enthusiasm. Communist society, however, will certainly have to be built not only on the basis of conscious effort of the majority for society's sake, but at the same time, for their own satisfaction and enjoyment. And for this the ground must be *prepared not only by a great expansion of technology and all the production forces*, but also *economically and socially, above all through division of labour* (breaking down its rigidity), *shortening working hours, providing opportunities for education and specialized training,* still further *relieving people of material and other cares* and by a much fuller *democracy in public life.*

Labour at the socialist stage cannot be of this nature; nevertheless it can be performed with a degree of public awareness. A distinction should be made, however, between awareness and enthusiasm. In the immediate post-revolutionary years people undoubtedly did work with enthusiasm, without being fully aware of the changes that had taken place. Enthusiasm was generated, as already pointed out, by the most obvious, external aspects. People did not need to know, and to this day most of them do not know, the changes that had been made in distributing the national income, or how the surplus product was distributed and expended. Yet they were capable of genuine enthusiasm. Then in the course of time the obvious changes in the nature of work, in its control and management and in various other factors were the most readily forgotten, people got used to them and work became a matter of routine. The younger generation, who did not experience the change-over and who now tend to compare their work and its results (often superficially on the basis of incomplete and distorted information) with the situation in the developed capitalist countries, are unable to conjure up the post-revolutionary enthusiasm for occupations which fail to satisfy them. It is not by chance that we find, on the whole, a degree of enthusiasm surviving longest in special campaigns (brigade work etc.) where the tangible results serve some exceptional needs of the community.

For a thorough *understanding* of the changed nature of work under socialism as compared with capitalism, we need profound theoretical training; it involves a grasp of the substance of Marxist political economy, not to mention other social sciences. Such an understanding is, naturally, still attainable by only a relatively small section of the community and should be seen as a process in the course of which people gradually and in a variety of ways acquire knowledge and change their outlook. Theoretical training is, understandably, not the sole factor, because day-to-day experience, too, can play its part. The latter would yield better results if, for example, people had a clearer picture of how the national income is distributed and expended, of the use to which the surplus product is put, and if they could play a fuller part in deciding these processes.

Even a deep understanding of the transformation of the social character of labour under socialism does not however, signify anything more than an understanding of the necessity and significance of optimum performance on behalf of society, of the necessary social distribution and expenditure of the fruits of labour. Labour itself, however, is not changed in the sense that monotonous and uninteresting or highly intensive work would even for socially conscious people become their prime want and concern. Such people have simply grasped its superiority to labour under capitalism and they will, therefore, be ready to defend the socialist economy against any attempt to restore capitalist conditions; but they will not be motivated in their everyday work by considerations other than those motivating the majority of their fellows.

From this we can deduce that for the majority of people the prime incentive to work does not, in the given technical and economic conditions, lie in work itself, but in *acquiring the necessary use values produced by others.* The majority are motivated by the desire to make sure of the highest possible level of material consumption, and in some cases of non-material consumption which the material things can provide. The incentive is always corrected to greater or lesser degree by social awareness and enthusiasm on the following approximate pattern: growing awareness and knowledge are manifested when together with interest in immediate reward there is a growing understanding that both immediate and long-term public needs also make demands on work. If the conflict between the immediate personal and social interests sharpens, the socially conscious can for a time work for the public welfare even at the price of sacrificing some of their personal material reward. But not even in the case of the most conscious people can this be the rule, because they, too, realize that many of these long-term contradictions are superfluous or can be overcome in other ways.

Enthusiasm, in some cases without fuller understanding, is manifested not only in socially necessary labour, but also, in case of need, in work for which personal reward is not expected. But such work, too, can only be a short-lived, exceptional occurrence at the socialist stage of development and cannot rule out the vital role of consumption which, operating through the medium of material reward, is the general incentive under socialism.

4. MATERIAL INCENTIVES

Understanding of the prime labour incentive under socialism implies a constant recognition of its influence on the *relatively independent decisions about production made by enterprises,* which should ensure that, in the long run, labour is expended to give the maximum returns for the whole working group. Naturally, the group in a socialist enterprise, and above all its management, will be more fully endowed with a sense of socialist consciousness and understanding of the social necessity of labour than many individuals. In the short term, this awareness can be manifested by the performance of socially necessary labour even at the price of a temporary sacrifice to the pockets of all members of the group (in the event of an increase in the contradictions between socially necessary labour and labour for which the enterprise can reap financial benefit). However, even in the case of the whole group and its management one cannot expect socialist consciousness to extend to performing regular and long-term socially necessary labour at the expense of lowering the group's material reward below the level they would receive for other jobs. *Hence for an enterprise group, too, the general, long-term incentive for concrete expenditure of labour will be to gain the highest possible material reward for its members.*

It would be idealistic to think that it is possible to lay down in detail from the centre what an enterprise should produce, thereby limiting the relative independence of choice and decision to a minimum. Only people closely associated with production can decide its actual course, both the quantity and, above all, the quality, and the interrelations of quantitative and qualitative development. Enterprise managements with their specialized knowledge will always have to decide the actual trends of production, although their decisions may be made in the context of overall macroeconomic plans and with their aid. Their practical decisions will always be guided both by reasoned knowledge and by definite economic interests, which at the socialist stage are still of necessity, and primarily, material interests.

In recognizing this we should also recognize that the *overall reward of an enterprise group, its wage fund, should be linked to the development of labour in such a way that it will stimulate the most effective expenditure of labour.* For an individual group to acquire the greatest number of use values from others (and this is the issue when we speak of wage funds), it will have to produce, within the limits of its sector, products that meet the needs of its customers, while constantly improving them and keeping costs down to a minimum. And enterprises should be urged by their own material interests to do this. Thus the closer their relatively independent decisions on production approach the optimum, the higher should be their wage fund, and vice versa. Analysing this requirement, we find that in practice it can only be met through commodity-money relations.

5. COMMODITY-MONEY RELATIONS UNDER SOCIALISM

An enterprise should in the first place produce use values for all its customers in proportions corresponding to demand, and progressively improve them or develop entirely new use values. There is no better judge of whether products are in fact use values of the kind required than the consumer. Therefore, *the first condition for an enterprise to acquire a wage fund in return for its operations is that the consumer should assess how far the products meet his needs. No one is likely to invent a better way than that linked to commodity production, whereby the consumer voluntarily, free of any administrative pressure, confirms the usefulness of commodities by buying them. This then is the first feature of commodity relations.*

Of course, an enterprise in exchange for its use values can receive use values from others only in proportion to the amount of socially necessary labour expended on the commodities exchanged. It will try to expend socially necessary labour only insofar as this labour is realized as value, that is insofar as it decides the exchange ratios or prices (in money exchange) of the commodities bought and sold. Consequently, if all enterprises produce use values for others, if they expend labour for others with the main aim of acquiring the largest possible wage funds (use values from others), then *the synthesis of these mutually contradictory endeavours is the realization of labour as value.* The fact that every socialist enterprise transfers a share of the value realized to cover social requirements makes no difference. This labour, too, which is destined for centralized social expenditure, has to be realized as a component of value in the process of exchange. *The average long-term necessity for mutually equivalent exchange is, therefore, not negated, but on the contrary emphasized. This is the second feature of commodity relations.*

Finally an enterprise has to build up its wage fund in direct proportion to the value realized. As a percentage of realized value, the size of the wage fund will rise and fall proportionally to the movements of the former. An enterprise will, naturally, be interested not only in realizing the maximum value, but together with this in producing the maximum volume of use values, i.e. in producing all its products productively (and at minimum cost), and moreover in turning out the very best, progressive use values. If then the growth of the wage fund of an enterprise can outpace the growth of total realized value thanks to cutting actual production costs as compared with socially necessary production costs and making use values superior to the general run, this will encourage the enterprise to follow such a course. It can be done again through commodity money relations as follows:

(*a*) *The wage fund rises in proportion to the actual growth of income* (gross or net), the share of which in total realized value (sales) rises the more, the lower are the material costs (or production costs altogether) with which the given value has been created and realized.

(*b*) The total value realized (sales) will be the greater, *the more the quality and usefulness of products rise above the average and the higher the prices obtained for them.*

This is the third feature of commodity relations.

Under the given conditions of labour no one has been able, or is likely to suggest a better way of interesting groups of producers in optimum operation than through the action of commodity-money relations. Each socialist co-operating group can, in effect, acquire commodities with the required use values from other units only to the value of which they have themselves produced commodities of a given use value for others. This is the essential substance of commodity relations. Their prime cause is confirmed as really being that under certain conditions of production determining the nature of labour and consumption as explained above, consumption is the foremost incentive for the work of groups producing for each other on the basis of advanced division of social labour.

More surprising than the recognition that socialist production rests on this essential commodity basis is the fact that this recognition has come so tardily and is meeting with such obstacles and ideological resistance. The explanation lies in those special features of socialist commodity production which justify us in referring to it as a special type of commodity production. In the past, however, these features were blown up to such an extent—both theoretically and in long years of practice—that the underlying substance of commodity production was lost to sight.

Before enumerating these features of socialist commodity production, we will briefly examine why this aspect of socialist production was rejected, or at the most acknowledged in a severely truncated form, for so many years.

The underlying theoretical cause is, in fact, that the founders of scientific socialism, Marx and Engels, were able in their day to acquaint themselves only with the private type of commodity production. They tied these relations to private production, and therefore supposed that with the extinction of the capitalist economy, commodity production would also disappear. Today we should clearly recognize that Marx and Engels were in their day unable to foretell the complexities of a socialist economy, and indeed they never set themselves such a task.

Only a hopelessly dogmatic interpretation of Marxist–Leninist theory is capable of denying the existence of new realities just because they were never stated and explained by the classics of Marxism–Leninism. On the contrary, the most scientific and fruitful understanding of Marxism–Leninism, one that genuinely applies its true theoretical method, presupposes that it will be continuously developed and enriched with new realities. The true proponents of this teaching are not those who deny the existence of socialist commodity relations because they contradict the letter of the classics, but those who in line with the realities of these relations undertake their theoretical elucidation and then help to extend and apply them in practice.

Very early, in the light of initial experience of the growth of the Soviet state, Lenin realized the need to use commodity-money relations. He stressed the importance of enterprise cost accounting, seeing it not merely as simple book-keeping, but linking it fully to the aim of harnessing the material interests of the enterprise. Unfortunately, he did not have time to work out and explain this method more fully and consequently he was unable to prevent its subsequent degradation to a mere formality.

Above all, there was no theoretical work to refute the idea that commodity production would disappear when private production had been replaced by socialist relations of production. Commodity production which was underlined by Lenin at the time of NEP was linked to private, small-scale production of the transition period. This explains the revival of theories about the abolition of commodities and money in the Soviet Union following the collectivization of agriculture and the ending of private production.

Stalin did, indeed, play a progressive role in countering these purely speculative and sectarian views and defending commodity–money relations. However, he committed other serious theoretical errors, which flowed in large measure from the state of the Soviet economy at the time. The consequences of these errors were operative for a long time both in economic practices in the Soviet Union and later in the economies of all other socialist countries. He put forward the theory that commodity–money relations are in the nature of a foreign element in a socialist economy which has to suffer them purely because their existence is forced upon it by co-operative forms of socialist ownership, which he regarded as inferior forms in which socialist principles were inadequately embodied.

He believed that in the socialist state sector there could be room only for accounting and recording of values in response to external relations (with co-operatives and other countries) and that genuine commodity–money relations could not exist between socialist state enterprises. These relations should also, in his view, be quickly eliminated from dealings between state and co-operative enterprises.

This theory of Stalin's, which was strictly adhered to during his lifetime and is still widely applied in practice, became a deep-rooted dogma with grave consequences for socialist economic growth. It magnified the special features of socialist production to an extreme. Although in their true proportions these features necessarily distinguish the socialist and capitalist types of commodity production, when magnified in this speculative way they lead in practice to a break down of the commodity nature of socialist production, thereby seriously aggravating the conflicts existing within commodity production.

In the economic debates of the twenties and thirties, with which present-day economists are gradually and with considerable difficulty becoming acquainted, many notable theoretical views were expressed on the utilization of commodity–money relations, the law of value and so on. Many of the views advanced by Soviet economists at that time were later suppressed and we are only gradually getting to know at least some of them. For the most part they were concerned with questions of the commodity–money mechanism in the period of *transition* to a uniform socialist economy, the relation of private agricultural production to socialist industrialization, resources for the industrialization drive, the balance and contradiction between industry and agriculture, etc. The market was, on the whole, still seen as belonging to an economy with several social sectors. One can find only some abstract ideas about the general necessity of using the market as an instrument of planned growth under socialism.

Rather better known are the discussions of economists (Marxist and non-Marxist) during the thirties and the immediate postwar years in the West concerning socialist planning, management systems, centralism and decentralism, prices and the market etc.

The Polish economist Oskar Lange,† writing in the early thirties, was among the first to link socialist planning with the market mechanism and to underline the role of balanced prices in ensuring effective distribution of resources within socialist industry. His outstanding contribution has been in connection with the structure of production, where he has drawn attention to the opportunities for substitution in production and consumption, to the presence of various alternative courses and the role of prices in securing the most effective variant. Unfortunately, his approach to the market fails to reveal the socio-economic basis that exists under socialism, too; he does not start from the intrinsic conflict between socialist labour and economic interests and, therefore, fails to show prices as being the necessary form in which this conflict can be resolved. Consequently, he is unable to put his finger on the true nature of the socialist market and the dialectics of the plan/market relation. Since his outlook was necessarily influenced by the views then prevailing among Marxist economists, that is that the market mechanism cannot operate together with socialist planning, he looked for a substitute to the market in balanced prices fixed at the centre and, in fact, was too ready to make concessions to a concept of socialist planning based on administrative priorities.

Understandably, no theoretician is able to go much in advance of his times, nor can he free himself altogether from the prevailing views. He can hardly be expected to come forward with findings that have to grow and mature in soil provided by accumulating, generalizing and analysing practical experience. At a time of rapid growth rates, when certain contradictions within this growth were still far from being as apparent as they are today, it was very much to the credit of an economist if he pointed to problems of structure, effectiveness, the market and prices under socialism, even if he was still unable to attack some of the 'axioms' of socialist theory, show up their fallacies and find a radical solution.

Credit for re-discovering all these notable theoretical contributions made in the first half of the century is due, above all, to Polish economists

† He was working at the time in the U.S.A.

who took the lead in the socialist countries by embarking in recent decades on a full discussion about socialist economic models and questions of economic synthesis. W. Brus, author of 'Socialist Economic Models', has made a notable contribution to current theoretical thinking by his attempt to formulate the essential substance of these long-past discussions and to find their relevance to the problems engaging us today.

Despite the tremendous value of the Polish work, even here we do not find an explanation of the *objective necessity* for the existence of commodity–money relations and the market in a socialist economy, nor of the *impossibility of resolving* economic conflicts when these relations are restricted or suppressed by the old method of administrative planning. The explanation of market relations is not sought in the inner contradictions of socialist labour at the given stage of the development of the productive forces and, therefore, the market does not appear as a necessary economic form of resolving these contradictions within the framework of socialist planning. Consequently, the decentralized management model is still regarded as just one of the possible models, while the share of *centralization* and *decentralization* in management is seen as a matter of knowledge and not as connected with the contradictions inherent in economic interests.

Let us now examine the real features of socialist commodity production and how they have been incorrectly magnified.

6. PROBLEMS OF CENTRAL PLANNING

When a socialist economy is brought into being, private appropriation is on the whole doomed to extinction. Revolutionary measures in the realm of power and the law enable qualitative changes to be made in the economic field. Individuals able to appropriate the fruits of another's labour disappear from the scene. Nor can individuals any longer sell commodities produced by others, they cannot use this exchange to acquire the necessary articles of consumption and means of production and they cannot appropriate surplus value. While a fundamental change takes place in the social character of co-operating groups in which workers and appropriators no longer confront each other, there is transformation of all the processes of distribution and exchange, too, and this conditions the break-up of private appropriation.

Its place is taken by social appropriation, which signifies a certain purposeful planning of the processes of labour, distribution and exchange for society as a whole, and regulation and co-ordination of group activities in line with the vital interests of all working people. Hence the cardinal feature lies in the fact that all labour is expended in accordance with the needs of society as a whole with the aid of a uniform social plan. However, this is the factor which above all in theory, but also in practice, has been enormously overrated.

The most typical theoretical exaggeration was the thesis that labour was by its very nature social and the postulation of this as an absolute concept. It was then considered possible for the uniform economic plan to be used as a means of ensuring that all products would correspond to the needs of the consumers and be produced with the highest possible social productivity. In consequence it would be possible under state socialist production to distribute all products directly to the consumers and, therefore, within this sector commodity exchange and the market would be unnecessary. If it were not for co-operative production, neither commodity production nor its allied categories would need to exist and production costs (for reasons of economy) could be entered in units of labour time. The theory was crowned by the argument that commodity production cannot exist in a system of state-socialist production because there are no separate owners to confront each other. This 'ownership' theory was then formally extended to the point of a special definition of the relations of production, which was supposed to demonstrate in the most general way (without definite historical backing, however) that the forms of ownership (without a precise definition of the content of this category) have always decided the modes of distribution and exchange.

Just because I at one time grasped this formal thread in Stalin's concept, I have first of all essayed in a more extensive work to refute his basic theory of production relations and ownership. Many colleagues, however, find difficulty in comprehending the connection between the analysis of production relations and ownership in general, and the definite suggestion that the necessity of commodity–money relations and their utilization under socialism be recognized. I am not concerned here with conducting a polemic at this highly abstract level; nor do I wish to refute incorrect ideas about labour planning under socialism by refuting Stalin's basic errors concerning 'ownership forms as the basis of exchange relations'. I think, however, that our brief historical recapitulation has shown that no appropriation exists either historically or logically without including distribution and exchange, and that ownership in its specific volitional and legal manifestations has never existed as a general social phenomenon without specific economic appropriation, i.e. without specific production, distribution and exchange activities.

Let us, however, return to a closer examination of the error involved in the proposition that the direct social character of labour is absolute. In the first place, this theory, in its entirety, is a tremendous simplification of the *process of cognition*, completely ignores the impossibility of a plan which will take into account all the manifold economic linkages which can hardly be matched in the complexity of their interrelationships by the growth and development of any other form of the movement of matter. Primarily, these are all the real linkages between the production of an enormous number of use values which are necessarily subjected to constant change and, on the other hand, the diverse assembly of wants which also follow their relatively independent course; to this must be added the high degree of social division of labour. Then there is the linkage between the trend of individual costs of producing use values and that of all the factors determining the growth of social productivity. Finally, there is the interlocking and dialectical interdependence between the trend of production costs conditioned by the trend of productivity, on the one hand, and the trend of wants and of the use values produced, on the other. While the movements of production costs and productivity exert a strong influence on the trend of wants and of the use values produced, the reverse is also true. Thus we can form an idea of the tangled web of connections and interconnections in a country like Czechoslovakia, for example, producing roughly one-and-a-half million types of use values.

It goes without saying that the planned progress of gearing the concrete and most productive social labour expended to the overall concrete wants of society cannot be carried out without a process of generalization and aggregation towards the centre of society. Only the most basic and general linkages among the highly aggregated economic factors can be recorded at the centre. It is not enough to take note of these factors, however. There must be management and organization capable of presenting the plan in concrete terms and guiding all decisions and instruments of management both in space (through a network of operative managements at lower level) and in time, i.e. through short-term plans and decisions as opposed to the long-range plan and forecasts. Conceding the need for such generalization and aggregation in space (towards the centre) and in time, there was, nevertheless, a failure in the past to recognize the enormous number of potential variants in economic growth, requiring that factors stemming from perpetually changing details should be truly generalized and aggregated from below up to the centre. Furthermore, it was not grasped that co-operating groups at lower levels especially the enterprises, should be given only overall guidance, while it is impossible for central assignments to be mechanically divided out and handed down from the top, which would imply detailed charting of day-to-day decisions for the enterpises from the centre. The need was not seen for enterprises to have relative freedom in choosing their own production programmes from the many possible variants within the planned, broadly defined course of economic growth.

Secondly, this theory drastically simplified the part played by interests within a socialist economy. It elevated the unity of interests among enterprises and society to the status of an absolute principle and completely overlooked the objectively-based, specific material interests of enterprise groups and the inevitable emergence of non-antagonistic conflicts between the centre and enterprises, and between different enterprises. The concept was, in short, that the socialist enterprises would always tend to make decisions fully in accord with the interests of society and that it would suffice to give individual members of an enterprise material incentives to fulfil a plan handed down from the top.

In reality, however, not only do the material interests of individuals and society conflict, but the material interests of all members of an enterprise group always tend to merge into a general interest of the entire enterprise in having the largest possible wage fund and this, naturally, plays a big part in shaping decision-making by managements. The way in which this wage fund is geared to performance then conditions decisions on enterprise operations taken by its executives.

Understandably, all previous economic stimuli which have generated a certain degree of mutual conflict between the operations of specific sector (branch or enterprise) managements bore the stamp of the existing system of administrative planning and management. This system, whereby, through a well-defined set of planning indicators, the attention of managements was almost wholly and unilaterally directed to the quantitative aspect of production, led inevitably to the neglect of quality and of the development of use values.

Central planning and management authorities, using all available indicators, were still able to do no more than regulate the volume of production, whether of very broad groups of products, or of a few selected items. Even the 'quality indicators' were, economically speaking, merely further indicators of quantity because in effect they simply set the trends of certain volumes of production (measured by value or by physical output) correlated to the labour force (productivity), or various other quantititative expressions of growth of production and labour expended (indicators of operating costs, manpower, productive fixed assets, etc.). Apart from a negligible number of technological development projects fixed at the top, none of these indicators were capable of deciding the development of actual use values, their improvement, replacement, the technology and techniques of their production, etc. Progress in quality, whereby production both satisfies and stimulates new needs, had to be left almost entirely in the hands of enterprise and plant managements, who by their intimate contact with production (including research and development) are alone fitted to carry it forward.

However, the qualitative development of use values, and the proportions in which they are to be produced (which again, with the exception of a few set assignments, cannot be fixed at the centre) are inseparably linked to the quantitative side of production. There is an intrinsically contradictory, dialectical connection between them. Work has to progress both quantitatively and qualitatively in order to ensure a growing amount of various use values as well as their production in new and improved forms. Moreover, some increase in the quantity of labour and its products is a condition of better quality and the development of use values, while improvement in quality is a condition of raising their output. Unbalanced growth on one or the other side sooner or later reacts to the detriment of the other. In other words, disproportionate growth of one or the other signifies its temporary expansion at the expense of the factor which in the long term accompanies and qualifies it.

For a time one can, in one or another social formation expand, for example, the quantity of production at the expense of improvement and progressive replacement of old types of use values by new ones. There comes a time, however, when the lag in development inevitably makes itself felt, including, of course, a lag in the technical qualities and productive capacities of the means of production. The latter is the main obstacle to further growth in volume of production (both absolutely and related to manpower). In short, where up-to-date, technologically progressive means of production are lacking, there is no hope of stepping up output when and as required. The same would be true of the opposite extreme, although it has not yet occurred in practice. If a disproportionate amount of labour were to be turned to improvement and to chopping and changing assortment programmes, a brake would be put on the growth of the volume of output. Only when all aspects of production are fully harmonized can rapid and steady growth of consumption be assured.

As already mentioned, it is no easy matter to acquire the knowledge necessary to ensure optimal growth of each branch of production and of social production generally. However, such growth becomes a matter of pure chance when neither the people in direct control of management (especially enterprise managements), nor those directly engaged in economic activity (operatives, salesmen etc.) have any reason to be interested in reaching the optimum and on the contrary, their interest is tied to one-track growth.

The administrative method of planning and management encouraged enterprises to adopt production programmes with such one-track, primarily quantitative aims. Targets were stepped up year by year by the central authorities in a mechanical way without adequate economic justification. Their instruments were planning indicators, a tightening control of the fulfilment of these one-track assignments, and ultimately the tying of all funds of material remuneration to these quantitative (in the economic sense) indicators. This, accompanied by rather generalized political and moral appeals for better technology and quality, was bound to encourage an undue stress on quantity at the expense of use values and advanced production methods. Enterprises concentrated on fulfilling and overfulfilling their annual planned assignments (volume of gross output, output of goods, net output, or gross output related to manpower) and they avoided anything likely to stand in the way of this aim. They, therefore, looked askance at technological change, product improvements (indeed, decline in quality was often suffered in silence) or putting new items into production.

Increasing the number of indicators planned and checked from the top can never be effective in transforming this one-track system into a stimulus to optimal growth. All practical attempts of this kind were bound to fail and all theories formulated on these lines have remained empty, impracticable abstractions. No one has been able to suggest how central indicators can be made to serve as substitutes for research, development, construction, designing, technological and other activities carried out by the enterprises. These provide the groundwork for improving quality and, in accordance with the economic incentives at work in the enterprise, they may be held back more or less, or more or less encouraged. Nor has anyone thought of a way by which central indicators can maintain a balance among all sectors of production and guarantee that every item will be constantly available in quantities corresponding to the fluctuations in consumer demand.

Under the old, detailed system of directive planning and management with production programmes aiming primarily at quantity and wage funds tied solely to plan results, concern for the size of wage funds exerted enormous pressure on enterprises to choose the one-track course of purely quantitative extensive growth at the expense of quality, effectiveness and socially necessary development. That is to say, not only insufficient understanding, but also the specific material interests of producers generated the growing contradictions between the concrete labour expended in an enterprise and the socially necessary development of labour.

In correcting these erroneous theoretical views we need to grasp both the necessity of commodity production under socialism, as previously explained, and the specific features of this type of production.

7. A SOCIALIST MARKET

By harnessing their interests through commodity exchange, socialist enterprises should be pressed to seek the most productive socially necessary, optimal production programmes. Commodity relations here, however, are between socialist co-operating groups in a system of planned co-operation covering the whole economy. Socialist enterprises do not work completely separately and independently of each other, according to their own interests and decisions, for a more or less unknown market. Their general course is co-ordinated and balanced by the macro-economic plan. The basic structure of their output programmes is regulated by overall planning. Technological and investment policies are under planned control and the training of personnel is organized with regard to the changes in the structure of the labour force. The plan also lays down the overall distribution of the national income and regulates the movements of key prices, price relations and the general price level. By these means planned regulation is extended to cover the whole field of market demand and its fundamental structure. In this sense we are theoretically justified in saying that the labour of society taken as a whole is, in the main, expended in a directly planned way and in harmony with the overall planned regulation of social demand.

This does not mean that all concrete labour expended is socially necessary labour. Contradictions are bound to arise—between the development of labour and the growth of needs, between the potential sources for raising productivity and the movement of actual production costs, between the prospects for improving use values and the normal course of their production, etc. In short, while it is possible by planning to raise the socially necessary content of labour, there is no way of guaranteeing that all labour expended will be identical with socially necessary labour. And for the very reason that the contradictions between the concrete labour of the enterprises and socially necessary labour cannot even be avoided in an overall, planned system of socialist co-operation, commodity–money relations are needed all the time to help overcome them. The contradictions, which partly stem from the specific material interests of the producers (interests arising from the objectively conditioned character of labour) coming into conflict with social interests, are felt by enterprises through losses of value on the market when their products fetch lower prices. On the other hand, optimal performance (harmony between concrete and socially necessary labour) brings gains in the realization of values.

In this sense there is no question, even with socialist commodity production, of equivalent exchange among enterprises of an arbitrary amount of expended labour, but of value equivalence (equal exchange of a socially necessary amount of labour). He who expends more labour on a certain type of commodity than is socially necessary loses, and vice versa. Whoever produces unwanted commodities, or more than are needed, loses, and whoever, on the other hand, produces new and better use values, for which demand exceeds supply for a time, is bound to gain.

In this manner the socialist market helps, within the scope of the macro-economic plan and through the direct contact of interests between producers and consumers, to encourage enterprises to undertake production of commodities that are in demand, steadily to improve their assortments while lowering production costs. This is a supplementary function of commodity–money relations, of the market, prices and money in resolving conflicts implicit in socialist labour, which planning can do a lot to keep in check, but cannot entirely eliminate.

The market to be regulated is, of course, socialist and in the main only socialist producers and trade organizations sell on it, while the means of production, too, are sold to socialist organizations, so that there is no prospect of capitalist production re-emerging. Nevertheless, it is essentially a real market, with real commodities, and real money, which are an expression of certain internal contradictions in social labour and therefore perform a real economic function, not merely that of formal accounting.

In this way the socialist stage of development sees an organic linking of social planning with commodity–money–market relations, and this is the basic feature of this type of commodity production. Its origin lies in the necessary and at the given stage insoluble conflict in social labour, which in its turn stems from the contradiction in the material production base of a socialist economy. This production base on the one hand requires that all labour in the economy be expended according to plan and directly linked in social co-operation, while on the other hand it has not yet made labour man's prime want and cannot yet provide for full satisfaction of his needs as under communism. While creating common interests of society as a whole, interests respected in planning, it also generates specific interests of groups and individuals, which come into non-antagonistic conflict on practical issues. These conflicts cannot be overcome all the time by planning changes in this or that economic activity from the top. But it is possible and necessary to utilize commodity relations and the direct interplay of interests between enterprises, and between producers and consumers.

Comprehension of this necessary relation between socialist planning and the socialist market, comprehension of the necessity, substance and special features of the socialist type of commodity production is the main theoretical factor which has contributed in no small measure to the search for a new and more effective system of planning and managing the national economy of Czechoslovakia.

8. CZECHOSLOVAKIA'S NEW SYSTEM

This theoretical groundwork was used in framing the principles of the new system of planning and management:

Planning procedure had to be changed primarily in the direction of restricting the central economic plan to questions of macro-economic growth based on realistic analyses of demand trends, technological-economic analyses and computing optimal solutions.

Enterprises should be free to frame their optimal programmes in relative independence and in harmony with production conditions and the market; therefore, they should not be hemmed in by rigid, subjectively framed and mechanically administered orders concerning volume of output.

Enterprises, which will have to assess their future market and make sure of getting the best possible returns, should be given a considerable voice in drafting long-range plans and, above all, in selecting investment projects with a view to their most effective use. All investments will be financed by the enterprises from their own funds or from credits. Major investment projects will be included in the long-range economic plan in order that the basic proportions of production may be regulated.

The centre should make use of financial levers to encourage fulfilment of macro-economic plans, which serve primarily as guidelines. These levers include the transfer and redistribution of part of the incomes earned by enterprises, credits and interest, prices, taxes, custom duties, export premiums, subsidies, etc. These methods will enable the central authorities to ensure that the necessary balance is maintained between accumulation and consumption within society, that the financial resources allocated by enterprises for material inputs are in harmony with the production and import of means of production, that a balance is kept between money resources and the volume of goods on the market, basic wage relations are established as between branches of production and that other similar macro-economic proportions are maintained.

With the relative stabilization of their transfers to the state treasury, enterprises will be able to react more readily to economic changes (prices, taxes, interest etc.), and, accordingly, make their own decisions on their production programmes, wage policies, technical development, investments etc. with a view to ensuring as far as possible a steady, lasting and maximum growth of the wage fund.

Since they will have to cover all their expenditure from income, their decisions will be aimed at getting maximum returns with minimum production costs. On the average, however, price relations will have to follow the relations and movement of socially necessary production costs (based on value, or value modified by the socialist production price), so that equivalent exchange between the socialist enterprises should as a general rule be maintained.

Takings will, with a few exceptions, grow more rapidly when performance is optimal, that is to say, not only when volume of output alone is stepped up, but when together with this products are put out in a well-chosen assortment and new, improved products are successfully put into production. Economic price movements will be the best guarantee of this. The prices of the new, improved products should be above the general level, while those of out-dated types, or of commodities put on the market in excess of demand, should drop.

The question of balanced prices is linked with the status of the producer (supplier) and the consumer (buyer) on the market. We cannot bypass their confrontation or the formation of balanced actual prices. In order to restrict opportunities for unilateral advantages, it is necessary under socialism, too, to curb tendencies to monopolize the market; all kinds of competition between enterprises should be encouraged and all available levers should be brought to bear by the central authorities to limit speculative activities without putting a brake upon economic, relatively free price formation. Market pressure, the prospect of being left with unsaleable goods on their hands and of getting into such financial difficulties that they would not be able to pay out bonuses and income-related shares to their employees—these are the only pressures which can be relied on to induce enterprises seriously to adapt their programmes to consumer demand, keep their output up to the mark, while cutting down on production costs and prices.

No official control (which can never reveal the true capacity and reserves of an enterprise), no rules and regulations, nor political and moral appeals can ever persuade an enterprise to relinquish voluntarily an established programme which affords good earnings to all employees. There will be resistance to switching over to new types, to changing techniques when the old ones seem good enough, to cutting prices when there is no incentive to do so, to bothering about innovations when one can operate to capacity on the old lines. That is to say, as long as producers' incomes have to be linked to their labour for society, and as long as no one outside the producing group is capable of estimating the capacities and practical trends of this labour, we shall need to leave some scope for the market mechanism and competition. In the event that this is not done, it will be impossible to avoid a serious lag in the quality of socialist production.

The purpose of this article has been to present a brief outline of the theoretical questions concerning market relations under socialism. In confrontation with the realities of socialist economies our knowledge will, no doubt, grow more profound and exact. I believe that the implementation of the new system of planning and management in Czechoslovakia will play a significant part.

THE COMPUTER AND THE MARKET

OSKAR LANGE

I

Not quite 30 years ago I published an essay *On the Economic Theory of Socialism*.† Pareto and Barone had shown that the conditions of economic equilibrium in a socialist economy could be expressed by a system of simultaneous equations. The prices resulting from these equations furnish a basis for rational economic accounting under socialism (only the static equilibrium aspect of the accounting problem was under consideration at that time). At a later date Hayek and Robbins maintained that the Pareto–Barone equations were of no practical consequence. The solution of a system of thousands or more simultaneous equations was in practice impossible and, consequently, the practical problem of economic accounting under socialism remained unsolvable.

In my essay I refuted the Hayek–Robbins argument by showing how a market mechanism could be established in a socialist economy which would lead to the solution of the simultaneous equations by means of an empirical procedure of trial and error. Starting with an arbitrary set of prices, the price is raised whenever demand exceeds supply and lowered whenever the opposite is the case. Through such a process of *tâtonnements*, first described by Walras, the final equilibrium prices are gradually reached. These are the prices satisfying the system of simultaneous equations. It was assumed without question that the *tâtonnement* process in fact converges to the system of equilibrium prices.

Were I to rewrite my essay today my task would be much simpler. My answer to Hayek and Robbins would be: so what's the trouble? Let us put the simultaneous equations on an electronic computer and we shall obtain the solution in less than a second. The market process with its cumbersome *tâtonnements* appears old-fashioned. Indeed, it may be considered as a computing device of the pre-electronic age.

II

The market mechanism and trial and error procedure proposed in my essay really played the role of a computing device for solving a system of simultaneous equations. The solution was found by a process of

† The Review of Economic Studies, London 1936 and 1937. Reprinted in O. Lange and F. M. Taylor, *On the Economic Theory of Socialism*, edited by B. E. Lippincott, Minneapolis 1938.

iteration which was assumed to be convergent. The iterations were based on a feedback principle operating so as to gradually eliminate deviations from equilibrium. It was envisaged that the process would operate like a servo-mechanism, which, through feedback action, automatically eliminates disturbances.†

The same process can be implemented by an electronic analogue machine which simulates the iteration process implied in the *tâtonnements* of the market mechanism. Such an electronic analogue (servo-mechanism) simulates the working of the market. This statement, however, may be reversed: the market simulates the electronic analogue computer. In other words, the market may be considered as a computer *sui generis* which serves to solve a system of simultaneous equations. It operates like an analogue machine: a servo-mechanism based on the feedback principle. The market may be considered as one of the oldest historical devices for solving simultaneous equations. The interesting thing is that the solving mechanism operates not via a physical but via a social process. It turns out that the social processes as well may serve as a basis for the operation of feedback devices leading to the solution of equations by iteration.

III

Managers of socialist economies today have two instruments of economic accounting. One is the electronic computer (digital or analogue), the other is the market. In capitalist countries too, the electronic computer is to a certain extent used as an instrument of economic accounting. Experience shows that for a very large number of problems linear approximation suffices; hence the wide-spread use of linear programming techniques. In a socialist economy such techniques have an even wider scope for application: they can be applied to the national economy as a whole.

It may be interesting to compare the relative merits of the market and of the computer in a socialist economy. The computer has the undoubed advantage of much greater speed. The market is a cumbersome and slow-working servo-mechanism. Its iteration process operates with considerable time-lags and oscillations and may not be convergent at all. This is shown by cobweb cycles, inventory and other reinvestment cycles as well as by the general business cycle. Thus the Walrasian *tâtonnements* are full of unpleasant fluctuations and may also prove to be divergent. In this respect the electronic computer shows an unchallenged superiority. It works with enormous speed, does not produce

† Cf. Josef Steindl, 'Servo-mechanisms and Controllers in Economic Theory and Policy', in *On Political Economy and Econometrics, Essays in Honour of Oskar Lange,* Warsaw 1964, pp. 552–554 in particular.

fluctuations in real economic processes and the convergence of its iterations is assured by its very construction.

Another disadvantage of the market as a servo-mechanism is that its iterations cause income effects. Any change in prices causes gains and losses to various groups of people. To the management of a socialist economy this creates various social problems connected with these gains and losses. Furthermore, it may mobilise conservative resistance to the iteration process involved in the use of the market as a servo-mechanism.

IV

All this, however, does not mean that the market has not its relative merits. First of all, even the most powerful electronic computers have a limited capacity. There may be (and there are) economic processes so complex in terms of the number of commodities and the type of equations involved that no computer can tackle them. Or it may be too costly to construct computers of such large capacity. In such cases nothing remains but to use the old-fashioned market servo-mechanism which has a much broader working capacity.

Secondly, the market is institutionally embodied in the present socialist economy. In all socialist countries (with the exception of certain periods when rationing was used) consumers' goods are distributed to the population by means of the market. Here, the market is an existing social institution and it is useless to apply an alternative accounting device. The electronic computer can be applied for purposes of prognostication but the computed forecasts have later to be confirmed by the actual working of the market.

An important limitation of the market is that it treats the accounting problem only in static terms, i.e. as an equilibrium problem. It does not provide a sufficient foundation for the solution of growth and development problems. In particular, it does not provide an adequate basis for long-term economic planning. For planning economic development long-term investments have to be taken out of the market mechanism and based on judgement of developmental economic policy. This is because present prices reflect present data, whereas investment changes data by creating new incomes, new technical conditions of production and frequently also by creating new wants (the creation of a television industry creates the demand for television sets, not the other way round). In other words, investment changes the conditions of supply and demand which determine equilibrium prices. This holds for capitalism as well as for socialism.

For the reasons indicated, planning of long-term economic development as a rule is based on overall considerations of economic policy rather than upon calculations based on current prices. However, the theory and practice of mathematical (linear and non-linear) programming makes it possible to introduce strict economic accounting into this process. After setting up an objective function (for instance, maximising the increase of national income over a certain period) and certain constraints, future shadow prices can be calculated. These shadow prices serve as an instrument of economic accounting in long-term development plans. Actual market equilibrium prices do not suffice here, knowledge of the programmed future shadow prices is needed.

Mathematical programming turns out be to an essential instrument of *optimal* long-term economic planning. In so far as this involves the solution of large numbers of equations and inequalities the electronic computer is indispensable. Mathematical programming assisted by electronic computers becomes the fundamental instrument of long-term economic planning, as well as of solving dynamic economic problems of a more limited scope. Here, the electronic computer does not replace the market. It fulfils a function which the market never was able to perform.

SOCIALISM, PLANNING, ECONOMIC GROWTH

SOME UNTIDY REMARKS ON AN UNTIDY SUBJECT

KURT W. ROTHSCHILD

I. 'FUNDAMENTALISTS' VERSUS 'INSTRUMENTALISTS'

The planning reforms in Socialist countries, taking their inspiration from the well-known blue-prints of Liberman, Trapeznikov, Šik and others, have called forth spirited reactions from many corners. The greater role to be played by the market, by prices, profit criterion, etc. has induced politicians and economists to ask profound questions with regard to the future of socialism.

Among the groups offering this or that interpretation we can detect some weird coalitions. Thus, liberal defenders of free market capitalism and conservative Marxists† combine in pronouncing that the introduction of market elements and profit criteria marks the beginning of the end of socialism and a return (welcomed or damned) to capitalist modes of production.

A similar situation arises in connection with the spread of 'planification' and other types of state intervention in capitalist countries. Here we find a union of liberals of the afore-mentioned type and some socialists (mostly of the right-wing variety) complaining or rejoicing that these are the first steps towards socialism. Among those who do not take this view that a silent revolution is on its way, the argument is frequently chosen that planification and all that is not 'real' planning. That is, this group, too, works under the assumption of a close and direct correlation between planning methods and socialism.

Against these 'fundamentalists' on both sides we have the 'moderns' for whom the extent of planning does not take on such a profound significance. While economists dedicated to capitalism naturally display a preference for the (unavoidable) market mechanism and socialist reformers show more interest in (theoretically possible) methods of central

---

† As soon as one enters the field of political opinions the prevalence of value-loaded terminology makes life rather difficult. The reader might quite rightly object to having the word 'conservative' connected with the term 'Marxist'. I trust, however, that the loose use of every-day jargon will suffice to convey who and what is meant.

planning, we find that planning and market elements are regarded above all as instruments to be used in varying proportions and to be judged by their efficiency in reaching certain limited objectives.

Thus the Polish economist Brus, after distinguishing a centralized and a de-centralized model of planning (the latter being defined as a planned economy with a built-in market mechanism), goes on to write: 'We are now faced with the problem of evaluating the centralized and de-centralized model of a planned economy with respect to their relative efficiency. It is not possible to pass any absolute judgements, because the usefulness of the first or second solution depends on many factors and on the concrete situation (quite apart from the fact that no solution can be adopted in its pure form). All that can be attempted in the following pages is a discussion of the advantages and disadvantages of the two approaches, in order to find out under which conditions the one or the other should prevail.'†

Here a purely instrumental view is taken of the problem how far planning and market elements can and should be mixed in a socialist economy. A similar attitude is taken by Dobb in his discussion with Bettelheim and the editors of the *Monthly Review*.‡ It is most forcefully expressed by the Czech economist, Šik (also quoted by Dobb) when he writes:

'Until recently, the connection between planning and the market was incorrectly understood and the concept of the market was applied to the socialist economy in a sort of shamefaced way. It was held, wrongly, that planned social co-ordination, planned management of production, was the absolute antipode of orientation on the market, of utilizing market levers. Planning was assumed to be an attribute of socialism alone, and production for the market a feature solely of capitalism... Our production differs from capitalism, not in that it should not meet the requirements of the market, but that it is a *different* kind of production catering for a *different* kind of market.'§

Similar 'undogmatic' views are also spreading on the 'capitalist' side. Thus Thomas Wilson, though thoroughly opposed to any kind of socialist planning, is at pains to show 'that planning and private ownership are not totally incompatible'.|| And with regard to economic development the World Bank economist Waterston expresses himself not less forcefully than Šik:

'The world-wide acceptance of planning as a means of achieving national development objectives has made academic the doctrinal debate about whether a country should plan. For most countries, the question now is how

† W. Brus, 'Die Entwicklung des sozialistischen Wirtschaftssystems in Polen. Bemerkungen zu einigen allgemeinen Problemen', *Hamburger Jahrbuch für Wirtschafts- und Gesellschaftspolitik*, 10. Jahr, 1965, pp. 164 ff.
‡ M. Dobb, 'Socialism and the Market', *Monthly Review*, September 1965, pp. 30–6.
§ O. Šik in *World Marxist Review*, nr. 3/1965.
|| T. Wilson, *Planning and Growth* (London, 1964), p. 16.

to plan. There are still those who equate planning with socialism or with central controls harmful to freedom and private enterprise, but these are "a dwindling band!"†

The present division between those who tend to equate planning and socialism on the one hand, market and capitalism on the other hand, and those who take a more instrumental view of planning and market methods, can only be understood in the light of the sharply formulated statements that were a special characteristic of the inter-war period. It was, I believe, only in this period that viewing markets and planning as mutually exclusive systems became almost an article of faith.

In the field of theory the trouble probably started immediately after World War I when Mises took resort to extreme formulations in his important and influential 'liberal manifesto'.‡ His 'all-or-nothing' approach has been aptly criticized by Dobb.§ In German bourgeois economics this bipolar view of planning and markets became later hardened into a basic methodological tenet under the influence of Eucken's teaching. He divided the economic world into two antagonistic systems of regulation: the 'ideal types' of centrally directed economies (*zentralgeleitete Wirtschaft*) where 'the direction of the entire every-day business of a community is in the hands of one central body', and market economies (*Verkehrswirtschaft*) containing two or many individual units with their own economic plans. 'Traces of other economic systems —apart from these two—cannot be found in the economic reality of to-day or in the past; it is also difficult to conceive that others can be found.'|| Such thinking in extreme 'ideal' types did necessarily blur the view for the instrumental aspects of planning and markets and their appearance in socialist and capitalist economies.¶

Among socialist theoreticians a similar strictly bipolar view of economic mechanisms could be detected. It found, for instance, succinct expression in Sweezy's brilliant exposition of Marxian economics,†† where he wrote:

'It follows that in so far as the allocation of productive activity is brought under conscious control, the law of value loses its relevance and importance;

† A. Waterston, 'A Postwar Prodigy: Development Planning', *Finance and Development*, The Fund and Bank Review, March 1965, p. 8. The excerpt is taken from Waterston's book: *Development Planning: Lessons of Experience* (London, 1966), p. 44.

‡ L. Mises, 'Die Wirtschaftsrechnung im sozialistischen Gemeinwesen', *Archiv für Sozialwissenschaften*, April 1920, pp. 86–121.

§ M. Dobb, *On Economic Theory and Socialism* (London, 1955), pp. 70–1.

|| W. Eucken, *Die Grundlagen der Nationalökonomie* (Jena, 1940), Part 3, Chapter 2.

¶ In a similar way the exclusive pre-occupation with the 'ideal' types of perfect competition and pure monopoly had blocked for a long time the approach to a fruitful treatment of reality where monopolistic and competitive elements intermingle.

†† P. Sweezy, *The Theory of Capitalist Development* (New York, 1942), pp. 53–4. (The page reference comes from the 1946 London edition.)

its place is taken by the principle of planning...Value and planning are as much opposed, and for the same reasons, as capitalism and socialism.'

But not only in theoretical treatises, in the everyday political discussions of pre-war days, too, the terms 'planner' and socialist were almost interchangeable, and a protagonist of the capitalist system was—at least before the Keynesian revolution—expected to be a staunch defender of *laissez-faire*.

2. CHANGING VIEWS ABOUT THE PLACE AND FUNCTIONS OF PLANNING

These shadows of the past colour many of the present-day discussions. They explain the strong emotional undertones which propositions for new combinations of planning and market mechanisms provoke in socialist circles (and similarly among advocates of the capitalist system).†

If planning were indeed more or less synonymous with socialism and market mechanisms with capitalism, then a socialist would have to be very suspicious of every shift from centralized planning to a wider use of market methods. But such a far-reaching equation of certain regulative instruments with social systems seems to be inadmissible. In this section we want to indicate that socialist views about the relation between planning and socialism have undergone considerable change in the course of the years and that in different periods different aspects of planning have been in the foreground. The review will be short and incomplete. But it should suffice to put the extreme planning-market plus socialism-capitalism dichotomy of pre-war vintage into proper perspective.

If we go back to classical Marxist thought we find socialists almost exclusively concerned with the basic problem of ownership and class divisions. Socialism's task is to end the special power of capitalists and open the road towards a classless society. This would also mean the end of an anarchic production for profit, the freeing of productive possibilities which could be used fully for the benefit of all mankind.

Little consideration was given to the day-to-day organization of this socialist economy. Planning was not so much regarded as the essence of socialism, but as the obvious way in which it should be run. Once

---

† Unfounded opposition arises, of course, not only from emotional sources of the above-mentioned kind, but also from vested interests threatened by the proposed changes. Thus some layers of the planning bureaucracy may fear a reduction in their social status when direct administrative interference is reduced. Similarly, some capitalists react unfavourably to planning measures, even if they benefit from them, because they fear their radius of uncontrolled power may in future be reduced. Thus Wilson in *Planning and Growth*, p. 16, stresses quite rightly that private capitalists will probably not sabotage planning measures under the condition that they themselves are associated with the officials in preparing a plan. In our considerations we neglect this problem of vested interests in the planning discussions.

technical progress had increased the size of production units and the social extravagance of isolated private decision power had been removed society would regulate its economic business in the same planned rational fashion as was done in pre-capitalist days. Marx did, of course, realize that the running of a modern economy is by no means a simple affair, and he stressed that the determination of a proper system of regulative values and the keeping of detailed accounts would be 'more essential than ever before'.† But the detailed problems of an extensive planning mechanism were not considered; they were left to the future.

The somewhat naïve way in which planning was originally taken as the self-evident return to natural and rational conditions is best illustrated in Karl Kautsky's popular introduction to Marx's economic teaching.‡ In the final chapter, which deals with the transition from capitalism to socialism, he stresses that there are only two ways to get rid of the contradictions of social production and private appropriation, with which capitalist markets present us: (*a*) a return to simple small-scale production, or (*b*) social ownership of the means of production. With the choice of the second alternative it seems to Kautsky quite self-evident that with social ownership production would again (!) be carried on in a planned way just as in pre-capitalist days when 'the natural mode of production was based on social labour planned in an organized fashion'.§ Kautsky, following Marx, acknowledges of course that extensive book-keeping would be required under modern conditions.

Kautsky also expressed the advantages which socialists expected from planning. 'In the place of anarchic production of commodities we get the consciously planned organization of social production; the rule of products over the producers has come to an end. Man, who has increasingly become master over the powers of nature, will then also be mastering social development'.‖ This point will be taken up again in § 3.

The vaguely considered planning aspect of socialism was suddenly pushed into the lime-light when socialism replaced capitalism in the Soviet Union and was on the verge of being victorious in Central Europe. The socialists who came to power had inherited the conviction that planning—more or less full-scale planning—would be the immediate and adequate system of regulating production. But now, under the stress of difficult, practical problems, it became clear that previous planning ideas provided no clue to an operational approach. In Russia, in the early years of the revolution, 'planning...was a propaganda phrase rather than an economic force'.¶

† K. Marx, *Das Kapital. Buch III: Der Gesamtprozess der kapitalistischen Produktion* (Berlin, 1951), p. 907.
‡ K. Kautsky, *Karl Marx's ökonomische Lehren* (Stuttgart, 1887).
§ Kautsky, *op. cit.*, p. 252.   ‖ Kautsky, *op. cit.*, p. 259.
¶ M. Dobb, *Soviet Economic Development since 1917* (London, 1948), p. 133.

This sudden appearance of socialism as a reality called forth (after 1917) an intensive, though rather short-lived theoretical discussion on the possibility and methods of planning, which for the first time delved more deeply into the details of the planning mechanism. The discussion had two focal points: Austria and the Soviet Union. The rise of planning debates in the Soviet Union had obvious reasons and does not need any explanation. In Austria the discussion was not only fostered by the revolutionary situation at home and the short-lived socialist revolutions in neighbouring regions (Hungary, Bavaria). The existence side by side of the individualistic Austrian school of economics—then at the height of its fame—and of a particularly theoretically-minded Socialist camp provided an excellent breeding ground for analytical discussions of this sort.

Post-first-world war Vienna has become well-known as the source of the most closely argued attack on central planning. It was put forward that planning was *in principle* unable to solve the problem of a rational allocation of resources, quite apart from any practical difficulties. This influential paper by Mises† of 1920, which later obtained a wider circulation when it appeared in English translation in Hayek's collection on planning problems,‡ was already fully refuted by an earlier article by Barone.§ But Mises' provocative essay was an important stimulus for a closer examination of the *intricacies* (if not the *impossibility*) of planning efficiently in the million-commodity-world of modern times.

The allocation problem had received little attention from socialists in earlier days. Now Mises' attack started one set of discussions among socialists in which the solution of the allocation problem became the *pièce de résistance*. Among the main contributors in the inter-war period we might name Taylor, Tisch, Dickinson, Hall, and Lerner.‖ The most distinct formulation of the problem and one form of its solution is contained in Lange's famous article on the economic theory of socialism.¶

For this group of writers the proof that socialist property relations can be combined with the allocation solution of competitive equilibrium theory was the primary task. By researching in this direction they were important fore-runners of to-day's instrumental attitude to market mechanisms and of contemporary decentralization proposals. But they were probably too fascinated by Mises' allocation puzzle and too dedi-

† Mises, 'Die Wirtschaftsrechnung im sozialistischer Gemeinwesen'.

‡ F. A. Hayek (ed.), *Collectivist Economic Planning* (London, 1935).

§ E. Barone, 'Il ministerio della produzione nello stato colletivista', *Giornale degli Economisti e Rivista di Statistica*, September and October 1908, pp. 267–93, 391–414. An English translation is contained in *Collectivist Economic Planning*.

‖ Some of the literature is quoted on pp. 173 and 176 of the second edition of J. A. Schumpeter's *Capitalism, Socialism, and Democracy* (New York, 1942).

¶ O. Lange, 'On the Economic Theory of Socialism', *Review of Economic Studies*, October 1936 and February 1937, pp. 53–71, 123–42.

cated to the frame-work of static competition theory. Even a non-Socialist writer like Schumpeter pointed out that the competitive equilibrium solution would only secure a short-run maximum and that 'only outright beefsteak socialism can be content with a goal such as this'.†

Side by side with this Mises-provoked train of thought intensive discussions on the method and aims of full-blooded planning developed in Austria and the Soviet Union. In the years between 1917 and 1925 Viennese socialists were heavily engaged in disputes about these themes. Among the main contributors we find O. Neurath, K. Polanyi, O. Bauer, O. Leichter,‡ and W. Schiff. The book on planning by the last-named author§ represented the culmination and—with the advance of fascism—the end of this debate.

Much of this early discussion turned round the question whether planning should be in physical quantities or whether monetary accounting should be used. Otto Neurath, a remarkable personality, was a forceful advocate of physical planning. In 1919 he proposed his system to the Workers' Soviet in Munich‖ as a guide to action, at the same time stressing the need for elaborate statistics. In Neurath's memorandum we find (for the first time?) socialism *defined* as planning. But he explains this stress on planning by the great poverty of post-war Germany. From this he deduced the need for strong social priorities which only a plan could secure.¶

Neurath remained fairly isolated with his demand for physical planning. With the recovery of the economy the emergency character of planning faded into the background. If we take Schiff's later work†† as representative of the main trends in the Vienna group we find already some remarks on money and markets (pp. 67/8), on the lack of a theoretically defined 'welfare function' (pp. 51/3), on wage differentials etc., which sound rather modern. In our context, however, it is of greater interest to see that planning is mainly desired for two reasons: to provide social justice and to avoid depressions. The growth and allocation aspects seemed less important in those days of crisis and mass unemployment. Thus Schiff expected that in an advanced country which could change over to socialism with its productive apparatus remaining intact, capital accumulation 'would not be carried out to any great extent' and 'the Economic Plan could consequently be given a more or less static character'.‡‡ We certainly have travelled some distance these past thirty years!

---

† Schumpeter, *op. cit.*, p. 184.
‡ O. Leichter gave a good summary of the debate in 'Die Wirtschaftsrechnung in der sozialistischen Gesellschaft', *Marx-Studien*, vol. 5, nr. 1 (Vienna, 1923).
§ W. Schiff, *Die Planwirtschaft und ihre Hauptprobleme* (Berlin, 1932).
‖ O. Neurath, *Wesen und Weg der Sozialisierung*, Gesellschaftstechnisches Gutachten vorgetragen in der 8. Vollsitzung des Münchner Arbeiterrates (Munich, 1919).
¶ Neurath, *op. cit.* p. 21.   †† W. Schiff, *op. cit.*   ‡‡ W. Schiff, *op. cit.* p. 48.

In the Soviet Union the discussion which dominated the twenties stood under the pressure to produce as quickly as possible practicable solutions.† Many of the technical problems discussed at that time have become prominent in the contemporary planification debates in capitalist countries. Thus the role of projections is analysed, the question is raised whether plans should be forecasts or programmes, whether they should mould the economy or—by making visible the underlying trends—just help it to follow its 'necessary' course in a smoother fashion.‡ As far as the aims of planning are concerned we find that they were largely determined by the war-torn and backward state of the Russian economy: structural changes and growth rates loomed in the foreground.

The urgent need to settle on a workable method of planning made it necessary to lead the discussions to some definite conclusion. In the end the method of balances was victorious. After World War II it was copied by the new Socialist states as the only available *practiced* pattern of full-scale planning.

The short sketch of the preceding pages shows that after World War I there had been important beginnings in the endeavour to clarify the role, methods, and aims of socialist planning. These discussions came to a more or less abrupt end at the beginning of the thirties. In Central Europe the rise of fascism killed the open development of Socialist and Marxist thought; and in the Soviet Union theoretical discussions were stifled in the Stalinist era.§ No clear-cut theory of planning had emerged in this short period. After World War II the lack of generalized experience and the tendency towards narrow 'practicalism' in planning matters was heavily criticized in the Soviet Union.‖

The dearth of theoretical discussions of the planning problem in the thirties—apart from the continued interest in Anglo-Saxon circles in the allocation problem under Socialism¶—and the onslaught of the great depression shifted the planning question increasingly to a purely practical-political plane. The fact that the Soviet Union alone among all the developed countries could avoid mass unemployment became a decisive experience. For millions of people the demand for socialism was mainly

† For a good summary of the early Soviet debate see Dobb's account of Soviet economic development, *Soviet Economic Development since 1917*. A fuller insight can be gained from the more recently published readings and commentary by N. Spulber, *Foundations of Soviet Strategy for Economic Growth*, Selected Soviet Essays 1924–1930; and *Soviet Strategy for Economic Growth* (Indiana, 1964).

‡ On this latter point Strumilin, for instance, expressed the view that in the short run plans would have mainly the function to forecast the likely development, while in the longer run they could play a more active role. See the quotation in Dobb, *op. cit.*, p. 326.

§ On this point see section I in Dobb's article on theoretical discussions among Soviet economists, 'The Revival of Theoretical Discussion among Soviet Economists', *Science and Society*, Fall 1960, pp. 289–311.

‖ Dobb, *Soviet Economic Development Since 1917*, p. 334.

¶ See above, p. 167-8.

dictated by their desire for full-employment planning. Planning, in the eyes of many, ceased to be a concomitant of socialism, a mere instrument: the plan, securing employment and income, was the most important fruit socialism had to offer.

This equation of socialism and planning among the working class and socialists led to a violent reaction on the other side. Since planning seemed to be the essence and the show-piece of socialism, it had to be fought lock, stock and barrel. Every single piece of planning had to be refused as the thin end of the bad wedge of socialism. The market had to be extolled as the one and only means of running a 'free' society. This view found its extreme formulation in Hayek's *Road to Serfdom*.†

Looking at these developments one is probably justified in seeking the roots of the extreme identification between capitalism and market mechanism on the one hand, and socialism and comprehensive planning on the other, in the special political setting of the inter-war era. With the changed politico-economic conditions of the post-war world this temporary simplification had to give way to a renewed consideration of the role and the aims of planning.

In the capitalist world it has been realized that another depression of 1932-dimensions would be the end of the capitalist system. Thus one has reluctantly taken note of the Soviet success in avoiding unemployment and depressions, and has admitted planning elements to an extent which would have been unthinkable in *laissez-faire* days. At the same time the transformation of the Soviet Union into a developed industrial nation and the addition of highly industrialized countries to the socialist camp have shown up the limitations of the traditional planning methods. We find a growing willingness to learn some lessons from the market mechanism.

These developments have led to the present situation which we have sketched in the first part of this essay. We experience a growing tendency to separate the fundamental capitalism-socialism debate from the planning-market debate. The two divisions are not completely independent, but the problems of market and planning mechanisms acquire increasingly special and purely instrumental aspects. We can no longer define or recognize socialism simply by the extent to which planning is used in the running of the economy. This calls for some considerations as to the place planning should occupy in socialism and what its aims should be. Some tentative remarks in this direction are the subject of the following section.

† F. A. Hayek, *The Road to Serfdom* (London, 1944).

3. PLANNING AND ECONOMIC GROWTH IN SOCIALISM

First of all it may be in order to stress that the *method* of planning will normally be much easier assimilated by a socialist society than in capitalism. That is, even if we shed all inherited dogmas, prejudices, habitual ways of thought, etc., we shall still find that planning, in so far as it is useful and desirable, is only in socialism the obvious, 'system-immanent' means of regulating production. With the means of production owned by society the planning of balanced development is—*where technically possible*—of such obvious rationality (as every big trust knows) that it would be absurd to neglect it. We find, therefore, that even those socialists who are very open-minded with regard to the introduction of new methods in running a socialist economy, take it for granted that planning will continue to play an important part, especially in the field of investment policy.†

In capitalism, on the other hand, we must reckon with institutional resistance against planning methods even where they would ease the running of the system without endangering its foundations. The more deeply probing defenders of the capitalist system are aware that the privileged position of private ownership can only be maintained, if some measure of private, uncontrolled decision-power is upheld. Once this prerogative is seriously undermined it could become obvious that ownership of big production units does not fulfil any necessary function in a modern industrial economy.

Planning beyond a certain minimum is, therefore, opposed even if its immediate outcome is regarded as beneficial. The fear of long-run effects of planning and of alternative uses to which planning may be directed after a change in government are sufficient to prevent a whole-hearted acceptance of planning measures. Utterances in this direction by anti-socialist politicians and writers can be found by the dozens. A brilliant analysis of this political aspect of planning in capitalist societies was given more than twenty years ago by Kalecki.‡ It may very well be that at some future date, when the methods of planning have been further developed, socialist societies will gain a marked superiority by their greater scope for a smooth adoption of such methods.

It should be noted in passing that this distinct difference between socialism and capitalism vis-a-vis the planning mechanism is not matched by a corresponding difference with regard to the market mechanism. There is no *fundamental* institutional barrier to the adoption of market

† See, for instance, Brus, 'Die Entwicklung des sozialistischen Wirtschaftssystems in Polen', pp. 154–73, or Dobb, *An Essay on Economic Growth and Planning* (London, 1960), p. 5. Also Šik has repeatedly stressed the need for over-all planning.

‡ M. Kalecki, 'Political Aspects of Full Employment', *Political Quarterly*, October-December, 1943.

mechanisms in socialist economies when and where it is desired. It is true that in cases where an existing planning machinery is to be reduced there will be strong resistance from the ranks of the planning bureaucracy. This is a disturbing factor which—as Parkinson has shown—is a common-place experience in all spheres of our bureaucratic age. This may make the shift from more planning to less planning, from centralized to de-centralized systems a difficult and protracted affair. But once the personal and psychological difficulties have been overcome, socialism *as such* has probably little to fear from a greater use of markets (provided the roads to private accumulation of productive capital and to monopolistic practices are efficiently blocked). There should be no parallel to the distrust in principle which capitalists display against a wide-spread introduction of planning methods.

When we pass on to the aims of contemporary economic planning we notice a remarkable similarity between socialist and capitalist plans. Development and industrialization is the foremost aim of all economically under-developed countries. In the developed nations the pre-war targets of aiding a proper allocation of resources and of securing full employment have become generally accepted. But more than ever before they are subordinated to the one over-riding aim of all plans: the achievement of high rates of growth. Growth is also the motive force for another dominant principle in modern planning, viz. the manipulation of structural changes.

There is obviously nothing wrong in adopting economic growth as a major target. Even the wealthiest nations can still do with more goods to reduce poverty at home, to contribute towards mitigating misery abroad. But the enormous extent to which growth is stressed in present-day planning ideology—much more so than in the less prosperous years of pre-war periods—calls for some special comment.

There can be little doubt that the preoccupation with planning for growth and its increased acceptance in capitalist countries has predominantly political roots. Theodor Prager has shown in a convincing manner† that it is the growth of the socialist sector, the 'competition of the systems', which has edged capitalists into acquiescence in government measures for full employment and growth which they would hardly have tolerated in an undivided world. Similarly, the growth problem now dominates the thinking of socialist planners to an extent which can only be explained by the force which growth rates have acquired in the battle of proving the superior economic efficiency of this or that system. There is some danger here that certain special targets, which should be a hall-mark of *socialist* planning, may get lost in the heat of the battle.

† T. Prager, *Wirtschaftswunder oder keines? Zur politischen Ökonomie Westeuropas* (Vienna, 1963).

Let it be said at once that I do not want to belittle the role which growth will have to play as a major target for a long time to come. The economy of many socialist countries is still so backward that for reasons of development and the acquisition of decent living standards economic growth is of the utmost importance (as it was for the Soviet Union in the inter-war period). And even in the advanced societies of to-day a growing economy is essential to satisfy modern man's desire to extend his experience and to move to new forms of consumption.

But socialists should be aware that growth as such and the constant extension of production and consumption is not an ultimate socialist aim and will not by itself lead to a new type of society and of man. Too great a preoccupation with it may even hinder such a development. Expansion for expansion's sake is a demon which haunts capitalist societies. Mrs Robinson has stated the problem quite clearly:

'The stagnationists, instead of welcoming the prospect of a period when saving would have become unnecessary, high real wages would have reduced the rate of profit to vanishing point, and technical progress could be directed to lightening toil and increasing leisure, regard its approach as a menace. This, of course, is a perfectly reasonable point of view if the aim of economic life is held to be to provide a sphere for making profits. Satiation of material wants is bad for profits.'†

The mechanism of capitalist societies thus makes running after growth a dire necessity. But need socialist planners adopt this attitude? Planning may no longer be a distinctive characteristic of socialism, but socialist planning can and should be different from other kinds of planning. Put in a nutshell, it should never be contented with full-employment and growth planning as such but should be dominated by questions like 'Full employment for what? How much and what kind of growth?' In asking such questions and in its capability of shaping certain growth patterns socialist planning should find its specific expression. This point has recently been very strongly put by Thomas Balogh.

'Thus the arguments for planning,' he writes, 'based on the need for faster expansion are compelling, but they need not lead to *socialist* planning. Faster expansion could be accommodated without socialism, without public enterprise or public ownership. It is—as it always was— at the moral and spiritual (or psychological) plane that the realization of the insufficiency and growing emptiness of a mere continuance of the present trends in the West leads one ever more insistently to socialism.' And again: 'It would be sad if our best hopes for the next 25 years would be limited to approaching today's American way of living. Something much more happy and satisfying is both needed, and possible.'‡

† J. Robinson, *Economic Philosophy* (London, 1962), p. 135.
‡ T. Balogh, *Planning for Progress. A Strategy for Labour* (London, 1963), pp. 37 and 38.

As socialist countries get wealthier the aims of socialist planning may in fact be shifted more and more in the direction of *specific patterns* of a new kind of life rather than being directed towards high rates of growth. Such a shift would certainly be in line with Marx's original visions. For him—as Adam Schaff has convincingly shown†—the intensive occupation with a new economic basis for society (and for new economic instruments) was subordinated to his search for a higher development of man which had been so dominant in his earlier writings.

One should not, however, trust that this shift in the emphasis of socialist planning will come automatically as production and incomes grow. The special historical situation in which socialism develops poses its special problems. The enormous lead of the United States in production and productivity over the rest of the world has important repercussions. The well-advertised standards originating from the profit-orientated growth patterns of the United States lead to demonstration effects from which no country remains exempt. This obviously hampers the development of new attitudes. It is only when the living standards in socialist countries have approached more closely those of the richest capitalist countries that it will be possible to judge how far the attraction of American-type consumption standards is merely a function of their big lead in real income. If socialist education and planning succeed in preparing the ground for new humanistic, non-profit-orientated patterns of living, the competition between capitalism and socialism should in the not too distant future move to new planes and no longer hinge on the decimal places of growth statistics.

One final point. We have presented the view that planning and market mechanisms are instruments which can be used both in socialist and non-socialist societies. We cannot decide 'how socialistic' a society is merely from the extent to which the one or the other method is used. Planning, it is true, will be more acceptable and probably more extensively applied in socialism than in capitalism. But so far we have maintained that the actual degree to which planning is used should be a purely pragmatic question to be decided on the grounds of economic and social expediency.

This view has now to be slightly modified. It was important to explode the primitive identification of central planning and socialism and to stress the instrumental character of planning. But once this has been achieved it may be in order to point out that to some extent planning may be more than an instrument: it may constitute an independent aim (among several others) of socialist endeavour. This aspect of planning is connected with the desire of man to be master of his own fate. Handed down by the renaissance and the French revolution it was taken over by

† A. Schaff, *Marxismus und das menschliche Individuum* (Vienna, 1965).

Marx who envisaged a society in which mankind would no longer be dominated by the 'blind forces' of the market. Viewed from this angle effective planning becomes desirable as a means of making 'man... master over social development',† even if it could be shown that market mechanisms—leading to unforseen combinations—may yield slightly higher growth rates.

At some future date it may appear as a joke of history that socialist countries learned at long last to overcome their prejudices and to dismantle clumsy planning mechanisms in favour of more effective market elements just at a time when the rise of computers and of cybernetics laid the foundation for greater opportunities in comprehensive planning. These two opposing trends will be with us for some time to come. They will necessitate a constant reconsideration of the proper relations between planning and socialism, between growth and other aims. If the rise of new dogmas can be avoided and a flexible approach is secured, the road should be open to a promising evolution of socialist systems of economic regulation.

† See above, p. 166.

SOCIALIST AFFLUENCE

JOAN ROBINSON

History has seen two methods of carrying out the accumulation necessary to install scientific technology. The first, which has been in operation for two centuries, relies upon individual acquisitiveness; the second,
which has been in operation for less than half a century, relies upon
socialist planning. Both have reached the stage where, in a number of
countries, the fruits of accumulation are now available to be enjoyed
in a high level of consumption, but in each the process of accumulation
has set up institutions and habits of mind which put obstacles in the way
of rational enjoyment.

I. PROBLEMS OF CAPITALISM

In England, the pioneer of private enterprise, the first stages of accumulation were carried out with the utmost brutality. In the later stages, with
the evolution of head-counting democracy, and now after the shared
experience of two wars, all classes have come more or less to accept the
ideal of a welfare state—that gross poverty should be eliminated; that
there should be equality of opportunity; that the great wealth of the
nation should be deployed, for, in some sense, the general good of all
its citizens.

The process of accumulation, however, cemented great inequality
into the system, and this is now an impediment to realizing the accepted
ideal. In principle, a democracy should be able to vote itself into egali-
tarianism through the tax system, but in practice the legal arrangements
favourable to property and the habitual acceptance of the class structure,
which were necessary to foster accumulation, now put up a resilient
defence of inequality.

The institutions of private property and great inequalities of wealth
were necessary to the process of accumulation in the manner in which
it was carried out. Universal suffrage and egalitarian ideals in the eighteenth century would have inhibited the industrial revolution before it
began. But now private property has become otiose. What does the individual share-holder contribute to the operations of a modern corpora-
tion? Private saving is a convenience for private families—it is no longer
necessary to aliment industrial accumulation. The gross investment that
corporations carry out from amortization funds and retained profits is

continually installing improved techniques, enlarging productive capacity without requiring 'abstinence' from anyone.

The shareholders and rentiers indeed, make a great negative contribution to industry, for much of the best talent of every generation is engaged, one way and another, in the lucrative business of swapping securities around amongst them and so is kept away from constructive activities. The notion that the Stock Exchange, with all its ancillary apparatus, is the most efficacious means of supplying finance to industry, compared to other available methods, is a figleaf which it wears to preserve its self-respect.

After the experience of the Thirties, full employment is an insistent demand. This, combined with the institutions of private enterprise, which limit the sphere of government expenditure, has led to the ugly situation where democratic opinion accepts the arms race as a useful expedient for maintaining prosperity.

The institutions of private enterprise leave the main initiative in economic affairs to a number of independent corporations which have developed a motivation of their own—a pursuit of *success* which includes but is not bounded by the mere pursuit of profit. It is now generally agreed that the interplay of the policies of these independent corporations cannot be relied upon to secure continuous full employment, a consistent pattern of development, or a viable balance of trade. A national 'plan' is now seen to be necessary to coordinate their activities. But their very independence and power of individual initiative, which was the main-spring of the private-enterprise system, now prevents the economy from developing organs to control them in the general interest. So far, 'national planning' at most consists in persuading them to remove gross inconsistencies from their individual programmes.

To direct their behaviour towards a democratically decided programme would be quite another matter. If we think of the nation as a family, how would it wish to dispose of its resources? The manner in which the public *does* spend its money is not a reliable guide, for all the arts of salesmanship, direct and indirect, are used to build up in the public a system of wants that provide a convenient outlet for profitable sales. There is a systematic bias in the pattern of production, dramatized in Galbraith's slogan: *private affluence and public squalor*, in favour of goods and services which can be sold piecemeal, so as to provide scope for profit, and against collective consumption which has to be financed by taxation. This bias is unfortunately fostered by economists who, when they purport to measure consumption as an indication of the standard of life, are really measuring only the sale of consumption goods.

Consider a middle class family with an income considerably above the national average but not great enough to saturate all their possible wants, and with sufficient education and self-confidence to resist advertisement and ignore the Joneses. In their notion of a comfortable standard of life beyond the obvious needs of food, clothing and amusement, a decent house ranks highest; the provision of education for the children; retirement pensions for the elderly and good medical help when needed. If a member has some disability, he will be kept as far as possible in the same comfort as the rest. Other wants are sacrificed, when need be, to satisfying these needs. Some scion, perhaps, finds comfort stuffy and goes out of his own free will to test his hardihood in a primitive world, but the family would by no means consider it a benefit to have the test of poverty thrust upon them.

The wealthy capitalist democracies have a great struggle to impose this scale of values upon their pattern of production. Housing, education, the health service are starved of funds. The elderly and the handicapped suffer. Pockets of squalid misery persist. The modern cry for 'growth' is partly an expression of the hope that a sufficient all-round proportionate rise in income will bring the bottom to a tolerable level without the necessity to interfere at the top.

In one respect latter-day capitalism has been remarkably successful— in avoiding serious recessions. This very success creates further problems. With continuous near-full employment superimposed upon the system of industrial relations and of wage-bargaining and price-fixing developed in other circumstances, inflation has become chronic and the system is extremely resistant to the institutions of an 'incomes policy' designed to preserve the value of money.

Finally, the spread of quasi-planning within each country runs into conflict with international anarchy, so that one government after another has to sacrifice progress towards a welfare state (whether gleefully or sadly) to the requirements of the balance of payments.

2. PROBLEMS OF SOCIALISM

In the European socialist countries, also, the toughest phase of accumulation has been accomplished. They do not have to contend with the heritage of private property and private enterprise. Without unearned income, the objective of equality of opportunity is less hard to attain, and differential earnings can be kept within acceptable limits. The distinction between profit and state revenue does not arise, so that resources can be allocated between industry and social services according to rational criteria. There can be no question of wilful independence of enterprises which are all organs of the planned economy. Inflationary pressure occurs during the phase of accelerating accumulation, because spendable income is then increasing relatively to the output of purchasable goods; but there is not the same pressure from the mere persistence of full employment to raise money-wage rates and prices. Defence expenditure is a burden to them. They have no need to fear that an 'outbreak of peace' would cause a slump, for the resources involved can be redeployed to useful uses with little delay. They suffer, indeed, like capitalist countries, from insufficient export earnings, but they cut their imports to fit and do not allow the tail to wag the dog.

On the other hand, the socialist method of accumulation has left its own legacy of obstacles to the enjoyment of the potential affluence which it has achieved.

Of these, the most serious is in the political sphere. Whether or not repression is 'necessary' for rapid accumulation, they have in fact occurred together, both in East and West. In England four or five generations passed between the time when Trade Union organizers were deported to Australia and when they are installed in the House of Lords. The corresponding reversal in socialist countries has occurred within a decade. It is against the background of this disturbing experience that economic reforms are being carried out.

The demand for reforms, which has been rumbling since 1956, has broken out most recently in Czechoslovakia, and is there most sharp and articulate. The following is based mainly upon Czech experience.

The economic system developed for the purpose of rapid accumulation was imitated from the Soviet Union and contained features which were not at all appropriate to the requirements of a small country highly dependent upon international trade. Moreover the Soviet system imposed not only necessary but also unnecessary hardships upon the consumer, for instance, the elimination of individual tradesmen, such as cobblers. The planners were taught to think that only investment goods were 'serious' and neglect of consumer interests became a virtue in itself.

The dogma that, under socialism, the share of investment devoted to Department I, which was identified with heavy industry, must exceed the share of Department II, meant a continuous effort to *accelerate* accumulation. The dogma was disputed, for instance in Poland in 1956, but policy in Czechoslovakia continued to be dominated by it. When the rate of growth slackened and actually came to a halt, the authorities could think of no remedy except more investment.

The organization of industry was a system of command from above which deprived the individual manager of authority and initiative. Planning was both rigid and clumsy. The criterion of success was reckoned in terms of gross output. The highest possible degree of self-sufficiency was aimed at. Trade, not only with the capitalist world, but amongst the People's Democracies, was heavily discouraged. The class war was carried to the second generation; children of middle-class parents were debarred from education. Much of this, which may have been unavoidable in the struggle for industrialization in the Soviet Union, was retrograde in Czechoslovakia, where there was a larger professional class and where more subtle methods of accounting and management had been developed in capitalist businesses. Even in Czechoslovakia, however, the heavy pressure to accumulate overrode all its drawbacks. It is reckoned that, not only national income, but *per capita* consumption was more than doubled between 1948 and 1960.

The methods which were successful in rushing to full employment and full utilization of resources have now become a fetter upon further progress.

The command system in industry led to inefficiency within an enterprise, both in the details of technique and in the handling of personnel. The method of reckoning in terms of gross output fostered waste of materials. The arbitrary system of prices made cost accounting useless as a check on efficiency. Dictating the plan to an enterprise in physical terms broke contact with the market, so that it was common for unsaleable goods to be piling up in the cellars of shops while the enterprise was earning premia for plan fulfilment. Foreign competition, as a control upon quality, was cut off, for no imports were permitted of goods which an enterprise could claim to make at home. Innovation within enterprises was inhibited by the exaggerated horror of risk which the command system induces.

Proposals are now being made to overcome these particular drawbacks of the present situation.†

The main lines of the central planning system are not to be affected. No one now supports the suggestion that prospective profitability should influence the allocation of investible resources in the central plan; nor, indeed, has anyone succeeded in showing what such a criterion would mean in operational terms. Overall changes that are to be made, for instance greater attention to agriculture and light industry and a relaxation in the general rate of accumulation, are to be made centrally in a coherent manner, but in detail much more autonomy is to be given to the individual enterprise. The enterprise will have control over minor investments and in the sphere of consumer goods, can choose its own product mix, to suit the indications of demand coming from retailers; in some branches it is given authority to vary its prices.

Gradually the system of absorbing the surplus through the turnover tax at various rates on different commodities will be liquidated. Each enterprise will be required to pay a tax of 10 per cent on its wage bill

† See Ota Šik 'The Problems of the New System of Planned Management', *Czechoslovka Economic Papers*, no. 5.

and 6 per cent on a valuation of its installed capital, and will then be instructed to earn its costs from the sales of its output. Management is permitted to dispose of its wage fund as it pleases, so as to introduce incentive schemes.

Between the ministries and the enterprises is to be interposed a system of trusts, each concerned with a particular industry. Efficiency is to be promoted by the trust imposing a system of prices based upon average (or better) performance (taking account of inevitable advantages or drawbacks of the situation of different enterprises), so that its worst managed firms will be penalized unless they can improve, while its best enjoy a stimulating reward.

No doubt these reforms can produce a dramatic improvement. The better performance of individual workers and more efficient deployment of teams, the elimination of wastage of materials, the rationalization of relations between suppliers within a trust, and above all the direction of production towards what consumers actually want to buy, should bring an upward bound in the standard of life that will hearten the reformers.

But it is not easy to see that they have evolved a viable system for continuing development. A great deal of experiment and adaptation still must be to come.

Management

The much-discussed question: whether there is commodity trade under socialism, is a somewhat metaphysical way of drawing the distinction between principals and agents in economic affairs. The housewife who goes shopping is a principal. She is spending the family's money for their benefit as she judges best. When she buys from a peasant, he also is a principal. (It is commodity trade on both sides of the market.) When she buys in a state shop she is dealing with agents. When the shop replenishes its stock from a socialist enterprise, both parties to the transaction are agents of the same principal.

The point of the distinction is that a principal uses his judgement while an agent is directed by rules laid down for him. A western economist may say that the housewife is maximizing utility under a budget restraint, the advertiser may be studying her motives to get her hooked, but she feels that she is doing what she wants to do; she need not account, even to herself, for why she does it. The distinction is not absolute. An agent must have *some* discretion. A principal is guided by law and tradition. The problem for the reforms in socialist management is where to draw the line. The top management of a capitalist enterprise, though legally agents of the share-holders, act as principals in the interests of the company. They need to make profits, since profits are necessary to secure the survival and growth of the company, but the pursuit of profit does not confine them to a narrow groove; there is a wide range of possibilities between playing safe and adventurous experiment. Moreover, in a world of uncertainty the pursuit of profit is expressed in short-cuts, rules of thumb and conventions of policy. Considerations of reputation and professional honour modify pure money-making. The management of a company feels 'a three-fold public responsibility, to the public which consumes its products, to the public which it employs, and to the public which provides the capital by which it operates and develops'.

When the management of socialist enterprises are given more autonomy, they will have the same three-fold responsibility, with contributions to the national budget substituted for the interests of the share-holders. Merely to instruct them to maximize net profit from the capital equipment with which they are provided is an inadequate guide. From a long-run point of view a contented labour force and satisfied consumers are essential to profitability—how weigh one against the other when their interests conflict, and each against short-period advantage? One of the evils of the present system is that proper expenditure on upkeep and repairs is sacrificed to short-run plan-fulfilment. An instruction to maximize net profit is no substitute for judgement in weighing the present against the future. Moreover, net profit is an *ex-post* measure. The decisions that have to be taken by management, about day to day operation as well as about long-run policy, are decisions about people and things. At best the instruction to maximize net profit is an instruction to act in a manner that may be reasonably expected to maximize profits over some future term. And what is it reasonable to expect?

In Czechoslovakia the proposal is, not to use net profit as a criterion of success, but to instruct management to recover the wage fund which they have been advanced, along with other expenses, from their annual operations. This is a remedy aimed at the crude evil of fulfilling a plan by producing unsaleable goods at unnecessarily high costs. It seems also to be intended to give the workers an interest in the efficiency and discipline of the enterprise in which they work without going the whole length of giving them the equity in it, on the Yugoslav model. (The wage fund is ensured up to 90 per cent, so that bad management would not be the disaster for a group of workers that a bankruptcy may be under capitalism.)

In practice, it seems, the autonomy of enterprises is to be much less than this scheme suggests. The trusts that have been set up for each broadly defined industry will give instructions to the enterprises in some mixture of physical and financial terms, which, no doubt, will be evolved as experience accumulates, while the overall plan is given to the trusts from above. The analogy, then, will be not with capitalist enterprises, but with cartels. A well-run cartel is by no means the worst form of management that capitalism has produced for its own purposes, but to adapt it to socialist purposes needs some care. The most obvious danger is that the officials of the trusts will develop an excessive patriotism for their particular industry and devote more effort to gaining favours for their enterprises from the centre than to subordinating them to it.

The Workers

In China, North Korea and Cuba, where revolutionary patriotism is still warm, the proposal to make greater use of monetary rewards as incentives to the individual worker is regarded with grave suspicion. It seems to them a denial of the moral content of socialism, which should appeal to public spirit and personal self-respect. Capitalist experience suggests that it is dangerous also from a purely economic point of view.

The money motive under capitalism has two sides, fear of loss and hope of gain. The first is far and away more powerful than the second, especially for a worker to whom loss of employment entails total misery. In the post-war era of continuous near-full employment, progressive management, to attract labour, to effect improvements in efficiency and to call forth effort from the men, offers increased earnings in various open or disguised forms. Every grievance, every demand, is bought off by offering more pay. It suits the progressive firms to do so, for by setting a level of costs that less efficient firms cannot cope with, they rob their rivals of their market as well as their labour force. But from the point of view of the economy as a whole it is a great nuisance, since money incomes rise faster than *average* output and so generate chronic inflation. When a man has got used to a certain pay packet, it becomes his necessary standard of life; to reconcile him to any change will need another rise. Even under capitalism there is an irresistible demand for fair (that is, more or less equal) relative earnings, so that less progressive industries and occupations have to follow the progressive ones in raising money-wages continuously. Moreover, once it is accepted that the motive for effort, above the bare minimum, is extra income, it becomes perfectly legitimate for individuals or groups of workers to prefer minimum effort with minimum earnings. Hard trades, like mining, become impossible to man.

Let alone morality, the socialist countries should consider the psychology and the economics of money incentives very carefully before they step onto this slippery slope.

Prices and Costs

General instructions to the enterprises in terms of net profit or gross receipts make sense only if the system of prices is sensible. One of the sharpest objections to the present system is the arbitrariness of prices.

The Czech proposal is to rationalize the system, gradually introducing prices based on costs, including the taxes on resources used (10 per cent on the wage bill and 6 per cent on assessed capital) which are to provide the fund for accumulation and general expenses of the state. Subject to covering total costs from total receipts, the enterprises have some freedom (in certain lines) to vary prices of particular products—for instance to adjust scales of prices for differences of quality.

So far as consumer goods are concerned, a system of prices based on costs cannot be completely satisfactory. For a long time to come there will be particular scarcities of supply relative to demand. A pattern of supply-and-demand prices has somehow or other roughly been established by differential rates of turnover tax. To move directly to a pattern of prices based on relative costs would fail to maintain a fit between demand and supply. Yet there is no reason why a particular enterprise should benefit (in easier profits) from the scarcity of the type of productive capacity it happens to command. Moreover, since the socialist sector of the economy 'imports' consumer goods from co-operative agriculture, and imports a great deal from capitalist and from other socialist countries, there are bound to be unforeseen changes in supply from time to time, which are more convenient to deal with by altering prices than by rationing. The remedy is for the office of price administration, which is an independent organ of the economy, to set final prices to the consumers so as to maintain an overall balance between sales and expenditure and as close a fit as possible between particular demands and supplies, without upsetting cost relationships by interfering with the prices of productive enterprises.

For the enterprises, to have prices adjusted to costs would bring order into chaos and permit some rational cost-accounting and calculations of efficiency to be undertaken. But is it satisfactory on its own merits? The basis of the proclaimed virtues of the competitive system in the textbooks is that each producer finds himself faced with a price in the market so that his profit depends on keeping his costs below it. In capitalist industry, of course, this situation does not really obtain. Prices are administered on a cost-plus basis, while competition runs into salesmanship and product differentiation. Will the socialist trusts avoid the evils of cost-plus?

Optimum Saving

Czech economists maintain that the cessation of growth in national income in 1963 came about in spite of an exceptionally high rate of investment in the preceding years.[†] To carry out investment faster than

---

† J. Goldman, 'Short and Long term Variations in the Growth Rate and the Model of Functioning of a Socialist Economy', *Czechoslovak Economic Papers*, no. 5.

the digestive system of the economy can absorb it is a vain sacrifice. But when a proper balance between physical investment, education and research ensures that current saving will increase future production, are there any principles in which the ratio of investment to consumption should be fixed?

In practice the capitalist nations have given up the pretence that private enterprise produces either the right amount or the most efficient form of investment (witness the fashion for planning) but the economists still discuss the problem in terms of the desirable rate of saving.

There is no way of judging, from the behaviour of individual families in a capitalist country, what people *really want* to save. The distribution of income between families, the general habits of the various classes, and the reliability of the social security system have a strong influence on private saving. Nor is it possible to judge the effect of incentives to save. It is a fallacy to say that interest is the 'reward' of saving. The reward of saving, in the capitalist world, is owning wealth. The fact that wealth can be 'placed' in assets that yield a return is only one of its advantages. The amount of saving that individuals do to acquire individual wealth cannot tell us anything about the amount of saving they *really want* to do to acquire collective productive capacity. Nor does the reaction of individuals to the return on placements give an indication of what their attitude may be to the return on social investment. The question has been open since Marshall's day, whether the typical family saves more or less from earned income at a higher rate of interest. The question concerns differences, say, between 3 and 7 per cent on gilt-edged placements. Now, it is generally estimated that the incremental capital/output ratio in a developing economy is of the order of 2 or 3. To be on the safe side, and to be sure that it is net, let us put it at 4. This means that saving today yields 25 per cent per annum in perpetuity. How much would you or I save at that offer? How do we know?

There is a more subtle difficulty in passing from individual psychology to social choice. The process of investment cannot be represented simply as sacrificing present for future consumption or vice versa. It is true that a sacrifice in current consumption can always be made, in conditions of full employment, by drafting labour into basic industry, but, after the heroic age of accumulation, such a policy is unlikely to be chosen. Consumption will not be allowed to fall below a level that it has once reached. The other way round, to increase current consumption by cutting investment is generally not possible (except by acting upon the balance of trade). The choice is rather between an increase in consumption in the relatively near future (by directing investment into light industry) and a greater increase in the more distant future (by maintaining investment in basic industry). Any path that is chosen has to be followed consistently and the possible paths are indefinitely various. There is no way in which signalling from the market can direct the choice between them.

This does not mean that the choice must be foisted upon the public by the whim of the authorities. The present revolt is largely a demand (in vague general terms) for consumption to rise as fast as may be. The very inefficiency of the present system provides a hump, so that it should be possible to increase consumption appreciably without cutting basic investment. After that, a wise strategy might be to bring about a further sharp rise in consumption, then to keep it almost stable for a few years while investment was directed to securing another burst later. Such a scheme (in spite of marginal utility theory) might give more satisfaction than a slow steady rise which would scarcely be noticed from year to year.

This is a new problem for the socialist countries. Up till now optimum saving has simply been the maximum possible investment; and in fact they have sometimes done more—imposing abstinence on their people which failed to fructify in increased productive capacity.

Investment Planning

The planning of investment is the key to economic control, and the authorities do not intend to relax their grip on it. In Yugoslavia the original conception of the economic reform was that investment funds should be allocated by the central plan to branches of industry and to districts, and that individual enterprises (now under the control of their own workers) should bid for shares. This system has evidently got out of hand, and the authorities instead of trying to get a grip on the plan again, have resorted to a temporary all-round credit squeeze. This has been a useful warning for Czechoslovakia.

Not only the overall rate, but the broad composition of investment must be planned centrally. Long-range decisions, such as the source of power, affect the whole of industry and all elements have to be made consistent with them. (This is precisely what has driven the capitalist countries to accept the necessity for planning.) In this sphere, improvements in methods are being sought, but there is no basic change in contemplation.

So far as the choice of technique for a given output is concerned, the enterprises must have considerable influence, since it is they who have concrete detailed knowledge of the problems involved. The charge of 6 per cent on assessed value of fixed capital is intended to induce economy. Once an installation has been set up, the enterprise ought to use it to the best advantage, and 6 per cent is neither here nor there. The charge is intended to curb demands for unnecessarily lavish extensions and re-equipment, and to affect the design of new installations. Presumably, with experience, the tax charges can be varied to express the scarcity of labour relatively to investible resources, but this could work only if prices are independently given. Cost-plus would make it ineffective.

Hitherto the socialist economies have approached the problem of the choice of technique in terms of the saving of future labour cost to be attributed to an addition to investment—they have had in mind something like a production function, or spectrum of known techniques. Czechoslovakia is the most mature in the sense of having reached an overall scarcity of labour. The amount of progress to be made by pure 'deepening' of the capital structure is presumably not very great. The problem now is to foster technical progress—to find out methods of production that save *both* future labour and present investment cost.

The worst feature of the command system is the timidity which checks experiment. There is considerable danger that mistakes made under the new system will be used by those who flourished under the old to press for a return to rigid planning. There is always a certain superficial plausibility in the argument that it is dangerous to allow a child into the water till he has learned to swim. The problem now is to find a form of economic organization which encourages initiative without being too lenient to wasteful errors.

Consumer Sovereignty

In all this what seems to be most lacking is some method to direct the use of the resources now available to 'securing the maximum satisfaction of the constantly rising material and cultural requirements of the whole society'. Now that the emphasis has changed from growth at all costs to raising the standard of life, there is an obvious need for the public to be given some means of saying what their requirements are. It is an illusion to suppose that market signals can guide the planners. Increasing consumption involves not only a consistent path through time, but a consistent composition of output. The goods that represent a rising standard of life are consumed in clusters—housing, electric gadgets and domestic power; sports goods, hotels and travel. The housewife knows what gadgets to buy only after she has been informed what the future price of power will be. Moreover, in a fairly egalitarian society, the demand curves for particular commodities are likely to be highly convex—elastic at small quantities, plunging abruptly to saturation after a certain point. The height of the demand price today does not tell the planners what increase in output would carry supply to the corner. Nor can it tell them anything about the effect of one man's consumption on the welfare of his neighbours. At some stage they will have to face the problems which arise from satisfying the constantly rising requirements of the whole society for motor cars.

The present system is just as much a system of producer's sovereignty

PART III

PROBLEMS OF ECONOMIC DEVELOPMENT

OBSTACLES TO ECONOMIC
DEVELOPMENT†

PAUL M. SWEEZY

I. BARRIERS TO CAPITALIST PRODUCTION

The United States is universally classified as a 'developed' country, indeed the most highly developed in the world. What does economic development mean for such a country? One possible definition would be in terms of overall economic growth: it might be said that economic development is deficient if the growth rate is inadequate to sustain continuous full utilization of the labour force and the stock of capital. A more general, and I think more satisfactory, definition would run in terms of the realization of the full potential of modern science and technology to promote the general welfare.

Whichever approach to the definition of development is adopted, it is clear that the performance of the American economy has been weak and disappointing in recent years. Apart from cyclical fluctuations, the unemployment rate has remained high and the rate of utilization of productive capacity has been markedly lower than during the early 1950s. These facts are in themselves enough to suggest that the gap between realization and potential has been widening, but even the most accurate statistics on the degree of underutilization of human and material resources—and in fact our statistics are far from accurate—would not provide us with a measure of the size of this gap. For it is widely recognized that if science and technology were fully exploited in the United States

† A few months before Paul Baran's death in March, 1964, he and I were each invited by Professor François Perroux, Director of the Institut d'Étude du Développement Économique et Social in Paris, to contribute to a symposium on the subject 'Blocages et Obstacles au Développement'. We corresponded about the invitations and, finding ourselves in complete agreement, decided to submit a joint contribution. His death prevented the carrying out of this intention: he never saw even a draft of my response to Perroux. Nevertheless, in organizing my remarks I was guided by the following passage from one of Baran's letters: 'I like the topic very much: the whole bloody "field" of economic development should be called that way: "Obstacles to Economic Development." We have the possibility of either going into some domestic aspects of the problem or trying to present a sensible view of the role played by imperialism. It would perhaps offer opportunity of saying once more and sharply that in addition to what imperialism does, one should consider and indeed emphasize what its role is in *preventing* what needs to be done.' The present essay is a revised version of my response to Perroux's invitation. I believe that it also expresses Paul Baran's views and that if he were alive he would have been more than willing to have his name associated as co-author of a contribution in honour of Maurice Dobb for whom he entertained warm feelings of friendship and admiration.

today, a vast increase in the productivity of both labour and capital could be achieved in a relatively short time.

What is the explanation of this poor performance? What are the obstacles that prevent the American economy from growing more rapidly and from making full use of its incomparable scientific and technological potentialities?

These are, of course, not new questions. They were raised in a particularly urgent form during the Great Depression of the 1930s, and several attempts were made to supply a theoretical explanation. The Keynesian schema pointed directly at a weak inducement to invest coupled with an excessive propensity to save as the source of the trouble. The savings function—or conversely the consumption function—was explained partly on psychological grounds but more importantly as a reflection of the distribution of income normal to capitalism. Taking the continued existence of the system for granted, as the Keynesians always do, this meant that the crucial variable was the inducement to invest. Following this line of reasoning, Alvin H. Hansen elaborated a theory of secular stagnation which Schumpeter appropriately named the theory of 'vanishing investment opportunity'. Historically, according to Hansen, a high level of investment was sustained by territorial expansion, population growth, and capital-using innovations. Beginning around 1880 or 1890, he thought, basic changes took place. The geographical frontier was closed, the rate of population growth began to slow down, and capital-saving rather than capital-using innovations became the order of the day. The impact of these forces was delayed by a variety of factors but finally hit with full force to produce the Great Depression and the subsequent stagnation of the 1930s.

Schumpeter effectively criticized this theory. He showed that it makes little sense to link the closing of the frontier in the nineteenth century with investment opportunities in the second third of the twentieth; that the connection between population growth and investment is not necessarily that postulated by Hansen; and that the change in the character of innovations from capital-using to capital-saving is a mere hypothesis, not a proven fact. In place of Hansen's theory of vanishing investment opportunity, Schumpeter proposed an essentially political theory of the stagnation of the 1930s. The more successful capitalism is, he thought, the more it engenders hostility among certain sections of the population, especially among the intellectuals. The Great Depression, which Schumpeter attributed mainly to the accidental coincidence of troughs in his three-cycle scheme plus maladjustments left over from the First World War, enabled these hostile elements to gain control of government; and their anti-business policies, embodied in the New Deal, undermined business confidence and hence the will to invest.

Schumpeter's theory was in turn subjected to a devastating criticism—by Arthur Smithies, himself a student and admirer of Schumpeter, in a paper delivered at the 1946 annual meeting of the American Economic Association. This should have cleared the ground for new efforts to produce a satisfactory theory of the 1930s—a theory of the obstacles to economic development in an already developed capitalist economy. But in the atmosphere of the early postwar years, bourgeois economics had lost interest in the unsolved problems of the 1930s, and the matter was allowed to drop out of sight altogether. Indeed so profound was the profession's lack of interest in explaining what happened during the 30s that almost no attention was paid to an extremely important book on the subject which was published in England in 1952. I refer to *Maturity and Stagnation in American Capitalism* by Josef Steindl, an Austrian economist who spent the war years at the Oxford Institute of Statistics.

At the theoretical level Steindl's achievement was to combine the two big advances of the post-1929 period, the Chamberlin–Robinson theory of non-competitive markets and the Keynesian theory of income and employment. Whereas earlier writers had treated monopoly and oligopoly as purely micro-economic phenomena, Steindl explored their relevance for the functioning of the system as a whole.† He showed that the introduction of monopoloid elements into a competitive model would have a twofold effect: on the one hand, it would cause a 'shift to profits' and hence indirectly raise the propensity to save; on the other hand, it would discourage investment in the monopoloid industries thus exercising a depressing effect on the inducement to invest. If one adds, as Steindl did, the essentially Marxian theory that the development of capitalism is necessarily characterized by a continuously rising degree of monopoly (to use Kalecki's term), one has all the elements of a logically complete and consistent theory of secular stagnation.

It should be especially emphasized that this theory, unlike Hansen's or Schumpeter's, attributes the difficulties of developed capitalism to endogenously generated changes in its basic economic structure. It therefore provides a new theoretical proof, appropriate to the conditions of developed capitalism in the second half of the twentieth century, of Marx's dictum: '*The real barrier of capitalist production is capital itself.*'‡

As for empirical evidence of the correctness of Marx's insight, need one do more than point to the American economy itself, dominated as it is by an ever smaller handful of giant monopolistic corporations and plagued by ever growing problems of unemployment, poverty, and

† Kalecki had already pioneered this road by introducing the 'degree of monopoly' into his dynamic model. He did not, however, attach great importance to the point.

‡ Karl Marx, *Capital*, Volume III, Chapter 15, § 2.

waste ? Here surely, in the most developed capitalist country in the world, capital has finally and definitively proved itself to be the real barrier of capitalist production.

2. TRANSFERRING THE SURPLUS FROM THE POOR COUNTRIES TO THE RICH

I believe that it can also be shown that under present-day conditions in the underdeveloped countries, monopolistic capital, even if it is indigenously owned, is a barrier to capitalist production. But in a brief essay it seems more important to focus attention on the effects on the development prospects of the underdeveloped countries of their relations with the advanced capitalist countries.

Apologists for capitalism and imperialism maintain that trade and investment between advanced and underdeveloped countries make a crucially important contribution to the development of the latter.

In the case of trade, it requires no elaborate argument to show that the truth is exactly opposite to this contention. From the earliest period of capitalist overseas expansion in the sixteenth and seventeenth centuries, the advanced countries imposed upon their victims a pattern of trade which ruined their pre-existing balanced economies and forced them to play a subordinate role as suppliers of raw materials and buyers of manufactured goods. Far from promoting development, this trading relation led to dependence and degeneration.

It is widely believed, however, that foreign investment by the advanced countries has a favourable effect on the underdeveloped countries. By putting part of their surplus at the disposal of the capital-hungry poor countries, so the argument runs, the advanced countries lay the groundwork for future development, and this in turn sooner or later makes it possible for the underdeveloped countries to break out of the confines of economic dependence which is the legacy of the past.

This theory is open to criticism from several angles. For example, it can be shown that most investment by the advanced countries in the underdeveloped countries is incident to and strengthens the trading pattern just described. But much more basic is the fact that the whole process of foreign investment is a method of transferring surplus from the poor countries to the rich and not vice versa.

Take the case of Britain in the heyday of its imperial glory. Between 1870 and 1914, Britain's net export of capital totalled £2,400 million. On the face of it, this seems to indicate a large-scale transfer of the country's surplus to other lands, many of them underdeveloped. But this is only one side of the coin. It is also necessary to take account of the fact that during these same years Britain's income received from foreign investments in the form of interest, dividends, and other remittances amounted to no less than £4,100 million.† In other words, while Britain was sending out with one hand, she was taking back much more with the other. On balance, the flow of surplus was not from Britain to the rest of the world but from the rest of the world to Britain.

The period of maximum American foreign investment has been the two decades since the Second World War, and official figures compiled by the Department of Commerce on its amount, distribution, rate of return, etc., exist since 1950. Between 1950 and 1961, the foreign assets of American corporations rose from $11,800 to $34,700 million, an increase of $22,900 million. During the same period net direct investment outflow totalled $13,700 million and direct investment income came to $23,200 million. It thus appears that during this period American corporations were able to take in as income $9,500 million more than they sent out as capital, while at the same time expanding their foreign holdings to the tune of $22,900 million. In the light of such figures, the characterization of foreign investment as a method of making surplus produced in the advanced countries available to the underdeveloped countries is nothing but a bad joke. Foreign investment is much more accurately described as a giant pump for sucking surplus out of the underdeveloped countries and transferring control over a large part of their productive resources to the great imperialist corporations.‡

Confronted with facts such as these, the apologists for imperialism have one last argument to fall back on. Without foreign investment, they say, the underdeveloped countries would never acquire the modern technology which, after all is said and done, is the real *sine qua non* of genuine economic development.

The importance of technology to economic development is of course not in doubt. But it is not only technology but also its control and the uses to which it is devoted which are important, and all the evidence goes to show that the technology which comes with foreign investment remains under the control of the foreigner and is used for his enrichment, not for the economic development of the receiving country. For the rest, the experiences of Japan and the Soviet Union, each in its own way, proves that an independent country determined to promote its own develop-

† The figures are from A. K. Cairncross, *Home and Foreign Investment, 1870–1913* (Cambridge, 1953), p. 180.

‡ It should be added that these official figures reveal only part of the reality. Huge sums are also transferred from the underdeveloped to the advanced countries in the form of royalties on patents, payment for unnecessary or nonexistent 'services' rendered by parent corporations to their subsidiaries, excessive charges for materials and parts, etc., etc. A further drain from poor to rich countries occurs when the wealthy classes in the former send their funds abroad to avoid taxation or possible confiscation. It has been estimated in testimony before a U.S. Congressional Committee that more than $10,000 million was deposited by wealthy Latin Americans in Swiss and North American banks during the 1950s.

ment cannot be prevented from acquiring the necessary scientific and technological knowledge and skills. There is even less reason to doubt that this will be true in the future now that some of the socialist countries have reached an advanced stage of economic development and stand ready to assist any of the underdeveloped countries that may show signs of wanting to develop on their own.

It follows from all this that no underdeveloped country can hope to initiate a genuine programme of development as long as it remains en-meshed in the trade patterns dictated and controlled by the imperialist countries, and allows a large part of its economic surplus to be sucked out by foreign capital.

But if this is so, and if it is also true that the desire for economic de-velopment constitutes an overwhelming political demand in nearly all the underdeveloped countries, one may well ask why so many of these countries remain, apparently willingly, within the imperialist orbit and continue to rest their hopes for development on aid of one kind or another from the advanced capitalist countries. In answering this question, so important to an understanding of the historical epoch in which we are living, I can do no better than quote the words of Andrew Gunder Frank, a younger economist whose work in the field of development, underdevelopment, and their dialectical inter-relations promises to be of great importance. Concluding an analysis which relentlessly exposes the widespread myth of United States aid to Brazil (and other Latin American countries), Frank poses the question as to why Brazil continues to tolerate a relationship which is so harmful to her own interests. The answer, he continues,

'is to be sought in the very Brazil–United States relationship itself. First, of course, the relationship does benefit *some* Brazilians with gains and power. These groups then apply this same power in efforts to maintain the relation-ship. Secondly, with time, Brazil becomes so dependent that breaking away involves such high costs in the short run that—whatever the long-run gains— many other groups, and especially any government, are loath to accept them. Thus in the short run, failure to receive credits to refinance the already exist-ing debt would force a cut of imports that are necessary in the same short run because in the meantime the same economic relationship has destroyed or prevented the creation of productive capacity that would obviate the need for these imports. If, going a step further out of the relationship, American in-vestments are threatened, the short-term cost, as the case of Cuba demon-strates, is the stoppage of all trade. In a word, Brazil and other similarly situated countries find themselves in a kind of debt-slavery relationship not unlike that of the peasant with his landlord-moneylender the world over, a relationship in which the very exploitation seems to make its own continu-ance necessary. Finally, for what it may be worth, and as the analysis by the American-trained Brazilian Ambassador demonstrates, the United States also supplies the economic science—and the ideology as well—which tries to demonstrate that this exploitative relationship is not only necessary but desirable.'†

The conclusion, I think, is inescapable: the first and most important obstacle to the economic development of the underdeveloped countries is their relationship to the advanced capitalist countries which dominate and exploit them. Until this relationship is either completely ruptured or totally transformed—and of the latter there seems to be absolutely no prospect in the foreseeable future—talk about overcoming the many other obstacles to economic development is at best naive and at worst deliberately deceptive.

† Andrew Gunder Frank, 'Brazil–United States Economic Relations', mimeographed, February 1963. An abridged version of this paper was published in the New York magazine *The Nation* of November 16, 1963, under the title 'Brazil: Exploitation or Aid?'.

CAPITALISM, SCIENCE
AND TECHNOLOGY

JOSEF STEINDL

I. CAPITALISM ACTS AS A BRAKE ON PROGRESS

This statement is explained by the fact that many good things could be done, but in fact are not done, because they are not profitable. The use of the profit criterion has ruled out the use of a vast amount of physical possibilities of production in the great depression, and has led to waste, though on a much lesser scale, again in recent years in the United States. I argued some time ago† that the braking of the economy in the 1930s was due to the growth of monopoly in modern capitalism, which led to a fear of excess capacity, and in this way discouraged investment. Recently‡ I have added another argument, namely that the bigger firms are the more they are inclined to sacrifice a high mathematical expectation of profit if by so doing they can get greater safety. This means that big firms will invest less in relation to their accumulated profits than medium firms, because they are less inclined to indebt themselves. In modern capitalism where the share of giant firms has become very large, the incentive to invest is therefore reduced in comparison to nineteenth-century capitalism. The indictment usually made against the profit incentive must thus be extended or shifted to the 'safety preference' inherent in modern capitalism.

Reducing investment in all probability means slowing the spreading of innovations, and the preoccupation with the firm's individual safety works against new methods and new products; it hits research and experiment harder than anything else because they are very risky. The brake therefore slows up technological progress.

2. CAPITALISM UNLEASHES UNCONTROLLED FORCES OF TECHNOLOGICAL DEVELOPMENT

The short-sighted exploitation of resources, heedless of results, is described in German by the appropriate term *Raubbau* ('rapacious exploitation'). The history of capitalism is a sequence of various forms and

---

† J. Steindl, *Maturity and Stagnation in American Capitalism* (Oxford, 1952).
‡ J. Steindl, 'On maturity in capitalist economies' in *Essays in Honour of Mihał Kalecki* (Warsaw, 1965).

types of *Raubbau*, if we generalize the meaning of the term in a way which will become immediately obvious. Marx concentrated on a special case of *Raubbau*, the exploitation of human beings without regard for their wellbeing and dignity, and heedless of the transformation of society which proceeds in the wake of exploitation. The case to which the term *Raubbau* originally applied is the exhaustion of natural resources like forests, agricultural land (the 'dust bowl'), hunting and fishing grounds. This immediately leads to an extended concept. The destruction of the natural habitat of man by pollution of water and air, upsetting the balance of animal and plant life, ruining the aesthetic values of nature. From this we are led to a further concept, the alienation of man not only from his natural habitat, but from himself, which happens in so far as human contacts are replaced by commercial or bureaucratic relations (men are ruled by machines as the inhabitants of 'Erewhon' feared, and are therefore dehumanized; the machine which directly controls men is, of course, the organization and the propaganda of firms, parties etc.).

The indictment against capitalism is that it exploits the possibilities of science and technology short-sightedly, heedless of the consequences even where these could be foreseen. It works in mad haste to turn into money new knowledge which has not been perfected or supplemented to protect against the evils which may arise from it. It insists on supersonic jets, motor car congestion, sedatives, patent medicines, thalidomide, food adulteration, and noise.

3. A CONTRADICTION

Between the brake on progress and the mad haste of exploitation there seems to be a contradiction. It is resolved if we remember that there are stages of capitalism. The mad haste of exploitation, threatening the very basis of the human resources of labour on which it was built, was characteristic of the industrial revolution. The brake was on in the mature economy of the interwar period.

What of the present time? The two indictments are, in a sense, both valid, and the contradiction is resolved as follows: capitalism works with mad haste to exploit commercially certain profitable applications of the technological and scientific development. It does very little itself, however, to stimulate and keep up this development, which would have receded to a low ebb but for one factor: war—or the armaments race.

We have to admit, however reluctantly, that a very great part of the major technological developments of recent decades has been stimulated by the last war, or the armament race since the war; atomic energy, radar, electronic computers, jet aircraft, rockets and the adventures in space, all have only thus been made possible.

The share of the government in the finance of all research development is 66 per cent in the United States, 61 per cent in Great Britain, and
78 per cent in France (data relating to 1961). The growing research
expenditure of the last twenty years does not belie the contention that
private concerns are reluctant to engage in risky ventures; their reluctance is overcome only because the government takes over a large share
in the finance of research.

We can hardly exaggerate the importance of the strange fact that to a
great extent our modern scientific and technological development owes
its existence to war. Although this has always been true it has never been
as strikingly evident as in the last decades. As we shall argue below a large
expenditure for research is nowadays indispensable for economic progress. Private entrepreneurial capitalism, as is shown by its meagre contribution to the finance of research and development, would by itself be
incapable of providing anything like the present stimulus to technological
innovation. But why is it that only war, or the threat of war, achieves results which are desirable for a peaceful life? This is because war gives
rise to a collective, organized, and planned effort, and no other occasion,
in a free enterprise system, is apparently able to achieve this result.† In
war, society in a sense regresses to earlier forms, in this case to a pre-
capitalist collectivistic organization such as existed, on a lower level, in
primitive types of society; these earlier types of organization are, on the
basis of modern technique, used very effectively to reach given targets
and aims. A big sustained armaments race seems to achieve some part
of this collectivism in certain fields at least.

The role of war in scientific development can be compared with its
role in producing a high level of employment. The capitalism of the 1930s
was radically altered when the war started and the unused capacity was
put to work for a target set by the government. It will always be one of
the most appropriate criticisms of free enterprise society that it is quite
unable—or rather, unwilling—to use collectivist forms of economic
organization for an attack on slums, poverty, disease and lack of education, while it *is* able to use all those techniques, repugnant as they are to
the business man's mind, when it comes to war, and to some extent also
in a state of continuous high tension when the shadow of war on an
enormous scale is sufficiently real to fulfil the function of an actual war.
It is hardly necessary here to explain how the expenditure on weapons
has contributed to high-level employment in the United States. A substantial proportion of the gross national product (about 10 per cent in
recent years), financed largely by profit taxes, is taken out of the market

---

† The hostility against collective action in advanced capitalist countries is so great that an
imbalance has developed between a relatively abundant provision of goods and a starvation
of the sector of public consumption, as Galbraith has shown (*The Affluent Society*, Chapter 18).

economy, and to this extent the Keynesian problem of offsetting the saving of the rich by additional spending is solved. The government expenditure in turn increases the utilization of capacity in the private business sector and stimulates investment there.†

The importance of war, actual or potential, to modern capitalism is such that one may doubt whether this system could exist with anything like its present vitality without it. This statement must be qualified as far as Western Europe is concerned: here the Keynesian or post-Keynesian techniques of public investment have been harnessed to a great extent to peacetime purposes, and the driving force behind the full employment policy is the fear of the political rather than the military enemy.‡

4. ROLE OF TECHNICAL PROGRESS IN CAPITALISM

The apparent contradiction between the two indictments of capitalism appears also in the following form: on the one hand, capitalism tends to apply the results of new knowledge too quickly, before they have been sufficiently tested and their implications considered. The obvious example is the drug thalidomide. On the other hand, industry is very slow in making use of the increased knowledge accumulated by the development of science. J. D. Bernal§ maintains that the span of fifty years which elapsed between Faraday's discovery of electromagnetism and the building of the first power station at the Edison Electric Illuminating Company of New York was determined mainly by economic factors; this is to say that the development might have been quicker if the demand for electric current for lighting purposes had been anticipated and the supply of electricity had been developed simultaneously with it by enterprising capitalists capable of understanding the connection between the two. More recently, the development of the fluorescent lamp and of television has been delayed by vested interests.

On the basis of this and similar experience one might argue, as I did in *Maturity and Stagnation in American Capitalism* that there is always a reservoir of unused scientific knowledge waiting to be applied. I was, however, wrong, as I see it now, in drawing the conclusion that new innovations do not affect the readiness of business to invest. The innovations which interest business are only those which promise quick results, and they are rare enough, so that their appearance does affect investment. According to a McGraw–Hill Survey in 1958, 39 per cent of large firms

† Steindl, 'On maturity in capitalist economies'.
‡ For a full statement of the thesis that the potential competition of 'the other system' accounts for the prosperity of Western Europe, see Theodor Prager, *Wirtschaftswunder oder keines?* (Vienna, 1963).
§ *Science and Industry in the Nineteenth Century* (London, 1953).

expected their Research and Development expenditure to pay off in less than three years, and another 52 per cent of large firms in more than three but less than five years.[†]

The weakness of the private capitalist confronted by science is therefore that he expects quick results and will not wait, or risk, beyond a point; this excludes many projects of great social urgency, and it also prevents him from taking a responsible attitude towards the incidental effects and implications (the 'external diseconomies', one might say) of an innovation.

5. THE LAW OF INCREASING COMPLEXITY OF LEARNING

In a recent paper Denison stated that '...in the past we have doubled and redoubled the number of college graduates, the number of high school graduates, the number of scientists and engineers completing either the B.A. or the Ph.D. degree, and the number of scientists and engineers engaged in research, but we have experienced little if any acceleration in the rate at which productivity has advanced...'[‡]

It is very tempting, and indeed quite right, to retort that a lot of research expenditure is devoted to military purposes and its eventual use for constructive purposes is therefore rather costly. Further, in Europe the growth rates of productivity *are* higher than they used to be before the war, and the surge of innovation *is* paralleled by an accelerated pace of economic growth. But these answers, reasonable as they are, do not meet the main question which goes much deeper.

The growth of productivity has been aptly described as a process of learning. It seems—and this is the answer to Denison's puzzle—that learning is becoming more expensive and difficult the more the stock of knowledge increases. The exploitation of knowledge is subject to increasing cost (or decreasing returns). This results from the fact that the whole complex of knowledge is interrelated and cannot easily be divided up like a cake. A division is attempted, it is true, by specialization, but the well known disadvantage of the specialist reflects the difficulty of dividing knowledge: he loses the possibility of linking up facts from different fields, and thus of realizing those fertile combinations of ideas which are a necessary condition for further progress. The growth of knowledge shows a certain analogy with the increasing complexity of big organizations, the bureaucratic giant concerns which are the standard example of decreasing returns to scale. The advance of the specialist

† D. Hamburg, 'Invention in the Industrial Research Laboratory', *Journal of Political Economy*, April 1963.

‡ Edward F. Denison, 'Measuring the contribution of education to economic growth', in *The Residual Factor and Economic Growth* (OECD, Paris, 1964).

means, in fact, the bureaucratization of science. But knowledge cannot be divided up in any way—between firms or by a policy of decentralization; it forms a compact whole which by its very nature cannot live and prosper in separate parts.

The increasing complexity of learning is shown in the difficulty that science students have in absorbing, and that their teachers have in conveying, the increasing 'substance' of science, which, it is alleged, doubles every ten years. The growing complexity results, of course, from the multiplication of new facts and the opening up of new fields: think of the extension of the astronomer's horizon in the course of the twentieth century, of the advance into the microstructure of the atom, of the study of low temperatures, of the acceleration of particles by the cyclotron, and so on. In each case the advance on these frontiers becomes progressively more costly.

Not only does it become more complicated, I maintain, to advance on a path of abstract progress as implied in the examples just quoted, but it becomes more complicated and costly to maintain a constant increase in productivity. The apparatus of production becomes more and more diverse and complex and an advance in one field only affects a small part of the whole. The improvement (operational development) of particular goods like the aeroplane becomes more and more costly without yielding proportionately greater results.

To this is added another fact. The innovations throw up secondary problems; and however blind those who exploit them are, they cannot disregard the most obvious ones: the refuse of atomic piles has to be safely disposed of, etc. In fact, a considerable amount of the cost of some facilities is due to the precautions which have to be taken to prevent them from doing harm.

At the bottom of the growing complexity of knowledge is a problem of information. The researchers, the ideas, the facts have to be linked to keep the process going. Every scientist knows that it is fast becoming an impossibility to keep acquainted with the results of current work even in a very special field.

There exists, it is true, a 'countervailing power' against the growing complexity of science—namely the unifying and simplifying tendency of theory at its highest level, quite apart from the didactic and pedagogic achievements of some scientists and teachers. But this development of theory in itself causes high costs—the generalization of a unifying theory is only reached once sufficient facts are known—and it may be slowed up by the scarcity of the high-powered scientists capable of these exceptional achievements.

If the 'law of increasing cost of learning' is accepted, an interesting consequence would seem to follow. To keep up a constant growth of productivity we shall have to shift more and more people to research, which in practice (on account of I.Q. considerations) finds a limit long before the whole working population is so occupied. It follows that there is a limit to the growth of productivity and that its growth rate will have to decline sooner or later. There is nothing very unpleasant in this result, if one believes, as Marxists fundamentally must do, that human wants are limited and a saturation can be achieved.

6. THE SORCERER'S APPRENTICE

Technological development during the capitalist period of history has fundamentally modified the biological and psychological conditions under which man lives, and thereby created enormous problems. The most obvious example is the population problem: we have a fertility designed for a race living under conditions in which death, among infants and mothers especially, takes a heavy toll, many times more than it does with us. We have not become biologically adapted to the conditions which we have created, and in a great part of the world the effects have not been remedied yet.

Another instance is the development of the technique of war. We are told by students of animal psychology[†] that the members of species which are by nature equipped with strong teeth, claws etc. (e.g. wolves) are subject to restraints in their fights among themselves which prevent them from endangering the existence of their own species, while the animals which are poorly equipped for fight (e.g. pigeons) are without this kind of restraint and, as far as their means permit, on occasion kill each other mercilessly. Obviously, man by nature conforms to the pattern of the latter group; subsequent to his acquisition of weapons, he developed restraints which, however, still left room for atrocious wars. The development of modern weapons has brought about a maladjustment, which could not be more glaring, between his mentality—appropriate in the above sense to an unarmed animal—and his equipment for struggle which in view of its supreme destructiveness is suitable only to an animal with a highly developed system of restraints in all kinds of internecine struggle.

Between these two examples—excessive procreation and ultimate destruction—there is the whole range of effects produced by technical progress which, as suggested above, tend to destroy or impair the natural habitat of man or which at the very least throw up problems which are difficult to solve, but which business men are not interested in solving (they do not care about the noise produced by the vehicles they sell, and they care only reluctantly about the trouble which their detergents produce in the sewers).

† Konrad Lorenz, *Das sogenannte Böse. Zur Naturgeschichte der Aggression* (Vienna, 1963).

The deepest of all the effects of technological development, via its impact on society, is on human relations. A great number of writers, artists and thinkers in the last hundred years who suffered from civilization saw in the rule of the machine over man the cause of his degradation. The machine, they felt, shapes society, and in the form of 'organization' produces a supermachine which from a means has become an end in itself. For Karl Kraus the 'machinery' of the first world war was the symbol of the degrading monster. In Kafka's *The Castle* we find a silent invisible bureaucracy, whose members are impossible to contact, and who rule our lives in ways which are beyond comprehension. The social machine, the organization, suppresses spontaneity, and this leads to an impoverishment of human relations and of life generally.

Technical progress is a child of war and of haphazard shortsighted business interests. As a consequence it is severely ill-balanced. We know how to go to the moon, but we do not know very well how to build cheaply suitable and decent houses for the earth dwellers. The effect of technical progress on our conditions of life, on our existence, is not given sufficient thought, and it is therefore a disintegrating force in our lives. It is not in any way controlled by us, but controls us by devious routes which are largely hidden from us, and it threatens us perhaps more than the forces of nature threatened primitive man. There is of course no question of stopping technical progress, even if we wanted to; it has gone too far for that. But it should be possible to direct, coordinate and intensify it, so as to anticipate some of its ill effects, and take precautions against them. But if we want to do that, if we want to gain control over technical progress, if we want to adjust ourselves to the conditions created by our knowledge, we can do it only by a collective organized effort. We must have a society capable of tackling these problems in the same concentrated and determined way in which our present society tackles the armaments race. This, I think, nowadays ought to be, in advanced countries, the major argument in favour of socialism, and it might perhaps also be a way of recapturing a clear idea of what socialism ought to be.

ON THE
POLITICAL COMPULSIONS OF
ECONOMIC GROWTH

THEODOR PRAGER

Economic growth, these days, is at the heart of politics everywhere, in the sense that people will not, and governments cannot, go without it for any length of time. In the economically underdeveloped countries, economic growth is essential in order to provide a basic living for the rapidly increasing numbers; there is now everywhere a sufficiently large and articulate minority at least which will no longer resign itself quietly to stagnation and sometimes deepening misery as an Act of God. In the industrial countries, economic growth is essential in order to provide reasonably full employment and also such steady increase in real income as people have come to expect; they will no longer accept unemployment of men and resources or even a freezing of living standards as the inexorable outcome of market forces too subtle or majestic to challenge. No ruling class or party can thus avoid working, planning or somehow providing for a measure of economic growth, whether in India or China, in the U.S.A. or the U.S.S.R. or, for that matter, in Austria or Hungary—for even in small countries it has become difficult for governments to put the blame for economic stagnation on world market or regional developments; they would not be allowed to get away with it for long.

It has not always been so, and it may be worth going briefly into the causes. In a way, one might think that the more the productive forces have advanced, the more material wealth has increased and the further the areas of dire poverty have been pushed back, the less urgent the need for further economic growth. But of course the very development of material resources and of know-how of all kinds, with its demonstration of the potentialities of wealth and of further growth, has made people more aware of their misery or at any rate of the gap between actual and potential living standards. With memories still alive of how coffee was dumped into the sea and wheat burned in the face of urgent need, there came the experience of the war which brought not only full employment but, in some of the warring countries, an actual improvement in the material living conditions of millions. It finally convinced people that hunger and unemployment were really totally unnecessary and nothing but the product of bungling and incompetence. If jobs and something like fair shares for all could be provided in war-time, very well, then it was up to those in charge to see to it that jobs and a decent living wage were available in peace-time as well. This, at any rate, was the feeling in countries like Britain, the U.S.A., and those in their orbit; and while it carried no earth-shaking revolutionary implications—after all, this was the winning side and the ruling oligarchies had not discredited themselves by kow-towing to Hitler but had, on the contrary, led the war against him—there was nevertheless enough dynamic in it to oust the Tories in Britain and to cause governments everywhere to promise full employment, social security, housing and even a measure of planning as a means of securing economic growth.

In continental Europe, the balance of political forces was more strongly disturbed, the hold of the old oligarchies more immediately threatened. In Germany and Italy, the ruling classes were held responsible, and rightly so, for resorting or surrendering to Fascism and dragging their countries into war and down to defeat. In France it was different but not so different as all that: for while the resistance embraced sections of all classes and almost all political groups there was a significant part of the possessing classes that had collaborated willingly enough with Hitler. At any rate, it was the working class (and the patriotic intelligentsia) which here, as elsewhere on the Continent, provided the spearhead of national resistance against German Fascism and the most active and loyal force in the crucial phase of post-war reconstruction; and there was an almost universal determination that things should be 'different' now; that the economic and social strongholds of big capital, held to be the source of economic stagnation and political repression, should not be allowed to be re-established; and that there should be jobs, decent wages, social security, adequate housing and economic as well as political democracy for all. The political composition of early post-war governments, the tone of their pronouncements and pledges, including that of nationalizing key industries and enterprises, the adoption, occasionally, of extremely democratic new constitutions (as in Italy) or declarations, even by Conservative Chancellors, that theirs would now be a 'new, revolutionary' land (as in Austria) reflected this atmosphere and balance of social and political forces; and it is worth recalling that even the stricken German working-class with its decimated cadres (how many of the old *Vertrauensmänner* were still alive in 1945?) and rather forlorn leadership managed to push through legislation providing for the nationalization of heavy industry in the key areas of Nordrhein–Westphalia and Berlin (though this was immediately vetoed by the Allies). The arguments put forward for nationalization at the time were by no means solely or even primarily based on economic reasoning—a fact frequently overlooked by present-day critics of nationalization; they were rather couched in political terms, pointing to the sinister part played by the Krupp and Thyssen and their opposite numbers in the big chemical and electrical engineering combines in providing funds and moral support for Hitler and his war.† But there was sound economic sense in the demand for nationalization, too.

First, there was the obvious fact that in war-ravaged countries only the state would, for a considerable time to come, be able to put the big plants of heavy industry on their feet at all; in that case, it was reasoned, and this re-enforced the political considerations mentioned, it might as well take over ownership, too. Once in charge, the government would have to see to it that jobs were safeguarded, for else the party (or parties) in power would have to take the electoral consequences. This made as nearly certain as could be that the government of the day would ensure an adequate flow of investment and working capital and also plan its own public investments in such a way as to provide orders for the nationalized plants. Finally, it was felt that, with a friendly government in power (and, it must be remembered, most early post-war governments were broadly based anti-Fascist coalitions which included leading representatives of the trade union and socialist movements), it would be easier to push through a measure of workers' control or 'co-determination' (*Mitbestimmung*) at the plant level which, again, would help to safeguard jobs and a 'fair share' in the fruits of labour.

Reviewing the first volume of Marx's *Capital* for a Leipzig weekly in 1868, Frederick Engels remarked that '*universal suffrage compels the ruling classes to court the favour of the workers*. Under these circumstances, four or five representatives of the proletariat are a *power*, if they know how to use their position...' (Engels' italics).‡ The ruling classes of Italy, Germany and of other countries eventually met this challenge by doing away with universal suffrage and establishing a rule of terror. They took a beating and, by 1944 or 1945, the workers had four or five representatives not only in the parliaments but in each of the governments of Europe. Perhaps they did not know how to use their power to anything like the full extent; but the restoration of parliamentary democracy itself and the measures of nationalization, minimum wage and social security legislation, Italy's early ban on factory dismissals, Austria's and Germany's restoration and extension of Shop Steward legislation, Ger-

† Thyssen may later have expressed regret at the fact; this does not undo the evil-doings perpetrated by his henchmen of the Alpine Montan Gesellschaft (since 1926 an affiliate of the German Stahlverein) even in the as yet free and independent Austria: not content with restricting local steel production for the sake of the German-based mills, they raised and financed the armed gangs of the Styrian *Heimatschutz* which first smashed the free trade union movement in Austrian heavy industry, then proceeded to shoot Austrian democracy to pieces and finally, on the occasion of the 'Anschluss', turned itself into the local branch of the Nazi storm trooper army.

‡ Karl Marx, *Selected Works*, Vol. I (London, 1942), p. 344.

many's provision for 'co-determination' in the iron and steel industries, France's, Holland's and Norway's reconstruction and development plans, etc. all created an atmosphere in which it was difficult to resort to the time-dishonoured practices of deflation and restrictionism. People would not be pushed around; unemployment would not be tolerated for any length of time; governments and employers alike had to think up something new and could not 'rationalize' plants and industries or 'correct' regional imbalances at the expense of workers' living standards or established ways of life, as of old. To re-quote an example given elsewhere, and entirely symptomatic of the winds of change: when American experts suggested to the Italian government that at least one in three of the country's shipyards should be closed down, on the grounds of inefficiency, surplus capacity and so on, it was they who suffered shipwreck, for 'in the present economic and political condition of the country, no government has the strength to close down industrial plants giving employment to tens of thousands of workers. Only within the framework of an expanding economy could such a decision become politically possible.'[†] Much as the political and economic position of Italy (of the late forties and early fifties) has differed from that of other countries, and much as it has changed all over Western Europe, it is still true that only within the framework of an expanding economy has the dismantling of shipyards or the closing down of mines or factories been politically possible; and in the comparatively few cases where it has been done governments have seen to it that new jobs were found in nearby existing or in newly established, and frequently government-subsidized, plants. By doing so, the state has everywhere contributed to the maintenance of the expansion itself.

Now this expansion was, of course, rooted in the first place in autonomous economic forces and impulses such as early reconstruction and modernization requirements, in the vast technological changes unleashed by the war, in the great and rising tide of investments of the oligopolies in search of new products, additional market outlets and of profits and super-profits. It is not suggested that the enormous and almost uninterrupted expansion of production and employment, of investment and consumption, of national product and income over a period of two decades has been the direct product of political deliberation and decision-taking; that post-war economic growth has been 'engineered' by governments and capitalist oligarchies concerned only with appeasing, gratifying and integrating the working classes into an increasingly planned and streamlined 'neo-capitalism'. The point is, however, that the phenomenon of an apparently reinvigorated and rejuvenated

[†] Mario Einaudi, Maurice Byé, Ernesto Rossi, *Nationalization in France and Italy* (New York, 1955), p. 217.

capitalist system cannot be adequately understood without regard to the fact of continuous state intervention and encouragement at all levels and all along the line, and that this was, in turn, prompted, to a larger degree than ever, by social pressures from below, unleashed by the national liberation struggle, the defeat of Fascism and the defensive role into which the capitalist oligarchies of Continental Europe (and in a lesser degree in Britain, too) had been pushed in the wake of these and related events. Economic growth had become a necessity, more than ever before, because only in this way could capitalism show reason why it should not make way for a radically different social order, and the old oligarchies for another kind of social leadership.

The suggestion, therefore, is not merely that politics and economics have become more intertwined than ever but that the political economy of the oligarchies had to proceed from the need to meet an elemental and often articulate challenge to its leadership from antagonistic social forces and anti-capitalist parties in circumstances where the renewed resort to naked repression had become practically impossible. After some attempts to dig in and fight back on the old ground there followed a gradual but complete re-orientation of strategy: propped by American political support and invigorated by American economic aid, the oligarchies launched forth on bold programmes of productive and social investment, modernization and trade liberalization, 'human relations' and productivity drives, streamlining of agricultural as well as of industrial structures and of 'social partnership'—with the Unions, where necessary, or over the heads of the Unions and directly at the plant level, where possible.

It has worked, it has worked 'miracles', and almost everywhere. The oligarchies have risen to the occasion; so much so that it is beginning to be forgotten how it all started. Yet it is of more than historical interest to remember that it was the changed relations of social power after 1944/45, the renewed dynamic of the underlying social forces, the unleashing of class conflict in the changed conditions after the war (but rooted in the struggle for liberation from the yoke of Hitler) which provided impetus and a new dynamic for the old system. The brutal repression of the Italian workers and poor farmers (who had been very much on the move in the early twenties) by Fascism produced two decades of economic and social stagnation; the repression of the German workers and democratic movement (preceded by extreme political polarization to Left and Right but with a large common denominator of strong anti-capitalist feeling) produced profound moral and cultural degradation and a lop-sided armaments-induced boom and ended in total collapse and waste land; but the pressure of the democratic and socialist movement unleashed after the war, while contained within a substantially unimpaired property structure, released powerful new productive forces and gave capitalism a new lease of life. It has managed to absorb the shock, it has converted the explosive stuff of nationalization and planning, of brimful employment and rising wages into elements of strength; it has even institutionalized a measure of 'co-determination' and converted it into a lever for working class integration into the system. It is a changed capitalism but it is capitalism still, and in spite of many persisting old and not a few new tensions and contradictions, frustrations and alienations, it works, and looks like being with us for a long time yet.

It does so, although—and again, in a sense, because—the challenge present from within has been powerfully re-enforced by a challenge from without. For nearly three decades the Soviet revolution and system remained an isolated 'accident of history'; now, similar patterns prevail over much of Europe and of East Asia, presenting an alternative to the capitalist mode of production. It is, naturally, a matter of debate as to how far it is an attractive alternative; let it be said at once that the social and economic condition of, say, Soviet Middle Asia looks more inviting to the poor farmers of Pakistan, Persia or Turkey than that of, say, Hungary or even Czechoslovakia to the workers of Austria or North Italy; and let it be admitted that those early high growth rates, once thought to provide conclusive evidence of the inherent superiority of centrally planned economies and an easy guarantee for 'catching up' very soon on the developed capitalist countries in most things that mattered, no longer yields unequivocal results: we all know the 'Radio Yerevan' crack about the coming year which was going to be 'middling': worse than the present year but better than the next. . . Nor are Marxists —they perhaps least of all—unaware of the grievous damage wrought to the cause of socialism by the crimes and follies of the Stalin era. But the point here is that the mere fact of capitalism losing out, of the old oligarchies swept from power in Eastern Europe, etc., has presented a serious challenge and threat to the capitalist oligarchies in Western Europe (and Japan), not militarily, or at least not primarily militarily but in terms of social power. To meet this threat, they have had to be on their toes; they have had to prove the superiority of capitalism in social and economic terms; they have had to make out a convincing case for maintaining the old property structure, or at least the case against 'costly experiments'. Capitalism, in other words, has to deliver the goods; and this has meant high priority for full employment and for adequate rates of economic growth.

It may be objected that this is a somewhat 'Eurocentric' point of view and that the strongest of all capitalist countries, the U.S.A., has been far less subject to such pressures so that, accordingly, neither full employment nor economic growth have held such undisputed sway in its

scale of priorities. Now it is, of course, true that the belief in Free Enterprise and The American Way of Life has, after taking some knocks in the
early Thirties, remained unshaken, and it is also true that the outside
challenge, in the shape of East European or East Asian Communism
looks rather remote (except to the brass hats in various walks of life).
Nevertheless, the mere threat of Western Europe, or the Third World,
'going Communist' provoked a massive response from the U.S. oligarchy
and government, to which the whole record of the last two decades,
from the Marshall Plan and 'Point Four' to the 'Alliance for Progress'
and Kennedy's growth targets for the O.E.C.D.-countries (let alone the
military build-up and numerous armed interventions) bear witness.

Moreover, the economic interdependence of the capitalist world is
such that strong movements in any of its more important sectors will
exert corresponding pulls in the other sectors. This has been exemplified
frequently enough in the case of crises and depressions but it also works in
the other direction. The politically induced expansionist bias of Western
Europe (much aided and encouraged, in its initial phase, by Marshall
aid and American prodding but later gaining a momentum of its own)
was a considerable counterweight to the crisis tendencies within the U.S.
economy; and it may thus be said that the social and political pressures
at work in Western Europe and elsewhere have helped the U.S.A. to
overcome its own bias towards orthodoxy and stagnation.

But this is not to belittle the crucial part played by the U.S.A. in
providing the means for getting European expansion going in the first
place. Looking back, over the first post-war years, it can easily be seen
that the Marshall plan was neither, as one side have claimed, a simple-
minded act of generosity by the American tax-payer in order to save
Europe from hunger and destitution; nor, as the other side has said, an
attempt to export America's crisis of over-production, etc. It was in
fact a gigantic piece of political investment to make European capitalism
a going concern again. By providing the lacking working capital, it
permitted the old oligarchies to get the process of production and accumulation into swing, thus enabling them physically and morally to
reassert to the full their claim to social and political leadership. Now,
there have been wars before, and destitution and the threat of revolution
in their wake, and victors economically capable of putting out a hand
of help; and there was the Hoover Mission after the First World War;
but never has aid been given on such a scale, in such a planned manner
and with such a true sense of purpose: about 20 billion dollars were
channelled into more than a dozen countries in accordance, very largely,
with real priorities, so that pre-war levels of production were everywhere
reached and surpassed within a few years and the basis laid for modernization all along the line—and in such a way that the old property struc-

ture was practically restored unimpaired. One is bound to ask, whence this extraordinary effort, whence this readiness even to go roughshod over old-established tabus (as when the Marshall missions insisted that the local governments work out detailed development plans for their basic industries etc., and devote the bulk of industrial E.R.P.-finance to such industries even when they happened to be nationalized!)—and one is bound to conclude that only an unprecedented external threat or challenge could have caused it all: the fear that else all Europe might 'go Communist'. Looking at the effect of Marshall aid, at the powerful impulse it gave to the restoration and further development of the productive forces in Europe, and the fillip to the American economy, one has to admit that the rivalry of the two social systems did a powerful lot of good to capitalism almost from the moment it got going.

Nor is it hard to see the connection between the social transformations in Eastern Europe and the social pressures within Western Europe: without the anti-capitalist sentiment and militant movements in the West, the U.S.A. might perhaps have written off Eastern Europe and left Western Europe to struggle along as best it could; after all, the latter's infrastructure, production apparatus and human potential was still sufficiently intact to allow restoration to take place, more painfully and more slowly of course but nevertheless of its own accord. Clearly, however, there was a risk that this might be accompanied by social transformations highly unpalatable to the forces of 'free enterprise' and the 'way of life as we know it'. Hence, indeed, the skill developed by European governments in playing on America's fear of Communism so as to obtain additional favours and at the same time a measure of independence from too much loving care and guidance from Uncle Sam; and hence also the more than average help given to such sensitive spots as Greece or Austria. But while the Americans were here to some extent becoming victims of their own propaganda there was nevertheless some truth in the assertion that 'else' there might be social unrest and a new swing to Communism. Western Europe simply could no longer afford massive unemployment, persistently low real wages or persistent extreme and overt social injustice.† For, as has been said (and one could quote dozens of statements to this effect): 'Today capitalism is only one of several economic systems...If it is true that the centralized command economies can guarantee full employment, the free market economies cannot afford the luxury of mass unemployment as this would no longer be tolerated...'‡ and while governments have been greatly concerned

† This has remained true to this day. 'Communist gains may inspire more government reforms' was the headline of a report on Italy's local government elections of 1964 in what is surely the most sober daily paper anywhere (*The Times*, 30.xi.1964).

‡ George N. Halm, *Wirtschaftssysteme. Eine vergleichende Darstellung* (Berlin, 1960), p. 1.

about creeping inflation (especially in Germany, with its hangover from the inflation trauma of the Twenties), they have been prepared to pay this price, too: 'Modern governments in the democracies of Western Europe appear more fearful of the prospects of unemployment than of inflation...Post-war governments, whatever their political coloration, almost universally preferred to err on the side of inflation rather than of deflation, and they have acted on that preference most of the time since the war...'† But it was not merely a question of avoiding mass unemployment but of expansion and growth: 'Expansion became a political necessity from the moment that the conflict between East and West took on the form of economic competition';‡ and 'growth theory, too, has a background in real life, i.e. the growth race of the old industrial countries of the West and the countries of the East'.§

These are economists speaking but the matter is put even more succinctly by a political philosopher: 'It was the very structure of existing civilization which was challenged and which had to prove its mettle anew as against a competing civilization';‖ while a physicist, reflecting on the follies of the Thirties and on the changes wrought since, first pays 'due credit to these two great men', Keynes and Beveridge, for debunking those of their fellow-economists who used to 'teach that the way to fight unemployment was to tighten our belts' but adds that 'we must not forget an even more important great fact. This was the strength of the U.S.S.R.; the strength which it had demonstrated in the war, and its growing economic and military power in the years after. In the presence of a mighty Russia the bankers had to give up their favourite game of throwing a spanner in the economic machinery. The politicians had to unbend too—the miracle of the European Economic Community became possible. Under the impact of communism, *laissez-faire* capitalism developed into something for which there is as yet no proper term. Only its result has got a telling name: the Affluent Society.'¶

We have, then, a confluence of pressures from within and without:

† *Europe's Needs and Resources. Trends and Prospects in 18 Countries* (New York, 1961), p. 28.
‡ Albin Chalandon, *Le Monde*, 8 June, 1960.
§ Gottfried Bombach, *Wachstum und Konjunktur* (Darmstadt u. Opladen, 1960), p. 7.
‖ Herbert Marcuse, *Die Gesellschaftslehre des sowjetischen Marxismus* (Neuwied,1964), p. 53.
¶ Dennis Gabor, *Inventing the Future* (London, 1964, pp. 16–17). Professor Gabor adds that 'this was a triumph of dialectics—though never admitted by Marxist dialecticians'. I do not know about dialecticians, but Marxists have certainly recognized the fact (that the new *Systemkonkurrenz* has had an immense impact on the West and contributed to those reforms and forward strategies which have made post-war capitalism such an unexpected success), and they have argued about it for years; see, for instance, the debate carried on in the Vienna Marxist monthly *Weg und Ziel* in 1957/8 and again on numerous later occasions; or my *Wirtschaftswunder oder keines? Zur politischen Ökonomie Westeuropas* (Vienna, 1963) which gives a full presentation of precisely this and related issues. In England, Maurice Dobb has repeatedly touched upon the subject, as, for instance, in *Capitalism, Yesterday and Today* (London, 1958), and, more fully, on later occasions.

on the one hand, the pressure from within, to create jobs and to utilize resources to the full, backed by 'inverted strikes' (as when the unemployed in Italy began to repair roads and ships, of their own accord and even without pay), by shop steward and union-inspired industrial investment and regional development plans (as in Italy, Austria, France, Belgium, etc.), by proposals to introduce and effectuate extra-budgetary public investments, as well as by electoral campaigns to ensure expansionist government policies generally; and on the other hand, the challenge from without, prompting the Marshall plan and reaching a high point with the so-called Sputnik shock which induced all major Western powers to re-assess their plans and impelled massive new investments into the armaments and space race, including such spheres as higher education and research and development.† Add to this the race for the favours of the so-called underdeveloped, the 'Third' world‡ and you have the social and political setting in which, of the whole spectrum of possible lines of action, 'Keynesian' pump priming, public investments, plentiful (if not always cheap) money, government subsidies to all and sundry and for all and sundry—investment and consumption, warfare and welfare—in a word, expansion and growth, became the dominant motif and line of action, in the face of orthodox opposition and in spite of frequent setbacks.

In his Inaugural Address to the Working Men's International Association in 1864, Marx described the carrying of the Ten Hours' Bill as 'the victory of a principle; it was the first time that in broad daylight the political economy of the middle class succumbed to the political economy of the working class.'§ One might, similarly, describe the promises and policies of full employment, of social welfare and of expansion and growth in the post-war era as the victory of a principle, as an important if a limited break-through of the political economy of Europe's working classes; for it was their 'presence' and pressure which to a large extent determined the broad orientation of bourgeois strategy and which forced the pace of government policy. One might object that

† 'For a long time the great number of scientists and engineers being produced each year in Russia was discounted on the grounds that their quality could not be high. The "sputnik" demonstrated two years ago that there was quality as well as quantity in the Russian effort. Since then we have had other evidences of Russian advances...' ('Co-operation in the fields of scientific and technical research', Report by Dana Wilgress, O.E.E.C., Paris, 1960, pp. 6–7).

‡ 'Without doubt the U.S.A. is still economically the most highly developed country to-day. But every student of affairs will note that their aid to the development countries is immeasurably greater than it would be without competition with the Soviet Union and the socialist countries. Their mere existence, even apart from such real assistance as they are giving, is a weighty motive for the capitalist countries to exert themselves beyond such intentions as they would have realized in the absence of (such) competition.' (Georg Lukacs, 'On the debate between China and the Soviet Union', Forum, Vienna, December, 1963).

§ Karl Marx, Selected Works, Vol. II, p. 439.

after all this has neither weakened the hold of bourgeois rule nor even inhibited the process of capitalist accumulation; one might point out that there was no special virtue in keeping so many wheels turning by way of armament orders; and that, by and large, there was at present less sign of an autonomous working class policy and effective pressure for far-reaching social change than there had been in the early post-war years. Well, neither was the statutory limitation of the working day thought to be likely to prove a fatal blow to capitalism; in fact, it gave additional impulse to rationalizing and modernizing the process of production and speeding the development of the productive forces generally (as did most social legislation, the pressure for higher wages, the gradual extension of general education and most other reforms won through in the course of capitalist history). Capitalism has managed to absorb the pressures and turn them to its own use. It has not, on that account, become any more harmonious or shock-proof; there are new tensions and conflicts building up. Now that growth has been with us for so long, people expect it to continue at much the same rate and they are setting their sights accordingly. Should growth slow down or even come to a near-stop, then the system might well, like a bicycle slowing down, begin to totter this way and that. Should the gap between the developed and the underdeveloped parts of the world continue to widen, there may well be explosions. Should the arms race continue unchecked, the consequences are only too calculable. So that, while capitalism in its main centres has proved an unexpected economic success, thanks to the pressures and challenges that have compelled it to exert itself, the prospects it offers to mankind, are now rather more sombre than even Marx envisaged.

ROLE OF THE 'MACHINE-TOOLS SECTOR' IN ECONOMIC GROWTH

A COMMENT ON INDIAN AND CHINESE EXPERIENCE

K. N. RAJ

I. MACHINES TO MAKE MACHINES

In analysing the growth and planning problems of underdeveloped countries Maurice Dobb has been concerned at least as much with the structural and technological constraints on investment as with the motivations underlying the saving-investment process in their respective institutional settings. He was one of the first economists in the West to recognize the possibility of the rate of investment in some of these countries being more crucially dependent on the already existing stock of capital than on the supply of wage-goods; and hence of the compulsion in such cases to enlarge first the equipment in capital goods industries. He was aware of the initial retarding effect this might have on growth of output on account of the diversion of some of the existing capital equipment to the manufacture of more such equipment, but pointed to the higher rate of growth of output which expansion of productive capacity in the capital goods sector would make possible at future dates.†

The theoretical implication that it might be useful in certain contexts to break down the capital goods sector in the Marxian scheme of reproduction into two sub-branches, one devoted to the manufacture of capital goods for producing capital goods (which for convenience has been termed the 'machine-tool sector' by Dobb) and the other manufacturing capital goods directly for the consumer goods sector, has been reflected to some extent in subsequent planning literature.‡ Only a few attempts have been made however to incorporate a 'machine-tool sector' into growth models and investigate the consequences for growth of altering the proportion of total investment allocated to this sector.

† Maurice Dobb, 'A Note on the So-called Degree of Capital Intensity of Investment in Under-Developed Countries', *Économie Appliquée*, 1954, no. 3, Reprinted in his collected papers, *On Economic Theory and Socialism* (London, 1955).

‡ P. C. Mahalanobis, 'The Approach of Operational Research to Planning in India', *Sankhya*, The Indian Journal of Statistics, Vol. 16, Parts 1 and 2, December, 1955, Chapter 6.

One of them (by Dobb himself) underlines the peculiar ability of the machine-tools branch within the capital goods sector to initiate and sustain a circular production process of its own and of thus 'breaking out of the determinism' laid upon the sector by the existing structural relations.† Other contributions on the subject have in addition brought out the dependence of this sector (as of other sectors) on intermediate goods, the braking effect this might have on rates of growth over a period of time, and of the more extended period of initial retardation which would have to be accepted for minimizing the impact of these braking effects on growth rates in the longer run.‡ No attempt has however been made so far to examine the empirical relevance of any of these questions in the context of the developing countries today.

The constraint that might be imposed on the rate of investment by the existing stock of capital would be absolute only if (a) production of capital goods requires the aid of capital goods, and (b) the domestic output of capital goods cannot be supplemented with imports. Interpreted literally these are extreme conditions unlikely to be satisfied in reality. There may be, for instance, some capital goods (perhaps of a not very sophisticated kind) which can be produced without the aid of capital goods; at any rate, as long as there is international trade, it should always be possible to supplement domestic production with imports.

On the other hand there are, in practice, limits to the scope for making capital goods with bare hands; at the very minimum some simple tools are essential, and for many purposes much more. When export earnings are stagnant, or there are other strong competing demands for the available foreign exchange, the extent to which imports can supplement domestic production of capital goods may also be limited. Given these conditions, the growth models in which a 'machine-tools sector' is identified as the sole source of capital goods for the larger capital goods sector is likely to have some relevance, even if the more rigorous conditions postulated by them are not wholly satisfied.

However, it is not essential that all the capital goods required for investment in the initial stages should be somehow produced within the economy.§ One could assume that there is to begin with not even a nucleus of the 'machine-tool sector' in the economy but that some foreign exchange is available to the economy which it could use to import capital

---

† Maurice Dobb, *An Essay on Economic Growth and Planning* (London, 1960), Chapter IV.

‡ K. N. Raj and A. K. Sen, 'Sectoral Models for Development Planning', *Arthaniti*, Vol. II, no. 2, May, 1959, and its expanded version entitled 'Alternative Patterns of Growth under Conditions of Stagnant Export Earnings' in *Oxford Economic Papers*, Vol. 13, no. 1, February, 1961; and K. A. Naqvi, 'Machine Tools and Machines: A Physical Interpretation of the Marginal Rate of Saving', *The Indian Economic Review*, Vol. VI, No. 3, February, 1963.

§ See Dobb, *An Essay on Economic Growth and Planning*, p. 144. It may of course be a realistic assumption to make that underdeveloped economies are in a position to manufacture some capital goods, even machine-tools of a not very high degree of precision.

goods of any kind.† This is a fairly realistic assumption to make, since most developing countries have in fact had some foreign exchange available to them through trade or aid and which, in principle, they could use for importing capital goods for either branch of the capital goods sector or directly for the consumer goods sector. The implications of allocating a high proportion of investment to the 'machine-tool sector' would then be reflected in the growth path corresponding to the case in which the bulk of this foreign exchange is used for importing 'machine-tools'.‡

Indian and Chinese growth experience since 1951 offers an opportunity for a comparative analysis from this angle. The economic structure of the two countries was strikingly similar at the starting point; both recognized the need to build up capital goods industries as part of their development programmes; total export earnings as a proportion of national income have been approximately the same in both cases; both had free foreign exchange available through trade and/or aid;§ both have had serious problems of food shortage and have had to import foodgrain on a large scale; but there has been a significant difference in the policies pursued by them in respect of the 'machine-tools sector'.

One must of course be careful not to attribute all the differences in growth experience in the two countries to this difference in development strategy, since there have been also other important differences in approach and policy as well as in the objective conditions. Nevertheless it is worth investigating in what respect the policies followed in regard to the 'machine-tools sector' is likely to have affected the subsequent development of their economies.

2. MACHINE-BUILDING IN CHINA AND INDIA

China has attached very high priority to machine-building, and to the 'machine-tool sector' within it, from the very beginning of its development programme. This will be evident from the following extract from its Five Year Plan (1953–1957):‖

The machine-building industry is the key to the technological transformation of our national economy. During the course of our First Five-Year Plan, we

† Raj and Sen, *op. cit.*

‡ K. N. Raj, 'Growth Models and Indian Planning', *The Indian Economic Review*, Vol. v, No. 3, February, 1961.

§ Thanks to the growing market for Chinese exports provided by other Communist countries in the 'fifties, China was able to secure a larger proportion of its foreign exchange through trade than India was able to during the same period. See K. N. Raj, *India, Pakistan and China: Economic Growth and Outlook* (Hyderabad, 1967).

‖ *First Five Year Plan for Development of the National Economy of the People's Republic of China in 1953–1957* (Peking, 1956), pp. 75–82.

must develop our machine-building industry on the basis of the growth of our iron and steel and non-ferrous metals industries...A heavy responsibility rests on our existing machine-building factories during the period of the First Five-Year Plan. We will ourselves manufacture from 30 to 50 per cent of the equipment needed for 156 projects which are being designed with the help of the Soviet Union; at the same time the machine-building industry is faced with many demands from various branches of the national economy. It is therefore necessary, on the basis of a higher technical level, to fully utilize and expand the productive capacity of existing machine-building works and to increase their production of new types of products. In this period, we must rely on our original enterprises as well as new and reconstructed enterprises that come into production to produce equipment for ron-smelting and steel-making, equipment for small and medium hydro-electric and thermal power industry; accessories and complete sets of equipment for the coal, non-ferrous metals, and cement industries; drilling machines together with accessories for the oil industry; various metal-cutting machine-tools; rolling stock and vessels needed for transport; and complete sets of equipment for textile, printing and dyeing, sugar-making, paper-making and food industries.

Official data do not reveal the proportion of total investment allocated for the capital goods sector as a whole or for the machine-tools branch within it, but an unofficial estimate suggests that over 5 per cent of the total 'capital construction investment' in the public sector went into machine-building in China's First Plan.†

The emphasis on machine-building was continued in the Second Plan. Though information on the progress made during the period 1958–1962 is much more scanty than for the preceding few years there is general agreement that there was spectacular growth of industrial production in the first three years of this period.‡ This has also been identified as 'the "take-off" period in Chinese machine building':

'Before then the industry had mainly confined itself to producing fairly simple medium-size equipment, providing parts to keep the old machinery running and complementing newly imported machinery...Starting with the Second Five-Year Plan, greater emphasis was put on the independent designing and production of complete sets of machinery and special tools, and advances are said to have been made in all sectors of the machine-building industry.'§

It has been officially claimed that 85 per cent of the machinery and

† Shigeru Ishikawa, *National Income and Capital Formation in Mainland China* (Tokyo, 1965), Chapter 4, Tables 11–13 and 11–17.
‡ Choh-Ming Li, 'China's Industrial Development, 1958–63', *The China Quarterly*, No. 17, January–March, 1964.
§ Harald Munthe-Kaas, 'China's Mechanical Heart', *Far Eastern Economic Review*, May 27, 1965.

equipment China needed for the Second Plan was produced within the country.†

The progress in machine-building in China has been not only in terms of the quantity produced but also in the range of the products and in the sophistication involved in their manufacture:

The pride of modern Chinese machine building is the 12,000-ton hydraulic forging press which went into regular operation in Shanghai (in March, 1965)...There are only about 20 similar forging presses in the world, and only a few countries—the United States, Britain, West Germany and Czechoslovakia—have yet manufactured them...The most significant fact is that China today is able to produce big high-precision machinery, the 12,000-ton forging press being but one of the more impressive examples. Among the more spectacular achievements claimed by the Chinese are steam-driven turbines with a capacity of 50,000 kilowatts and water-driven turbines with a capacity of 72,500 kilowatts...China is also able to produce blooming machines with rollers measuring 1,150 mm in diameter and equipment for an iron-melting works capable of producing 1,500,000 tons of iron a year. Oil refineries with a capacity of one million tons and fertilizer factories producing 100,000 tons of nitrogenous fertilizers per year must also be counted among the achievements of the last few years. As for sophistication: 'Some of the more mature techniques in the world, such as electronic tornardo welding, round arc gears, electrical processing techniques and powder metallurgy, are beginning to be applied extensively.'‡

India had a somewhat later start, as the emphasis on capital goods industries was evident only with the beginning of its Second Five Year Plan in 1956. Though the importance of machine-making industries was recognized in this Plan, the investment allocation was relatively small to begin with.§ Moreover the lags in implementation and the consequent shortfalls in performance have been considerable in this sector of industry both in the Second and Third Plans.‖ It is not therefore surprising that,

† Po I-po, 'The Socialist Industrialization of China (written for *Cuba Specialista* of Cuba)', *Peking Review*, No. 41, October 11, 1963. Quoted in the article cited above by Choh Ming-Li.

‡ Munthe-Kaas, *op. cit.*

§ Of the total planned investment of Rs. 4800 crores by the public sector in the Second Plan, only a little over 1 per cent was allocated for machine-building industries; in addition, there was an allocation of about the same magnitude for the private sector of the economy. As indicated earlier, machine-building absorbed over 5 per cent of the total 'capital construction investment' in the public sector in China's First Plan. Since working capital was almost entirely neglected in the investment estimates for India's Second Plan, its 'total planned investment' corresponds fairly closely to China's 'capital construction investment'.

‖ An appraisal attempted in 1958 of the progress of the Second Plan contained the following observation: 'In the field of engineering industries, there will be shortfalls in respect of structural fabrication and in respect of all types of machinery, except sugar machinery...' (*Appraisal and Prospects of the Second Five Year Plan*, May 1958, p. 73). Similarly a mid-term appraisal of the Third Plan says: '...progress on the part of private industry has lagged behind in a number of key areas, such as alloy tool and stainless steel, steel castings, steel forgings, machine tools, fertilizers, cement, paper and newsprint and in some chemical industries' (*The Third Plan Mid-term Appraisal*, November, 1963, p. 4).

according to an official estimate, only about 55 per cent of the total requirement of machinery and components in 1965–66 (the last year of the Third Five Year Plan) could be met out of domestic production and the rest had to come from imports.†

It is also worth noting that, of the machinery and components produced in India in 1965–66, well over two-fifths (in value) took the form of transport equipment and machinery for consumer goods industries (such as cotton, sugar, paper and tea). Another two-fifths was accounted for by electrical machinery and motors, electric transformers, power-driven pumps, boilers, diesel engines, cranes, tractors and the like, not all the output of which can be regarded as contributing to the 'machine-tool sector'. Machine-tools, heavy equipment and metallurgical machinery, and such other products as can be regarded as the output of this sector accounted perhaps for not more than about one-eighth of the total value of the machinery and components produced in the country in 1965–66.‡

The continued dependence of India on imports of machinery and equipment on a large scale§ has no doubt meant that it has often been able to install better-quality products manufactured in the more advanced countries and therefore often embodying more recent improvements in technology. However, as will be evident from the following observation made by a Western visitor who inspected comparable industries in both countries, India has had to pay a price for this in terms of development of technical expertise and skill within the country:

It was instructive to compare two new chemical fertilizer plants, one in Nangal (Punjab) and the other at Wuching (Shanghai)...Wuching cost $25 million, makes 100,000 tons a year, employs 2,400 people for an average $30 a month—and is completely Chinese in design, construction and operation. Nangal cost $65 million, produces 375,000 tons a year, employs 3,500

---

† Perspective Planning Division (Planning Commission), *Notes on Perspective of Development, India: 1960–61 to 1975–76*, April 1964, Appendices, Table C. 34.

‡ Perspective Planning Division, *op. cit.* Table B. 4.

§ The inability to manufacture machinery within the country has not been of course the only factor responsible for the dependence on imports. Some of the other factors at work, and the consequences, will be evident from the following comments of the Member in charge of Industry in the Indian Planning Commission: 'For one thing, there is an omnipresent, though unspoken, inferiority complex in the field of industrial production. Goods and machines will sell only if they have a foreign brand or patent name. Even industrialists who loudly and bitterly complain of the market resistance to their indigenous products, strain every nerve to obtain foreign brands when they procure equipment for themselves...Foreign collaboration, apart from royalties and the stultification of indigenous capability, invariably brings in its train a bias for the import of foreign machinery. The foreign collaborator is interested even more in exporting his machinery than in exporting the know-how...Our current troubles have arisen out of the fact that the new industries set up with imported equipment and know-how and dependent upon imports of components and raw materials have not been able collectively to develop an export potential adequate to take care of the import requirements and service obligations of foreign loans and royalties.' (S. G. Barve, *Problems of Industrial Growth in India*, Planning Commission, Government of India, May 1966, pp. 10–12.)

people for a similar average wage—and sixty foreign technicians supervised the installation of the latest British, French, German and Italian machinery. Wuching is home-spun, almost amateurish, but with a lived-in look; Nangal is elegant and efficient but the Indian staff look almost out of place, scared to touch their sophisticated surroundings.†

3. COMPARATIVE GROWTH RATES AND IMPORTS

Judged in terms of the realized rate of growth of national income it seems unlikely that Chinese economic growth in the last fifteen years has been much faster than the Indian. It was certainly faster during the period 1952–57 but, after the setback in agriculture following the Great Leap Forward and the series of droughts, the difference in the average rates of growth over the period as a whole is probably not very large.

In the important sector of foodgrains, for instance, output grew in India at a compound rate of about $2\frac{1}{2}$ per cent per annum during the period 1952–1962. Such evidence as is available on China suggests that its rate of growth of foodgrain production has also been at best only of the same order.‡

The rate of growth of industrial production (of the factory-type) in China has been clearly much faster than in India, though it is difficult (on account of the different concepts and weights used in the respective index numbers) to guess how large the difference has really been. For

† Dick Wilson, 'The Tortoise and the Hare', *Far Eastern Economic Review*, April 8, 1965.

‡ 'According to a publication of the Communist Party of China (*Proposals of the Eighth National Congress of the Communist Party of China for the Second Five Year Plan for Development of the National Economy, 1958–1962*, p. 18) the total output of grain in the country had, in the period before the Revolution, touched a peak of 150 million tons in 1936. This included about 11 million tons of soya beans and 6 million tons of potatoes, both of which are often shown in Chinese agricultural statistics as part of foodgrain. Output of rice in 1936 was only a little over 57 million tons and of wheat about 23 million tons, the rest being coarse grains of various kinds.

As a result of war and the subsequent dislocation of the economy agricultural output declined in the following years and was lower than this pre-war peak even in 1951. It was only in the following year that the pre-war peak was exceeded. 1952 is therefore a good base-year to use for measuring subsequent Chinese agricultural growth as it is for India. (See for the above and other official data quoted in the following paragraph the publication of the Government of China in 1959, *Ten Great Years*, p. 119).

By 1957 total foodgrain output (excluding soya beans but inclusive of potatoes) amounted to 185 million tons, compared to a little over 154 million tons in 1952 and 139 million tons in 1936. After the aberrations of the Great Leap Forward in 1958 ended in near-fiasco there has been an almost complete statistical black-out and official sources are therefore no longer available. But there is a well-supported estimate of Edgar Snow (after a visit sponsored by the Government of China) which places the total foodgrain output in 1960 at 152 million tons (See Edgar Snow, *The Other Side of the River*, London, 1963, p. 624). This was probably the worst year for China in the last decade. Recent visitors to China have been told that the harvests in 1963 and 1964 were very much better and that in the latter year the output was about 10 per cent above the 1957 level. If this is a correct estimate the 1964 output is likely to have been about 204 million tons, which is just about one-third higher than in 1952. (K. N. Raj, *Indian Economic Growth: Performance and Prospects*, Allied Publishers, 1965, p. 10.)

instance, according to official Chinese estimates, the net value of industrial output increased at a rate of over 40 per cent per annum during
the period 1958–1960 (which was in fact a period of spectacular growth of
industry); estimates made by scholars in the West indicate a somewhat
lower rate of growth, approximately between 25 and 30 per cent per
annum.† In India, the rate of growth of output in the four established
industries of the pre-Independence period (cotton textiles, jute textiles,
tea and sugar) declined from $4\frac{1}{2}$ per cent per annum in the period 1951–
56 to around $2\frac{1}{2}$ per cent per annum thereafter (mainly on account of inadequate growth of demand for their products); but output in other
industries—more particularly the chemical, metallurgical and engineering industries which received the bulk of the investment after 1955 and
carry a weight of 50 out of 100 in the official index numbers of industrial
production—has grown at a rate of over $11\frac{1}{4}$ per cent per annum in the
period, 1955–1963.‡ Since the share of modern manufacturing industry
in the total national output of both countries was relatively small to
begin with, it is however unlikely that this difference in the rate of growth
of industrial output during this period could have made a substantial
difference to the overall rates of growth of national income.

As rough approximations one might therefore guess that, if the rate of
growth of national income in India during the last fifteen years has been
of the order of a little over $3\frac{1}{2}$ per cent per annum (as official estimates
indicate), the rate of growth in China during this period could not have
been more than $4\frac{1}{2}$ to 5 per cent per annum.§ This by itself is not an
impressively higher rate.

The much more striking difference in performance has been the fairly
high rate of investment maintained in China in recent years with only
marginal dependence on imports of machinery and equipment. Complete industrial plants and other equipment had accounted for 60 per
cent of China's total imports from the Soviet Union in 1958, and 63
per cent in 1959, when the value of the total imports from the Soviet
Union was about 570 million and 860 million roubles respectively; their
share fell to 12 per cent by 1962, by when the value of the total imports
from the Soviet Union had fallen to 210 million roubles.‖ This is indica-
tive of the trends in China's trade with the rest of the Communist
countries. The decline was no doubt partly offset by increased trade with

† Choh-Ming Li, *op. cit.*   ‡ K. N. Raj, *op. cit.*
§ There are reasons to suspect that the official national income statistics underestimate the
rate of growth in India and that the actual rate has been probably of the order of 4 per cent
per annum. But if the rate of growth of national income in China is taken to be about 30 to
40 per cent higher than in India (on account of the higher rate of growth of income from
industry) a similar upward adjustment has to be made in the assumed Chinese rate. The
growth rate in China would, of course, be lower if the growth of foodgrain output has not been
as high as is assumed above.
‖ Choh-Ming Li, *op. cit.* Table 6.

non-Communist countries but it is significant that, despite such increase, the value of machinery and plant imported into China from the non-Communist world was only about $140 million in 1964.†

The rate of investment in China since 1960 has no doubt been lower than in the years of the Great Leap Forward, but gross investment appears to have been still not less than 15 per cent of the gross national product.‡ This reduction in the rate of investment does not however appear to have been primarily due to inadequate supplies of machinery, though the non-availability of specific types of equipment for which domestic capability had not been fully developed is likely to have been a contributory factor in slowing down the pace of investment in some high-priority sectors. The more probable explanation is that the very high rates of investment reached in the period of the Great Leap Forward (estimated at 30 to 40 per cent of the gross national product) and the corresponding rates of domestic saving could not be maintained after the sharp fall in agricultural output in 1960.

It must be remembered that, after 1959, China's foreign exchange position has been under severe pressure for three reasons:

(a) Export earnings fell sharply after 1959.

Exports from China (computed from partners' official statistics)

$ million

	1959	1962	1963	1964
To Communist countries	1615	925	800	700
To Non-Communist countries	615	585	727	970
Total	2230	1510	1510	1670

(b) Heavy imports of foodgrain were necessary due to the drought, the average import for the period 1961–1963 being about $5\frac{1}{2}$ million tons per annum. Even in a relatively good year like 1964, about two thirds of the total foreign exchange earned from non-Communist countries had to be spent on importing food-grain ($400 million), raw cotton ($90 million), fertilizer ($65 million), and crude rubber ($65 million).§

(c) China was repaying the loans taken from the Soviet Union and completed full repayment by 1965 (thus gaining the distinction of

† Dick Wilson, 'Peking's Trade Plans', *Far Eastern Economic Review*, May 20, 1965. See also Colin MacDougall, 'China's Foreign Trade', *Far Eastern Economic Review*, January 27, 1966.

‡ Y. L. Wu, *et al.*, *The Economic Potential of Communist China* (Stanford Research Institute, Technical Report No. 2, October 1963). Wu's estimate, which places the investment rate at over 20 per cent of the gross national product, is cited in the article by Choh-Ming Li referred to earlier. For some observations on the difference made by the relative prices of investment goods in China, see K. N. Raj, *India, Pakistan and China: Economic Growth and Outlook*.

§ Data for exports and imports given above are from Dick Wilson's article on 'Peking's Trading Plans' referred to earlier.

being perhaps the only developing country now not to have any foreign debt).

In these circumstances, if China had not already built up the machine-making sector to the extent it did, the cut in the rate of domestic investment necessitated by foreign exchange shortage is likely to have been very much sharper than has actually been effected during this period.[†] This also suggests that, once the setback in agriculture is overcome and conditions become favourable for raising the rate of saving once again, the Chinese economy will be able to grow at a much faster rate without foreign exchange becoming a serious bottleneck in stepping up the rate of accumulation.[‡]

India presents a sharp contrast. It has been heavily dependent on foreign aid, both on account of the difficulties it has faced in raising the rate of domestic saving and its continued reliance on imports of machinery and equipment on a large scale (for sustaining a lower rate of investment than in China). Imports of machinery alone account now for about 30 per cent of India's total import bill,[§] and according to the preliminary estimates for the Fourth Five Year Plan the share of machinery and components in total imports will still be around 40 per cent in 1970–71.[||] Since the estimated deficit on current account in balance of payments (to be financed by foreign aid) is of about the same magnitude as the estimated imports of machinery and equipment, and as the estimates allow for a sharp increase in the rate of domestic saving during the period of the Fourth Plan, it is clear that, even if savings increase as postulated, the investment programme will be crucially dependent on the availability of aid. In other words, for raising the rate of capital accumulation, India faces both a saving and a foreign exchange problem, while China has not only succeeded in raising the rate of saving much above the level in India but has very nearly broken the foreign exchange bottleneck as far as investment is concerned.

[†] China has of course still a serious foreign exchange problem which is reflected in inadequate supplies of intermediate goods, and consequently in the existence of unutilized capacity in several industries (including apparently even steel).

[‡] It is of interest to note that, in the Soviet Union also, imports of machinery met as much as one-fourth of the total machinery requirements in its First Five Year Plan, but supplied only about 1 per cent of the total requirements by 1935. The share of imports went up after the Second World War but still accounted for no more than 5 per cent of the total. See Richard Moorsteen, *Prices and Production of Machinery in the Soviet Union, 1928–1958*, (Harvard 1962), pp. 92–93. See also, in this connection, an interesting article by M. Perel'man on 'The Economic Competition between the U.S.S.R. and U.S.A. in the Field of Machine-Tool Manufacture', *Planovoe Khozyaistvo*, 1963. No. 12; translation available in *Problems of Economics*, November, 1964.

[§] Government of India, *Economic Survey, 1965–66*, February 1966, Table 6.3.

[||] Perspective Planning Division, *op. cit.* Table F. 1. The estimate of total imports here does not allow for imports of agricultural products from the United States under P.L.480.

NATIONAL ECONOMY PLANNING
AND THE DEVELOPMENT OF
NATURAL SCIENCES

SH. YA. TURETSKY

I. THE CONNECTION BETWEEN SCIENTIFIC ACTIVITY
AND ECONOMIC PLANNING

Scientific development in the widest sense is dictated by the constantly increasing need of society to expand its material and cultural wealth. An ever greater knowledge of nature is the basis for the development of the productive forces, and at the same time opportunities for scientific development, and especially for the technological use in production of the most recent discoveries, increase as productive relations are developed. Only when every social barrier to the development of the productive forces of society has been lifted are all restrictions on scientific and technical progress removed. Only in conditions of socialist production has science obtained the full benefit of the direct productive forces of society. Scientific activity has become the most important object of economic planning, and economic planning itself comes within the domain of scientific activity.

To study the influence of scientific progress on the rates and proportions of social production it is important to define the limits of the connections between the development of the natural sciences and economics. Of course, political economy studies the productive relations of people, and not the relations between society and nature; however, not people in isolation, but in the context of their relationship with nature, the source of all productive activity.

It would be incorrect to assume that the analysis of the development of the productive forces and the factors conditioning this development in terms of scientific and technological progress has nothing to do with the study of economic laws and lies beyond the scope of economics. To formulate the problem in this way would impoverish economics and isolate it from the other sciences. The connection between economics and the natural sciences begins in the initial stage of the exchange of matter between society and nature and concerns all stages of production and all forms of activity.

To elucidate the way in which the development of the economy and of economics itself depends on scientific progress is of major importance in the development of economic thought under conditions of socialism. But this is only one side of the problem. It is no less important to discover the role of economics in the development of the natural sciences. In what does this role consist, and what is its importance in a socialist society?

First of all, the study of the extent and composition of the material and spiritual needs of society is an immediate, direct task of economics. This determines the need for natural resources, and to obtain these requires the development of science and technology. The discovery of natural wealth, its extraction, reproduction (for biological resources), processing and treatment right down to the final product depends on the labour resources of society and their use, on the accumulated basic funds and on the condition and use of the implements of work.

On the border of economics and natural sciences the solution of the problem of the two aspects of the product is given in practice by the ratio of the socially necessary expenditure of labour on its production to its social usefulness; and, in conditions where the law of value applies, by the ratio of the value of the goods to their use value. The ratio of expenses to the potential use value of the final product, received from this type of raw material, or from other interchangeable materials, can be used as a criterion in applied problems in the development of various natural sciences (chemistry, physics, biology, geology, etc.) which affect the interrelation of society and nature.

Economics must give (define) an economic criterion for the development of the natural sciences, must telescopically determine the order in which scientific research into the further knowledge of matter is undertaken, taking the perspectives of economic development and a more efficient use (with lower consumption of labour) of the force of nature into account. To take only one of many possible examples, in the sphere of geology. The important point is not that the geologists have discovered the secrets of the earth's core, or that a technical solution of the problem of very deep drilling has been found. It is also necessary that the total expenditure on extraction should be justified, i.e. compensated for by the saving in productive or personal consumption, so that the final product is not made dearer, and the total productivity of social labour is increased.†

An efficiency criterion stipulates the necessity for seeking new and more acceptable variants of scientific discoveries which can be utilized

---

† It has been said that half the gas reserves and a third of the oil reserves lie at depths exceeding 3500 metres. According to the calculations of the experts, to drill to a depth of 3000 metres now takes two to three months, the next 1000 metres takes three to four months, and the next 500 metres takes ten months.

in practice. Thus the problem of constructing superconductors which transmit electricity over long distances without loss has been solved. However, additional expenses arising from the use of these materials (in their present variant) exceed the saving made. The total level of expenditure also limits the use of the highly efficient (hydrogen-oxygen) fuel element, of foodstuffs produced chemically, and of other scientific discoveries. There is also great scope for reducing the cost and increasing the use of atomic energy.

On a long-term perspective the scientific solution of the problem of thermo-nuclear synthesis will not only provide all people for centuries to come with power resources, but will create a practical basis for the transformation of nature (climate, river flow, etc.) for the benefit of mankind.

Of course, the criterion of economic efficiency in the development of the exact sciences cannot have a universal value; it principally affects the choice of the best of several alternatives when the general theoretical aspect has already been solved. One can hardly speak of criteria of economic efficiency in relation to the working out of the fundamental theoretical principles of science, or of its abstract methodological principles.

We can formulate three basic aspects of the theory and practice of comprehensive socialist development which require study and development in connection with further scientific and technological progress. These are:

(1) Changes in the proportions between final and initial production, resulting from further scientific knowledge of the forces and materials of nature and a fuller use of natural wealth and the substances extracted from nature. These lead to higher rates of reproduction and new intersector proportions: a different optimal relationship between the rates of development of the mining, agricultural and processing sectors, a choice of the optimum trend in the development of more promising and feasible types of production. This results in a change in the structure of the material economic balance and in new estimates of the efficiency of capital investment and its distribution.

(2) Changes in proportions between labour and natural substances, the wider use of natural factors to increase the productivity of social labour; changes in the distribution and use of labour and labour resources of society.

(3) Acceleration of the process of production and circulation and a change in the relation between them.

An uninterrupted increase in the level of material welfare and spiritual development of each member of socialist society, both for the people of today and for future generations, makes it essential to consider the economic aspects of all problems connected with the increase of natural resources and their fuller use, their transformation in the shortest possible time into products with the maximum possible usefulness.

In other words, efficiency is determined by the ratio of the amount of raw material to its usefulness and by the rate of transformation into the final product. Essentially this product is necessary for reproduction of the working force, and under socialism it is inseparable from the conditions for the all-round development of man.

2. EFFICIENCY IN THE USE OF NATURAL RESOURCES

We can distinguish between two forms of natural resources: (*a*) the forces of nature, and (*b*) the matter of nature. The first are used to obtain all forms of energy, e.g. wind and water power, solar energy and thermonuclear energy of the future.

These forms of energy do not 'go into' the final product—they are used up in the production process; but the value of the energy is transferred to the final product. Energy is used for the rapid transformation of raw material into the final product with definite physico-chemical and biological properties required by society. Such a basic distinction between the forces of nature and the raw material resources, which are the initial sub-strata of the material wealth, is important in establishing the proportions in which these two initial forms of natural wealth should be used, and thus for the direction of scientific research in the development of science, and for ensuring the unity and connections between power and the raw materials balance.

The problem is that the raw material of many classical forms of energy resources (basically organic substances) can also be used as material for creating final products. This applies not only to wood, which is to a large extent burnt even today, but also to such minerals as oil, natural gas and coal. The relation between mass (weight) and energy in these forms of energy differs completely. Hence the search to raise the proportion of total energy supplies which are of the most economical form, i.e. have the largest mass of energy relative to the mass of initial substance.

Labour consumption on obtaining energy today comprises almost 60 per cent of all labour consumption in the extraction industries. Of the total weight extracted today in industrially developed countries roughly half goes on fuel and in a number of countries the transportation of fuel accounts for 40–45 per cent of all freight.

At the same time, the potential energy directly contained in many natural forces (which cannot be used as raw material) is hardly used; for example, the plasma of the earth's upper crust, solar energy, the tides, and so on. Of the direct forms of energy, the force of natural waterfalls (hydraulic energy) is comparatively more widely used in certain countries (especially in the U.S.S.R. and the U.S.A.), although even so hydro-energy accounted for only 2 per cent of the world's total energy consumption in 1960.†

The use of direct natural forces for energy needs is restricted in many cases not by the scientific or technological possibilities, but by the economic limits, and primarily by the large capital capacity, the need for large investment over a long period of time compared with the use of traditional energy sources.

In the long run the amount of raw material resources will grow, not only because of increased extraction, but also as a result of the release of considerable material means used as energy sources. To achieve this further scientific research is required in physics (the use of atomic energy, the control of thermonuclear synthesis, and so on), in chemistry (photosynthesis, the creation of a fuel element, and so on), in geology (reaching the earth's upper crust), in biology and other fields. Given the varying degrees of durability of the use of different forms of direct natural forces, it is already important today to determine the economic criterion for efficient use of power.

In addition to this change in sources of energy a no less important problem in the next ten years is the fuller use of the potentialities of traditional energy resources. Today less than 2000 calories of each ton of potential energy of 7000 calories is usefully used; the balance is irretrievably lost. The total efficiency of energy resources in the world economy is just over 25 per cent, and in the U.S.S.R. it is today about 30 per cent.

There are good grounds for suggesting that in the foreseeable future the efficiency factor will reach 50 per cent, which is equivalent (on the scale of fuel extraction in the U.S.S.R. in 1963) to an increase in output of more than 500 m. tons of fuel, and saving of labour of 1,200,000 workers. It should be mentioned that it took a century (from 1860 to 1960) to increase the efficiency in the world economy from 10·4 to 26 per cent.

The increase in the efficiency factor to 50 per cent will not only be facilitated by a change in the structure of energy resources, but also by basically new methods of energy transformation, for example, the construction of a magnetic hydrodynamic generator, which directly con-

† In certain economically underdeveloped countries the long-term domination by monopoly capital led to the extravagant use of material resources. According to the data of the Indian scientist Homi Bhaba, in India 75 per cent of energy (in the form of heat, power, traction and light) was produced by burning cow dung. In India in 1951 224 m. tons of dry cow dung was burnt as fuel, and this is equivalent in heat production to the total annual extraction of coal in the Ruhr. This is a huge loss to agriculture (depriving it of fertilizer), sharply restricts the productive resources of the country, and keeps the standard of living of the people at an impoverished level. In pre-revolutionary Russia more than 60 per cent of energy (not counting live traction power) was produced by burning wood in furnaces.

verts fuel into electricity without a motor. Here the efficiency is twice as high as usual.†

Higher efficiency is obtained in electrochemistry by the creation of a fuel element or current source for which the chemical energy is converted directly into electricity. This is obviously a matter for the future. The same applies to transistor quantum generators with an efficiency factor approaching 100 per cent.

The limit to the amount of the final product is the amount extracted from nature (or produced in agriculture). This means that the theoretical limit to the material index (the ratio of the weight of the final to the initial product) is unity. But it does not follow from this that the social usefulness of the final product is directly proportional to the product of the growth in the initial product and the material index. It is also necessary to take into account improvements in the use value of each unit of the final product, its capacity for satisfying the ever growing social needs by increases in reliability, durability, quality, etc.

The 'scissors' between the initial product, extracted from nature and the final product will also be reduced by further knowledge of the properties of matter, the transformation and fuller use of these properties in the course of processing.

Together with the wider uses of many kinds of natural resources which are now burnt, the possibility of making better use of extractable raw materials is constantly growing. Today only part of the raw material is usable in the production of the final product; a large proportion is irretrievably lost as waste or is used in a repeated cycle with additional expenditure of labour. For example, only 35–40 per cent of the initial weight of iron ore, one of the basic forms of mineral raw material, enters into the final product.‡ The remainder is lost or wasted in various ways. The utilization efficiency factor of plastics is about 92–95 per cent. However, they are still expensive, and although they can successfully replace certain non-ferrous metals they are hardly competitive with iron and steel. In the case of iron ore, developments in physics and chemistry will create vast new possibilities for the more efficient use of the ore.

Huge reserves of increased production at lower cost lie in the use of many forms of vegetable raw material, particularly wood. By comparison with the pre-revolutionary period the efficient use of wood in the U.S.S.R. has grown noticeably. With a fuller use of the raw material

† When discussing the social usefulness of energy, its efficiency, one must mention the idea of creating an artificial biological muscular motor, i.e. a controllable muscle with efficiency several times higher than a machine motor, and also the experiments with biological electricity (produced by different bacteria).

‡ The slagheaps of the future will be a universal material for the construction of dams, reservoirs, elevators, silos, bridges, for the manufacture of decorative panels as a substitute for marble, granite, and so on.

the volume of wood which can at present be produced will provide an increase in the final product of not less than 2·5 to three times in physical weight and four to five times in use value.

A sharp increase in the efficient use of wood is a very important factor in forest protection and reproduction, affecting soil fertility, navigability of rivers and so on; and, like all plant life, forests participate in the conversion of solar light energy into chemical energy (photosynthesis), guaranteeing biological life. As yet the conversion of primary solar energy into chemical energy and the creation of organic substances are not part of the productive activity of man. The scientific discovery of the secret of photosynthesis will in the distant future provide for the 'extraction' of chemical or electrical energy direct from the sun. The possibility of using this discovery (like any other) in industry will depend on the degree of savings such extraction will ensure.

Forest riches, like other forms of plant life are (technically speaking) the most accessible on the earth's surface to direct consumption, and so have been destroyed steadily over the course of centuries.

Meanwhile, the huge biological resources of the world's oceans, accessible only at a certain level of technical civilization, at present remain almost untapped. Although the nutritional resources of the ocean are four times larger than those of the land, today only one per cent of the food products (calculated in calories) which are consumed by the world's population is satisfied by means of the biological resources of the ocean. Mineral resources hidden in the depths of the ocean too (oil, ore, magnesium, bromine, gold, silver, radium, uranium, etc.) are used only in very small quantities.

The problem of using natural resources more fully and efficiently, as one of the important factors of the economy of social labour, has a direct relation to the establishment of a long-term model of the final product. This question cannot be ignored in seeking the optimal variant of the proportions of the processing industries, and also of the best material composition of the initial products, taking into account their use properties and the reduction in the time required to transform the initial into the final product. A long-term model of reproduction worked out in this way reveals a whole system of proportions, based on the maximum results with the minimum expenditures.

3. THE PROCESSING OF RAW MATERIALS

In each sector taken separately and, even more so, in each separate enterprise, the share of expenditure on material increases as a consequence of the further division of labour and strengthening of the material connection arising from the development of new sectors and enterprises manufacturing parts and semi-finished goods on a large scale. As we know, this tendency of technical progress to increase the proportion of material costs and to reduce that of labour costs reflects the growth of the productivity of social labour, the increase in the organic composition of expenditure (and under capitalism the organic composition of capital).

We have seen from the development of the natural sciences that fuller use of the materials extracted from nature, the conversion of all, or almost all, the initial into the final product and an increase in the social usefulness of each unit of the final product require an increased amount of labour to process what was previously regarded as waste, and often also to improve the use property of the product. Even now, to adapt raw materials for the needs of society a great amount of labour is required, but the conversion of a larger proportion of this raw material into the final product and the increase in its use value by means of processing outstrip the growth of labour consumption calculated per unit of initial raw material. This means that the labour consumption per unit of social usefulness of a product is considerably reduced. The increase in the use values of the final product will continue to outstrip the increased labour consumption. Theoretically it is possible to triple the volume of the final product of many forms of raw minerals and fuel with an efficiency of 0·3–0·4. The increase in labour consumption will be much less. However, the total change in labour consumption will outstrip the increase in the primary raw materials which can be extracted.

A natural substance is a pre-requisite for the creation by the activity of labour of the variety of use values which determine in the aggregate the material resources of society and the national wealth.

'Being an activity intended to adapt materials to this or that purpose [labour] requires matter as a prerequisite. In different use values the proportion between labour and raw material varies greatly, but use value always has a natural substratum. Labour, as an activity, directed to the adaptation of raw material in one form or other, is a natural condition of human existence, a condition of exchange of matter between man and nature, independent of all social forms.' †

If we analyse the possibilities of development of the productive forces, starting from those afforded by progress in the natural sciences, we can assert that the proportion of the value of the final product which is made up by expenditure on processing and treating primary materials will increase at the cost of a relative reduction in the expenditure on their extraction. This hypothesis is justified and is supported both by an ex-

† K. Marx, *A Contribution to the Critique of Political Economy*, N. Stone (Ed.) (Chicago, 1904), p. 33.

amination of the corresponding dynamic series of the economic development of the U.S.S.R. over almost fifty years† and by long-term data on the development of other countries.

In the long-term the total labour consumption will increase principally in the processing industries and in the intermediate sectors, where primary raw materials are transformed into the desired final product.‡

This is true not only of mineral-processing industries, but also of those which process (and reprocess) vegetable and animal materials: the food industry and several light industries. In fact, the coefficient which characterizes the ratio of the final to the initial product produced from agricultural raw material is as high as 0·8–0·9.

As technology and culture develop and the standard of living of the people improves the manufacture of food products is brought to a point where they are almost completely ready to eat. This determines the establishment and development of the food industry, and the expansion of the degree of preparation of food products, canning, confectionery, etc. The labour consumption increases, but this is more than compensated for by the much greater saving in domestic preparation of food (the difference is four- to five-fold).

This process of complete preparation also applies to light industry. The development of sewn-wear, knit-wear and habadashery industries needs a considerable amount of labour, but simultaneously releases a very much larger amount of the labour which was uneconomically used in sewing, knitting and making articles by hand.

Calculated per unit of use value, the value is reduced, but the ratio of the labour to the materials changes in the case given to the advantage of the social expenditure of labour.

The size of the increase in the total expenditure and total capital investment calculated per unit of raw material for its complete use (its conversion into the final product) has a strictly defined optimum. The difference in these additional expenditures must be less than the costs (including capital investment) required to extract and transport the equivalent volume of raw material. The ratio between these quantities reflects the increased productivity of social labour on the scale of the whole economy. It is accompanied by a change in the distribution of

† See 'Extensive Socialist Reproduction and the Economic Balance', *Izd. vo Mysl'*, 1964, p. 40.

‡ While the development of the processing industries depends on the amount of extracted raw materials and energy resources and their use, the extraction of these resources depends greatly on the processing industries producing improved equipment (durable and ultra-durable materials). For example, the direct transformation of heat into electricity requires materials which are heat resistant up to 2500–3000 °C.; and the rapid progress made in motor construction is related to the durability and heat resistance of materials.

labour and of the means of production between industries and between the different economic regions.

In the longer run, a radical change in the ratio between labour and raw materials appears with the development of the mass industrial manufacture of food products, such as the products of synthetic chemicals. We have the picture, as yet improbable, of the disappearance of agriculture in the very distant future. This means that the most important social and economic problems of the inter-relation of town and country will disappear; the huge mass of labour now employed in the production of raw materials and final food products will be released. The productivity of social labour will be increased many times.

4. REDUCTION IN PRODUCTION AND CIRCULATION TIME

Scientific and technological progress in its turn directly affects the production time; the length of the working period and the time required for the influence of natural processes on production. In the case of the working period, two contradictory tendencies can be observed. It decreases under the influence of a reduction in, for example, the production phase of electrical energy, smelting (the direct restoration of iron from ore), the manufacture of cloth (non-woven materials) and so on. At the same time increased quality, durability and reliability often require an increased working period, especially when the product is carried to the stage where it is ready for use. The increase in the proportion of machines and other precise mechanical engineering devices, the manufacture of which requires a great amount of skilled labour, operates in the same direction. However, intensification and reduction of the production phase speeds up the processing and reprocessing of the product. With a given level of technology and skill, there is a strictly defined optimum reflecting the relation between the increase in the rate of production and the increase in quality.

The very limited data which exist about the dynamics of the work period provide evidence of a notable acceleration in the U.S.S.R. over the last 20–30 years in the smelting and processing of metals, the production of cement, the construction of buildings, etc.

In the extraction industries bore-hole drilling, mine-working and so on have speeded up. The time required for the production of many articles of consumption, especially the baking of bread, the preparation of leather and sewing of footwear, has been considerably reduced. Despite the different factors influencing the production period, the tendency towards a systematic reduction is undoubtedly the dominant one.

The reduction in the length of time needed to produce many products is greatly helped by the fact that less time is required for natural processes to act. For example, the development of the chemical industry, especially petro-chemicals, and the increased use of chemical processes in many industries, has contributed greatly to the reduction of production time. With the wide use of modern methods (electricity, ultrasonics, and so on) the drying of wood and many other materials is done much quicker. Plastics can be produced much faster than the metal, wood and building materials for which they are a substitute.

The effect of the reduction in both the components of the time required for production is an increase in the specific weight of the work period, i.e. in the active influence of labour on the object of labour with a more efficient use of equipment.

Scientific and technological progress affects circulation time at least as much as (and possibly even more than) production time. Circulation time (including the length of production time in the sphere of circulation and transport) considerably exceeds production time. This applies to almost all forms of fuel (especially coal and wood), cement, metals and metalware (from the extraction and transportation of the ore to the production and delivery to the region where the machines are to be used). Seasonal factors in agricultural production necessitate the lengthy storage of many foodstuffs and raw materials.

Circulation time, and especially the time during which the product is being transported, depends, as we know, on the location of the productive forces, the distance between the producer and the consumer, traffic speed, and the number of stages through which the good passes.

Further specialization of production and division of labour, subdivision of the manufacture of parts and semi-finished goods, the allocation of casting, tool-making and repair work to independent enterprises and industries—all increase the distance between the separate stages of the productive process. At the same time, freight transport of parts, semi-manufactures and so on is done on a more co-operative basis. Specialization produces an increase in circulation time with a reduction in production time by the rational division of labour. This is one of the many factors in the effect of scientific progress on circulation time. One must also take into account the continual reverse tendency towards a reduction in circulation time due to changes in the composition of energy and raw materials, the development of pipelines and electrification, and of electronics, the reduction in size of many means of production, the increased nutritive properties of foodstuffs, the greater production of egg and milk powder concentrates, and other factors.

The change in the structure of the fuel balance: the increased proportion of liquid and gaseous fuel, is accompanied by the development of pipelines which increase the speed of transportation many times in comparison with rail or water transport.† Changes in the outlook for energy resources together with the intensified use of direct natural forces, the creation of fuel elements, the increased role of atomic energy, will contribute to a reduced need for fuel transport.

Transportation of certain types of raw material is even now interlaced with production processes. Thus, pipelines are used not only for transportation of wood, but also for hydrolysis. The effect of natural processes upon the manufacture of products in some cases takes place simultaneously with its transportation (dyeing, etc.). Classical political economy considered (and it was correct at that time) that production and circulation (transportation) processes were separated in time, and that in transportation the use value of the goods being transported did not alter. Scientific and technical progress have brought about many changes in earlier economic laws connected with the period of production and circulation—the production cycle.

At present, fuel transportation charges comprise one of the main items determining the cost of power generation. Further rapid development of electrical energy production on the basis of local resources, long distance transmission and creation of a single high-voltage transmission network will considerably reduce the circulation period of power production. Generation and consumption of electrical power almost coincide in time. When the problem of using superconductors for long distance transmission of electricity without cables has been solved, the concept of energy circulation time will change radically.

The perspective of thermo-nuclear synthesis control, the generation of enormous power out of minute matter, will clearly eliminate the need for transporting fuel. Calorific value per unit weight of thermo-nuclear fuel is about one million times greater than that of ordinary fuel. Deep and extra-deep boring will reveal vast natural power and mineral resources in places where they are not at present extracted and to where fuel and raw materials have to be transported from great distances. Many types of resources will become available locally, and this will reduce the need for transport and improve the circulation time.

The processing of agricultural products is shared by various industries; the production stages from the growing of the raw material to the output of the finished product are interrupted and are separated by great distances. The problems of territorial remoteness and the dividing up of a single production process are overcome by transporting raw materials, semi-manufactures, etc. The circulation time here is exceptionally large.

---

† The role of pipelines is not restricted to the conveyance of liquids and gases. In the distant future it may be possible to transport solids by pipeline. The development of pneumatic techniques will enable mainline hydraulic pipelines to be used to send solids across very great distances.

In the manufacture of a similar chemical substitute continuity of production within the petro-chemical combine is achieved; many stages of
circulation are unnecessary, there is less dependence on transport for the
different production stages.

The development of electronics, the reduction in size (miniaturization)
of equipment and the increased usefulness of each unit of weight and
volume of materials reduce the influence of the transport operation on
the unit use value. Achieving maximum usefulness from minimum material, we can directly affect the size of the transport operation.

The analysis of the effect of the progress of the natural sciences on the
production and circulation time leads to the conclusion that in the future
the circulation time will be greatly reduced, and will fall relative to the
production time.

ON THE POSSIBILITY OF
CONSTRUCTING A MODEL OF THE
TRANSITION TO SOCIALISM
IN ITALY

ANTONIO PESENTI

I. TYPES OF PLANNING

The subject may seem somewhat strange—rather like a discussion on the sex of angels transposed into a modern key. But the fact remains that in Italy the non-socialist Left, to justify its refusal to unite with the more advanced sector of the socialist front, resorts not only to the usual ideological objections, but also to the plea that the Communists cannot produce any practical 'growth model' that might represent an alternative to the existing plan and would modify it by degrees but not impair the smooth functioning of the system now governing the process of reproduction.

This line of argument, which is undoubtedly just a political pretext, relies on the ideology of the 'growth model', which in our day has become a veritable myth, especially in petit-bourgeois minds. I have no intention of humouring this myth, but it does answer an objective requirement, especially for the middle strata of society, who want every programme of structural reform to proceed by successive stages, each of which must be reasonably stable and functional.

I would like to say at once that I have no intention of discussing whether it is possible to devise abstract models of an Italian 'transition to socialism', as an idealistic variant of the growth model ideology would require. Any number of models of this kind could be constructed, but they would serve no purpose. Reality with all its complexities and its own developments would undertake to destroy them. But even if we wanted to construct a properly realistic model of an 'Italian transition to socialism', we should find ourselves faced with insuperable difficulties. In a situation of intense class struggle, with its revolutionary desire to transform the whole structure of society in accordance with socialist principles, successive phases of political and economic stability are created, each of which lasts only a short time. Even if each of these phases represents a step in the same direction and a gradual transition to socialism, the

various functional relationships and the individual parameters are continually changing in a way which is very difficult to foresee. By its very
nature the political struggle is free and creative, and it cannot be reduced
to schemes amounting to anything more than indications of what is
possible and how coherent the programme is.

There have been several attempts in Italy to formulate 'econometric
models' for development, based both on overall programmes and on
schemes for individual sectors. The Pieraccini Plan for the years 1966–70,
which has not yet been debated or approved by Parliament is based upon
an econometric model. Previously, though with less econometric precision, attempts had been made to devise a pattern of development on
the basis of the so-called Vanoni Plan of 1955.

The Vanoni Plan really consisted of extrapolations of existing trends;
it was, in other words, a kind of co-ordinated assemblage of foreseeable
data, which did not imply that the objectives of economic policy would
be transformed by the plan into binding decisions. It might seem that the
Pieraccini Plan is something more than a simple projection of existing
trends—since it is based on quantitative hypotheses drawn from reality,
and sets more exact aims to which development must be adapted. But
even this is not sufficient since it does not provide for any *qualitative* or
structural changes in the existing functional relationships. In other words,
the objectives are not transformed into binding obligations.

Experience ought to have taught us that without an analysis and an
identification of the functional relationships and of their qualitative
variations, whether spontaneous or due to government intervention, it is
not possible to construct a realistic model, that is to say one which can
form a basis for decisions and has some analogy with actual developments. The same might be said of the patterns for individual sectors,
even when they appear to be less complex; and of regional projects like
the 'Green Plan for Agriculture' or the 'Plan for the Industrialization
of Southern Italy'.

Marxist criticism has already pointed out that this experiment proves
the truth of the Marxist principle that the economy consists of relationships between men, and not between things; that economic development
is not a phenomenon of quantitative growth, but one of continual
qualitative modifications. The latter must always be borne in mind; it is
impossible to establish quantitative targets by isolating the process of
development from the institutional framework within which it takes
place. The Marxist critical analysis has shown that even interventions on
the part of monopolistic state capitalism in its various forms, if they do
not impose actual qualitative restrictions implying modifications of the
structure, merely stimulate the process of capitalistic reproduction as
it exists in the present imperialistic phase, and thus heighten those

cumulative effects which are characteristic of this process. Such interventions strengthen the functional relationships inherent in the monopolistic structure, as well as the expansion and power of monopolistic capital, and by aggravating the existing contradictions they upset all the abstract quantitative forecasts of the 'planners'.

2. CHANGES IN FUNCTIONAL RELATIONSHIPS

The economic programme of a revolutionary party is of course always obliged to set certain quantitative targets, but it must be stressed that such targets are achievable only if they are accompanied by far-reaching qualitative modifications of economic relationships. This is inevitable because it has to satisfy the demand, so insistent in various strata of society and especially among the bourgeois middle classes, for a form of economic development based on an economic balance which is dynamic, but will consist of several stages each of which must have a reasonable stability. When occasion arises, the problem is naturally solved by political action. But is it possible, without attempting to construct a complete model, to evolve some scheme, however summary, having an economic or econometric character?

It seems to me that we ought to start from the functional relationships which explain the type of development most suitable for the more advanced capitalistic societies, and especially for those, like the Italian, in which structural modifications are still in progress, in the sense that capitalistic relationships are still evolving towards their most mature forms. It is well known that in such societies, which from the quantitative point of view are not yet 'mature', the annual rate of increase of the national income may be high, while the inequalities arising during the process of growth may be acute. In Italy, for example, between 1949 and 1963, the annual growth-rate of national product was 6·3 per cent. There were also large changes in the contributions of the different production sectors: the percentage of the industrial sector rose from 50 per cent of the net product in 1920–38 to 64 per cent in 1949–63, of which 49 per cent was in the manufacturing sector. The share of the agricultural sector declined from 18·9 per cent in 1920–38 to 7·9 in 1949–63. Agriculture also lost about three million units of labour, whereas manufacturing industry increased its labour force by about 1,300,000 units, the total active population remaining approximately stationary during the period 1951–61. Production per worker between 1949 and 1963 thus increased by 6·3 per cent in agriculture, 7·2 per cent in industry and 6·6 per cent overall. These quantitative results, which are a concise expression of a rapid process of development, were achieved, as is well known, owing to the existence of special conditions favourable to capitalistic development, namely the presence of large numbers of unemployed or under-employed workers, low wages, which increased at a rate lower than the increase in productivity, and a growing demand, stimulated by government spending and by the expansion of the capitalistic market both at home and abroad.

A development of this kind naturally strengthened the capitalistic relationships, with serious social consequences such as the depopulation of the poorest areas of peasant production leading to economic and social impoverishment and mass emigration of labour.

At the same time the accumulation of huge reserves in the hands of the dominant monopolistic groups boosted the influx of capital into the less monopolistic sectors (agriculture, food and textile industries, etc.), and thus accelerated the process of concentration. This in turn widened the gap between the rates of development in the various regions and social classes, and revealed the increasing inadequacy, both absolute and relative, of the education system and general infrastructure.

The fact that Italy is still being changed from an agrarian-industrial into an industrial country involves enormous social expenditure. This transformation is being undertaken in a world that is not standing still: the rate of technological progress in the more advanced economies increases rapidly every year, and the process of concentration, not only of financial resources, but also of production, is likewise advancing rapidly. But in Italy a backlog of a hundred years has to be made good, and this is also characterized by an accentuation of the 'dualism' between North and South.

The objective requirements of such a situation may be summarized as follows: (a) A need for a vigorous and rapid expansion of public spending in order to modernize the infrastructure; not only soil reclamation, the road system, ports, etc., but also education and health services, economic and social organization, scientific research, etc. (b) The second essential is the achievement of full employment of the labour force. This is not only a 'political' aim, in harmony with the fundamental demand of the workers as stated in the Constitution, but an economic objective which in Italy is an extremely complex matter, since there exists not only the 'visible' unemployment, but, as is well known, a high rate of concealed unemployment or under-employment. Many of the workers lack qualifications and experience and consequently their productivity is low. A further large percentage are employed in sectors such as agriculture and retail trading, where the output per man-hour is extremely low. It therefore becomes necessary to employ large numbers of unskilled workers, to redirect labour to more productive sectors, and to train the new or existing members of the labour force who may be capable of achieving promotion to a higher grade. This problem, however, is not insoluble and is in keeping with the requirements listed under (*a*), since public expenditure on economic infrastructures makes it possible to absorb large numbers of unskilled workers immediately. (*c*) In the private sector of the economy it is generally recognized that there are two top priorities—an increase in agricultural production per head and a reduction of the social costs of distribution. (*d*) Lastly, another objective on which all are agreed is the ensuring of a more stable rate of growth in the industrial sector.

Every plan claims to have found solutions for these problems, even if the quantitative targets and the economic policies differ. Heavy public expenditure with a view to increasing the external economies by developing the infrastructures is generally admitted to be necessary, even if many people prefer to spread the programme over a period in order to avoid putting too heavy a burden on the State budget by incurring expenses considered to be excessive in relation to private spending and the national income. There is also the problem that these sectors tend to have very high capital–output ratios.

However, the general unanimity regarding the need to bring the infrastructures into line with the demands of the modern economic structure is due to the fact that *in themselves* economic intervention and investment in the infrastructure sector do not properly belong to the field of 'structural reforms'. In other words, they can *help*, but do not change, the functional relationships governing the economic development of a system. If we want to make them help to consolidate *new* structural relationships, the system of production must be changed. From the economic viewpoint, this also applies to the problem of school reform. It is true that in this sector there is a lot of talk about 'reforming the schools', and it is likewise true that in this sector class antagonisms are considerable and acute. But the word 'reform' undoubtedly has a concrete political connotation when it is used to denote a renewal of the scholastic structure on democratic lines as well as a renewal of the trends in cultural and technical training, though from the economic point of view technical and professional training forms part of the system.

3. REFORM OF AGRICULTURE AND INDUSTRY

When we come to the aims listed under (*c*) and (*d*), however, we find ourselves involved in the class struggle, and here basic reforms of the functional relationships are being discussed or fought for.

For the Italian economy a problem of capital importance is an increase in the supply of agricultural products and a reduction of unit costs, or in other words a renewal of agriculture by means of a cultural transformation and an increase in the productivity of labour. But how can this quantitative result be achieved? Certainly not within the framework of the present functional structures, a fact of which all the political parties are well aware. A scheme for capitalistic development, coupled with the elimination of production relationships based on outdated forms (such as métayage, various forms of profit-sharing leaseholds or large estates) and of the gradual elimination of peasant holdings and their replacement by capitalistic agricultural undertakings, has not been chosen by the dominant class because it would have involved heavy social costs and would also have caused a swing to the Left among the peasant masses. Instead, an intermediate solution has been chosen: with the aid of State subsidies and the expenditure of vast sums, attempts have been made to support the medium-sized peasant and middle-class holdings and to eliminate the more backward structures, while at the same time encouraging improvements in agricultural methods. Such a policy can only attentuate and spread over a longer period of time the process of destruction of peasant undertakings. It cannot change the type of development, which is more and more dominated by financial capital. In fact, when inserted into the framework of the general economic system, a policy of this kind is powerless to prevent the gradual subjection of agriculture to monopolistic control, as regards both input of capital goods, needed for agricultural production, and the output for the process of maintenance, sales organization and the industrial processing of agricultural products.

The Communist programme aims at changing the social relationships existing in country areas and advocates an overall agrarian reform, the watchword of which will be: give the land to the peasants. This presupposes the abolition of outdated pre-capitalistic systems and the extension and strengthening of a new kind of peasant ownership. Freed from exploitation by financial capital, aided by simultaneous reforms in the industrial sector and encouraged to group themselves into associations of the co-operative type, which they approve of and want, the peasants would be in a position to create large agricultural undertakings embracing the whole vast arc of productive agricultural activity, from the purchase of the equipment needed to the industrial processing of agricultural products. In this way it should be possible to create new social conditions and bring about a much-needed increase in productivity.

Corresponding suggestions have been made for the distributive sector, in which productivity is also very low. Here too, in order to counter the penetration of monopolistic capital by way of the big stores, forms of association are advocated which would attenuate and render less burdensome the necessary transfer of productive forces to productive sectors. The fundamental question is, how to alter the functional relationships in the field of the basic productive sector, i.e. industry? It is here that there comes into play the fundamental process of accumulation which is responsible for the well-known cumulative effects.† These heighten the economic and social contrasts and are recognized by everybody, while all the political parties agree in demanding measures which will guarantee a smoother economic development. But those who do not wish to alter the existing economic system are trying to deal with the effects instead of tackling the causes, and as we have said, the programmes they put forward fail to take into account the qualitative changes which are indispensable if we want to ensure a regular, more stable economic development.

Viewed in the abstract and within the limitations imposed by the provisions of the republican Constitution, it would not be a difficult task to alter the above-mentioned functional relationships. There is already a large amount of State ownership of the means of production in sources of power and in steel, machinery, chemical and other industries, and the activities of this sector could be further co-ordinated and extended. The necessary mechanism also exists for the control of investment and basic price-levels, for the identification and restriction of the process of self-financing and regulation of profits. In all these cases precise proposals for democratic reform have been put forward, with due respect for existing institutions, and these proposals have the approval of the masses. Thus, in this sector too, the programme has been co-ordinated from the political as well as from the economic point of view. The aim is, of course, still full employment, starting from the presumption that trade-union demands stimulate the system and that the independence of trade unions must therefore be guaranteed. It rejects the so-called incomes policy, which in view of the present situation means nothing more than the freezing of wages to the benefit of profits. Moreover, trade-union demands, provided they are restrained by a sense of independent responsibility, cover not only the field of wages, but also the problems of control in the factories and the structure as a whole. In other words, these demands must act as a continual spur to the productive process, aiming at the achievement of a new equilibrium on a higher level.

As regards the specific sectorial, local, qualitative and quantitative targets, the programme envisages an active participation from below; this is the result of a close study of claims, of redevelopment plans in towns, districts, regions, and even on a national level, with the participation of elected bodies—parties, trade unions and economic institutes. It may seem that this method, when co-ordinated on a national basis, might well set impossible targets, but a realization of the possibilities, of the relationship between aims and means, has now been achieved which will forestall or limit any such risk. The starting-point will be the actual situation, and not some abstract hypothesis.

† This problem is discussed in more detail in the author's essay 'Attivita finanziaria e programmmazione' in *Rivista di Diritto Finanziario e Scienza delle Finanze* (March 1967).

If some other type of development is preferred to the existing pattern it will be necessary to break the vicious circle of the present accumulation of capital and replace it by another system of accumulation and distribution of the surplus value created by society.

This other type of accumulation could be achieved by increasing the accumulation of public funds needed to counterbalance the increase in social investments, by encouraging personal savings and by making the accumulation of resources by individual undertakings more uniform. This would naturally imply some form of control over price and profit levels.

The possibility certainly exists in the abstract, but it needs to be made concrete.

In private capitalistic undertakings the volume of production, or supply, and the process of investment, which is the basis of future production and the force underlying overall demand, depend on many parameters, in the first place on the present or hoped-for profit. A *natural and necessary rate of profit* does not exist. If we wish to operate on the basis of a programme or plan of development, in a market which can provide the necessary working capital and credit facilities at a low cost, the rate of profit loses much of its functional value. Of course, from the national point of view, taking the system as a whole, it is necessary to establish an overall rate of necessary accumulation, but within this framework an enterprise may be satisfied with some pre-established rate of profit, even if it is not high. A more uniform rate of profit can be obtained by the method of what I call 'equalization funds' (*casse di conguaglio*).

The Italian Constitution stipulates that private economic initiative shall be free, so long as this initiative is not harmful to the public welfare and does not prejudice the security, liberty and dignity of the individual. As things are at present, a capitalistic enterprise is free to invest its own capital 'how', 'to what extent', 'where' and 'when' it likes. Hitherto, pressure has been brought to bear on such decisions only from outside, indirectly and with the aid of various types of incentives. But any planning that really wants to direct economic development in such a way that economic and social inequalities are reduced or avoided, ought, at all events in the case of large enterprises, to lay down not only where the factory is to be built, which is particularly important in a country like Italy which has to reckon with the dualism between North and South; but also the type of product. In other words, it ought to control investment by a system of official permits and recognize that the policy of indirect incentives and disincentives is inadequate and costly.

New investments financed by issues of new shares and debentures are already subject to official permission. It would merely be a question of strengthening the existing system and making it democratic, instead of bureaucratic. It would not, therefore, be difficult to restrict the freedom of initiative of the big corporations as regards 'where' and 'how' their money should be invested.

It might be more difficult to restrict their liberty with regard to the amount to be invested. In certain circumstances, if it does not think the moment opportune, an enterprise is unwilling to invest its money. Although the procedure would have to be less rigid and would be less efficacious, I still think that it would be economically possible to 'compel' firms to invest, either by substituting public for private enterprise, when the latter is lacking, or else by creating economic conditions of such a kind that the capitalist would have no loopholes, i.e. *he would not be able not to invest*. This, however, would involve a relationship that would not be direct and immediate, as in the previous cases.

4. ACCUMULATION AND GROWTH

Any form of 'transition to socialism', even in a mature country with plenty of modern infrastructures, must presuppose a high level of public expenditure—both current and for investment and transfer purposes—destined to cover the cost of the reforms and the creation of new social and economic structures. Such expenditure is even more essential in a country like Italy, where the overall structure is, as we have already said, quite incapable of meeting the requirements of a modern economy. This requisite, if it is to be satisfied, presupposes a high rate of accumulation and the acquisition by the public administration, by direct means (public savings) or indirectly, of a considerable share in national savings. A high rate of accumulation is also needed to cover the investments necessary in order to increase the overall productivity of the whole economic system.

This high rate must be achieved with due regard for two economico-political limitations. The first is that the so-called 'social' investments in the economic and organizational infrastructure for the most part lead to little or no direct and immediate 'productivity', but to an indirect 'productivity' difficult to estimate, the effects of which are spread over a long period, and for this reason the general ratio of capital to income will at first tend to rise. The second requisite is that democratic planning starting from the bottom, with the participation and approval of the masses, must satisfy the immediate demands of consumers and must be based on complete freedom of the trade unions and not imply a wage-freeze.

It can be argued that the Harrod–Domar model is over-simplified and that it disregards the principle of general economic interdependence and the continual changes in functional relationships. I accept these criticisms if it is a question of establishing a model of economic planning which must be econometrically precise regarding all the economic relationships prevalent in the economic life of an advanced country. Nevertheless, I still think that we can gain from it some idea of the 'potentiality' of a system as a whole, in other words it can show whether or not a programme is feasible.

In Italy, those who agree with these criticisms of the so-called aggregate models are fond of quoting as an example the present Pieraccini Plan, the beginnings of which have already been contradicted by reality. The central nucleus of this plan is the Harrod–Domar equation which, in its simplest formula, $y = \alpha/K$, shows that y, the annual rate of increase of monetary income in a given country is equal to α, the average propensity to save of the people as a whole, divided by K, the capital–income ratio.

If, for example, we want the rate of total annual development to be 5 per cent and the ratio of capital to income is 3, then the amount saved must be equal to 15 per cent of the national income. It is pointed out that the Pieraccini Plan, which is based on its own forecast of an average increase of national income during the five-year period at a rate of 5 per cent per annum (which has not yet been achieved), categorically stipulates a marginal capital–income ratio for productive investments of 3·1. For the so-called social investments, the yield on which is far smaller than that obtained from productive investments, the capital–income ratio has been calculated as 9·36. If we combine these two ratios, we get an overall ratio for the entire Italian economy of 4·76. Consequently, in order to get an annual growth-rate of national income of 5 per cent, the savings of the community would have to be almost 24 per cent of the national income.

Obviously, these figures have not been achieved because they have not been converted into binding obligations. Entrepreneurs have been left free to operate as they choose, and government action, instead of restraining them, has encouraged these reactions, while the whole economic policy has tended to restore the process of capital accumulation desired by dominant monopolistic capital. Nevertheless, as an indication of 'possibility', the argument was, and is, realistic and based on experience. Given the extent of the still unutilized productive forces a growth rate of 5–6 per cent per annum can be achieved.

In the period 1949 to 1963 private consumption accounted for about 60–62 per cent of the national income, public consumption for 11–14 per cent, and investment for 20–26 per cent. 'Savings' amounted to less than the surplus value created, because part of the surplus was absorbed by objectively unproductive consumption or by unproductive categories which live on the surplus created. In industry, in fact, the annual surplus value, according to official statistics, fluctuated around 38–46 per cent of the gross product.)

Within the category of private investment, we find that the figures show a gradual percentage decrease in the sectors of direct production, e.g. agriculture (14 per cent in 1951, 8·47 per cent in 1964), industry (38·55 per cent in 1951, 26·82 per cent in 1964), transport (14·52 per cent in 1951, 13·95 per cent in 1964), while there has been a rise in housing (the percentage has been more than doubled, rising from 16·34 to 36·67) and in other sectors which are not direct producers. Although it is difficult to make a precise estimate, it is reckoned that the capital per unit of labour during the period under review has almost doubled in agriculture and has remained stationary in industry, while in services the index figure has risen from 100 to 153.

With a proper policy to eliminate certain items of luxury consumption, to reduce prices by means of increased productivity, and to achieve a more equitable distribution of income, the flow of money spent on consumption could be directed into other channels, thus effecting a real 'saving'. Moreover, items at present considered as private consumption would become part of public expenditure (education, health, housing in part, etc.). Public consumption, which at present takes 12–13 per cent of gross income, might thus rise to 15 per cent. In fact, by rationalizing the present public expenditure in accordance with schemes resting on a solid foundation, an increase in social expenditure of 3 per cent, in relation to the gross national income, would be sufficient to ensure the execution of the various sectorial plans and reforms.

Naturally, other problems of a financial nature will arise, and these will have to be solved and will involve an increase in public expenditure for transfer of income, e.g. various types of compensation payable in instalments to those who will suffer losses as a result of these reforms.

The ability to allot an average of 25 per cent of the national income to investments should make it possible not only to achieve full employment, but also to budget for an annual growth-rate of income of around 5 per cent per annum. It will be necessary to regulate and direct investment, and to this the objection might be raised that it would 'discourage' the formation of savings, which in a capitalistic country tend to become concentrated in the retained reserves of firms. But if we bear in mind what has been said above, the increase in public saving—which at present represents from 3·5 to 4·5 per cent of national income and 25 per cent of national savings—and also in personal savings might compensate for any reductions in saving by entrepreneurs.

Social investments have never reached 10 per cent of the national income. Here too, there ought to be a real increase, and a transfer from the private to the public sector. A real increase of such investments will be necessary to cover the above-mentioned expenditure on improving the infrastructure and to increase, with public help and the participation of the public administration, the investments in agriculture, in public and private building and in industry itself.

Our studies reveal the 'possibilities' of the system as a whole and tend to show that full employment of the labour force can be achieved together with a drastic reduction in emigration abroad of the most active and efficient elements, and the absorption of unemployment even among unskilled workers who will be able to find jobs more easily in public works, while the transfer of workers from unproductive to productive sectors and a greater productivity thanks to the better training of the younger elements will likewise be guaranteed.

We also believe that it is possible, by means of taxation and other measures (e.g. contractual saving), to increase voluntary personal savings. These, given a change in the distribution of the savings of undertakings by means of 'equalization funds' or through other financial institutions, should acquire greater importance and serve to restore the necessary equilibrium. This is feasible, though it is recognized that the 'propensity to voluntary saving' may tend to diminish when there is a more balanced distribution of income accompanied by an increase in social security.

Naturally, these considerations of a general character, showing that an overall programme of reforms in the socialist sense can be realized, also leave unsolved the specific problems of a rational distribution and utilization of resources, according to territorial areas and sectors of production. But these problems could also be solved if the political will to solve them were there, together with participation from below.

5. ECONOMIC ANALYSIS AND CLASS STRUGGLE

It is not possible to tie reality down, even if a central organization exists which controls all the national resources and can endeavour to utilize them in the most productive and rational way in the interests of the community at large, starting from the principle that production must serve mankind, and not mankind production, and that the aim of social productive activity is to ensure the satisfaction of all demands, of all the needs of human society, and not the realization of the biggest profit possible.

In a system under which most of the productive resources are in the hands of private capitalists and a bitter struggle is being waged to alter the basic functional relationships, accompanied by the consequent subjective economic reactions, it is pointless to make quantitatively exact forecasts of 'parameters', 'co-efficients', or other relationships.

In such a situation, we have already gone a long way if we can demonstrate the logical coherence of the relationships we wish to maintain and the economic possibility of realizing the aims we have set. Their realization, however, will be the fruit of a class struggle, or of a political struggle, which amounts to the same thing, and this, although it may draw nourishment from economic analyses of this kind, is nevertheless quite independent of them.

PART IV

ECONOMIC GROWTH IN HISTORICAL PERSPECTIVE

WORLD ECONOMY IN
TRANSITION (1850–2060)

SURENDRA J. PATEL†

It is now nearly two centuries since the publication of Adam Smith's *An enquiry into the Nature and Causes of the Wealth of Nations* (1776); and Karl Marx's *Capital* (1867) was published exactly one hundred years ago. In the course of these years, profound changes have taken place in the world economy. Their full significance has rarely been assessed, and their implications barely analysed. The preoccupation of the economist with the contemporary concerns may have been in part responsible for this weakness. And yet there is little doubt that the overall balance-sheet of how the wealth of the nations has expanded could have a considerable relevance to our appreciation of the prospects over the decades to come. The task of drawing up such a balance-sheet is indeed difficult; for there are many entries which form areas of relative darkness, and others which are under dispute as to whether they belong on the debit or the credit side of the ledger.

There are many questions for which it would be helpful to have answers. How great a stride has the world economy taken in the last hundred years? How does it compare with the earlier centuries? What were the overall rates of growth? What are the main features of this economic transition? Do they yield any guide-lines for the future? What prospects can one reasonably expect for the next hundred years? The economists' tools for measuring progress are yet too weak and the content of the future too uncertain to yield much precision in any such exercise. The progress of science may unravel unthought of possibilities. In the process, many new commodities and services may emerge; different ways of satisfying existing or new needs may arise. Man has just taken the first faltering steps towards leaving the age-old bonds of the earth; the strides in space may well open up new dimensions in astro-economics. The image of the future world economy, therefore, cannot but be foggy. And yet, an understanding of the past movement and its implications for the future would seem to be of sufficient significance to hazard guesses, no matter how weak in foundation and approximation to reality they may prove.

† The views expressed herein are personal, and need not be attributed to the organization, the United Nations Conference on Trade and Development in Geneva, of which the author is a staff member.

This study begins with a broad review of the changes in the world economy up to the midpoint of the last century, and then summarizes the main features of the change since then. These indications are then used for outlining the prospects for the next century and analysing their significance. An exercise like this can hardly have precision as its aim. It main purpose is to point out the broad sweep of the movement, rather than measure each step as it was taken.

I. CHANGES UP TO 1850

Over the last 6,000 years of its settled existence, most of mankind has spent most of its active time in making a living—that is, finding food, clothing and shelter. The conquest of the struggle for survival seems to have formed, in one way or another, the core of human endeavour. The most sensitive minds devoted themselves to it. The founders of the world's greatest religions promised to their faithful followers an entry to heaven. Reformers emphasized changing habits of individual behaviour and social institutions. Philosophers and political scientists suggested altering forms of governments. Revolutionaries called for radical changes in the existing balance of social power. In all these speculations, there was always an overriding preoccupation with the promise of an easier economic lot for the average person. The proposed solutions were all designed to procure some kind of an eternal affluence.

The economic historian has no means of measuring the levels of average real income that prevailed in the past. Civilizations rose and fell. Centres of culture and power shifted. Technical and scientific progress continued. Despite all this, the real income of the average citizen in most centres of civilization must have changed but little up to the mid-point of the last century.† According to Professor Kuznets' estimates, only five countries (the United States, Great Britain, Switzerland, Canada and the Netherlands) had attained an average annual per capita income (in 1952–1954 prices) of $200, or slightly higher, by 1850.‡ The average for the whole of North America and Europe could not have been much higher than $150—or only $30 to $50 more than in the poor countries today, or presumably then.§ These five countries together accounted in 185r for around 60 million people and some $12 billion (in 1952–54 prices) worth of output, or much less than what is now produced

---

† J. M. Keynes, 'Economic Possibilities for Our Grandchildren' (1930) in his *Essays in Persuasion* (London, 1931), p. 360; T. W. Schultz, 'Reflection on Poverty within Agriculture' in the *Journal of Political Economy*, Vol. LVIII, No. 1, February, 1950, pp. 7–9; for approximate data, see Colin Clark, in *Review of Economic Progress*, Vol. 1, No. 4, April 1949.

‡ S. S. Kuznets, *Six Lectures on Economic Growth* (Glencoe, 1959), p. 27.

§ See the author's 'Economic Distance between Nations: Its Origin, Measurement and Outlook' in the *Economic Journal*, Vol. LXXIV, March 1964; some of the conclusions in the following section are also based on this study.

in one city, such as London or New York. This difference can hardly be considered major, since requirements for food, clothing and shelter were much higher in colder climates in those areas than in the tropical or semi-tropical climates in the poor countries.

Without claiming much precision, some idea may be given of the order of magnitude of the growth of population and total and per capita real output up to 1850. The world population is estimated to have increased about two and a half times between the year of Christ's birth and 1650—from 200–250 million to some 550 million. It doubled in the next two hundred years and doubled again in the century thereafter.† All in all, a five-fold increase (from 200–250 million to 1171 million) between the beginning of the Christian era and 1850. The growth rate for the whole period was around one per cent per decade—lower for the period up to 1650 and higher thereafter.

Even rough estimates of the growth of total and per capita income are not available. But the magnitude of the change may be suggested by *a priori* reasoning. As pointed out earlier, the average real income in North America and Europe, the most advanced parts of the world economy, was around $150 (in 1952–54 prices) in 1850. This is not much higher than the rock-bottom level necessary for subsistence. One might even suppose that it was as low as only one half this level at the beginning of the Christian era. But since world population increased nearly five-fold, and since per capita output is assumed to have doubled, we can conclude that the total output might have risen some ten-fold, or slightly faster than one per cent per decade; and the growth rate of per capita output—doubling in 18 centuries—would come to about 4 per cent per century, or less than what many countries have recently achieved every year.

The growth rate of per capita income must thus have been negligible for the period as a whole, though there were times of spectacular spurts forwards as well as slides backwards. But throughout this period, the rise in per capita income could not possibly have been steady even at a very modest pace. Let me illustrate it thus: even if per capita income could have risen by a mere one per cent per decade, it could have, if the rate were maintained, increased about seven times in 2,000 years, twenty times in 3,000 years and fifty times in 4,000 years. At that rate, the average real income in Egypt, Sumer or Greece at the height of their civilizations would have been no more than $2 to $5 in present prices—or only one-twentieth to one-fiftieth of what it was around 1850. Human existence in any form would have been simply impossible at that level. The built-in steadiness of economic growth was thus to appear on the world scene mainly after 1850.

† W. S. Woytinsky and E. S. Woytinsky, *World Population and Production* (New York, 1953).

The world economy in the pre-1850 period provided a classic illustration of the model of 'dynamics of political economy'† as elucidated by Ricardo, Malthus and Mill. 'The power of population' marched almost in line with the 'power of production'.‡

2. THE ECONOMIC EXPLOSION SINCE 1850

Into this world of near stagnation, the Industrial Revolution introduced a highly explosive force. Although dated to begin in the last third of the eighteenth century, its impact on raising the level of average living was very small indeed until about the middle of the nineteenth century. Even in Great Britain, the country of its origin, the spread of new techniques was limited mostly to textiles, transport and coal until 1850.

The new techniques were to have a profound influence in raising the average level of living in the industrial countries in the period following 1850. For the purpose of statistical convenience, the industrial countries, as defined here, include the United States, Canada, Australia, New Zealand and the whole of Europe. This is obviously a simplification for hardly any of these countries could really claim this attribute in 1850, and some of them not even by 1960. The economic evolution of these countries since 1850 has a profound significance for any analysis of the future outlook. Let me summarize some of the elements which have a major importance in assessing the future prospects.

(1) The population of these countries rose nearly threefold between 1850 and 1960—from 300 million to 850 million. The increment alone was equal to the entire world population in 1650. The annual growth rate rose from less than 1 per cent per decade in the period preceding 1850 to nearly 1 per cent per year in the subsequent period. Undoubtedly, there was a population explosion. Its growth rate had increased tenfold.

(2) In the same period, the total output of goods and services produced in these countries had expanded over 20 times—from $45 billion (in 1960 prices) in 1850 to $930 billion in 1960. In these 110 years of an intense outburst of economic activity, the industrial countries alone produced over one-third of the entire real income, and two-thirds of the total industrial output generated by the labour of all mankind in the preceding 6,000 years. The economic explosion was indeed much more powerful than the population explosion.

(3) Against the annual expansion of population at under 1 per cent, output increased at 2·8 per cent per year, or nearly three times as fast.

† The phrase was used by John Stuart Mill at the beginning of Book IV, 'Influence of the Progress of Society on Production and Distribution', of his *Principles of Political Economy* (1848).
‡ David Ricardo, *The Principles of Political Economy and Taxation* (Everyman's Library edition), Chapter V.

In consequence, the real level of per capita income rose from an average of about $150 (in 1960 prices) in 1850 to $1,100 in 1960—or sevenfold. This was obviously much larger than in the preceding history. The 'dynamics of political economy' in which the population and output kept pace with each other ceased to apply to these countries almost from the year of the publication of Mill's classic.

(4) Although the impact of the economic explosion was so powerful, the annual growth rate involved was relatively modest compared with recent experience. The total output increased at about 2·8 per cent per year against an annual growth rate of population of under one per cent. The pace of economic growth was three times as fast as that of population. The differential between these two growth rates was responsible for the force of the economic explosion.†

(5) The grouping together of so many diverse countries and looking at only two points of time (1850 and 1960), however, gives a misleading impression of the growth rates. It is well known that all these countries did not begin their development at the same time. As the process of growth spread from its original centre to the other countries, there appears to have been a steady rise in the growth rate of overall and per capita output. The long-term annual per capita growth rate was 1·2 to 1·4 per cent in England and France; 1·6 to 1·8 per cent for Germany, Denmark, Switzerland, U.S. and Canada; 2·1 to 2·8 per cent for Norway, Sweden and Japan; 4 per cent or higher, depending upon the estimator, for the Soviet Union, and as high as 6 per cent and above during the last 15 years for a number of countries both in the East and in the West. The progressive tendency in the per capita growth rate to rise suggests that the latecomers to industrialization appear to have clearly benefited from the accumulated treasure-house of world technology. They could short-circuit the jump from one stage of technical development to another by a massive adaptation of the existing knowledge.

(6) One more facet of the economic 'explosion' may be explored here. It relates to the transformation of output. Up to the Indistrial Revolution, agricultural output accounted for half or more of the total nearly everywhere. Since then, however, its share has continuously fallen—from 50 per cent or more to only about 10 per cent; and that of industries has correspondingly risen from under 20 per cent to about 40 to 50 per cent. The complete reversal of the relative shares of agriculture and industry would thus seem to be the most distinctive feature of economic growth.

† In the essay cited earlier, Keynes had already drawn attention to 'the power of compound interest'. In economic dynamics, the differential between two growth rates is of extreme significance. Thus, although the growth rate of output was only 3 times as high as that of population, per capita income rose over 7 (and not 3 times) in 110 years. If the differential were to remain the same, but if the growth rates were to be 2 per cent for population and 6 per cent for output, per capita output could expand over 45 times in a century.

In the 110 years under consideration, agricultural output in these countries rose four- to five-fold (at 1·4 per cent per year); industrial output on the other hand expanded nearly forty-fold (at 3·5 per cent per year). These relationships seem to suggest that in the process of development, the expansion of agricultural output soon reaches a ceiling beyond which, if continued, it merely generates difficult-to-dispose surpluses.

Within the group broadly classified as 'industry', the output of light industry increased more than twenty times between 1850 and 1960, or approximately at the same annual growth rate as that of total output or the service sector (excluding transport and communications); heavy industry on the other hand expanded over a hundred-fold. As a result, there was a complete reversal of the relative shares of these two in the total industrial output, with the share of heavy industry rising from under one-third to over two-thirds of the total.

3. THE OUTLOOK FOR THE NEXT CENTURY

The image of the world economy a hundred years hence can hardly be determined with any precision. The present generation is not even dimly aware of the shape of things to come. And yet, the review of the past century and some of the pointers for the near future may be used as a basis for an illustrative exercise. The main purpose of any such exercise cannot clearly be to affirm that such and such developments will take place. Economists do not possess Cassandra's gifts of prophecy; and in any case, even Cassandra, owing to her non-fulfilment of reciprocal favours to Apollo, had to be content with never being believed by her contemporaries. But the exploration of the main contours of the probable developments may serve the purpose of indicating, not the final destination but, at least the general direction of economic growth. For the purpose of analysis, countries are grouped into two broad categories: (1) the industrial countries as defined in the preceding section; and (2) the pre-industrial or the developing countries covering the rest of the world.

(1) *Industrial countries*

The average per capita income for this group was $1,100 in 1960. This group consists of two major sub-groups: the OECD countries, or the developed market economies, and the socialist countries in Europe.

(*a*) *The OECD countries.* The plans and programmes for this group expected an annual growth of total income by 4·2 per cent, and of per capita income by over 3 per cent for the twenty years from 1960 to 1980. Recent experience has lent a more optimistic tone to these general targets. No estimates are available for the period after 1980. But let it simply be assumed that the growth will continue, say, at 4·2 per cent per year;

in consequence, the per capita output for the group could increase 19 times between 1960 and 2060—or from \$1,200 to \$23,000 (in 1960 prices) by 2060.

(*b*) *The European socialist countries.* The perspective plans for these countries for 1960 to 1980 envisage an annual growth rate of over 7 per cent for total and 6 per cent for per capita income. At that rate the average income could rise some 3·2 times by 1980—or above the anticipated average level of the OECD countries. No projections have been formally undertaken for the subsequent period, but let it simply be assumed, even as an obvious understatement, that these countries would not plan for attaining by 2060 a per capita income level particularly higher than \$23,000 (in 1960 prices), projected for the OECD countries. In order to achieve this, their annual growth rate of per capita output for the period 1980 to 2060 would have to be under 2·75 per cent, or less than one-half of the expectations for 1960 to 1980.

According to these assumptions, the outline of development in these industrial countries would proceed as follows:

	1850	1960	2060
Population (in million)	300	850	2,400
Income (billion \$ in 1960 prices)	45	930	55,000
Per capita income (1960 \$)	150	1,100	23,000

In the two centuries since 1850, population will have expanded 8 times, per capita real income over 150 times and total income over 1,200 times! For those who would be tempted to dismiss this exercise as an outrage to statistical sanity, let it be remembered that the implicit annual growth rates (1850 to 2060) are: 1 per cent for population, 3·6 per cent for output and 2·6 per cent for per capita output. A century along these lines is already a part of history, and the process is simply being extended for another century at a rate of expansion which is about the same as that since 1850 (minus the inter-war stagnation).

(2) *Developing countries*

But what about the developing countries? How can one postulate any reasonable assumptions about their prospects of development? The last century of their near stagnation is obviously no guide to the future. But it is this burdensome past which has so often weighed heavily on the development economists' pessimistic outlook about their future. I have discussed at length elsewhere the reasons why such a pessimistic outlook is uncalled for.† The main considerations regarding the prospects for the growth of their income and population may be briefly summarized here:

† See the author's *The India We Want: Its Economic Transition* (Bombay, 1966).

(a) *Expansion in income.* (i) According to the conventional national income estimates, the average per capita income of the developing countries was about $120 in 1960, against $1,100 for the rich countries. A number of studies in recent years, including the pioneering work of Gilbert and Kravis, have conclusively shown how inadequate the present methodology is for the comparisons of per capita incomes of different countries with differing price and employment structures. At least two important reasons tend to understate the level of per capita income in the developing countries: the exclusion of the housewives' services, and the relative prices of the products of the agricultural, handicraft and the service sector. If adjustments are made for these, the comparable level may well be two to four times higher—or about $250 to $400. The economic distance between the rich and the poor countries would, accordingly, appear to be much narrower than commonly suggested.

(ii) The experience of development during the last fifteen years has not been as discouraging as is often made out. A group of experts concluded in 1951 that even if the developing countries invested sums equal to 20 per cent (fully one-half of these were to be provided by external aid) of their combined national income, they would only succeed in raising their national income by 2·5 per cent per year.† The incremental capital output (net) ratio was implicitly supposed to be as high as 8:1! Actual experience has been much more promising. Between 1950 and 1965, the developing countries (excluding China and other Asian socialist countries) raised their income by some 85 to 90 per cent or at an annual growth rate of about 4·4 per cent; and the incremental capital output (gross) ratio was in the neighbourhood of 3:1, and lower if the figures on net output and investment were to be compared. But even this average picture is misleading, since it excludes China and other socialist countries, which account for nearly one-third of the population of the developing countries. Moreover, it also lumps together those countries which developed faster and those that did not.

Adjustments to unravel these confusing knots are difficult indeed. But let me separate the main pieces. (1) The evidence is not easy to procure for the growth of the Asian socialist countries with some 800 million people. Despite difficulties over some years, their annual growth rate since 1950 may be presumed to be around 7 per cent. (2) Fourteen non-socialist developing countries with a population of over 450 million experienced an annual growth rate of 5·5 per cent and above.‡ (3) The remaining developing countries (about 900 million people) had an annual

† United Nations, *Measures for the Economic Development of Underdeveloped Countries* (New York, 1951), p. 78.
‡ United Nations, *World Economic Survey 1963*, Part I, 'Trade and Development: Trends, Needs and Policies' (New York, 1964), pp. 21, 37.

growth rate slightly under 4 per cent, though significantly higher than the forecast made in 1951. Three large countries, India, Pakistan and Indonesia, with 650 million people formed the dead-weight pulling the average of the group low.

If these pieces are put together, we find that three-fifths of developing population (in group 1 and 2 shown above) increased their annual output two and a half-times between 1950 and 1965; the annual growth rate was in the neighbourhood of 6·5 per cent. Pessimistic perspectives would thus seem to be based on the development economists' self-created miasma rather than reality. And among the remaining, intensive search is going on for accelerating the tempo of growth; they have already set high targets—over 6 per cent growth per year—in their new development plans. They may fail again, and perhaps once more again but eventual success can hardly be doubted.

(iii) The experience of the last fifteen years should be taken as only the beginning, as the first faltering steps of a child learning to walk. In comparison with the preceding half a century, the developing countries have, during these 15 years, raised their output four to five times as fast, and put more real investments in the economy and more students in the institutions of higher learning. Capital formation has already reached 16 per cent of the gross domestic product and a continuation of the past marginal rates, could by 1970 raise it to 20 per cent or above. Educational advance has brought the enrolment in the first, second and third levels to the stage where Western Europe was on the eve of the first World War; and at the present rates of advance, the developing countries could attain the educational profile of Western Europe by 1980 and of the U.S.A. and the U.S.S.R. by 1990 or 2000. The growth points have thus been slowly built up, and the search is going on to surmount the weaknesses. Planning in one form or another has been adopted as an instrument of policy, and the public sector is emerging as the driver of the engine of expansion.

(iv) International attitudes and policies, though slow in changing, may also alter. For a period as long as a century, one can mention the hopeful points: disarmament and use of part of these resources for development; changes in trade flows and the international division of labour; and some progress towards a redistribution of world income.

(v) Many difficulties still remain unresolved and new ones may arise. Nor does it necessarily follow that all the developing countries will succeed equally and at the same time in accelerating the pace of development. But as emphasized in § 2, the growth rate of output has progressively tended to rise over the last century, and this trend can be expected to continue. The modest objective of the U.N. Development Decade is to raise the rate to 5 per cent per year; and pressure is already building up to set the sights higher. Success may not immediately follow the declarations, but its eventual attainment can hardly be doubted. The growth rate I have assumed is therefore high—over 5 per cent.

(*b*) *Growth of population.* The growth of population of the developing countries accelerated recently—from under 1 per cent per year between 1850 and 1950 to around 2·2 per cent in the last fifteen years. With greater success in reducing mortality rates, it could be expected to rise in the near future. But how long will this rise continue? The death rate has now fallen to about 25 per thousand. It may soon reach 15, and eventually 10 (but not below), or about the same as in the industrially advanced countries at present. Since the birth rate has hovered around the ceiling of 40 to 45 per thousand, it is obvious that the net growth rate of population could not cross the upper ceiling of 3·5 per cent per year.

Once the ceiling is reached, how long will it continue at that level? The question has been answered often with a great deal of alarm rather than clarity. My feeling is that the transition to low birth-rates, like that to low death-rates, is likely to come much faster than expected at present. The techniques of birth-control are on the threshold of revolutionary changes. Efficient, easy-to-use and cheap methods are now being tested. The pills and the infra-uterus devices provide the examples. And the conventional barriers against their use may soon crumble with a grudging green signal from the Pope. The way would then be open for an international agency, such as the World Health Organization, to initiate, like the 'anti-locust', 'anti-malaria', 'anti-illiteracy' and 'freedom from hunger' campaigns, a world-wide drive for 'freedom from birth'. Even if every single woman of child-bearing age in the developing countries were to be provided with these devices, its total cost would barely come to half a billion dollars—not such a large order to reduce the birth-rate to near zero. This is obviously an illustration, simply meant to emphasize the possibility of the decline in birth-rates arriving much earlier than imagined now.

With this as a background, I am assuming that the average annual growth rate of population of the developing countries is unlikely to be much higher than 1 per cent for the hundred years to come—higher in the first two decades, but drastically falling thereafter. The population of these countries may as a result rise three-fold, or from 2,150 million in 1960 to, say, 6,500 million.

(*c*) *Per capita income in 2060.* As stressed earlier, the real comparable per capita income of the developing countries is about $250 to $400 rather than $120. If the objective set was to abolish the Unequal World over the next hundred years, it would then imply raising the level of real per capita income of the developing countries to that assumed above for the developed countries, that is to $23,000. This would mean increasing it some 70 to 75 times, or at an annual growth rate of 4 to 4·5 per cent. Since population is assumed to increase at 1 per cent per annum, it follows that the total output would have to be increasing at 5 to 5·5 per cent per year—or at a pace only slightly higher than between 1950 and 1965, and than the objectives of the U.N. Development Decade.

The expansion may appear spectacular, but it merely represents the terror of growth at modest compound rates, cumulated over a long period.† Its size is in fact smaller than what is assumed to take place in the industrial countries between 1850 and 2060. The difference is simply in the time-horizon—the developing countries telescoping in one century what the others attained in two centuries. It is thus possible under not particularly unreasonable assumptions to conceive of the economic distance among nations, which has widened in the last century, being overcome in the next. If the growth rate is somewhat lower for income and higher for population, the result may come about a decade or two later. But that, and not hopeless centuries, is the approximate size of the development problem.

4. THE WORLD ECONOMY AT MID-TWENTY-FIRST CENTURY

At the growth rates assumed—about 3 per cent for the industrial countries and over 5 per cent for the developing ones—the average per capita income in the world of 2060 could be in present prices as high as some $23,000. For a family of four, it could mean over $90,000.

Whether this level should be considered too high or too low would depend on a number of unforeseen factors. But it may serve some purpose to compare it with what we know today about the richest families in the richest country, the United States.

(1) *The pattern of expenditure*

Top one per cent of all the spending units in the United States received 9·5 per cent of its total income in 1946; the average for the group was $16,800, and their savings-income rate was 38·4 per cent, which varied within narrow limits (37 to 43 per cent) between 1919 to 1945.‡ In 1947,

---

† In the dark days of the Great Depression, Keynes drew attention to the possibility of growth by citing the illustration of probable growth of the treasure of £40,000 with which Drake returned to England in the 1580s. Cumulating at 3¼ per cent per year, every single pound of it could have become £100,000 by 1930. See his *Essays in Persuasion* (London, 1931), p. 362.

‡ The data on the United States, shown in this section are derived from the following publications: S. S. Kuznets, *Shares of Upper Income Groups in Income and Savings* (New York, 1953), pp. 176–77; during 1919–38, the top one per cent received as much as two-thirds of all dividends paid to individuals (p. 130); United States Department of Commerce, *Income Distribution in the United States* (Washington, 1953), p. 84; and *Statistical Abstract of the United States* (Washington, 1963), p. 400.

only 52,000 families out of a total of 37 million had an annual income before taxes of $50,000 and over. The average income of this 0·14 per cent of the total families was $89,533, or, say $90,000. Coming to a more recent period, 125,440 units out of a total of 48 million received in 1960 taxable individual income in excess of $50,000 per year; their total gross income was $11·5 billion and they paid $4·3 billion as federal taxes, or 38 per cent of their income. Average annual income per unit was about $90,000.

Thus, 125,000 of the richest families (4 out of one thousand) in the United States received an average annual taxable income of $90,000— or about the same as would result by 2060 as an average for all the families in the world, if the growth rates assumed in this study are realized. These families at present paid over one-third as taxes and saved another third. The normal consumption needs of the richest families were met by spending no more than one-third of their average income—the other two-thirds provided for part of the public expenditures and private investment. If these proportions were to hold for 2060, their implications may be indicated by the following exercise.

In the United States, public expenditures for goods and services are currently running at about $500 per capita (of which nearly one-half for military expenditure), and gross capital formation at over $400 per capita. A large measure of these are contributed by the top 10 per cent of income groups. By 2060, however, with per capita income as high as $23,000 it should be possible, given the present tax and savings ratios, to have for these two purposes sums which are over 20 times higher on a per capita basis than now. If it is assumed that military expenditures are nil or negligible, the per capita level of public expenditure in 2060 A.D. for every citizen of the world could be some 40 times higher in real terms than in the United States at present.

These magnitudes are so high that one is tempted to suggest, on the basis of present knowledge of course, that long before these Olympian heights are scaled, mankind would be content to consider its basic economic problem as resolved. It may well be satisfied with achieving somewhat lower targets either at the same rate of growth in a shorter period, or at a lower growth rate in the same period. For the marginal utility of the increased output at that level is bound to be, in any case, very low, if not in fact near zero.

(2) *Pattern of output by industrial origin*

The growth outlook may be subjected to further analysis by estimating the probable changes in the industrial origin of per capita income. The past developments and the conjectures for the future are shown in the table below.

Changes in the Structure of per capita Output, 1850, 1960, 2060

Sector	1850	1960	Estimate 2060	1850	1960	Estimate 2060
	in U.S. $ in 1960 prices			share in percent.		
Agriculture	60	120	230	40	10	1
Industry	30	480	4,000	20	40	17
Rest of the economy	70	600	(18,770) (?a)	40	50	(82)(?a)
	170	1,200	23,000	100	100	100

Source: For 1850 and 1960, author's 'Main Features of Economic Growth' in the *Indian Economic Journal*, March, 1964; and for 2060, text of this study.

Note: Data for 1850 and 1960 relate only to industrial countries in the West; for 2060, however, they refer to the whole world.

(*a*) See the text for an explanation.

The share of agriculture in total output in the industrial countries has fallen from over 40 per cent in 1850 to only 10 per cent in 1960. With a per capita agricultural output of $120 at present, these countries are faced with agricultural surpluses. Whatever the future level of overall income, it is unlikely that the absolute quantum of per capita agricultural output would rise significantly. Its share may well fall to 1 per cent, or even lower, by A.D. 2060.

The share of industry, on the other hand, has risen from less than 20 per cent in 1850 to 40 per cent in 1960. In recent years, it has stabilized (and fallen in the United States) implying that it is no longer growing faster than the overall output. There is a certain limit to the consumption of industrial goods: one car per every adult, and perhaps one as spare for the family; one television set in each room; more of the still-to-be-invented goods; and so on. But ceilings may soon be reached for many items. As a result, it is more than likely that, like agriculture in the last century, industry would begin losing in relative importance over the next century.

How low this share will fall cannot be easily indicated. A rough and ready manipulation of the data for the richest families in the United States (referred to above) suggests that the per capita consumption of industrial goods in this group may be in the neighbourhood of $3,500 per year; even this figure is almost equivalent to one-half of the per capita consumer expenditure in this income-bracket. In addition, their per capita share in the nation-wide use of industrial goods for investment and public consumption may be estimated to be about $500. All in all, about $4,000 per capita for the top income-brackets. This level may be assumed to become the average for every single individual in the world of 2060. It would then form only 17 per cent of the projected per capita income.

If the assumed rates of growth and the level of income for 2060 A.D. are to be realized, an overwhelmingly important share of the expansion (83 per cent) would thus have to be accounted for by the service sector. As shown in the table above, real per capita service output would have to rise from $600 in the industrial countries in 1960 to nearly $19,000 by 2060 A.D. It should then account for 82 per cent of per capita or total output.

The richest top income group in the United States, to which reference was made earlier, probably spends at present no more than $3,000 to $4,000 for services on a per capita basis, or only about one-fifth of the projected average service output in 2060 A.D. But in a world as affluent as postulated here, it would not be easy to find people who would be simply offering services to others by 'holding their hands'—at least, not on a commercial basis.

If the projected level and proportion of the service output were not to be made available, it would imply the attainment of a lower growth rate than suggested here. This would seem to reinforce the conclusion derived above from the analysis of the pattern of expenditure that the probable growth level may well fall below the one calculated for 2060—that is, either the growth rate will be lower, or, perhaps, the time-span shorter.

5. CONCLUDING REFLECTIONS

In a survey as sweeping and an exercise as speculative as this, it would indeed be easy to tear holes. The assumptions may be questioned; and others may attempt to reconstruct the outline with a different set. Nor is it necessary for me to insist that my set is 'better' or 'more realistic' than the others. The exercise is like a journey through uncharted oceans, and one can only think in terms of the plausibility of a particular course. Although the assumptions are heroic, I am inclined to believe that they are plausible. Any change in them is likely to be in the neighbourhood of a percentage point of 'pace' of growth and a decade or two in 'time'. But the impact of any such alteration of assumptions on the broad conclusion of this study—that the world is set for an incredible economic explosion in the century to come—could not but be marginal.

(1) The experience of the past century and the probabilities for the next, suggested in this study, are shown graphically in fig. 1. The economic dynamics for the world economy as a whole for these two centuries may be summarized as follows: population rising from 1,170 million in 1850 to around 9,000 million by 2060, or under 8 times; and net income (in 1960 prices) from $130 billion to $150,000 to $200,000 billion, or some 1,200 to 1,500 times. But these could be the results of innocent-looking annual growth-rates (one per cent for population and 3·5 per

cent for output) cumulated for the two centuries. It is presupposed that the industrial growth which began within a tiny triangle in England in the post-Napoleonic years would have embraced most of mankind during these years.

(2) This may be dismissed as an exercise in euphoria. The post-war discussion on prospects for the developing countries has been dominated by a good deal of pessimism. In this respect, the contemporary development economist may derive comfort from being in distinguished com-

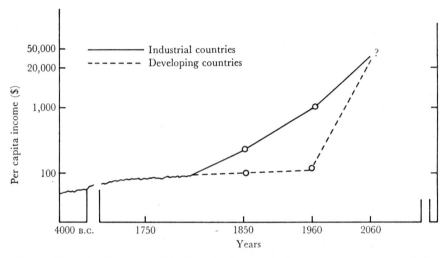

Fig. 1. Illustrative Dynamics of the Growth of per capita Income 4000 B.C. to A.D. 2060 in U.S. dollars in 1960 prices (semi-log scale).

Note: the chart indicates merely the broad sweep of movements at selected points.
Source: see text.

pany: the founding fathers of political economy in the nineteenth century were mostly pessimists (Ricardo and his law of diminishing returns, Malthus and the spectre of population, and Mill and the stationary state).

The discussions that followed in their wake in the nineteenth century were full of forebodings: the exhaustion of natural resources, the virtues or otherwise of this or that policy concerning foreign trade, tariffs, taxation, currency, budgets, labour legislation, social and political reforms, revolutions and what not. And yet, in the hundred years to follow, the income of the nations of Europe, the centre of their pre-occupation, was to expand over twenty times (and their wealth even more). The pessimists may have performed a role by pointing up the weaknesses; but their prognosis can hardly be considered to have been right. One wonders whether the contemporary development debate may not share the same fate. Keynes' warning, in the Preface to his *General Theory*, on the power of survival of old ideas, may be relevant here. He stated:

The difficulty lies, not in the new ideas but, in escaping from the old ones, which ramify, for those brought up as most of us have been, into every corner of our mind.

(3) The analysis in the preceding section suggests that mankind's preoccupation with growth itself may well terminate, or at least water down, before the projected high-point is reached. 'From the sweat of thy brow, thou shalt earn thy bread' was a useful, and indeed a necessary, injunction in the age of relentless toil. But with scarcity disappearing for an increasingly wide range of products, one need not wonder if the choice were to be more and more in favour of leisure and pleasure rather than output and accumulation. After all, since the first May Day demonstration in the United States, the average work-week has fallen from some 70 hours to about 35, with most of the decline having taken place in the last 30 years.† In the process of future growth, the work-week may fall to 8 hours or less (one eight-hour day or four two-hour working days in a week); at the projected income-level, the marginal utility of not working could be considerably greater than of working.

(4) But an economic transition of this magnitude could, surely, not be attained without creating a whole host of new problems. A large part of the intricate framework of the world's religions, philosophy, social and political thought, and institutions was built up when the scarcity of earthly goods formed the epicentre of mankind's speculations and struggles. With scarcity pushed away to the periphery, it can hardly be doubted that this whole edifice would require a fundamental reconstruction. The precise directions of this cannot be indicated at this stage; but the need for searching for them would seem to be urgent. It is perhaps time now to open up the widest speculation aimed at a profound rethinking of our values and refashioning of our institutions.

† See J. K. Galbraith, *American Capitalism: The Concept of Countervailing Power* (Boston, 1952).

SOME RANDOM REFLEXIONS ON
SOVIET INDUSTRIALIZATION

E. H. CARR

Nobody will doubt that industrialization is a major problem of the contemporary world, or that Soviet power and prestige owe much to the process of industrialization carried out in the U.S.S.R. The purpose of the present paper is not to examine the achievements, the failures or the costs of Soviet industrialization, but rather to investigate its specific place in the framework or perspective of industrialization considered as a historical phenomenon making its appearance in different contexts of time and space.

Much attention has recently been given by western writers—not without a side glance at current problems of industrialization in Asia and Africa—to Russian industrialization as an instance of industrialization in a 'backward' economy. Any country embarking on industrialization is, in one sense, by definition 'backward'. But something more than this is clearly meant. Gerschenkron, who has elaborated this theme at length in his collection of essays *Economic Backwardness in Historical Perspective*, distinguishes between the British, German and Russian types of industrialization, the British type being treated as the norm in relation to which the German, and *a fortiori* the Russian, types are economically backward. (American industrialization, which Gerschenkron does not discuss, presumably conforms to the British type.) Germany, and *a fortiori* Russia, on the threshold of industrialization were countries 'where the basic elements of backwardness appear in such an accentuated form as to lead to the use of essentially different institutional instruments of industrialization' (*op. cit.* p. 16). The key to the institutional differences Gerschenkron finds in the fact that, while British industrialization was the product of individual entrepreneurial decisions, the German type (of which French industrialization was a variant) placed the main initiative in the hands of the banks. 'The continental practices in the field of industrial investment banking must be conceived as specific instruments of industrialization in a backward country' (*op. cit.* p. 14). The Russian type represented a further stage of backwardness. The state substituted itself for the banks as 'the *agens movens* of industrialization'; indeed, 'the policies pursued by the Russian government in the nineties resembled closely those of the banks in Central Europe'. This was partly the result of military policies, especially of strategic railway construction. But 'these policies only reinforced and accentuated the basic tendencies of industrialization in conditions of economic backwardness' (*op. cit.* p. 20). When we reach the Soviet period things are still worse. 'The Soviet experiment in rapid industrialization' followed 'a pattern of economic development which before First World War seemed to have been relegated to the role of a historical museum piece'; it was something 'anachronistic, or rather parachronistic'—which did not, however, prevent it from proving 'immensely effective' (*op. cit.* p. 149).

The distinctions thus drawn between British, German and Russian experience are for the most part valid and suggestive. But in a work which professes to place economic backwardness 'in historical perspective', a more critical look at the perspective may be appropriate. Some romantic nostalgia for the earlier (British) type of industrialization may be condoned. What is less admirable is the attempt to treat it as a model which later industrializations failed to follow. Though Gerschenkron disclaims any intention of setting up a norm of industrialization, the application of a criterion of backwardness inevitably leads to this result. 'The industrial history of Europe appears not as a series of mere repetitions of the "first" industrialization, but as an orderly system of graduated deviations from that industrialization' (*op. cit.* p. 44). One of his favourite concepts is 'substitution' with its implication of the inferior or factitious; in Russian industrialization, 'the government's budgetary policy was effectively *substituted* for the deficient internal market' (*op. cit.* p. 126). The Russian type was a deviation from the German type which was itself a deviation from the British.

Great Britain provided the first recognized modern example of the historical phenomenon which we know as industrialization; and nineteenth century writers, including Marx, treated British industrialization as a sort of *Ur*-Industrialization from which the process spread to other leading countries. But this went with an acute consciousness of the darker sides of what came to be known as the 'Industrial Revolution'.[†] The orthodox nineteenth century view (Toynbee, the Hammonds, the Webbs) was that its immediate effect was to impose severe sufferings and hardships on the worker. This did not preclude the view that its ultimate effect on the worker was beneficial (though this was denied by the Marxists): the orthodox pre-1914 economic historian Cunningham wrote of 'the inevitable difficulties of transition' and of 'the terrible suffering which was endured in the period of transition'.[‡] It would have seemed

[†] For the origin of the term see G. N. Clark, *The Idea of the Industrial Revolution* (Glasgow, 1953).
[‡] W. Cunningham, *The Growth of English Industry and Commerce* (Cambridge, 1925), vol. ii, 668, 617, quoted by R. M. Hartwell (see below).

at this time paradoxical to hold up the British process of industrialization as a model or norm from which other industrializing countries would diverge to their detriment. On the contrary, other countries were congratulated on having been lucky enough, as late-comers, to avoid some of the worst evils of the British industrial revolution.

The consequences of industrialization for the British working class have recently been the subject of sharp controversy and rapidly changing attitudes, ably summarized by R. M. Hartwell a few years ago in an article in the *Journal of Economic History*.† The argument took a characteristic and instructive course. In the 1920s a number of economists and economic historians (Clapham, Hutt, Gregory) minimized or denied even the short-term sufferings inflicted on the workers by the introduction of the English factory system (the term 'revolution' was now avoided). In the 1930s the controversy was 'relatively quiescent'. In 1948 Professor Ashton returned to the defence of capitalism against the charge of having inflicted intolerable hardships on the industrial worker, and has since been followed by an ever growing host of disciples and imitators. (Among American intellectuals a similar rehabilitation of big business has been undertaken, having been inaugurated by articles in *Fortune* of December 1949 and April 1952). Hartwell sagely concludes: 'Interpretations of the industrial revolution in England have not depended entirely on unbiased analysis of the evidence; to an important extent they have resulted from particular attitudes towards social, political and economic change.'

One could have been explicit. Before 1914 English industrial society was self-assured enough to digest without discomfort any criticism of its origins. The traumatic experience of the Russian revolution of 1917 put it on the defensive, made it sensitive to such criticism, and rendered the conception of revolution distasteful. It became invidious to agree with Marx, or to write the same things about English economic history as were written by Soviet historians. This was the mood of the 1920s. In the 1930s, by way of reaction against Hitler, the climate of opinion became temporarily more sympathetic to Marxism and to the Soviet Union; and a truce was called in the battle of the English industrial revolution. After the second world war, opinion again turned sharply against the Soviet Union and against Marxism; and the view that the English industrial revolution had inflicted hardship and suffering on the worker was once more unacceptable. The chronology makes it clear that these writers were not primarily concerned with British industrialism. No doubt unconsciously—for historians rarely know what they are up to—they mirrored successive changes in attitude to Soviet industrialization. In order to show this up as a falling away from the original British model,

† Vol. XIX (1959), No. 2, pp. 229–49.

any attempt to equate the two processes must be warded off; the threatened *tu quoque* must be refuted. It is interesting to note in passing that, while the American argument convicts Soviet industrialization of 'backwardness' on the ground of its failure to maintain private enterprise, the British argument does the same on the ground of its failure to live up to the humanitarian standards of British industrialization.

These controversies are none of my present business. I shall not attempt to contest the advantages of private enterprise or the view that Soviet industrialization was responsible for the deaths of more people, or made more people more unhappy, or raised standards of living more slowly, than British industrialization. Such arguments, taken by themselves, do not seem to me to lead anywhere. Nostalgia for the past seldom makes for good history. Any perspective based on the explicit or unspoken assumption that the initial British industrialization through private enterprise and the market was a 'normal' or 'advanced' mode of industrialization, from which 'backward' countries have regrettably, though perhaps to some extent unavoidably, diverged, seems to me not only highly idiosyncratic but essentially unhistorical. It might indeed be claimed that the concept 'normal' has here no meaning, and that, viewed historically, twentieth century Soviet industrialization is more 'advanced' than any eighteenth or nineteenth century industrialization, not in any moral or political sense, and not merely in a temporal sense, but in the sense in which automated production in a large factory is more 'advanced' than production with hand tools in a small workshop.

The crucial point about the beginning of the process of industrialization is the character and origin of the resources needed to set it in motion. Great Britain and the Soviet Union are alike (and unlike most other industrial countries) in having industrialized without the benefit of foreign capital. In both countries, the industrial revolution was facilitated by an agricultural revolution and by the establishment of a primitive mining industry, and would scarcely have been possible without these assets. In most other respects Soviet industrialization diverged so far from British industrialization that it serves little purpose to regard the latter as a model. These divergences were due mainly to the difference in time, but partly also to the legacy of earlier Russian experiments in industrialization.

The first experiment was the work of Peter the Great. This, though it had its precedents in seventeenth century western Europe, was so remote from the classical pattern of 'industrialization' afterwards set by the English eighteenth century industrial revolution that it is commonly ignored in discussions of the subject. Peter the Great's industries worked exclusively on government orders (though some of the establishments were in private ownership), and fell into three groups: iron works producing armaments and military equipment; textile factories producing uniforms for the army and sail cloth for the navy; and a building industry engaged on public works of various kinds. Conscious imitation of western Europe, and desire to emulate western power, were a major factor in these foundations. The labour employed was peasant serf labour drafted in large numbers into these new industrial occupations. Technical processes were primitive and undeveloped; capital equipment was at the outset negligible. Some of the industry created by Peter declined or collapsed after his death.† But much of it survived and set the pattern of Russian industrial development for a century and a half. Historical traditions and habits of mind die hard; and it is in survivals of a primitive Petrine conception of industrialization (and of the primitive economic conditions which went with it) rather than in the modern clash between 'market' and 'planning' conceptions of industrialization that we should look for traces of Russian 'backwardness'.

The second phase of Russian industrialization began in the second half of the nineteenth century, and was marked by three major developments. The emancipation of the serfs opened the way to the creation of a 'free' labour market and of an industry employing 'workers' in a modern sense. The arrival of the railway age in Russia had paved the way for large schemes of railway construction, dictated mainly by military needs, but relying on foreign materials and foreign example. The growth of a large potential consumer market led to the establishment of a mass textile industry using foreign machinery and foreign technicians. These three developments were overtaken by, and merged in, the wave of intensive industrialization through foreign investment (including foreign loans to the Russian Government) which swept over Russia in the fifteen years following the conclusion of the Franco–Russian alliance in 1891. Since the aim was to build up Russian military strength, investment through state channels was directed primarily to the heavy and capital goods industries (including communications), and state orders rather than the market dictated the character of the end product. In brief, this phase of Russian industrialization had the following characteristics:

(1) It was set in motion and directed by the state. Much of it (including railway construction) satisfied military needs; many of the foreign loans which financed it were governmental loans granted for political motives.

(2) Its normal form was the large unit working with complex modern machines and requiring large capital investment.

(3) It was concerned primarily with industries producing capital

---

† A. Kahan in *Journal of Economic History*, vol. xxv, No. 1, March, 1965, pp. 61–85, argues that the decline has been exaggerated by Russian historians anxious to minimize Peter's achievement.

goods, not consumer goods. This was only partly due to military needs and to those of railway construction; in a period of advanced technology, the production of the means of production had a natural priority.

(4) It involved the recruitment and training, at short notice, of a primitive peasant population, entirely unused to urban life, to labour discipline and to mechanical processes.

(5) It required, owing both to its political orientation and to the technological complexity of modern industry, a substantial element of central direction and organization.

Following the dismissal of Witte, the disaster of the Russo–Japanese War and the revolution of 1905, some of the steam went out of the process. Between 1906 and 1914 industrialization in Russia proceeded at a substantially slower rate than in the eighteen-nineties; foreign loans and state financing of industrialization declined; the banks grew more powerful, and to some extent replaced the state as dispensers of long-term credit to industry. In Gerschenkron's analysis, this represented a certain 'westernization' or 'Germanization' of Russian industrialization (and hence an advance), under which 'the mode of substitution tended to approximate the pattern prevailing in Central Europe'. It was no longer the state, but the banks, which were 'a substitute for an autonomous internal market'. Gerschenkron regards this as a 'continuation of growth in changed conditions', showing 'elements of relaxation and "normalization" in the industrial process'. He believes that 'industry may have been passing at this time through a period of dynamic preparation for another great spurt', which 'of course never materialized' (op. cit. pp. 135–37, 142). He implies, without actually saying it, that industrialization in Russia might, given time, have reverted not merely to the intermediate German, but to the basic British, model: this would have constituted the maximum of 'relaxation and "normalization" in the industrial process'. It is probably correct that between 1906 and 1914 Russian industrialization came nearer than at any other time to the pattern of industrialization of western countries industrialized with the aid of private foreign capital. It is also true that industrialization in this period attained a lower rate of growth than in the eighteen-nineties when state capital was more actively engaged and state intervention continuous, and that it owed much of such impetus as it had to the achievement of the earlier period.

But this is only half the story. The conditions of Russian industrialization, though in some respects—notably in the primitive technical and social organization of Russian agriculture—more backward than those in which English or German industrialization has taken place, were in other respects more advanced. When Russia industrialized, the age of the large-scale factory unit, of machine production and of the conveyor belt was already well on the way. The demands of this type of industry were fundamentally different, both materially and psychologically, from those of the earlier industrial revolutions. It may be that the peasant recruited into a rapidly expanding Russian industry was more 'backward' than his English predecessor. But the industry into which he was recruited was more 'advanced'. The second factor was perhaps more decisive for the course of development than the first. The discussion seems to be obscured rather than facilitated by the introduction of such concepts as 'advanced' and 'backward', or 'norms' and 'deviations'.

It is against this complex background that the history of industrialization in the Soviet Union has to be traced. The main issues of Soviet industrialization, or of a resumption of pre-revolutionary programmes of industrialization, remained latent for almost ten years after the revolution. Revolution and civil war damaged factories, destroyed machines, and dispersed the labour force. In 1922, after the introduction of the New Economic Policy, Soviet industry touched its lowest point. Thereafter recovery was rapid, and by the end of 1926 production in general was back to its pre-revolutionary level. This 'restoration period' presented few problems of policy. The overriding aim was to bring factories and machines back into use and to reassemble a labour force. Demand exceeded supply; and almost everything that could be produced found an eager market. Owing to wholesale damage to blast furnaces in the Ukraine, and the catastrophic fall in the production of pig iron, metal industries lagged behind the rest. The fourteenth party conference in April 1925 sanctioned an investment programme to revive them. But this implied no special emphasis on heavy industry or on the production of capital goods. The Red Army had been demobilized and military expenditure cut to the bone; and no great works of construction were undertaken at this time. At the conference which adopted the resolution, Dzerzhinsky explained that 'the fundamental base of our metal industry as a whole...is the consumer market'; it was there that 'the whole strength and future of our metal industry is to be found'.† What was afterwards invoked as a Marxist 'law' of the priority of the production of means of production over the production of goods for consumption had no place in Soviet theory or practice in this period. The 'special conference on the restoration of fixed capital in industry' (OSVOK), which was set up by Vesenkha early in 1925, and issued a number of reports in this and the following year, showed no preference for capital goods industries. Throughout this time, the only consistent advocates of industrialization in the later sense of the term were Trotsky and his followers, together with the economist Preobrazhensky, whose famous essay on 'Primitive Socialist Accumulation' dated from the autumn of 1924.

† *Izbrannye Proizvedeniya* (1957), ii, 83–4.

By the end of 1925 it became clear that the 'restoration period' was nearing its end, and that major decisions of policy would shortly be called for. It was freely pointed out that industry could not be expected to maintain the rate of growth of the past four years once existing means of production had been rehabilitated and brought back into use. Henceforth the rate of growth in industry would depend on decisions how much to invest and in what to invest. The new mood was registered in the resolution of the fourteenth party congress in December 1925, which bound the party to 'pursue a policy aimed at the industrialization of the country, the development of the production of means of production, and the formation of reserves for economic manoeuvre'. But the decision of principle was subject to a variety of interpretations, and, in particular, said nothing about the tempo of industrialization. Bukharin at the congress had consoled himself, and the more cautious among his hearers, with the admission that 'we shall move forward at a snail's pace'; and a few months later Stalin compared the ambitious Dnieprostroi project with the perversity of the peasant who neglects the repair of his plough in order to buy a gramophone. Progress was made. Even the Dnieprostroi plan, which made sense only on the prospect of an indefinitely expanding demand for power from newly created industries, was approved in the autumn of 1926. Two other major construction projects approved in 1927 were geared to agricultural policy—the Turksib railway, whose main purpose was to carry Siberian grain to the cotton-growing regions of Central Asia, and the Stalingrad tractor factory. Generally speaking, the assumption prevailed that industrialization would proceed at a tempo, and in conditions, which did not involve unduly serious pressures on the peasant or on the industrial worker. A latent incompatibility between the principles of the New Economic Policy and the principles of planning was only dimly perceived.

This period of compromise, wishful thinking and evasion of the real issue ended in 1927. In the summer of that year, food shortages occurred in the large cities—showing that a policy of mild appeasement of the peasant, unsupported by mass production of consumer goods, did not suffice to guarantee grain supplies; official prices for important commodities could not be held, or led to a wide divergence between these prices and free market prices—showing the impossibility of combining reliance on the market with extensive price regulation; and currency inflation could no longer be concealed—showing that the stable currency was not strong enough to resist the pressures on it. The crisis, accentuated by the failure of the grain collections in the last months of 1927, made some shift in policy inevitable. The choice was, broadly speaking, between two courses. Industrialization could be stepped up, reliance on the market abandoned in favour of systematic planning, and more emphasis placed on the production of capital goods as a prelude to more intensive industrialization. This was what the opposition demanded. Or the tempo of industrialization could be reduced, and the emphasis transferred to the production of consumer goods for the market. This was the line more or less openly preached, though with some cautious reservations, by Bukharin and Rykov, and widely supported in the party; on the record of the past two years, it seemed the most likely line for the party to take. In fact, once the opposition had been expelled at the fifteenth party congress in December 1927, Bukharin and Rykov were branded as heretics, and policies of rapid industrialization, with emphasis on the production of capital goods, more vigorous and intensive than the opposition had ever dared to contemplate, were adopted. The central problem of Soviet industrialization is how this came about.

The pace of industrialization seems to have been determined mainly by two contributory factors. One was the war scare in the summer of 1927 following the breaking off of relations by Great Britain in May of that year. This was said to have aggravated the shortage of supplies by encouraging hoarding; and for the first time for many years it concentrated attention on military defence. The needs of rearmament stimulated, or reinforced, the case for the rapid development of heavy industry. Lenin had proclaimed not only that heavy industry was 'a fundamental basis of socialism', but that without it 'we shall perish altogether as an independent country'.† Historians with a liking for the 'might-have-beens' of history may wish to speculate whether the tempo of industrialization would have been slower if the Soviet leaders had not in 1927 felt themselves isolated in a hostile world; or alternatively what, if the tempo had been slower, would have happened to the Soviet Union in 1941. These speculations are not particularly profitable. But the security motive in the drive to catch up with the west by rapid industrialization should not be overlooked.

The second factor was the increasing weight of unemployment. Unemployment was a difficult category to define precisely in Soviet conditions. Though an urban phenomenon, its main source was rural overpopulation. In the middle nineteen-twenties the Soviet Union, having recovered with extraordinary rapidity from the casualties of war and civil war, was in the midst of a 'population explosion' which was increasing the population at the rate of 2·2 per cent per annum; and this resulted in a steady influx of peasants into the towns for unskilled seasonal work, especially in building. (Rural population was increasing only by 1·6 per cent per annum, urban population by 5·1 per cent.) Some of the unemployed had no experience of wage-earning beyond a few weeks of casual labour. Statistics kept independently by the trade unions

† For these quotations see *Sochineniya* (5th ed.), vol. XLV, 209, 287.

and by Narkomtrud varied widely. Both sets were incomplete, but both in 1927 returned a total of well over a million unemployed; and the opposition estimate of two millions was not unreasonable. The existence of this large untapped source of energy naturally invited the view that it should be put to work in ways which would increase the national wealth and power. The creation of new industrial enterprises seemed the only, though long-term, solution for an intractable problem. To increase production was the only way to take care of an expanding population. In the controversy about Soviet industrialization, most western critics have found themselves on the side of Bukharin and Rykov, some on humanitarian, some on economic, grounds (the two not being always clearly distinguished). But it has not been fashionable to speculate what would have happened to the rural population if a lower rate of industrialization had been adopted. The example of India does not suggest that Bukharin's policy of 'snail's-pace' industrialization, and avoidance of undue pressures on the peasant or the worker, would necessarily have solved the population problem. The Gosplan economist Bazarov once predicted that, if agriculture were reconstructed and the countryside flooded with consumer goods, there would be no way out but to spend on aid to the surplus population not hundreds of millions, but milliards, of roubles.†
Such speculations and comparisons do not, however, lead any further than others canvassed in this essay; and I think that we need to take a rather more detached look at the aims and methods of Soviet industrialization in a wider context.

A well-known work on industrialization, which was originally published in Germany in 1931 (an English version appeared in 1958), and made no attempt to discuss Soviet industrialization,‡ distinguished three phases through which countries commonly pass in the course of their industrialization. The first, or initial, phase is marked by the predominance of consumer-goods industries. In the second phase capital-goods industries advance rapidly, and may approach half the output of consumer-goods industries. In the third phase, the output of capital-goods industries equals that of consumer-goods industries with a tendency on the part of the former to expand still more rapidly, pointing to a fourth phase (not considered to have been reached anywhere in 1930), in which capital-goods industries would outstrip consumer-goods industries. The significant feature of this process has, however, been its accelerating character and the shortening of the phases, so that major industrial countries which had begun to industrialize much later than

---

† *Planovoe Khozyaistvo*, No. 2, 1928, p. 45.

‡ W. G. Hoffmann, *Stadien und Typen der Industrialisierung* (Kiel, 1931); *The Growth of Industrial Economies* (Manchester, 1958). A perfunctory half-paragraph on Soviet industrialization on p. 100 of the English version was evidently an addition, since it referred to works published in the nineteen-fifties.

Great Britain—the United States, Germany, France, Sweden—had before the end of the nineteenth century caught up with Great Britain, and entered the third phase on equal terms with her; and these countries were joined after the First World War by Japan where industrialization did not begin before 1860. Moreover, countries where industrialization did not begin before 1890, or even before the First World War, had by the nineteen-fifties entered the third phase; Canada, Australia and South Africa were cited as examples. This rapid progress was attributed partly to absence of competition from 'old-established craft industries', and partly to 'action taken by governments to foster capital-goods industries'.†

With this picture in mind, can we try to place Soviet industrialization in the perspective of a train of events set in motion by the English industrial revolution and continuing in our own time with the industrial revolution in Asia and Africa? When industrialization began in Great Britain in the middle of the eighteenth century, manufacture was still *manu*facture. The individual entrepreneur working with a dozen or a score of 'hands' was the typical unit of production; tools and machines were of the simplest kind; the capital investment required to float such enterprises was very small. It may be true that the British economy was somewhat more advanced—in the sense of having larger resources in capital and skill—when it embarked on industrialization than the continental and Russian economies of a later date when they started on the same course. But the much more significant fact is that, in the conditions of the latter part of the eighteenth century, far smaller capital resources and less technical know-how were needed to set the process of industrialization in motion. The problem of capital accumulation, which bedevilled the later types of industrialization, arose only in the second stage of British industrialization, when internal resources had multiplied sufficiently to cope with it. When continental Europe embarked on industrialization in the middle of the nineteenth century, the essential conditions had changed. Railway construction dominated the process. Large units of production, heavy and complicated machines and large investments of capital were the order of the day. When Russia followed the same path fifty years later, technology had made further advances, and these developments were further intensified. Hence the progression from the primitive British model of industrialization by the private entrepreneur through the more advanced continental model of financing and control by the banks to the still more advanced Russian model of financing and control by the state, already discernible in the Russian industrialization of the eighteen-nineties.

The conclusion I should like to draw is that Soviet industrialization

† Hoffmann, *op. cit.* pp. 80, 91–2, 100.

is neither a unique phenomenon, nor a deviation from an established and accepted model, but an important stage in a process of development which began two centuries ago and still looks to have a long history before it. The specific feature of Soviet industrialization is its association with a planned economy, though planning is neither so complete an innovation as is sometimes believed nor confined so exclusively to the Soviet and post-Soviet economies. This can be illustrated from the principal features of planned industrialization in the Soviet Union.

(1) The unit of planning in the modern sense is the nation, and the agent of planning is a governmental authority. Historically, national efficiency was the first motive of planned industrialization: of this Russia in the eighteen-nineties provided an early example. The planning of national economies in the First World War falls into this category. The early Soviet advocates and theorists of planning were consciously inspired by the German war economy. But, in a broader sense, national planning is simply a culmination of the long process which has replaced the individual craftsman or trader by the small business, the small business by the large share company, and the company by the mammoth trust or combine. The national planning authority presides over a group of combines. The nation has developed as the largest, and in modern conditions most efficient, unit of economic control. Economic groups or combines of small nations are the next logical step in the process.

(2) Planning means the replacement of 'spontaneous' market controls by conscious decisions of a central authority, of 'individual' rationality by 'social' rationality. Troglodytes of *laissez-faire* maintain—or used to maintain—that social purpose is necessarily irrational. It is of course true that society is composed of individuals, and that decisions taken in the name of society may be oppressive in regard to some individuals, just as decisions taken by some individuals may be oppressive in regard to others. But once we recognize the Hobbesian state of nature as intolerable, and have ceased to believe in the automatic harmony of interests, we are compelled to accept the hypothesis, which lies at the root of planning, that major economic decisions must be taken not by individuals or groups in pursuit of their own interests, but by an organ acting in the name of society as a whole. Planned Soviet industrialization was the first explicitly to proclaim this principle, which is now tacitly accepted—though sometimes with grudging reservations—in all major countries.

(3) All industrialization rests on the tacit assumption that, productivity of labour being higher in industry than in agriculture, the basic criterion of the economic level of any nation is the relative weight of industry in its economy; the Marxist doctrine of the destiny of the proletariat lent special importance to this factor in the drive for Soviet industrialization.

It followed from this proposition that, in any advanced programme of planned industrialization, priority would be given to the expansion of capital goods industries, which would raise productivity most rapidly. This development, as has already been shown, was also a feature in pre-Soviet industrialization; and the foreshortening of the process, bringing about this development more rapidly in later examples of industrialization, has also been noted elsewhere. It would be meaningless to attempt to assess the relative weight of these general trends and of the impact of Marxist doctrine in hastening this development in Soviet industrialization. But this was the background of the controversy with Bukharin and Rykov on the tempo of industrialization and on the priority of capital-goods and consumer-goods industries.

(4) Finally, Soviet industrialization was marked by a different attitude to foreign trade, due largely to specific Russian conditions. In the process of British industrialization the export of consumer goods, and later also of capital goods, had been of crucial importance. In the later stages, Great Britain became dependent on imports of food and, like other western European countries, of many of the raw materials required by advanced industries. None of these conditions obtained in Russia. Russia was an exporter of agricultural products and was well supplied with almost all essential raw materials, and was on the other hand an importer of the products of industry, both consumer goods and especially capital goods—a state of affairs which industrialization was designed to remedy. While therefore in Great Britain foreign trade and the international division of labour was thought of as an integral part of the economy and an instrument of progress, in Russia it was a badge of inferiority and backwardness, of a situation in which Russia was an 'agrarian colony' of the industrial west. The drive for self-sufficiency was from the first very strong in Soviet industrialization, partly because it seemed to be obviously practicable, and partly because it was the only road of escape from western tutelage and dependence on the west. The fear of western hostility also made it important in military terms. Foreign trade was regarded empirically as a way of obtaining some foreign product which was for the present indispensable but which might some day be replaced by a Soviet product.

But, though a cult of self-sufficiency and a cautious attitude to foreign trade were easily explicable as a result of the Soviet environment, they also represented a general trend in modern industrialization. While it is not clear that industrialization diminishes the volume of foreign trade, it certainly alters its pattern. It is perhaps unlikely that the export of textiles will ever be resumed on the scale familiar in the nineteenth century. At the height of the industrialization crisis in the Soviet Union in the late nineteen-twenties, 85 per cent of all industrial imports were capital goods. The same pattern is likely to be followed by other industrializing nations, and will for some time provide a stimulus to the capital-goods industries of the older industrial countries. But much of this process at present rests on a precarious foundation, which was never available to the Soviet Union, of 'aid' rather than trade. The future of international trade in an industrialized world is still a somewhat remote speculation. The trend towards self-sufficiency exhibited by the process of Soviet industrialization seems likely to spread: even the geographical maldistribution of raw materials is a less acute problem in the era of synthetic substitutes. A tendency for international trade to be concentrated on the most advanced and complex industrial products may perhaps be foreseen. Here too Soviet industrialization seems to illustrate a specific stage in a world-wide process of development.

ASPECTS OF SOVIET
INVESTMENT POLICY IN
THE 1920s

R. W. DAVIES

This article first examines some of the views about investment policy current in the U.S.S.R. in the late 1920s, and then tentatively discusses the practical impact of investment policy on industrial development in this period.

I. THE DISCUSSION

By the end of 1925, planned industrialization was firmly accepted as the major goal of Soviet economic policy: the alternative course of concentrating investment on agriculture had already been dismissed. Three principles of industrialization policy were generally accepted in contemporary Soviet writings. Firstly, it was agreed that a wide range of new industries must be established, so that the Soviet economy could become more or less self-sufficient, and independent of the capitalist world. A large literature was published in the middle and late 1920s about the proposed new industries which would produce machine tools, industrial equipment, motor vehicles and tractors; the importance of developing the engineering industries was particularly stressed (see the famous resolution of the fourteenth party congress in December 1925).† There was also a particular effort to encourage the growth of modern industries such as chemicals and electric power, which were felt to be growing points in world technology. Secondly, partly as a corollary of this first principle, priority was to be given to the producer goods industries. In the summer of 1925, the Supreme Council of National Economy (Vesenkha), responsible for administering state industry, declared the development of 'heavy' industry more rapidly than 'light' industry to be 'a healthy, progressive phenomenon' which marked 'the necessary second stage of industrial growth'.‡ Thirdly, industrial development must be based on advanced Western and particularly American technology. Advanced technology had been a persistent theme in Soviet publications throughout the vicissitudes of the first years of Soviet rule. In 1920, the GOELRO plan for the electrification of Russia had

† *Direktivy KPSS i Sovetskogo Pravitel'stva po Khozyaistvennym Voprosam*, i, (1957), p. 562.
‡ *Perspektivy Promyshlennosti v 1925–1926 g.* (1925), p. 108.

been grounded in a belief in a new technological revolution made possible by electrification; and Krzhizhanovsky, principal architect of this plan, had made widely publicized statements about the potentialities of modern technology in Soviet conditions.† In March 1925, TsIK, the Central Executive Committee of Soviets, recognized that fixed capital in industry and transport must be 'recreated' in a way which would 'serve as a technical foundation for the socialist society which is being built'.‡ By 1927, the need for 'modern technology' had become a cliché of all the Soviet leaders from Rykov to Kuibyshev.§

When stated in these general terms, these three principles of the policy of industrialization were accepted within the party with almost as little resistance as industrialization itself. Bazarov was almost alone in his challenge to the first principle, self-sufficiency, on the grounds that it would be more efficient to concentrate on a few industries in which production could be sufficiently large to make cheap mass production possible.‖ The second principle, priority to producer goods industries rather than consumer goods industries, was also generally accepted by the party and by the non-party experts. Here, as with the whole policy of priority to industry rather than agriculture, the difficulty turned on the weight which was to be attached to the principle in practice. At first it was taken to be subject to the constraint that its application must not involve a rupture of market equilibrium and a threat to the standard of living of the population as a whole and to the 'link' with the peasantry. But from the end of 1927 onwards official policy was prepared to accept a larger increase of investment in industry in general and in the producer goods industries in particular than the market could bear; and this brought Bukharin and most of the non-party experts into opposition to official policies.

The third corollary of industrialization, that it should be based on modern technology, was also universally accepted as a general principle. But there was great uncertainty and confusion about how far it should be taken in practice. Two broad lines of approach can be distinguished. The first was less radical, and placed the main emphasis on extending and re-equipping existing factories rather than on constructing new ones. Such new factories as were required should, it was argued, have a technical structure adapted to specific Russian conditions. They should be built on a smaller scale than the most advanced American factories and their technology should be labour-intensive rather than capital-intensive.

† See *Soviet Studies*, vol. XI, 1960, pp. 297–99.

‡ *Direktivy KPSS i Sovetskogo Pravitel'stva po Khozyaistvennym Voprosam*, i, (1957), pp. 506–7.

§ For examples see *Pyatnadtsatyi S"ezd VKP(b)* (1962), pp. 974, 1008–9; *SSSR. Tsentral'nyi Ispolnitel'nyi Komitet, 2 Sessiya 4 Sozyva* (1927), p. 250; *XV Konferentsiya VKP(b)* (1926), p. 194.

‖ See A. Erlich, *The Soviet Industrialization Debate, 1924–1928* (Cambridge, Mass., 1960), pp. 60–75.

The alternative approach, much more radical, placed the main emphasis on the construction of new modern factories of the American type, with large capacities and using a high proportion of capital in relation to labour. The two schools of thought, which Mezhlauk dubbed the 'crumb-collectors' and the 'fantasists',[†] were contrasted by an official of Vesenkha:

There are two approaches to capital construction. In the conservative English approach, improvements are introduced with difficulty, extra buildings are added to every existing factory, and individual shops are re-equipped; in one enterprise, you can trace the whole history of industrial progress. The other approach is the American one: a new factory is really built from scratch, in a new place without harmful traditions; the old works carries on as long as it can make a profit, and is then scrapped.[‡]

The case for the less radical approach was an economic one. It was argued that the market was too small to permit the construction of mammoth enterprises, and that the scarcity of capital and the abundance and cheapness of labour in Russia made it necessary to use capital sparingly. With a given capital outlay, production would be maximized if capital were used so as to maximize output and to absorb as much labour as possible, so that the capital/output and capital/labour ratios were minimized.

The alternative case for the policy of constructing new American-type factories rested on the belief that modern technology was so productive that if introduced in sufficient quantities it would sweep aside the limitations imposed by the backward agrarian environment and the existing technical level in industry. Just because of its backwardness, Russia could use the last conquests of science and technology:

We have in front of us a process like that by which a young capitalist nation, in undertaking the mechanisation of its production, borrows machines, appliances and productive methods which are the last word in capitalist practice from the arsenal of its capitalist neighbours, and does not go through the preliminary stages of mechanisation.[§]

It was also argued that planning made it possible to introduce technology which capitalism could use only in theory:

the real *kingdom of machines* which are not enemies but friends of mankind is not behind us but in front of us.[||]

[†] *Torgovo-Promyshlennaya Gazeta*, 13 October, 1927.
[‡] Birbraer in *Predpriyatie*, No. 6, 1928, p. 19.
[§] *Planovoe Khozyaistvo*, No. 2, 1926, p. 15; for other examples of this view see J.-M. Collette, *Politique des Investissements et Calcul Economique* (Paris, 1964), p. 130.
[||] *Planovoe Khozyaistvo*, No. 2, 1926, p. 15.

In economic terms, the argument in its extreme form seems to have been that in the long run major technical changes would make the present cost equations, including the capital/labour cost ratio, irrelevant; in order to get to the new set of equations, you could not start from what was cheapest given present parameters, but must introduce new technology into the existing situation in large lumps. American mechanization, Aleksandrov asserted, could not be transferred in part, or the necessary savings in costs would not be achieved: '*it is necessary that at a given enterprise everything from beginning to end should be mechanized*', and that complete new enterprises should be introduced one by one. The first major schemes would also serve as an attractive force, 'an example of culture in construction, an example proving the possibility of adopting American technology in our conditions'.†

In all these discussions about investment policy, the arguments about particular problems thus tended to turn on the conflict between the immediate need to economize in the use of capital and the long-term goal of a modernized capital-intensive economy. Let us look at each of the disputed issues in more detail.

New enterprises

The major argument in favour of extending existing enterprises rather than constructing new ones was that it required less capital per unit of output. The calculations were never very reliable. The amount of capital required tended to be underestimated in all proposals, whether they were for extensions to existing works or for the construction of new ones—it was known that a low estimate would be more readily accepted. The problem was strikingly illustrated in the case of the iron and steel industry. The initial estimates for new iron and steel works implied a capital cost of some 150 roubles per ton of capacity, while the equivalent capital cost in the case of extensions to existing works was generally estimated at less than 120 roubles.‡ Only one major extension scheme was actually undertaken in the late 1920s—the extension to the Kerch works. Here the approved capital cost per unit output when the work started was only half that of other planned extensions,§ and far less than that estimated for new works. But once the work was started the estimated cost of the Kerch investment nearly trebled in the course of two years, and became larger than that of constructing a new works of similar capacity.‖ However in the meantime the estimated cost of new works,

† *Torgovo-Promyshlennaya Gazeta*, 18 November, 1926.
‡ Compare A. P. Serebrovsky, *Rationalizatsiya Proizvodstva i Novoe Promyshlennoe Stroitel'stvo SSSR* (1927), pp. 104, 106; *Torgovo-Promyshlennaya Gazeta*, 10 July, 1927.
§ *Torgovo-Promyshlennaya Gazeta*, 25 May, 1926.
‖ *Torgovo-Promyshlennaya Gazeta*, 16 May and 21 June, 1928; *Pravda*, 8 September, 1928.

which had not even been started, also somewhat increased.† In this uncertain situation of rising estimates, attempts were even made to show
that new works could be constructed more cheaply than extensions to
existing works: one Vesenkha report claimed that new iron and steel
works would cost only 175 roubles per ton of capacity while extensions to
existing works, producing it is true a higher grade of metal, would cost
as much as 203 roubles per ton.‡ But as a general rule it was agreed that
the capital/output ratio was much lower for extensions to existing works
than for new ones. In the agricultural engineering industry, for example,
it was calculated that 2 roubles extra output per year could be obtained
per rouble invested in existing works as compared with only 0·74 roubles
planned from the new works at Rostov.§ The proposed new railway
wagon works at Nizhny Tagil was to cost 44 million roubles; five existing
works, if recapitalized, could produce the same output for an investment
of only 10 or 15 million roubles. ‖

The other major argument in favour of extending existing factories
was that new factories would tie up capital for several years while extensions to existing ones could be completed much more quickly. The
new works at Nizhny Tagil would take five years to construct; existing
works could produce the same output within one or two years.¶ The
existence of a lag was admitted by the protagonists of new works;††
Preobrazhensky even used the fact that there would be an average delay
of three years before new factories were completed as an argument, in
view of the necessity of constructing them, for greater urgency.‡‡

The economic case for the alternative of constructing new enterprises
was argued in terms of the lower production costs of the output which
would eventually be produced. The tractor industry offered a very obvious case: it cost five or six times as much to produce tractors in the shop
established at the old Putilov works as to purchase them from abroad;
production costs at the new works at Stalingrad were planned to be not
much higher than the price of foreign tractors§§ (however the argument
was spoiled within a few months when the cost of a Putilov tractor fell
to that planned at Stalingrad). ‖‖ Lower production costs in industry was
a major objective of economic policy throughout the 1920s: lower costs
would make possible both the higher industrial profits which would
finance future industrialization and the reduced industrial prices which
would satisfy the peasant. Thus Kaktyn' argued that industrialization

---

† *Torgovo-Promyshlennaya Gazeta*, 8 January, 1929.   ‡ *Ibid.*
§ *Torgovo-Promyshlennaya Gazeta*, 16 May, 1928.
‖ *Soyuz Sovetskikh Sotsialisticheskikh Respublik. IV S'ezd Sovetov* (1927), p. 233.   ¶ *Ibid.*
†† See for example Kaktyn' in *Bol'shevik*, No. 6, 1927, pp. 22–25.
‡‡ *Bol'shevik*, No. 6, 1926, p. 64.
§§ *XV Konferentsiya VKP(b)* (1926), p. 122; *Torgovo-Promyshlennaya Gazeta*, 21 October, 1926.
‖‖ *SSSR. Tsentral'nyi Ispolnitel'nyi Komitet, 3 Sessiya 3 Sozyva* (1927), pp. 11–12.

'provides its own practical justification and will be accepted by the whole country and particularly its peasant section only on condition that *industrial output is made cheaper as a result*'.† The decree on rationalization issued by the central committee of the party called for the establishment of new enterprises 'on the basis of the latest achievements in science and technology' and for 'fundamental re-equipment' of existing industry, together with the maximum use of capacity, as essential requirements of successful rationalization.‡ The five-year plan, in all its variants, postulated the reduction of industrial costs as a key requirement for financing the investment programme.§

It was also suggested by the protagonists of new factories that the possibilities of extending existing factories were extremely limited. In August 1926, for example, Vesenkha of the Ukraine predicted that the 1928–29 plan for iron output could not be met by the existing works, and that the construction of new iron and steel works must therefore immediately be started in the Ukraine.‖ A year later Serebrovsky asserted that 'the technical base we have inherited is almost completely utilized, and the task is mainly not to recapitalize industry but to construct new works and factories'.¶ These assumptions proved premature. Without new factories the Ukraine in fact reached in 1928–29 the amount of iron planned for that year in 1926; and a critic of Serebrovsky pointed out that while it was true that existing capacity was nearly completely restored, considerable possibilities existed of extending the capacity of existing factories.††

Finally, it was frequently argued in support of the construction of new works that general social and economic benefits could not always be reflected in straightforward calculations in terms of present costs. Thus in the case of Dnieprostroi, Aleksandrov pointed out that in order to estimate the annual gains from the project the benefits to agriculture and transport from the improvements to the Dniepr river should be taken into account as well as the savings from the reduced cost of cheap electric power.‡‡

Large-scale factories

The main argument against constructing enterprises which had a large capacity rested on the small size of the Soviet market. Thus in the case of electricity, the low consumption meant that power produced by large stations would need to be transmitted over long distances incur-

---

† *Bol'shevik*, No. 6, 1927, p. 27.   ‡ *VKP(b) o Profsoyuzakh* (1940), p. 308.
§ See R. W. Davies, *The Development of the Soviet Budgetary System* (Cambridge, 1958), pp. 194–97. (The short-term effect of the pressure to reduce production costs on the pattern of industrial investment is discussed on p. 302 below.)
‖ *Ekonomicheskaya Zhizn'*, 3 August, 1926.
¶ Serebrovsky, *Ratsionalizatsiya Proizvodstva i Novoe Promyshlennoe Stroitel'stvo SSSR*.
†† *Bol'shevik*, No. 17, 1927, p. 99.   ‡‡ *Ekonomicheskaya Zhizn'*, 10 December, 1926.

ring additional capital costs as well as power losses in the transmission lines. The problem of sales arose much more acutely in the case of all manufacturing industries. The new Dniepr and Nizhny Tagil railway wagon works were each planned to have an annual output which at 5–6,000 was far smaller than was usual in the United States;[†] it was nevertheless at first doubted whether the railways would be able to buy all their output. The problem of sales also worried the planners in the new tractor and motor endustries, in engineering generally, and in such consumer industries as footwear. Even on the assumption that the state could create its own market, severe restraints existed on the size of major factories owing to the shortage of investment funds. Total annual industrial investment was only a small fraction of that in the United States or even Britain, and in these circumstances the decision to establish a number of major new industries in the U.S.S.R. meant that the scale of major plants was restricted—one of Bazarov's main arguments for concentrating investment on a small number of industries was that this would make large-scale mass production possible.

Critics of large units also pointed out that some of the proposals for large factories merely involved the vertical integration of a number of fairly small units. There was a tendency to try to build huge combines in which the whole production process from raw material to finished good took place. Engineers argued that such combines were now out-of-date; and pointed out that Ford had shown that the production of components could take place in small factories in small towns and villages, where the cost of production could be lower, with the result that the advantages of mass production were combined with the virtues of decentralization.[‡] The Rostov agricultural engineering factory was particularly strongly criticized as a conglomeration of a number of units producing different products; time could have been saved by building each of them separately in sequence. Its defenders replied that the conglomeration of the units on a single site made it possible to provide common preparatory shops and services.[§] In the textile industry, some critics of the conservative-minded engineers who ran its scientific and technical council condemned them for unthinkingly advocating the construction of large factories when in the United States small highly specialized factories had been shown to be more efficient and easier to administer.[||]

In spite of these arguments, it was already widely believed that the new factories which were to be constructed should be as large as or larger than contemporary Western factories. Gosplan asserted in 1926 that

[†] *Torgovo-Promyshlennya Gazeta*, 29 July, 1928.
[‡] *Torgovo-Promyshlennya Gazeta*, 15 and 30 June and 7 July, 1928.
[§] *Torgovo-Promyshlennya Gazeta*, 13 July and 3 August, 1928.
[||] *Torgovo-Promyshlennya Gazeta*, 31 March, 1928; and see the reply by Professor A. Fedotov in the issue of 27 May, 1928.

large coal-mines must be the basis of the new Donbass.[†] The GOELRO plan in 1920 had already been based on a centralized network of what were considered large modern power-stations; nevertheless, a review of electric power construction in 1927 concluded that the power stations GOELRO had proposed, with turbo-generators of 10 thousand kW capacity, were too small: the aim should be to construct power-stations which had a capacity of 300,000 kW and which used generators each of which had a capacity of 60,000 kW or more. The case for such developments rested primarily on economies of scale. The large generators, for example, would use a minimum amount of steam per kWh, and could be fed by high-pressure boilers requiring a small capital outlay per kilowatt of capacity.[‡] Sales difficulties could to some extent be overcome by standardization and specialization, to which a great deal of attention was devoted. Kuibyshev defined a 'rationalized enterprise' as 'one which engages in mass production on a large scale, of standardized quality, and sizes, and applies continuous flow production as the best organizational and technical method'.[§] But even in the West the short-term prospects for the widespread introduction of mass production were exaggerated in the 1920s; Kuibyshev admitted that in Soviet conditions the universal use of continuous flow production would result in the saturation of the market within three or four years.[||]

The economic argument in favour of large factories was sometimes supported by the argument that large units could be more easily controlled from the centre and thus persuaded to adopt a progressive technological policy. At the same time the concentration of industrial workers into large units was believed by Marxists to result in greater political awareness and activity. One writer summed up the case for large factories succinctly when he claimed in the case of the textile industry that they were more profitable, that it was easier to give proper technical leadership where the units were large, and that '*politically such factories are a mighty proletarian fortress for us*'.[¶]

Capital-intensive technology

In the U.S.S.R., labour was cheaper and more abundant in relation to capital than in the West generally and the United States in particular. There was therefore a strong economic and social case, at least on short-term considerations, for using more labour per unit of capital in every investment project than in the more advanced countries. Some economists even argued that 'labour-intensity' per unit of capital should

[†] *Torgovo-Promyshlennya Gazeta*, 13 June, 1926.
[‡] *Ekonomicheskoe Obozrenie*, No. 10, 1927, pp. 139–40.
[§] *Torgovo-Promyshlennya Gazeta*, 29 August, 1928.   [||] *Ibid.*
[¶] *Torgovo-Promyshlennaya Gazeta*, 12 May, 1928.

be the main criterion for judging the desirability of an investment.[†] On these grounds, industrial investments were proposed which would absorb large numbers of under-employed artisans, and it was argued that agricultural investments should be directed into labour-intensive crops such as maize. Many experts who strongly supported the construction of new and even of large factories nevertheless believed that Western technology should be applied more labour-intensively in the U.S.S.R. The general case was put bluntly by Professor Fedotov of the scientific and technical council of the textile industry:

Our capital is at a minimum, it is very expensive and at the same time there is a sufficiently large reserve of labour. In America however capital is cheap and labour is expensive...In our conditions our aim must be that machines, which are dear here, should produce the maximum product; here the more intensive use of personal labour must be given second place.[‡]

A professor in the metal industry even more bluntly contrasted 'the industrial structure of a mature industrial country' with 'the structure of a country which has only just crawled out of colonial conditions and is freeing itself from handicraft (*kustar*) habits'.[§] Professor Derzhavin, a leading official in the textile scientific and technical council, described the wish to use the most up to date equipment as 'revolutionary romanticism'.[||] In practical terms the textile engineers argued that highly priced equipment which was suitable in the United States often did not pay in Britain and the U.S.S.R.; and in particular questioned the quite extensive development in the U.S.S.R. of the production of automatic Northrop looms to replace the simpler Platt looms, complaining that this manufacture had been organized without their participation.[¶] The Northrop loom, a United States design taken over by a British company, automatically fitted new spools; in the Platt loom they were fitted by hand. It was reported that pre-1914 Moscow factories had been 'strongly occupied with the idea of going over from simple mechanical looms to automatic'; and in 1924–25 the production of Northrop looms had been organized 'under the influence of a few people from the Ivanovo–Voznesensk trust', so that by early 1928 they were produced at four factories. A study of the two types of loom arranged by the scientific and technical council of the textile industry purported to show that the running costs of the Northrop loom were not much lower.[††] These engineers also suggested that if the looms were to be used it was appro-

[†] See Collette, *op. cit.*, pp. 27–30.
[‡] *Torgovo-Promyshlennaya Gazeta*, 27, May, 1928.
[§] Cited in *Torgovo-Promyshlennaya Gazeta*, 6 July, 1928.
[||] *Torgovo-Promyshlennaya Gazeta*, 28 July, 1928.
[¶] *Torgovo-Promyshlennaya Gazeta*, 27 April and 29 June, 1928.
[††] See *Puti Industrializatsii*, No. 2, 1928, pp. 43–46, and No. 11, 1928, pp. 46–49.

priate, because labour was relatively cheap, to work them for three shifts instead of the one shift normal in the United States, and to have fewer looms per worker; it was also in general correct to run textile machinery faster than in the United States even though this meant using more labour and involved some deterioration in quality.† Experience at a Tver factory showed that, on the assumption that capital was amortized at $7\frac{1}{2}$ per cent and bore an interest rate of 12 per cent, the saving from faster running could be about 3·8 per cent of manufacturing costs, though this calculation made no allowance for any deterioration in quality.‡ Such evidence, although in this instance it was disputed by the technical manager of the Stalingrad spinning works,§ seemed to show fairly conclusively that in terms of the cost structure which existed in 1928 more labour-intensive methods were more profitable. And behind these arguments in terms of existing costs there lurked the view, firmly held by many non-party experts, but not often expressed in print, that Soviet industrial labour was overpaid in terms of its economic value, and that in view of the abundant supply of labour there was no economic justification for the Soviet government to maintain substantially lower working hours and higher real wages than had been paid before the war.

The approach of these experts was rejected as technically reactionary and mistaken in its facts. One critic claimed that they had been educated 'under the strong influence of British technical thought, which is ossified in its development', and failed to realize the importance of placing industry on a higher technical basis. ‖ An article entitled 'The Technical Revolution in Danger' declared that the principal scientists and engineers responsible for the metal and textile industries were incapable of achieving the technical revolution.¶ In more specific terms, the protagonists of the most advanced Western capital-intensive technology argued that both labour costs and skills were in fact already higher than before the war, so that more mechanization was economically justified; skilled as distinct from unskilled labour was already scarce and would become more scarce as a result of the introduction of a seven-hour day— 'the Soviet Union has already ceased to be a country of cheap labour'.†† The correct policy must be to establish a new technical basis for industry and to create a highly-skilled working class; this would enable the problem of the relatively low standard of living of the Soviet working class to be solved.‡‡

† *Torgovo-Promyshlennaya Gazeta*, 27 April, 27 May and 20 June, 1928.
‡ *Torgovo-Promyshlennaya Gazeta*, 26 June, 1928.
§ *Torgovo-Promyshlennaya Gazeta*, 1 July, 1928.
‖ *Torgovo-Promyshlennaya Gazeta*, 24 June, 1928.
¶ *Torgovo-Promyshlennaya Gazeta*, 6 July, 1928.
†† *Torgovo-Promyshlennaya Gazeta*, 27 April, 24 June and 28 July, 1928.
‡‡ *Torgovo-Promyshlennaya Gazeta*, 6 July and 16 August, 1928.

The division of views about investment policy which has been described cannot be explained simply within the framework of the struggle within the party. Enthusiasm for the latest Western technology, and for embodying it in major new projects, was an important trend throughout the 1920s, and was found outside as well as within the party. A number of non-Communist engineers were associated with the technologically ambitious GOELRO plan, and they and others played an active part in the preparation of plans for large new works in the iron and steel and other industries.† By 1926, Professor I. G. Aleksandrov, the engineer who was the principal designer of Dnieprostroi, had like Krzhizhanovsky become known as a major public advocate of the construction of large modern works.‡ In 1925 and 1926, much of this enthusiasm of non-party experts was channelled into the 'hypotheses' for a five-year plan prepared by the Special Commission on the Restoration of Fixed Capital (OSVOK) of Vesenkha, which incorporated proposals for many of the major new factories which were eventually built in the 1930s. Enthusiasm for new construction on American lines was also found among factory managements. A critical commentator in the journal of the Red Directors suggested that:

With very, very many of our business managers, technicians and engineers, the huge majority of them, the conviction has long been deep-rooted that the rationalization of industrial economy is uninterruptedly connected with its fundamental re-equipment and renewal, with the construction of new enterprises. . . this idea is one of the substantial obstacles in the business of rationalizing the existing economy. Hopes for a quick re-equipment *ab initio*, dreams of 'Americanization' of our industry, plans and projects of new building jobs have so seized the thought and will of our officials that they have an almost contemptuous attitude to the humdrum everyday work on improving, simplifying and cheapening the existing economy, which the well-known appeal signed by comrades Rykov, Stalin and Kuibyshev calls for.§

On the other hand there were many complaints of the persistence of conservatism and adherence to traditional methods and out-of-date technology among both economic administrators and factory managements. A characteristic resolution from a Ukrainian congress on rationalization, held in October 1926, asserted:

Our production is grounded in traditions and experience. Sometimes, however inadequate something might be, it is stuck to, and any innovation is met with suspicion. It is not so easy to follow the path of struggling for new technology and for establishing new traditions; to break up the old to which

† See for example *Byulleten' Gosplana*, No. 6–7, 1923, pp. 52–53; *Planovoe Khozyaistvo*, No. 7, 1926, p. 71 ff.
‡ See for example *Torgovo-Promyshlennaya Gazeta*, 18 November, 1926.
§ *Predpriyatie*, No. 10, 1926, p. 13.

we are accustomed, with which we grew up. The cause of this is our backwardness, our general cultural backwardness and in particular our technical backwardness.†

Within the party there was at first no clear-cut division of views. The supporters of the Left Opposition, and notably Pyatakov, Preobrazhensky and Trotsky, were certainly more or less consistent adherents of the construction of new modern factories. But within the party majority, and among senior party economic administrators, there was at first great confusion. At one time Vesenkha, while Kuibyshev was present, even resolved that investment should be concentrated on factories 'which survive in competition with countries leading in technology, or at least come near to doing so'.‡ At this time Rukhimovich, a leading official of Vesenkha and a strong advocate of industrial expansion, while accepting the view that modern enterprises should be constructed in every industry as models, was cautious about the extent to which investment should be directed towards new factories, and argued that no general answer was possible;§ he also criticized what he stigmatized as a 'universal tendency' to design unnecessarily large works.‖ But the group around Stalin gradually became identified with the policy of concentrating investment on new, large and capital-intensive factories of a modern American type. The crystallization of policy was dramatically symbolized as early as 1926 when Stalin changed his position about Dnieprostroi. In April 1926 he sceptically compared it with a peasant buying a gramophone instead of repairing his plough;¶ by the end of the year he had become one of its principal advocates. Kuibyshev, who became president of Vesenkha in August 1926, emerged as one of the strongest supporters of the construction of new works. In November 1926, he defended Dnieprostroi on the grounds that it would bring about qualitative changes in technology;†† and at the fourth Congress of Soviets in April 1927 he criticized business managers who wanted to allocate a higher proportion of total investment to the expansion of existing factories.‡‡ In 1927, the journal of Red Directors reversed its policy of a year earlier and attacked the 'passion' to repair and restore out-of-date enterprises even when restoration was dearer than constructing a new factory.§§ During 1928, the advocacy of large new capital-intensive factories became official policy. This decision was closely associated with

† Cited in *Predpriyatie*, No. 6, 1928, p. 24.
‡ *Ekonomicheskaya Zhizn'*, 27 February, 1927.
§ *Ekonomicheskaya Zhizn'*, 23 February, 1927.
‖ *Torgovo-Promyshlennaya Gazeta*, 16 June, 1928.
¶ E. H. Carr, *Socialism in One Country, 1924–1926*, Vol. 1 (London 1958), pp. 355, 535.
†† *Istoricheskii Arkhiv*, No. 3, 1958, p. 44.
‡‡ *Soyuz Sovetskikh Sotsialisticheskikh Respublik IV S'ezd Sovetov*, pp. 255, 384–87.
§§ *Predpriyatie*, No. 7, 1927, p. 8.

the larger decision to force through rapid industrialization in spite of the resistance of the peasantry. In March 1925, TsIK, the Central Executive Committee of Soviets, while cautiously approving a policy of technical modernization, had also asserted that it was necessary 'in all measures concerning industry and transport to start by considering the development of agriculture and its production for the market'.† In October 1928, the central committee of the party, in a message to the Moscow organization which opened the public struggle against the Right wing, firmly and unconditionally declared that in spite of the strained situation and the goods shortages the rate of development of industry in general and of heavy industry in particular must not be reduced, and coupled with this a renewed assertion of the importance of new technology:

We have finished the process of restoration of the national economy. We have entered the period of its recapitalization, the period of the direct socialist transformation of the economy on the basis of new technology.‡

By this time the variant of the five-year plan prepared by Vesenkha in August 1928 proposed that between October 1928 and September 1933 as much as 47 per cent of investment in industry should be in new factories, even though they would only produce 20 per cent of total industrial output by the end of the plan period.§ The journal of the Red Directors now gave a firm answer to the problems of technical policy:

Can any of us insist on a 'little hold-up' in the construction of new blast-furnaces? The iron and steel industry needs new giant enterprises, the chemical industry needs new works and factories, and so do a whole number of other industries.‖

The policy of rapid industrialization and the drive for modern technology reinforced each other: a rapid pace of industrialization made it possible to envisage the kind of expenditure which was required for a programme of constructing major new factories on American lines; and the need to fulfil this programme was used as an argument to reinforce the case for more rapid industrial expansion.

2. INVESTMENT POLICY IN PRACTICE

These discussions about policy were taking place in the context of the first practical decisions about the shape of industrial investment. This section considers the influence of the conflicting ideas about investment in practice before the end of the 1920's.

† *Direktivy KPSS i Sovetskogo Pravitel'stva po Khozyaistvennym Voprosam*, i, (1957), pp. 506–7.
‡ *Ekonomicheskaya Zhizn'*, 19 October, 1928.   § *Pravda*, 2 September, 1928.
‖ Vl. Sarabyanov in *Predpriyatie*, No. 10, 1928, p. 11.

The view that Soviet industrial development should be based on modern technology and on large new capital-intensive factories had a substantial practical impact. At the level of the individual industry, several attempts were made as early as the mid-1920s to introduce modern technology: the most striking was in the oil industry, which was highly profitable, and used its profits to undertake a major programme of of modernization.† At the level of the factory, technical modernization was also attempted on a smaller scale. Thus the *Krasny Vyborzhets* works in Leningrad introduced electric smelting and electrified loading and unloading in one of its shops, and decided to replace its old steam boilers by electric power.‡ The individual industry and factory did not act entirely autonomously. In deciding to modernize, they were partly responding to pressures from the government, and, in some cases, from the market, to reduce their costs. But decisions by industry to introduce new technology cannot be entirely explained in terms of pressures from the centre or of a clear economic motivation. When the Donbass coal industry undertook what was described as 'the Americanization of getting and loading',§ this had the effect of reducing its costs, but, as was usual at this time, no proper calculations were made of the expected financial return. ‖ An autonomous enthusiasm for new technology, based on general confidence in its desirability, was undoubtedly present.

Other pressures tended to constrain the impulse towards new technology. These were partly institutional. Local and republican authorities controlled resources which could be used for new investment; and while they were sometimes anxious to establish impressive modern factories under their own control, the smallness of the amount of resources available for each project tended to result in wasteful investment and in a large number of new starts. As industrialization got under way, republican and local industry was increasingly starved of investment resources, and central controls were introduced over investments undertaken at republican and local level; these investments were therefore of diminishing importance as an autonomous factor. But all industry, including industry administered by the all-Union Vesenkha, was subject to short-term pressures which modified the drive towards new technology. Two major pressures will be discussed here in some detail: the pressure to increase output and the pressure to reduce production costs.

The pressure to increase output

In a situation of capital scarcity, the pressure from the central government for increased production tended to drive the pattern of capital

---

† See *Bol'shevik*, No. 9, 1927, pp. 42–43.   ‡ *Predpriyatie*, No. 7, 1927, pp. 64–66.
§ *Predpriyatie*, No. 1, 1926, pp. 95–96.
‖ See *Pervye Shagi Industrializatsii SSSR 1926–1927 gg.* (1959), pp. 88–90.

spending towards those investments which were less costly in capital, and away from investment in new capital-intensive factories. Three ways in which this happened can be distinguished. Firstly, investment was used to bring back into operation older factories or industrial plant which had been closed down in the earlier 1920s owing to their high production costs. This was a common occurrence in 1925–26 and 1926–27, as production approached the pre-war level; a series of official reports attributed a large part of the failure of costs to fall in these years in industry as a whole, and the actual increase in costs in certain industries, to the high costs of bringing older factories and equipment back into use.† The shortage of machine-tools, which had almost all been imported before the first world war, was so great that according to one report most factories were using all their pre-war stock of machine-tools and were also skimping repairs so as to keep them in production as continuously as possible;‡ however, there were reports in other industries of available capacity which was not yet utilized.§

Secondly, as a result of the pressure to increase output, investment tended in practice to be used to extend the capacity of existing works rather than to construct new ones. Plans to undertake major new schemes of industrial construction were sometimes rejected owing to their high capital costs. Thus the original five-year plan for the sugar-refining industry drawn up by a sub-commission of OSVOK proposed that only a quarter of the proposed increases in output should occur in existing works; the rest should come from new factories. This approach, later described as 'industrial romanticism', was gradually modified; successive drafts of the plan in 1926 and 1927 reduced the number of new factories planned and the total claim of the industry for capital investment.‖ In order to obtain a more rapid increase in output, industries and trusts sometimes violated the instructions they had been given from the centre about the allocation of their investments, and switched resources from the construction of new works to the extension of existing ones. Thus a Vesenkha commission reported that in 1926–27 both the Vesenkha department in charge of the fuel industry and the Donbass coal trust had switched resources in this way, so that 40 per cent of the allocations had not been used for the intended purpose.¶ The restoration and extension of existing factories usually proved less costly in capital, so that such switches saved capital as well as producing results more quickly; in Yugostal, for example, in 1925–26 an investment was required of less

† *Torgovo-Promyshlennaya Gazeta*, 17 and 22 September and 28 November, 1926 and 17 July, 1927.
‡ *Predpriyatie*, No. 7, 1927, pp. 27–32.
§ See, for example, *Torgovo-Promyshlennaya Gazeta*, 7 September, 1927.
‖ See *Torgovo-Promyshlennaya Gazeta*, 18 January, 1928.
¶ *Torgovo-Promyshlennaya Gazeta*, 13 January, 1928.

than 7 roubles per additional ton of pig-iron as compared with a minimum cost of 25 roubles to build a new furnace.† But the resulting production costs were higher. Sometimes the hasty expansion of existing
capacity proved expensive in capital as well as in production costs. It
was claimed, for example, that the production of the *Elektrostal'* works in
Moscow was trebled, at high cost, 'under the influence of the requirements of the moment', in preference to a more rational development
which had been planned elsewhere.‡ Between 1925 and 1927, in the
course of the drive to make full use of existing capacity in the engineering
industry, shops in 16 factories were retooled and re-equipped to produce
textile machinery and shops in eight factories were converted to the
production of Diesel engines; and several factories tried to produce
agricultural equipment and railway wagons and failed because of lack
of orders. Such small-scale attempts to introduce new technology in the
form of new products were reported to be wasteful of investment and at
the same time to result in high production costs because of the small scale
of production and the lack of specialization, and were used as an argument for closer central co-ordination.§

Thirdly, the pressure for output sometimes led trusts and industries
to undertake the construction of new works in a hasty or unplanned way.
This particularly tended to happen when the pressure for more output
resulted in a shortage of inputs essential to an industry; the industry or
trust was consequently driven towards an investment policy which increased the amount of backward integration. The Ukrainian iron and
steel works had their own coal-mines even before the revolution; more
were established in the 1920s. In order to obtain electric power, industry
tended to erect its own power plants rather than wait for the completion
of the regional power-stations of the GOELRO plan. These investments
were often expensive in capital and their cost of production was always
high.||

The effect of such hasty *ad hoc* decisions to construct new factories was
inevitably that these new factories tended to be small. The most striking
example of this was in the coal industry. The original intention was to
concentrate on developing large modern pits; but in June 1926, the
Soviet government itself approved a programme of developing a large
number of medium-size and small pits to overcome the fuel shortage.¶
During the first two years of this programme, the capital costs of these

† *Torgovo-Promyshlennaya Gazeta*, 17 September, 1927.
‡ *Predpriyatie*, No. 8, 1928, pp. 32–33.
§ *Torgovo-Promyshlennaya Gazeta*, 1 and 17 September, 1927; *Predpriyatie*, No. 8, 1928, pp.
30–33.
|| *Pravda*, 1 March, 1927; *Torgovo-Promyshlennaya Gazeta*, 17 and 22 September, 1926 and
1 March, 1927.
¶ *Torgovo-Promyshlennaya Gazeta*, 13 June, 1926.

small and medium pits, while much less than for large pits, were considerably higher than had been planned; and they produced only half the planned output, at a cost per ton which was higher than had been expected.† However, the pressure for more output did not work entirely in the direction of small units. The tendency towards backward integration which has already been noted resulted in large conglomerations of factories or departments under single administrative control; the total unit was large, though the amount of particular items which was produced in the auxiliary shops or factories would often be small, and production costs high.

The pressure for more output in conditions of capital scarcity also inhibited the attempt to invest in a capital-intensive manner. In spite of the objections of the enthusiasts for the latest American technology, modern equipment and new technical processes often used more labour per unit of capital than in the West. In the oil industry, for example, there were far more men per drill than in the United States.‡ Instead of the proposed mechanization of a factory 'from beginning to end', a high degree of mechanization of major processes was often accompanied by a low degree of mechanization of auxiliary processes: the coal industry provides some clear examples here.§ In contrast to the conflicting principles of 'capital-intensity throughout' or 'labour-intensity throughout' the practical solution was thus either to use capital-intensive processes in a labour-intensive way or to combine capital-intensive and labour-intensive processes under the same roof. The capital-labour ratio was also lowered by using capital more intensively. In the cotton textile industry a three-shift system began to be introduced in 1928. In the case of many of the new factories, such as the Stalingrad tractor factory, the number of shifts planned per day was increased when the projected capacity was raised.

To sum up the effects of the pressure for increased output: it tended to encourage investment in restoring and extending existing factories rather than in constructing new ones; when this pressure impelled the construction of new factories to overcome bottlenecks in production or supplies, these factories were small, even when they formed part of a large trust, and did not use advanced technology. At the same time the pressure to increase output modified capital-intensive programmes in such a way as to maximize output per unit of capital.

† For details see *Pervye Shagi Industrializatsii SSSR 1926–1927 gg.*, pp. 102–109.
‡ *Bol'shevik*, No. 9, 1927, p. 43.
§ *Pervye Shagi Industrializatsii SSSR 1926–1927 gg.*, p. 89.

The pressure to reduce costs

The reasons for which the government actively pursued the aim of reducing production costs have already been discussed. However, the pressure to reduce costs was not simply conveyed to enterprises through government orders, though these were important. In the middle 1920s, many products could find a market only if their prices were sufficiently low. Trusts also had an incentive to reduce costs in those cases, particularly frequent in the engineering industries, in which imported products were cheaper than home production even though they paid a high import duty; the effect of this differential price was that consuming enterprises tried to obtain a licence to import rather than buy at home. Trusts and industries in any case had some incentive to make a profit, and this gave them an autonomous incentive to reduce costs (and to increase the output of these goods which were most profitable).

In the long term, attempts to reduce costs necessarily encouraged at least those technologically more advanced kinds of investment which were economically efficient. Preobrazhensky stressed that '*the extension and technical re-equipment of industry is the main means of reducing prices*';[†] and similar views were expressed by Aleksandrov, Mezhlauk and others.[‡] But the short-term effects of the pressure to reduce costs were more complicated. It certainly inhibited the use of out-of-date equipment. Thus Vesenkha of the Ukraine pointed out that the re-opening of closed iron and steel works was 'economically inexpedient in view of the fact that equipment is to a considerable extent worn out and out of date'.[§] In Sverdlovsk, the president of a trust declared during a costs reduction campaign that it would 'go as far as the mass closing of unprofitable enterprises'.[||] In a number of industries, older high cost plants were in fact closed at various times in the 1920s. But on the other hand the cost reduction campaigns also favoured investment which would yield quick as well as high returns; and tended to encourage rapid adaptations of existing factories rather than the construction of new ones. In September 1926, in the course of a campaign to reduce costs, Rukhimovich attacked the tendency to be '*diverted with the latest "American" equipment*' even when less outlay would give greater savings; and cited a new glass works the output of which would still be more expensive than imports.[¶] A year later Kuibyshev, in a report on costs, attacked 'playing at America' and the use of the new equipment 'for the sake of new equipment'; he called for rationalization which was subordinated to the interests of costs re-

† *Bol'shevik*, No. 6, 1927, p. 64.
‡ *Torgovo-Promyshlennaya Gazeta*, 22 September, 1926 and 17 July, 1927.
§ *Ekonomicheskaya Zhizn'*, 3 August, 1926.
|| *Torgovo-Promyshlennaya Gazeta*, 14 October, 1927.
¶ *Torgovo-Promyshlennaya Gazeta*, 17 September, 1926.

duction and supported investment which would be quickly recouped and would have a direct influence on costs.† In their struggle to obtain higher output and to finance a higher general level of investment, Soviet leaders like Kuibyshev who supported radical technical change were nevertheless driven towards cheap and expedient solutions.

It is difficult to make a general assessment of the result of the interplay of the various factors influencing industry and policy towards industry in the 1920s: the rival technological policies, the pressures to increase output and reduce costs, and the changing market situation. Different pressures often led to confusion or conflict in investment decisions. The Lugansk loco works offers a characteristic example of the uncertainties which resulted. At first, it was decided to re-equip and extend the existing works; but a technical survey concluded that the factory was too out-of-date and that a new one should be built. The construction of this new factory was delayed because of lack of resources; and meanwhile the existing factory was given very small allocations for capital repair. However, in the course of 1927 the urgent need for the output of the factory led to a decision that the existing factory should after all be quickly reconstructed.‡

For industry as a whole, three main periods may be tentatively distinguished. In the first period, between 1923 and the beginning or middle of 1925, production rose rapidly; but at the same time a policy was pursued of concentrating production in the largest and most modern of the existing factories. As late as 1925 and even 1926, in major industries the number of industrial units which were actually working was far smaller than in 1913 or in 1922, even though production was several times as large as in 1922 and was approaching the pre-war level.§ The policy of concentrating production was a major factor in the impressive reduction in costs which occurred in 1924 and early 1925,‖ though a successful policy of wage restraint was also important. The second period runs from the middle of 1925 to the end of 1926 or the early months of 1927. Although efforts were made to reduce costs in this period, the main emphasis in practice was on increasing production through the bringing back into operation of older plant; costs were at best stable though wage increases now played some part in the failure of the costs campaign. The third period may be dated from the beginning of 1927 to the be-

† *Torgovo-Promyshlennaya Gazeta*, 14 August, 1927.
‡ *Torgovo-Promyshlennaya Gazeta*, 28 August and 30 November, 1927; *Istoricheskii Arkhiv*, No. 3, 1958, pp. 49–52.
§ See for example *Pervye Shagi Industrializatsii SSSR 1926–1927 gg.*, p. 87; *Predpriyatie*, No. 10, 1927, pp. 62–64.
‖ *Torgovo-Promyshlennaya Gazeta*, 17 September, 1926.

ginning of 1929. In this period the government succeeded in increasing output while at the same time reducing industrial costs substantially: increases in output were primarily a result of investment in improving and extending existing factories; investment efforts were concentrated on piece-meal developments which would increase output while somewhat reducing costs—but again as in 1924 a successful policy of wage restraint was an important factor. Developments in the second and the third period revealed greater possibilities of increasing output at existing factories than had been thought available in 1925: production increased more rapidly between 1925 and 1929, and with a smaller investment of capital, than the OSVOK plan, for example, had proposed.

During both the second and third periods the policy of concentrating investment on the construction of new factories was put into effect, at least in part. In spite of the counter-pressures which have been described, the proportion of capital investment spent on new factories in industry planned by Vesenkha increased each year, and rose from about one-eighth of the total in 1925–26 to about one-third in 1928–29.[†] This was an impressive increase. However, it was smaller than that planned in 1925 by OSVOK, which wanted new factories to receive one-third of industrial investment over the whole period October 1, 1925 to September 30, 1930.[‡] Moreover, much of the investment in new factories was in smaller projects which could be rapidly completed. While an appreciable advance was made in the technical level of industry in these years, the large new long-term projects, which were to form the backbone of the first five-year plan, were frequently postponed, and received allocations which were smaller than had been originally planned: only Dnieprostroi, the Turksib railway, and the Stalingrad tractor factory received more than trivial sums before the autumn of 1929. By the eve of collectivization, the principal organizations for designing the major new works had been established and were hard at work; and contracts had been signed with the principal foreign consultants. But the big push was yet to come. The delay was due to several factors. It was difficult to organize and prepare such major projects. The projects were resisted by many of the leading economists and engineers who were advising the government. But the delay was to a considerable extent a result of the pressures on government and industry which resulted from the immediate desire or need to increase output and reduce costs.

From the end of 1929, the situation changed rapidly. Total annual investment in industry increased several-fold. The major new projects were given a large share of total investment. A technological revolution

---

† See *Osnovnye Momenty Rekonstruktsii Promyshlennosti*, ed. S. V. Minaev (1931), p. 57; *Ekonomicheskoe Obozrenie*, No. 10, 1929, pp. 121–3; *Bol'shevik*, No. 4, 1927, pp. 35–6.

‡ *Torgovo-Promyshlennaya Gazeta*, 18 July, 1926.

began. Even so, the kind of technological compromises which took place in the later 1920s still occurred. In the 1930s, the introduction of the most modern technology was concentrated on certain industries. In the case of other industries, proposals for their technological transformation which had been made in the 1920s were dropped: the building materials industry continued to produce timber and bricks rather than reinforced concrete; the railways used steam locos rather than Diesels; much of the new development proposed for the chemical industry did not take place; some important types of industrial equipment continued to be imported. New industries were established with large factories employing modern technology, such as the heavy industrial equipment industry and the tractor industry; and new modern plants were built in older industries such as iron and steel. But even in the modern industries, as Professor Granick has shown, capital-intensive and labour-intensive processes operated side by side.†

A NOTE ON INVESTMENT CRITERIA

A great deal of attention was paid at this time, among both economists and politicians, to the problem of the criteria to be used in comparing proposals for investment. In May 1927, a commission including Kuibyshev and Rukhimovich was established to investigate the effectiveness of investment, and production costs, in metal and engineering works.‡ In July of the same year, Rukhimovich congratulated Sokolovsky and the group of officials concerned with costs in Vesenkha for taking industry through a school of learning not to ignore cost and output calculations when making an investment.§ This discussion of the merits of different projects and alternative technologies very often involved attempts, usually of an unsophisticated kind, at measuring the return on capital.‖ The indicator most frequently used was the additional annual output per rouble of capital invested. Using this indicator, Shanin and Sokolnikov argued that relatively less investment was required in agriculture than in industry.¶ Capital/output or equipment/output ratios were published for all the major industries;†† the not surprising conclusion was reached that the producer goods or heavy industries required more investment per unit of output than the consumer goods or light industries. This indicator was recognised to be unsatisfactory as it merely showed the least capital-intensive investments; it provided no measurement either of the 'need' for a particular

† *Quarterly Journal of Economics*, May 1957 and *American Economic Review*, May 1957 and May 1962.

‡ *Pravda*, 11 May, 1927.   § *Torgovo-Promyshlennaya Gazeta*, 17 July, 1927.

‖ A careful comparative analysis of Soviet discussions on investment criteria will be found in J.-M. Collette, *op. cit.*, to which I am indebted for its valuable insights.

¶ *Bol'shevik*, No. 4, 1926, p. 89; No. 2, 1926, pp. 65–87.

†† See for example *Materialy Osobogo Soveshchaniya po Voprosam Vosstanovleniya Osnovnogo Kapitala pri Prezidiume VSNKh SSSR*, Seriya III, vypusk 1 pp. 35–39, vypusk 4, pp. 24–28; *Perspektivy Razvertivaniya Narodnogo Khozyaistva SSSR na 1926/27–1930/31 gg.* (1927), pp. 89–91.

factory or of the savings in production costs as compared with existing factories or alternative investments. In a market economy, need and costs savings combined could be measured in terms of profit per unit of capital; but in the U.S.S.R. in 1925–29 most prices were already fixed by the state. Producer goods' prices were relatively low, so that in these industries the capital/profits ratio was relatively high, and provided no criterion of the relative desirability of investing in one type of production rather than another. The problem of taking account of need was not dealt with quantitatively: in support of investment in the producer goods industries it was merely argued in general terms that from the national-economic point of view 'enterprises not giving a profit can nevertheless be very important', and that to concentrate investment on the consumer goods industries would contradict national-economic interests.†

The capital-output ratio also showed that less capital and equipment were required to extend old factories than to construct new ones.‡ The main alternative method of measuring the effect of an investment was in terms of the savings in production costs. This measure gave a more favourable verdict on capital-intensive technology; new factories fairly systematically showed lower production costs per unit of output than extensions to old ones. J.-M. Collette points out, 'les critères de rendement [output per unit of capital] stimulent les investissements modestes, rapidement amortis, tandis que les critères de prix de revient [costs] stimulent l'application des techniques modernes'.§ It is not surprising that Trotsky described the price at which electricity could be produced per kilowatt-hour as the 'decisive control instance' in deciding upon capital investment projects in the electric power industry.‖ The additional capital invested was sooner or later recouped by the savings in production costs. The effect of an investment, the rate of return on it, can be measured by calculating annual savings in production costs as a percentage of the cost of the additional investment (the inverse of this figure shows the number of years in which the investment pays off, and is known as the period of recoupment). Such comparisons were occasionally made in the 1920s. The construction of a new railway wagon works at Nizhny-Tagil was defended on the grounds that it would produce wagons for 7,000 roubles each as compared with a cost of 9,000 roubles at existing works: the new works would produce 5,000 wagons a year, and the saving of 10 million roubles a year in production costs was said to justify a capital cost of 42 million roubles.¶ Capital and current costs of hydro-electric and thermal power stations were compared on the assumption that a 10 per cent rate of repayment on capital was appropriate.†† Gipromez calculated that two-shift working in the assembly shop of the Stalingrad tractor factory

---

† *Perspektivy Razvertivaniya Narodnogo Khozyaistva SSSR na 1926/27–1930/31 gg.*, pp. 65—66.
‡ *Materialy Osobogo Soveshchaniya po Voprosam Vosstanovleniya Osnovnogo Kapitala pri Prezidiume VSNKh SSSR*, seriya III, vyp. 4, pp. 24–28.
§ Collette, *op. cit.*, p. 76; a qualification of this view is discussed on pp. 297–305 above.
‖ *Ekonomicheskaya Zhizn'*, 23 July, 1925.
¶ *Torgovo-Promyshlennaya Gazeta*, 26 October, 1927.
†† *Bol'shevik*, No. 3, 1926, pp. 59–61.

would be uneconomical because the savings in equipment would be out-weighed by higher production costs within $1\frac{1}{2}$ years.[†] Vesenkha reported that in 1926–27 1·8 million roubles in current costs had been saved by mechaniza-tion in coal mines as compared with outlays on mechanization of only 2·8 million roubles in 1925–26 and 4·2 millions in 1926–27.[‡] Some interesting attempts were even made at a rudimentary 'costs-benefits analysis'. For instance, calculations for Dnieprostroi announced at the end of 1926 showed that a total investment of 145–150 million roubles would bring an annual saving, including indirect benefits to agriculture and transport, of between 43 and 59 million roubles; saving in foreign exchange would be 45 million roubles.[§]

Although references to the 'effectiveness of investment' and the need to calculate it were frequent at this time, no standard rate of return or period within which investment should be recouped was established. The use of a rate of return to compare investment in *different* industries came to be looked on as bringing the criteria of capitalism into Soviet economic calculation: an economics textbook, pointing out that 'to say that investment in one industry is x times more effective than in another is to say that its output is x times more necessary than the output of another', argued that no such quantitative statement was possible for industries whose products were non-substitutable because use-values could not be compared quantitatively.[||] Thirty years later, the calculation on a computer of shadow prices which would indicate production requirements began to be considered a practical possibility.

[†] *Torgovo-Promyshlennaya Gazeta*, 15 April, 1928; this argument was later rejected.
[‡] *Pervye Shagi Industrializatsii SSSR 1926–1927 gg.*, p. 90.
[§] *Ekonomicheskaya Zhizn'*, 10 December, 1926.
[||] E. Khmelnitskaya, *Ekonomika Sotsialisticheskoi Promyshlennosti* (1931), p. 545.

THE HISTORICAL SETTING OF
SOCIALIST PLANNING
IN THE U.S.S.R.

RUDOLF SCHLESINGER

I. INTRODUCTION

During the half-century which has passed since the days of October, the assessment of planning by the outside world, and even the part played by it in our general assessment of the Soviet revolution, has greatly changed. For us who were young in those days, the Bolshevik revolution was all-important as an answer to the problems raised by the horrors of World War I. Socialist intellectuals in Central Europe had sufficiently studied their Marx to be conscious of the eventual importance of planning, but the issue of its realization during the years of the civil war, and immediately afterwards, appeared less relevant than the basic need for survival of which we were very conscious, comparing our own defeated revolutions with the victorious Bolshevik one. We were, of course, conscious of the specific problems raised by Russia's backwardness but found no specific association between them and the fairly generally accepted task of socialism to overcome the anarchy of capitalist production. Even that acceptance was not as overwhelmingly strong as in later days; it was emphasized only in a few of the diverse plans for 'socialization' which were abroad, in our part of the world, during 1919 (and on which we even had systematic teaching in the special courses established by our Austrian T.U.C. to prepare students for their part as teachers in the newly-established schools for Works' Councillors). Otto Bauer, the leader of the Social Democratic party and, on the whole, not a right-winger, in his book *Der Weg zum Sozialismus*, and also in the first 'Socialization Law' of the Austrian Republic, paid his tribute to Guild Socialism. He even asserted that, reacting against the centralization of war economies (the very experience on which Lenin, in his *Will the Bolsheviks Retain State Power?* had based his anticipation of a possible success), public opinion demanded from 'socialization' not centralization but only greater social justice.† This was more or less his private and

---

† Notwithstanding the precisely opposite approach taken in Engels' Preface to the 1884 re-edition of Marx's *Misère de la Philosophie*, in explanation of the attitude taken by the founders of Marxism as early as 1847.

(since in Austria the economic depression soon set in) only very temporary exercise, but even we left-wingers criticized him for allowing in his concepts far too great a part to private ownership in the means of production rather than for insufficient planning.

In 1920, Eugen Varga, a left-wing Social Democrat who had come to communism on the basis of his experiences as a member of the short-lived Hungarian Soviet government, wrote his book on *The Issues Facing the Economic Policies of Proletarian Dictatorship*—by far the best one on these problems published in those days, and much later, in the West;† the individual issues were tackled in a highly practical way, as problems of survival. I think I commit no undue indiscretion if I state here that we German communists, when preparing in 1923 for the assumption of power, in our parliamentary propaganda as well as in the preparations of the first measures of the new government, followed no considerations other than those for (*a*) making the transition as acceptable as possible for as broad as possible a part of the German people (and thereby reducing to a minimum the strength of our opponents in the unavoidable civil war), and (*b*) tackling the ensuing war-economic problems, without devoting more than very general thought to the possible consequences of the necessary short-term measures for the following reconstruction. I must honestly confess that the contradiction inherent in the Soviet land-reform of 1917–18, with the ensuing necessity to solve it by forcible collectivization of agriculture, came fully into my mind only when the Soviet evidence available since 1956 made it clear how little a part had been played in the correction by voluntary decisions of the peasantry, and to what extent, hence, extreme centralization followed from the conditions in which power had to be assumed. I still believe that Lenin was right, and so, in *principle*, was Stalin when deciding—so far as individuals had anything to decide once the life or death of the Russian revolution was involved—in favour of the 'correction'.‡ If I had any hesitations on this point I would be convinced by a glance at the position of the underdeveloped countries which are now facing the problems of pre-revolutionary Russia—though things will certainly be easier for them with the Soviet experience, including mistakes to be avoided, before their eyes. But the clearer one's mind becomes on these problems and the more one accepts Oskar Lange's description of original communist planning as 'a war economy *sui*

† Unhappily, this book is virtually unknown in the west even amongst Marxists who, perhaps, remember just Lenin's critical marginal notes which take its merits and general approach for granted, as they were in those days.

‡ Rudolf Schlesinger, 'A Note on the Context of Early Soviet Planning', *Soviet Studies*, Vol. XVI, pp. 22 ff. The argument is supplemented in my article 'On the Scope of Necessity and Error, some observations on Dr. Lewin's article' (published *ibid.* Vol. XVII, pp. 162 ff.), *ibid.* Vol. XVII, No. 4, pp. 353 ff.; Maurice Dobb, 'The Discussions in the Twenties on Planning and Economic Growth', *Soviet Studies*, Vol. XVII, pp. 198–208.

generis',† the more one realizes the limitations of the general validity of the Soviet planning experience.

But I have jumped well ahead of what I wished to state in these preliminary remarks. Bukharin's *Economics of the Transformation Period* reached us when the New Economic Policy, which rendered obsolete the book (and, in particular, its concepts of a 'withering away of money'), was already in operation. I do not think that any west European communist ascribed particular value to this concept (in general, we had learned to regard the treatment of money and market problems as central as a characteristic of lower-middle-class utopian socialism), though we took for granted Bukharin's (and Lenin's) treatment of the transition period as one during which the old incentives die down while the new, socialist, ones gradually emerge; so also the identification of those new social motives with the growth of planning. About the details of the GOELRO plan I learned much later, in my capacity as a research worker on the U.S.S.R.; during my actual stay and work there in the critical years of 1925–27 we were concerned with the peasant question in its capacity as a problem of power at least as much as in that of securing the start of planning, the speed of which followed from the need to prepare for a war of external defence, possibly against a united West. In my boyhood I had laughed at the aesthetic consistency aimed at by the authors of the diverse 'socialization' projects—why should I, ten years later, when experiencing the life-and-death needs of a socialist country for more steel, electricity, guns and tractors, bother excessively about details when the only thing absolutely certain to anyone who had even the smallest experience in the administration of that giant and backward country was the prospect of such details remaining 'underfulfilled' when being translated into social practice?‡ If anyone had taken the phraseology about 'fulfilment and overfulfilment of plans' seriously on the national scale— not in that some good factories should partially make good the short-

---

† Oskar Lange, *Entwicklungstendenzen der modernen Wirtschaft und Gesellschaft* (Vienna, 1964).
‡ A western Marxist way of putting this problem is Maurice Dobb's statement (*Soviet Economic Development Since 1917*, London, 1948, p. 239) that the first five-year plan had embodied a serious miscalculation of the expected improvement in labour productivity, in particular of the required expansion of the labour force. Yet not the mere co-ordination of production factors (even so far as these were concerned the Soviet planners would have been babes if they had seriously expected every piece of machinery and every train-load of raw materials to arrive in time at the necessary place) but the transformation of the labour force itself was in question. It was natural for the plan propaganda to emphasize the educational aspects but I would not doubt that the planners themselves when elaborating on higher orders, 'minimum' and 'optimum' variants, thought not just of objective factors such as harvests, international market conditions, etc. but also of the possibility of a situation in which the policy makers might have to put the responsibility for the (inflationary) consequences, in particular as regards the promised improvement of mass-standards of life, on insufficient efforts, with the implications that more consumer goods could be produced when efforts improved.

comings of many others—he would have been forced immediately to question the compatability of such phraseology with quantitative planning.

The Great Depression in the West put full employment (and 'overemployment') as realized in the U.S.S.R. in sharp perspective. Western Social Democrats were right when stating that an unemployed worker in Great Britain or Germany (as long as he received benefits, a point on which these authors preferred to be silent) was better off than an employed unskilled worker in the U.S.S.R. but this could not affect the basic fact that *without* large-scale and planned industrialization the Soviet worker would have been *much worse off*, and that there are other things at least as important as household baskets. In those days Soviet planning made its first major impact upon non-socialist thought in the West: however strongly the shortcomings and errors were emphasized (an enormous anti-Soviet propaganda machine took care that they would not be overlooked) the very emphasis put by orthodox economics on the alleged impossibility of large-scale planning resulted in the fact that its success *in essentials*—and, subsequently, the Soviet achievements enabled by it—was news; while, outside the activities of the interested lobbies, the shortcomings had to wait for their day of publicity. That day came after Stalin's demise, when the U.S.S.R. could not be satisfied with fulfilment *in essentials*—survival and growth—and had to look for the answer to the question of how to improve upon what had been achieved.

In the West, at the same time, 'liberal' economics, at least on paper, attempted a come-back, as had happened already after World War I. I emphasize the words 'on paper': a few years after the establishment of the German Federal Republic I was told, by a leading, and non-socialist representative of the social sciences, 'we have much more planning than we dare to profess in public'. At least in specialist studies on the location of enterprises and the subsidies required to prevent a falling-back of regions less favoured by market conditions, it is now frankly recognized that the much advertized 'free market economy' is incapable of securing orderly development.† I do not suggest that the kind of planning enforcing itself by the logic of things upon its very opponents is related in kind to the planned economy of the U.S.S.R.—the opposite is true:‡ but, certainly, the success of Soviet planning has broken the taboos obstructing the diverse possible applications of the planning approach. In principle, it has become generally accepted in large parts even of the non-socialist world, and in particular in the developing countries.

† See the articles by W. Giel and W. Guthsmuths published in *Raumforschung und Raumordnung*, Bd. XXII (1964), No. 3/4.
‡ Rudolf Schlesinger, 'Some Observations on the Historical and Social Conditions of Planning', *Economics of Planning*, Oslo 1965.

2. THE NATIONAL AND THE INTERNATIONAL ELEMENT IN
THE BACKGROUND OF SOVIET PLANNING

Soviet planning would have been inconceivable had it not fulfilled some long-standing national needs, but its realization would have been impossible without the international element in the background of the leading party. The great sacrifices required for Russia's transformation presupposed ideological energies which, in the state of the world then (as distinct from our era of colonial revolutions) could hardly be provided on other than an international basis. The hope for early revolutions in at least some west European countries served as a scaffold during the first and most difficult period, though in the short term even a German revolution would only have brought a limited release for struggling Russia. In the long term, everything depended upon the possibility of making the German economy much more efficient than it was by the application of socialist planning: many miscalculations amongst Russian socialists depended upon the erroneous conception that west European capitalism had developed in its womb all the necessary elements of a socialist society by 1882, when Marx and Engels wrote their last common Preface to the *Communist Manifesto*, or at least by the beginning of the twentieth century, when Hilferding wrote his *Finanzkapital*. But the main contribution of socialist internationalism to Soviet planning had been made already before the October revolution (and, *a fortiori*, before the foundation of the Communist International) when it enabled the Bolsheviks to proceed in full intellectual independence of either of the two power blocs fighting World War I, and of the ideologies propagated, in particular, by the western bloc, the interests of which were identified by the Liberals and by most Mensheviks with those of Russia's regeneration. The perspicacity with which, even now, half a century after the event, Lenin is reproached in a large literature for *not* having played the western game in 1917, provides a remarkable illustration of the capacity of 'cold wars' to preserve arguments into times when, in any sober assessment, they should appear as obviously refuted by the facts. However ridiculous the efforts to denounce Lenin's betrayal of democratic values allegedly inherent in the western alliance, the association of the liberal tradition with that alliance has been brought about not merely by western propaganda and by widespread misunderstanding of the actual character of French or British institutions, but by the actual conditions in which Russia's industrialization had started under Witte.

Since the days of Peter I, the needs of defence provided a main motive for Russia's industrialization in general, and for the comparatively strong development of the heavy iron industries in particular; in all its stages, that development proceeded at the expense of agriculture. For

Witte, at the end of the nineteenth century, the central task was the development of the Russian railway system, now including Asia, to be pursued by a protectionist policy and by the encouragement of foreign investments. In the conditions of the time, France was the natural supplier of such investments; since Tsarist Russia was not the safest investment place for foreign capital, its main attractive power rested in its military importance in the event of a European war. In this, the interests of the foreign investors—or of the government influences guiding them—coincided with those of the rising Russian bourgeoisie whose own demands for domestic reform coincided with what was desirable from the standpoint of foreign investors; a strengthening of Russia's western associations might strengthen the bourgeoisie's position against Tsarist autocracy, with its strong German associations.

For the same reasons, though with opposite evaluations, a few conservative advisers of the Tsar, in particular Durnovo,† were capable of assessing soberly the prospects of a war in which the ruling group had little to gain but everything to lose. In view of the complete permeation of Russia's economic life by western high finance they could not have their way (nor would it have preserved Tsarism, which might easily be removed by bourgeois reactions to the concessions required for an appeasement of Germany). Yet their attitude, too, had a firm economic background: Durnovo had been one of the main spokesmen of the agrarian—in the conditions of the time, landlord-aristocratic—reaction against Witte's industrialization policies.‡ Russia could avoid involvement in World War I on the side of the western allies, with consequences destructive to the existing regime, only if that regime decided to turn her permanently into an agrarian *Hinterland* of Germany: this was impossible already in 1902, not to speak of 1914, as was well recognized by the regime itself.§

† See his Memorandum submitted to the Tsar in February, 1914, first published by A. Tarle in *Byloe*, No. 19, English translation in A. Golder, *Documents on Russian History 1914–1917* (New York, 1927).

‡ See Theodore H. von Laue, *Sergei Witte and the Industrialization of Russia* (New York, 1963) pp. 84 and 277–9.

§ Tribute was paid to it for such a capacity to overcome its ideological and family links with the German regime by so characteristic a representative of the liberal attitude (in the Witte tradition) as V. I. Grinevetsky, a man whose merits as an economist, in particular as regards the preliminary conditions of economic planning, his Bolshevik fellow-economists did not fail to recognize (cf. Krzhizhanovsky in *Planovoe khozyaistvo*, 1925, No. 7, p. 17). He reproached the Russian revolutionary intelligentsia, with the exception of the small group of right-wing Social Democrat defencists (to which he himself was close) for having pursued an allegedly utopian ideology and thereby brought Russia into a condition of complete dependence on foreign capitalists. (*Poslevoenniya perspektivi russkoi promyshlennosti*, Kharkov, 1919, pp. 79, 64 ff., 181 ff.) The preface to the book is dated 30 June, 1918; it is possible that Grinevetsky allowed himself to be impressed by the German successes of the first half of that year and in 1919, when the book came out, simply transferred such acceptance of superior capitalist power to the western allies then at the height of their supposed strength (the book

How could Russia emancipate herself from that dependency—and, as a by-product, how could Russian socialism get the international socialist movement out of the alternative of serving either of the competing monopoly-capitalist groups as a specialized propaganda-agency 'for workers'? No particular political genius was required to see, in the late autumn of 1917, that a separate peace with Germany and some redistribution of the big estates was unavoidable—General Verkhovsky, Kerensky's last Minister of War, was undiplomatic enough to make the point, for which he was sacked, five days before the October Revolution.[†] Any military dictator who might subsequently have come to power in consequence of a Bolshevik defeat would have concluded a separate peace with the Germans in order, of course, to save as much as possible of the big estates while shifting the responsibility for the harsh terms of the peace upon the left-wing, thereby justifying the White terror. Yet no one except the Bolsheviks could have raised the energies required for Russia's reconstruction. They could do it precisely because they had been a 'defeatist' party, free from the responsibility for the war and from the links which bound all the other parties to western financiers and factory owners.

So far, the relationship of Bolshevik planning to the bourgeois inheritance was negative. It was, however, positive in two main aspects. *First*, the preparatory work performed by the capitalist war economy was recognized, provided only, as Lenin explained in *Will the Bolsheviks Retain State Power?*, that state capitalist planning, as developed by the German war economy[‡] was combined, in Russia, with the conquest of political power by that class which could turn what otherwise would be an instrument of bureaucratic arbitrariness into a tool for the building of the new society. *Secondly*, the Bolsheviks accepted a whole catalogue of main tasks of the reorganization of the national economy which already in 1918 was taken for granted by specialist opinion. As early as March 1918 the Academy of Sciences had offered the Soviet government its collaboration in the exploration and development of the country's

was published during Deniken's advance into the Ukraine). Such vacillations of intelligent right-wing Social Democrats illustrate what the Bolsheviks—and Russia—owed to their allegedly 'utopian' internationalism.

† The documents are reproduced in Browder and Kerensky (eds.), *The Russian Provisional Government 1917*, (Stanford, 1961), Vol. III, pp. 1735 ff.

‡ In his *Poslevoenniya perspektivi russkoi Promyshlennosti*, Grinevetsky, faithful to his glorification of war-time collaboration with the bourgeoisie, kept his reference to the war-economic councils of 1915–16 which allegedly represented the culmination point of creative and collective energy hitherto achieved in Russian history. He only neglected the 'bagatelle' that in its practical results it proved a failure: it really could not be quoted as evidence in favour of anything except of a policy of class-collaboration, which had long since failed. The Bolsheviks would be interested in experiences of bourgeois planning *which yielded practical results* yet emphasized the need for a precisely opposite class-setting so as to ensure that the results could be utilized in the desired direction.

natural resources: when the offer was discussed by Sovnarkom Lenin†
put forward, as the main problems to be studied by the scientists, rationality of location, suitable amalgamations and concentration of production in a few large-scale enterprises, independence of the existing Soviet
territory from the Ukraine and other German-occupied territories,
electrification and transport and the energy supply of agriculture. Larin,
commenting on the offer of the academicians, had described the development of the Kuznetsk coal basin (which, in fact, had to wait for the
first five-year plan), the electrification of the Petrograd industry (which
started with the building of the Kachira works, the first fruit of the
GOELRO plan), and the irrigation of the Turkestan cotton areas; a
decision adopted by the first congress of economic councils in June 1918,
emphasised the need for shifting the heavy industries to the Urals and
West Siberia.‡ In 1918 this idea, which would eventually provide a
main line of the first five-year plan, was clearly conditioned by the external situation of Soviet Russia; it was bound to be put into abeyance
by the changing fortunes of the civil war. As to the practical needs, there
was a near consensus of specialist opinion, though an author such as
Grinevetsky,§ still thinking in terms of the railway age, i.e. grouping his
positive suggestions round this axis and expecting reconstruction from
the attraction of foreign investments, would express his preference for
the development of the East in terms other than those of the technologists and scientists who appealed to the new fervour of creative imagination brought into Russian life by the Bolshevik revolution. The party
not only gave a positive reply to these suggestions, but, as evident
already in Lenin's notes of April 1918, emphasized the need for qualitative change in the very technological field, which would turn industrial construction into the creation of a new society. Krzhizhanovsky's
article on the electrification of Russian industry, published in January
1920, developed Posnikov's forecast, at a pre-war conference of
electro-engineers, that just as the bourgeois age had been an age
of steam power, so the proletarian age would be an age of electricity. When elaborating the idea in his speech at the Moscow party
conference on the GOELRO plan, Lenin sharpened the point by
describing communism as a combination of (political) Soviet power and
electrification.

There is no point in searching for scientific precision in formulas
intended to draw the people's attention to the essentials of socialist
planning; we need not even devote excessive attention to the question
how far this result could be achieved with the means of publicity then

---

† *Sochineniya*, 5th ed. Vol. 36, pp. 228–31.
‡ E. H. Carr, *The Bolshevik Revolution, 1917–1923*, Vol. II (London, 1952), pp. 366–7.
§ Grinevetsky, *op. cit.*

available.† In any case, Soviet planning suffered a temporary setback when, after the end of the civil war, the restoration of a market economy capable of satisfying the most elementary needs moved into the foreground. But the basic foundations had been laid: they included a continuation of concepts developed by advanced pre-revolutionary technological opinion with the requirement for qualitative changes, which should ensure a social result exceeding a mere continuation of the slow growth observable in pre-revolutionary Russia. Whether Lenin's condensed formulas were quite correct or not, their methodological approach would protect the first five-year plan against the danger of turning into another Witte experiment.

3. SHIFTS IN THE FUNCTIONS OF PLANNING

In early 1924, Bukharin,‡ arguing against the Trotskyists—and, by implication, against the leftist ideas of his own earlier period—explained that central planning, though necessary in times of war, had become obsolete. After the victorious conclusion of the civil war, Bukharin found, the plan could not be established at once, 'from above': it could develop only gradually, with the growth of the socialist large-scale industry, under the continuing and co-ordinating pressure of the working-class state. In his opinion, under the New Economic Policy, the class struggle proceeded as a molecular struggle of the diverse economic foundations in the framework of a market economy. The former, military, struggle could end with a clear victory: the essence of the present struggle, however, was the economic competition of a system state capitalist *in form*§ with the dispersed cells of the small-scale economy. Since, in the U.S.S.R., the large-scale economy was controlled by the proletarian state, its triumph in economic competition with small-scale enterprise would imply the victory of socialism.

† Four months after Lenin had described the GOELRO plan as 'our second party programme', Stalin, a member of the Council for Labour and Defence, on the occasion of an illness found at last time to read it (Stalin, *Sochineniya*, Vol. V, pp. 50–51); as late as June 1921 Lenin found it necessary to enquire, in the Gubernia, not only about the question how far the party decisions in favour of propaganda for the GOELRO plan had been carried out, but even about the availability, or otherwise, of at least a copy of the plan in the province's main library (Lenin, *Sochineniya*, 5th ed. Vol. 43, p. 288).

‡ Nikolai Bukharin, 'The Liquidators of our days' (in Russian), *Bol'shevik*, 1924, No. 2.

§ These words are italicized in the original so as to emphasize that the enterprises of a socialist state operating according to capitalist rules could not in substance be capitalist, even state-capitalist: still, the atmosphere differs greatly from that current one year later when the Leningrad opposition was attacked for describing the Soviet state enterprises in such terms. Of course, the Leningrad group intended, by that description, to emphasize the workers' right to defend their interests against 'state capitalist' enterprise; Bukharin pursued the opposite aim of demonstrating that its victory in competition with small-scale enterprise implied the triumph of socialism.

To Bukharin, planning thus appeared as the coordination of the competitive action of the state-controlled cells of the new order. There is no indication of what should happen if that competition, after yielding initial successes—as it did during the first six years of the New Economic Policy—should land in a *cul-de-sac* because of a failure of privately controlled agriculture to support industrial growth to a degree sufficient for the development of state industry and for securing the country's defence against attacks from its hostile environment. But precisely from the need to overcome that type of crisis emerged those forms of planning which Oskar Lange described as 'a war economy *sui generis*': far from achieving its end, as Bukharin suggested, with the storm of the Perekop, it had to tackle the transformation of the structure of Soviet industry in times of peace, and has to tackle it further in other underdeveloped countries.

Bukharin did not envisage planning as a central institution of the present Soviet economy. For the time being, it could not aim at maximum satisfaction of social needs with the available resources since the state controlled only a section of the national economy: what elements of planning were available had to be directed primarily at broadening such control by operations on the market. But what was to be done if the measures required to secure the agrarian basis necessary for industrialization should explode the market framework? Half a year before Bukharin wrote that article, his former friend in left-wing days, Eugene Preobrazhensky, reacting against the 'scissors' crisis' (which, in general, formed the background of the re-opening of the party argument), had explained† the necessity of some burdening of the peasantry in the interest of industrialization, 'primitive socialist accumulation'. In all instances, he said, *some* kind of extra-exploitation of the peasantry had formed the basis of industrialization: in the socialist case, however, it would proceed, not in the interest of an individual ruling class but of the new society as a whole; it would decrease to the extent that socialist industry became capable of standing on its own. Like all his contemporaries, Preobrazhensky took the market economy of the N.E.P. period for granted (it is incorrect to describe him as an advocate of eventual collectivization though his suggestions, if realized, were bound to lead to a situation which would have made collectivization unavoidable at an early date though perhaps more organically than happened in the actual course of events). In his opinion, the necessary exploitation of the peasantry had to proceed in the market, by exchange of the agricultural

† In *Vestnik Kommunisticheskogo Akademii*, 1923, No. 8. An English translation (by Brian Pearce, introduced by A. Nove) of the whole of *The New Economics* by Preobrazhensky, the decisive chapters II and VI of which reproduce those essays of 1923, was published in 1965 by the Clarendon Press, Oxford. In an Annex, Preobrazhensky's reply to Bukharin's misrepresentation of some of his views is given.

products against industrial ones at 'non-equivalent prices'. Hence the price disproportions, as evident in the 'scissors', were the consequence not of any mistakes, corrigible within the framework of the market economy, as the party majority believed, but of the inherent laws of 'primitive socialist accumulation'. They represented the form in which the necessary 'tribute' was raised from the peasants in the interest of the state industry and also of their own future, since the country could not advance without industrialization. As to the forms of transition, Preobrazhensky hoped that state farms would successfully compete with the peasant economy. Correctly, as the future was to show, he approached with great scepticism the capacity of the existing types of agricultural co-operatives to operate from a standpoint higher than that of the peasants' urge for profits. He did not foresee a situation in which the struggle between the public and the private sector would proceed *within* the kolkhoz, requiring thus a series of state interventions against the latter's autonomy. But even if he had foreseen an explosion of market relationships by the suggested 'non-equivalent exchange' between industry and agriculture it was politically impossible to suggest surgery before the attempt had been made to raise from the peasants the food required for industrialization at such prices as were compatible with the new investments (the attempt was, in fact, made during 1927–29: its breakdown led to enforced collectivization by 'revolution from above').[†] No political group—not even the Trotskyists, to whom in his personal allegiances he belonged—dared to support Preobrazhensky's proposal: so far, Bukharin was wrong when, slightly demagogically, he described (in *Bol'shevik* 1924, No. 15–16) Preobrazhensky's concept as 'The economic platform of the opposition'. Preobrazhensky, on his side, proved his consciousness of what he was working for in 1928, when he was to lead the opposition of the exiled Trotskyists against their leader who, in his personal hatred of Stalin, refused to recognize the reality of the latter's turn towards industrialization.[‡]

The tasks of the five-year plans had to be solved in the framework of the 'war economy *sui generis*': this objective fact would have excluded a conception of planning as absolute optimization of the use of the available resources, even if the mathematical tools required for the application of such an approach in a fully planned economy had been available, which they were not at that time.[§] But the impact of the Soviet approach of consistency planning coincided with the Great Depression in the West, soon to be followed by the development of ordinary war economies all

† Schlesinger, 'A Note on the Context of Early Soviet Planning'.
‡ I. Deutscher, *The Prophet Unarmed* (London, 1959), chapter VI.
§ Bazarov in *Planovoe khozyaistvo*, 1926, No. 1, p. 12. But see Dobb, 'The Discussions in the Twenties on Planning and Economic Growth'.

over the world. In such a setting planning, as opposed to the 'free play of economic forces' dear to economic liberalism yet compromised by the Great Depression, was valued in itself: for this very reason the period failed to elaborate the arguments necessary in support of planning once the specific grounds prevailing during the Great Depression and during the industrialization of the U.S.S.R., not to speak of war economics proper, had come into abeyance. K. Mannheim, in the most general of terms, defined planning as 'foresight applied to human affairs, so that the social process is no longer *merely* the product of conflict and competition': it appears as a transition process, as '*reconstruction* of a historically developed society into a unity which is regulated more and more by mankind from certain central positions', i.e. by a certain élite. Yet since he is far from defining that élite from the standpoint of class-struggle, as its historical product which eventually should achieve a combination of the technical needs of planning with those of self-government, his definition remains formal. For Mannheim, the aim of the planning process is the end of 'history, the unforeseeable, fateful dominance of uncontrollable social forces'.† This is a far cry from Engels, to whom the triumph of communism was the end of the *pre*-history of mankind, the transition from a molecular and uncontrollable to a self-controlled and conscious direction of social development.‡ In the background of Mannheim's concepts stands the Benthamite, administrative utopia, in the practical realization of which well-meaning municipal councillors prescribe to the tenants of municipal flats whether they are allowed to keep pets and what plants they have to grow in their gardens, thereby provoking an anti-planning reaction whenever the opposite evil, capitalist anarchy, has lost some of its horrors, and criticism of mistakes committed in planning obscures its basic achievements.

Clearly enough, Mannheim's argument is conditioned, not only by its timing at the opening of a major war, but also by the strong impact made on many western intellectuals by the appearance of fascist successes, and by the image of the U.S.S.R. at the time of the 'personality cult', *a fortiori* at a time when *any* system operating in the U.S.S.R. had to represent a war-economy, without qualifications; arguments such as Mannheim's would hardly be used today by western social scientists. In his *Soviet Impact on the Western World*, written in 1946, E. H. Carr treated a general acceptance of some kind of planning as a main part of that impact: notwithstanding a growing reluctance of western social scientists frankly to recognize this fact (to which I have referred above) it is, in substance, hardly open to questioning. But for this reason we are facing

† *Man and Society in an Age of Transition*, London, 1940; cf. in particular pp. 74–75, 152 and 193. My italics.
‡ *Anti-Duehring*, pp. 190–1 in *Marx–Engels*, Selected Works, Vol. II.

the question of which *type* of planning can now be regarded as universal.†
The industrially developed socialist countries are now in transition from
a period characterized by a mere emphasis on the continuity and inherent consistency of growth, to emphasis on optimization of the plans
so as to secure the best possible satisfaction of existing needs with the
available resources.‡ Planning thus has to assume the functions associated in western-type economics (and also in developing countries, to
whatever extent nationalization of means of production is applied)
with the market. In such a setting the question arises whether, with an
increasing range of purposes to which the planners' attention is devoted,
the 'war economy *sui generis*'—even in so broad a sense as to include not
only defence but also the points of gravity in industrialization—by
absorbing the 'cushions'§ fully loses its character as 'partial equilibrium
planning' and thereby raises qualitatively new problems. It is possible
to describe the Khrushchev-phase in the development of Soviet socialism
as one in which the broadening of the purposes to be tackled by planning
was already realized but a solution to those qualitative new problems
not yet found.

4. SOME CONSIDERATIONS ABOUT THE LIKELY PLACE OF SOVIET PLANNING IN THE HISTORICAL PROCESS

It is always risky to attempt a projection into a broader context of a
certain line of development of one's own days—even if it extends over so
long a period with such manifold changes as Soviet planning has shown
up to now. There is not only the risk of faulty assessment (in that case,
the failed effort would still have some value as a stimulant), new and important aspects may be overlooked by an author although one or two
decades later others, and he himself, may recognize that already in his
days they were well in the process of growth. Fifteen years ago even
authors who were strongly convinced of the world-historical importance
of the emancipation process of the colonial world would hardly have
recognized the modifications which it was to introduce into general
concepts of planning, to what extent it was to confirm, and to what to
refute, an assessment of the Soviet experience as valid for one, be it even

† Schlesinger, 'Some Observations on the Historical and Social Conditions of Planning'.

‡ Lange, *op. cit.* p. 136. At an earlier stage of the development, eighteen years ago yet in
correction of a statement made by him twenty years before, Maurice Dobb (*Soviet Economic
Development since 1917*, pp. 3 and 21) stated that 'Soviet planning in the period in which this
book deals was primarily occupied...with such questions as the rate of investment, the
location of industry and the development of new sources of power and raw materials, transforming the very constants of economic geography'. The chronological conditioning of this
statement is important: for the future, Dobb's earlier definition (quoted on p. 3) may become
relevant again.

§ Charles Bettelheim, *Les Cadres Socio-économiques et l'Organisation de la Planification Sociale*
Problèmes de Planification, 5 (Paris, 1965).

giant, country only. It is easy to imagine possible courses of events, in the West as well as in the developing countries, which may make the Soviet experience appear as either very individual, or *very* typical, indeed.

Most of the efforts made before, and during the first period after, World War II to describe the success of the Bolshevik revolution as a local phenomenon were based upon an opposition of the Russian to the 'classical' west European development. So far as those efforts started from the Marxist scheme, they overlooked the fact that in the *Communist Manifesto* the supposedly central role to be played by Germany in the expected revolution was based upon the coincidence of the two factors characteristic of Russia during the decisive period of 1905–17: the survival of 'feudal residua' (in particular, a stratum of latifundia-owners virtually controlling the state apparatus) while a working class, with interests opposed to those of the bourgeoisie, was already in existence. The founders of Marxism had obvious delusions about the realization of the second condition in the Germany of 1848, and, in fact, about the objective conditions for the realization of socialism in pre-monopoly capitalism in general; but this is irrelevant for a theoretical assessment of the issue since the Russian situation of 1917 clearly came under the heading, and further examples are bound to evolve as industrialization proceeds round the world. If China, because of the choice of a non-capitalist way of development, failed to provide another classical example, India, some Latin-American countries, or even the Congo—provided that the present regime can be stabilized for the decades required for some industrialization—may easily supply the new examples. Hence the problem rests, not on the occurrence of objective socio-economic situations of the 'Russian' type but upon the power-political conditions which may turn such objective conditions into instances of socialist planning.

During the first period after the end of World War II, western criticism of the Bolshevik revolution was mainly based upon a revival of the Menshevik approach; after a—fortunately passing—interlude of explanations by 'criminal conspiracy' during the last years, in particular in the United States the tendency has grown to look for particular explanations for the failure of the Russian revolution to comply with the supposedly valid scheme of liberal democracy.† Reasons for the failure of Russian middle-class 'society' to dissociate itself in time and with suffi-

---

† Theodore H. von Laue, on p. 46 in the symposium published in the American *Slavic Review*, Vol. XXIV, No. 1 (which, in general, is fairly typical of the tendencies here described) states that Russian history in the Soviet period might be understood 'not in terms of Thermidor [i.e. of a reduction of a radical revolution to its objective, bourgeois-democratic contents. R.S.], but perhaps of a twentieth-century version of Peter I's service state'. Yet amongst the participants in that discussion, Prof. von Laue is one of those who gives strongest recognition to the fact that the revolutionary crisis, which approached maturation already on the eve of the war, as well as Russia's involvement in it, were involved in her initial stage of industrialization.

cient energy from the decaying autocracy, and thereby to preserve some chances for its right-wing Socialist allies were forecast already in the first programme of Russian Social Democracy (of 1898); analogous phenomena are experienced regularly by the Americans themselves whenever they attempt to support presumably 'democratic' alternatives to communism in ex-colonial countries. Their 'successes' in the 'cold war' are bound to operate in the same way as the western alliance operated in the preparation of the Russian revolution—with the difference only that, with the Soviet example in existence, the success of the operation would not be such a matter of touch-and-go as was the original. Hence more opportunities for the formation and operation of 'war economies *sui generis*' are likely to come into existence, aside from resources planning in underdeveloped countries which aim at a gradual transition; so also in the U.S.A. itself, efforts to apply planning methods in order to escape from the dependence of its prosperity upon the 'war-economic complex'.

However clear the inevitability—in more than a few examples—of the 'war-economy *sui generis*' we remain with the question whether its function, like that of war economy proper, is merely temporary, bound to dissolve itself into something unspecific as soon as the countries applying it have lost the specific characteristics of underdevelopment. W.W. Rostow's concept of 'stages of industrial development' (which not without reason has been described by its author as a 'non-communist manifesto') is a characteristic example of American arrogance but it is easy to imagine a course of history in which societies of that type, presumably strongly influenced by their competition with the countries of the Soviet type, form one sub-species of the social formation likely to predominate about the end of this century, while the countries of the Soviet type, themselves strongly affected by competition with the 'western' capitalist type, form another one; the limits between the two becoming extremely fluid as the two 'camps' lose their rigidity, which might be unavoidable in a prolonged period of peaceful competition. Similar conclusions as regards the possibility of different social systems may be reached from the opposite side if, with Charles Bettelheim† 'socialist market economies' are treated as a contradiction in terms while 'true', i.e. fully consistent, central planning for an economy treated as a gigantic concern is regarded as exceeding the presently achieved level of the forces of production: in either case the conclusion is already implied in the assumptions.

A strong case for 'convergence', at least in appearance, emerges from a mere starting from dogmatic assertions about either system, which are bound to break down in a period of prolonged peaceful competition. As a socialist, I find nothing wrong in the destruction of so-called 'applications' of Dialectical Materialism such as Lysenkoism, or of assertions

† Bettelheim, *op. cit.*

of an allegedly inherent superiority cf central distribution of all goods rather than of the closest possible contact between suppliers and consumers: such breakdown of definite applications also involves such definitions of Dialectical Materialism and Marxist economic theory as imply such conclusions. Yet at the time immediately preceding and following the Bolshevik revolution these definitions were absent: I do not believe that I and my contemporaries became worse Marxists for having grown up without them—most of us never got much taste of them—though I would agree that an easier task confronts those who can shape their God, or bogy respectively, from the textbooks of the Stalin period, the by-product of the war economy. On the other side, for those who detest public expenditure other than for military purposes, and identify freedom with the not-so-free competition of private capitalist enterprises, 'creeping Bolshevism' is involved in every act of nationalization and in the very fact of competition with the communist countries in welfare and similar services. The desire to fight these types of extremism provides an *emotional* argument in favour of the assumption of a 'convergence' of the two competing socio-economic systems, difficult though it is to establish beyond the recognition of certain commonplaces such as that *every* socialist country existing in our days uses certain market institutions while *no* political regime in any developed capitalist country can afford mass-unemployment. (On the other hand, those who wish to refute the 'convergence' hypothesis on the basis of easily observable phenomena, for example in the sphere of 'superstructures', may easily find themselves in the position of having proved the very opposite from what they intended, namely the identity of the development trend claimed by them as particularly socialist with progressive trends all over the world.)†

Yet it is quite mistaken to test the qualitative novelty of the planning system which has come into being by the Russian revolution from the standpoint of a comparison of any number of individual institutions (quite apart from the unavoidable differences in such institutions on grounds of differences in historical background, geographical conditions, etc.). Only the *dynamics* of the operation of social systems can decide the question of whether we are facing mere local processes which enabled, and may still enable, some underdeveloped countries to make up for their temporary backwardness, or a system of basically new social

---

† A characteristic illustration is the statement, in J. Elias' article on the Czechoslovak Family Law in the East German *Staat und Recht* (July 1965, p. 1078), that certain progressive institutions are to be found in the Family Law of only the most advanced capitalist states while they are general in the law of socialist states, including the less developed ones. Quite apart from its correctness or otherwise, this statement amounts to an assertion that, in this particular field, socialism is an institutional device by which economically backward states can reach, or even surpass in details, the level of more developed ones with private ownership of the means of production.

phenomena. Even supposing that limits are drawn to the replacement of market forces by planning, because of the latter's very nature† or in view of the insufficient level of productive resources,‡ it in no way follows that the sector of social phenomena accessible to planning in a society aiming at its maximization is equivalent in quality to that without which, in our days, no industrial society can preserve near-full employment and tackle the other tasks today taken more or less for granted in industrially developed societies. The assertion of a basic identity of the two types of 'planning', is, indeed, a mere implication of the assertion that the 'market' accepted everywhere as a setting where elemental economic forces can preserve, or restore, certain equilibrium conditions is identical with the treatment of such equilibrium conditions (plus individual interests shaping them) as the standard for a society's approach to its basic development problems (and, hence, presumably also to the respective scope granted to 'spontaneous' and planned processes). It is perfectly true that, because of geographical and technological conditions, even a regime based upon private enterprise, if it existed in the U.S.S.R., would be bound to have a much larger nationalized sector in transport than has the U.S.A.§ but it is also true that, though many countries with different regimes have the variety of regional conditions and national backgrounds making a federal system highly desirable, the socialist countries manage them, and in particular their economic basis, much more successfully than do Canada or India. This is not just due to ideological differences: although the multi-national character of a state, in a system based upon private enterprise, forms an obstacle to the development of consistently democratic attitudes there is nothing in basic Canadian or Indian state ideology which would prevent a broadminded treatment of the French Canadian or the Indian 'language' questions. The point is simply that a system operating by planning (with market elements and even a private sector admitted as concessions to the limitations put to planning by the present stage of development of even the most developed economies and of planning methods), disposes of the tools with which it can comparatively easily tackle all the manifold contradictions which arise, and are bound to arise on a much larger scale if scientific progress should produce technological mass-unemployment, between short-term economic and social rationality.‖ This would hold true even if the differentiations exist-

† See Zygmunt Bauman's article on 'The Limitations of "Perfect Planning"', and also the articles by W. Brus, Jan Tinbergen and D. Granick published in *Co-existence*, Vol. III, No. 2, July 1966. For a critique of the one-sided application of directive methods on the one, market methods of guidance on the other hand see Yosef Pajestka's article in *Problemi Mira i Sotsialisma* 1966, No. 1.

‡ Bettelheim, *op. cit.*   § Raymond Hutchings, *Soviet Studies*, Vol. XVII, p. 290.

‖ Schlesinger, 'Some Observations on the Historical and Social Conditions of Planning'; W. Pavlenda, 'Ways of Solving Economic Underdevelopment in national regions as illustrated by the experience of Slovakia', *Co-existence*, Vol. III, No. 1, April 1966.

ing and arising say at the end of this century between the 'industrially developed' societies should be assessed 'only' on the scale of the differences existing, at the time of predominant 'feudal' relationships, on a large range between serfdom and individual family enterprise. The question relevant in this connection is not so much where competing societies stand at a given moment but in which directions they are bound to move.

The difference in approach may affect the life or death of mankind. The conception of the economic process as directed towards the marketing of the output produced in a given system of property relations tends, so far as it is directed towards the production of status symbols, to reproduce a society fairly static in substance while the need for technological progress produces a specific type of market: the military-aggressive one which, on its part, produces certain ideologies, those of 'cold' and not-so-cold war which are required to keep that market going and society static. This vicious circle, full of dangers in the thermo-nuclear age, can be broken only by an orientation of planning towards the needs of the reproduction process, of material goods and of opportunities for cultural life made possible by material wealth and by conscious participation of the people in a social production process directed towards the satisfaction of their own needs. We must state in all clarity that the Keynesian demand for 'full employment', even if guaranteed by building pyramids, digging holes, or building atomic submarines, whatever advance it may have signified against *laissez-faire* liberalism, in the thermo-nuclear age is not only obsolete but positively harmful. The basic question today is: full employment *for what*?

As against this fundamental issue, the technical question of how to use the existing institutional recipes for getting maximum output from the available resources should be regarded as subordinate. Different principles pursued in the direction and use of investments would result in renewed institutional divergence as soon as a new technological revolution, at present noticeable only in its embryonic forms, should create conditions of plenty even in absolute terms. These divergences would materialize even if in a large majority of instances the quest for the most suitable methods of guidance† should result in preference for methods based upon unit autonomy as opposed to administrative ones, and hence the largest possible development of 'socialist market economies' during the intermediate period were taken for granted. This would hold true in particular for those countries who first took the socialist way, nearly by definition because they were backward at the time and hence faced urgent production tasks for more decades to come.

† This is the terminology applied by the CPSU on the eve of its XXIII Congress. See Rumyantsev's article in *Kommunist*, 1966, No. 1.

SOME PROBLEMS OF
URBAN REAL PROPERTY
IN THE MIDDLE AGES

R. H. HILTON

There has been, over many years, a good deal of discussion among economic historians about the part played by the ownership of real property as the source of the initial capital for the development of trade. W. Sombart, misled, according to his critics, by the study of the backward towns of medieval Germany, thought that the foundation of the fortunes of the urban patriciates was the income received from ground rents. Pirenne's persuasive writings substituted a theory of early urban growth which attributed merchant fortunes to the exploitation of long-distance trade. Sapori and others follow Pirenne, and minimize the real property contribution to early merchant and urban fortunes.[†]

But there has also been a swing away from Pirenne, without, necessarily, a return to Sombart. Contemporary historians are not inclined to underestimate the great development of international commerce in the twelfth and thirteenth centuries. However, they tend to see some continuity between the developed patriciate of the period of efflorescence and the petty nobles, feudal officers and other small urban landowners of the tenth and eleventh centuries. Even if the urban oligarchs of the era of the so-called 'commercial revolution' were primarily bankers and merchants, there may have been, at an earlier date, an important element of real property in their family fortunes. Furthermore, as Pirenne and others have emphasized, merchant fortunes, whatever their origin, were frequently invested in land.[‡]

Although there has been among historians a general interest in the problem of the part played by landed property in laying the basis of

[†] A. E. Sayous in his introduction to Sombart's *L'Apogée du Capitalisme* (1932) expresses the criticisms of a follower of Pirenne. The most recent support for Pirenne's general line will be found in H. van Werweke's edition of Pirenne's *Histoire Economique et Sociale du Moyen Age* (1963). A. Sapori's *Studi di Storia economica medioevale* (1946) contains the best of his generalizing articles, but on Sombart see especially his *Le Marchand Italien au Moyen Age* (1952).

[‡] See J. Lestocquoy *Les Villes de Flandre et d'Italie sous le Gouvernement des Patriciens* (1952) for a general reconsideration of the Pirenne position. Supporting evidence from studies of individual towns is too numerous to quote, but it should be mentioned that E. Fiumi has strongly reaffirmed the purely mercantile origin of the Florentine patriciate, in 'Fioritura e decadenza dell' economia fiorentina: Nobilta feudale e borghesia mercantile', *Archivio Storico Italiano*, 1957.

early mercantile wealth, there has been less interest in the distribution of urban landed property in the central and late middle ages, as though this were no longer of practical or theoretical interest. In view of other well-documented features of the social, economic and political life of towns from the thirteenth century onwards, this is perhaps natural. It would, however, be of some interest to establish whether or not rent from urban real property continued to form an important part of the incomes of the mercantile and industrial upper classes; whether or not there was any tendency for the concentration of ownership of urban real property; and if so, whether this concentration was in the hands of a recognizable and distinct social group.

An enquiry on these lines is rather different from those which, by examining the histories of individual merchants, show how successful families often acquired properties and even merged into the landowning aristocracy. It would start from the standpoint, not of the individual, but of the total available amount of real property in the town—or as near to the total as documentation will allow. It would not concern itself with the investment of merchant capital in agricultural land. To make significant generalizations, we ought, of course, to draw on evidence from a wide range of towns. In medieval Europe there was enormous variety, ranging from big centres of industry, banking and trade to minor market centres. One should not expect similar answers about real property holdings from them. This essay will be confined to a few towns of the English midlands for which there is some useful evidence of the type required. One of them, Coventry, was, from the thirteenth century, a prominent cloth manufacturing centre, perhaps by the second half of the fourteenth century the third largest town in England, after London. Even so, it was, by (say) Italian standards, small. The others, Gloucester, Worcester and Warwick were administrative centres and regional market towns with a certain manufacturing element. Though smaller than Coventry, they were fairly representative of the middle rank of medieval English towns.

Between the eleventh and the thirteenth centuries, there was evidently a considerable expansion of the urban occupied area. Not only did the built-up area spread laterally and spill beyond the town walls into the suburbs, but unoccupied land within the walls was also used for building. Perhaps the latter provided the more significant multiplication of living space. How far can we measure this? It is easier to guess what was happening than to give exact figures.

The earliest units of urban land of which we have medieval records sometimes give the spatial dimensions of the plot without indicating what, if anything, was built on it. An example is the *haga* or haw, or enclosed plot along the north wall of Worcester granted by the Bishop of Worcester in 904 to the alderman of Mercia and his wife Aethelflaed, daughter of Alfred of Wessex.† It measured twenty-eight by twenty-nine by nineteen rods. If we take the risk of assuming that these rods contained five and a half yards, the haw was between three and four acres in area. But this example comes from a period which many historians would regard as pre-urban. Most regard the eleventh century, at the earliest the tenth (in Italy for example), as the initial phase of the great period of urban growth. In England it may (hestitantly) be measured in Domesday Book (1086), the most comprehensive and reliable piece of quantitative evidence from any European country at that date. In this record, many different terms are used for the basic units of tenure in the towns—messuages, houses (*mansiones*), tenements, burgages among others—but in all cases it is almost certain that the term referred to an area of land rather than to the buildings (if any) on it. The term 'burgage', indicating a tenure which gave rights as well as implying obligations, became generalized in succeeding years, but continued to imply an area of land rather than the dwelling or other building. The area varied from place to place. In Lincolnshire, at the time of Domesday Book, it seems that there were six or seven burgages to the acre.‡ The burgages of those towns, many newly founded, of the twelfth and thirteenth centuries, which were given the laws of the Norman town of Breteuil, usually contained more than half an acre, in one case six acres.§ When the Bishop of Worcester founded Stratford-on-Avon, round about 1196–8, he divided the borough area into burgage plots of three and a half by twelve perches, just over a quarter of an acre.‖ At Worcester, according to some deeds of transfer, some urban tenements were of considerable size. In 1250 a draper sold to a cleric his capital messuage of nearly four acres. In 1307 a house and a three-acre garden were sold. Both of these sites were within the town wall.¶

Whatever the variations in the surface areas of these early haws, messuages or burgages, it is obvious that they were usually much more extensive than the ground-plan of the average medieval two-or three-bay house.†† By the end of the thirteenth century, at the peak of a period of urban as well as rural population expansion some plots may not have been built on, may even have been cultivated. Most, however, had been split up, sub-let and built over by houses, cottages, shops, inns, work-

† A. J. Robertson, *Anglo-Saxon Charters*, (1939), No. XIX.
‡ J. W. F. Hill, *Medieval Lincoln* (1948), p. 35.
§ M. Bateson, 'The Laws of Breteuil', *English Historical Review*, Vols. XV and XVI.
‖ William Dugdale, *Antiquities of Warwickshire* (1656), p. 514.
¶ *Original Charters relating to the City of Worcester* (Worcester Historical Society), ed. by J. Harvey Bloom (1909), Nos. 1073, 1074, 1100.
†† The bay was normally about twelve to fifteen feet long.

shops and stables of varying size and rental value. Topographical research, based on deeds and rentals, can illuminate this process by which the intra-mural area of our medieval towns were built up.

But other problems arise as well, of economic and social rather than of topographical history. Some of the midland urban rentals may in part solve some of these problems, while posing others.

In the early Norman period, in the midland towns as elsewhere, the principal ground landlords were the king and the ecclesiastical and secular nobility. In Worcester, the bishop had ninety 'houses' (*mansiones*) half of which were sub-let to Norman nobles, the most important being the sheriff, Urse of Abitot. The Abbot of Evesham had twenty-eight messuages and the king and five nobles had fifteen between them. In Warwick, the king had 113 'houses', his barons (of whom the most important was the Benedictine Abbot of Coventry) had 112, and nineteen burgesses owned their own messuages. At Gloucester, 542 'houses' were distributed between the royal demesne (300), the archbishop of York (60), St Peter's Abbey (52) and some twenty other lords.† Stratford-on-Avon, of course, had one principal ground landlord, the Bishop of Worcester. Coventry, probably entirely rural at the time of the Domesday survey was divided from the twelfth century between the Benedictine Abbey (which became the cathedral priory) and the Earl of Chester.‡

These principal landlords drew varying rents from burgages (or whatever else the unit of tenure might be termed). Some were only a few pence, as in the case of the Gloucester 'landgable' payments.§ A higher rent was not uncommon. In newly-founded towns, and elsewhere, 12d a burgage was not uncommon. This was the burgage rent at Stratford-on-Avon. By comparison with the rent from arable land this was considerable. || But, of course, it gave burgess privileges and was in lieu of all services. The fact that landlords were able to attract settlers with these relatively high rents illustrates the twelfth century urban boom. But with the considerable rise in prices which continues to the end of the thirteenth century, these burgage rents became much less valuable to the principal landlords. It was the burgage tenants who sub-let who were in the best position to profit from the rising demand for town property, as we can show by a comparison of burgage chief rents with the rents of sub-let properties.

† Domesday information for Worcester and Warwick in *Victoria County History, Worcestershire*, I, p. 294, and *ditto, Warwickshire*, I, p. 299. Information for Gloucester, 1096–1101, printed in *Rental of Houses in Gloucester, 1455*, ed. W. H. Stevenson, (1890), p. XIX.

‡ M. D. Harris, *Life in an Old English Town* (1898), p. 32.

§ W. H. Stevenson, *op. cit.* passim.

|| M. de W. Hemmeon, *Burgage Tenure in Medieval England* (1914); *Red Book of Worcester* (Worcester Historical Society), IV, ed. M. Hollings (1950), p. 481 ff.

An official survey of 1280 of Coventry† gives a number of examples of the subdivision and sub-letting of burgage tenements. Master Richard Burton and his wife Petronilla had a holding consisting of nine burgages, many of them subdivided; three watermills; half a dozen cottages; a couple of crofts; and a complex tenement held by a sub-tenant. For these holdings they were both paying rent to the overlord, and receiving rent from sub-tenants. The complications can be simply illustrated from one group of holdings for which they paid 34s. 6d. to the Prior of Coventry, overlord of his own half and lessee at that date of the half of the borough which had once belonged to the Earl of Chester. This payment was for four burgages and a watermill. Unfortunately the rent of the watermill cannot be separated from that of the four burgages, but burgage chief rents were seldom more than 2s.‡ We may safely assume that the four burgages were responsible for not more than 10s. of the combined rent paid to the Prior. But these four burgages were sub-let, one complete for 5s., one with two cottages for 9s., the rest being sub-divided into thirty cottages and thirteen curtilages or garden plots. The total rent from the sub-letting came to nearly £5. Another example is from the property holdings of Peter Baroun who had seventeen and one third of a burgage and two cottages for which he paid to the principal ground landlords 14s. 1d. These were not sub-divided to the same extent as the Burton property; twelve burgages were sublet complete, fourteen cottages being carved out of the rest. Even so the total rent from the sub-letting was 39s. 2d. If we knew about the sub-sub-letting which undoubtedly happened, but which is not recorded, the total profits from the property would be seen to be even greater.

Similar profits accruing to intermediate tenants can be observed at the same date in Warwick. As one would expect in this smaller and less wealthy town, the recorded subdivision of burgages was much less developed.§ Thomas Payn, a Warwick burgess who bore the ephemeral title of 'mayor', held a dozen burgages for low rents from the Earl of Warwick and from a number of ecclesiastical landlords, as well as three of which he was principal landlord. His rent income from his sub-lettings was nearly four times as great as the rent he had to pay out. The average burgage rent that Payn paid to the Earl of Warwick and to St Mary's Collegiate Church averaged just over 8d. though he had to pay between 1s. and 4s. to his monastic landlords. He was, however, sub-letting some of his burgages for 8s. to 10s., although some other rents for sub-let burgages were kept at a traditionally low level.

† In manuscript in the Leigh Collection at the Record Office, Shakespeare's Birthplace, Stratford-on-Avon. This is a copy of part of the great survey of which most has been printed as the *Rotuli Hundredorum.*

‡ Four other burgages were held by the Burtons of the Prior for 1s., 2s., 1s. 4d. and 6d.

§ In another manuscript version of the 1280 survey, Public Record Office, E. 164, Vol. 15.

In these two surveys of 1280 we see considerable remnants of the burgage system of the earlier period. In Warwick, in fact, the whole tenanted area, apart from eighteen tofts and four cottages, were reckoned in whole or fractional burgages, possibly occupying much the same surface area as at the time of the Domesday survey. At Coventry, while there were many tenements, messuages and cottages which may or may not have originated in whatever original area it was that was divided into burgages, the burgage system was still prominent. At Stratford in 1252, as one might expect from the date and circumstances of its original foundation the burgage tenements were still the only ones that counted, apart from a few stalls and shops. But this information is in the bishop's rental, and he would not necessarily be interested in sub-letting.

By the fourteenth century the 'burgage' is less prominent. If the towns were filling up with buildings, especially buildings of a more permanent character than those of the twelfth century, it would follow that, in the later rentals and deeds of transfer, houses and shops rather than burgages should feature largely, although often enough the house and the land are described together. In Stratford there are no more rentals for the whole town after that drawn up for the episcopal overload in 1252. But in the fourteenth century begins a series of rentals of the Holy Cross Gild and the other gilds which were soon to be amalgamated with it, probably the most important property owners in the town. The earliest of these is dated about 1328, and they continue until the sixteenth century. In the middle of the fourteenth century, the Holy Cross Gild was still subletting burgages, half burgages and tenements as well as buildings, but as time goes on, the buildings rather than the house sites predominate. The contemporary gild accounts, mainly occupied with building and house repair costs, show clearly that the gild recognized the importance of house rents. From about £6 in 1355 the gild income from its urban property rose to nearly £50 by the end of the fifteenth century. To begin with, an element in this increase resulted from the amalgamation of the gilds, but it was mainly due to the buying up of property, the improvement of existing property and to the erection and letting of new buildings. Rents varied a great deal according to factors which cannot be calculated, but the impression is that they were, in general, going up in the fifteenth century. The contrast between the old, low, burgage rent and that paid for new houses still occasionally appears. In a rental of 1446, for instance, the gild lets out two burgages, one in Evesham Lane for 8d. and one in Rother Street for 1s. 8d. But a new tenement in the corner of High Street, sub-let to a tailor and a shoemaker, and which certainly occupied less space than a burgage, was bringing in 36s. 8d.†

† The records of the Stratford-on-Avon Holy Cross Gild are in the Shakespeare's Birthplace Record Office, and are calendared by F. C. Wellstood (in MS). See T. H. Lloyd, *Some*

Two Warwick rentals of the fifteenth century, drawn up for the principal ground landlords, St Mary's Collegiate Church and the Earl of Warwick, present interesting contrasts to the 1280 survey which we discussed above. In 1424 the College was receiving rent from some eighty or ninety tenements, cottages, crofts and gardens in the urban area.† Rents varied greatly. In the absence of details about the rented property there must be some doubts as to the reasons for these variations. It is probable, however, that the frequent rents for 1s. or less are old burgage rents of the type we have been discussing, and in a rental of this type there are naturally no indications of rents taken from sub-tenants. There are, however, some recent economic rents which were paid to this chief lord, such as 18s. paid from a newly built tenement in the Horsecheaping, leased for a term to the tenant. In the Earl of Warwick's rental of 1482‡ much of the archaic burgage framework was artificially preserved. This is partly because this is a rental of an ancient principal ground landlord still drawing income from burgages which had undoubtedly been long since sub-let by the tenants. Partly, too, the relative economic stagnation of Warwick in the fifteenth century must have slowed down the break-up of the old tenurial system. The burgages were only paying small sums, normally less than 1s. However, the earl's rent income from some hundred and sixty or seventy tenants included a number of improved, or economic, rents, called farms, not, of course, from archaic burgage tenements but from buildings. Since these were economic rents, signs of very recent change show them moving in a downward direction. Even so, cottages were let at 4s. or 5s., messuages for sums varying between 8s. in Castle Street and 26s. 8d. in High Street.

Moving to the more active economic milieu of Coventry, we find these tendencies further advanced. Already by the middle of the fourteenth century, the deeds which bear witness to land transactions indicate an abandonment of the 'burgage' terminology still used in 1280. Apart from the original and copied deeds, the main sources are early fifteenth century rentals of the urban properties of the Coventry Cathedral Priory cellarer and pittancer,§ and a late fifteenth-century rental of the property of the powerful Holy Trinity Gild.‖ In 1411, about a quarter (thirty-six) of the properties held from the priory's pittancer were held

Aspects of the Building Industry in Medieval Stratford-upon-Avon (Dugdale Society, 1961), and *The Medieval Gilds of Stratford-on-Avon and the Timber-framed Building Industry* (Birmingham University M.A. thesis, 1961).

† Public Record Office, E. 164, Vol. 22. I am grateful to Mrs Dorothy Styles for lending me her transcript of this document.

‡ Public Record Office, DL43/9/21.

§ The Coventry Cathedral Priory cellarer's and pittancer's and rentals are in the priory's register, Public Record Office, E.164, Vol. 21.

‖ *Records of the Gild of the Holy Trinity, St. Mary, St. John the Baptist, and St. Catherine of Coventry*, ed. G. Templeman, (Dugdale Society) 1944.

'in fee'. Many of these, as well as tenures in fee held from the cellarer, paid 1s., others less. These may be relics of burgage tenure. Sub-tenancies are occasionally mentioned but there is no information about the rents paid by the sub-tenants to the priory tenants, so there is no knowing exactly what was the increase in rental value implied in the difference between the rent in fee and the rent paid by the sub-tenant. However, two-thirds of the pittancer's tenants were in fact holding for life or lives or at will, and these of course would tend to be the same sort of economic rents as sub-tenants of tenants in fee would be paying.†

Peter de la Mare held in Cosford Street by indenture for life a big tenement with a tavern built in stone, called the New Inn, paying 20 mks (£13 6s. 8d.), and three other tenants each held for life, a shop, hall and chamber above (*super*) the said tavern for 33s. 4d. a year each. Margaret Halle held a tenement for life, with a tavern, for £4. She sub-let to Adam Swelte, a cardmaker, but for what rent is not stated. A chandler, James Fynche, paid £4 a year for a tenement in Smithford Street which he held by indenture for life. John Barrow paid £3 for a big tenement and two cottages with a garden where there had once been six cottages. He had a sub-tenant, William Stille, but this sub-tenant's rent is not given. These are among the highest rents for which there is evidence, and the rental of the Holy Trinity Gild for 1486 suggests a similar level. In this rental, as in those of the priory, precision is impossible because the size and nature of the property is not given in sufficient detail. However, cottages fetched between 4s. and 12s. and some of the wealthier tenants, great merchants with familiar names, were paying over £4 for their tenements.

There is a Gloucester town rental of 1455 which was principally compiled to record the old, low, landgable rents payable by the principal tenants to the town authorities from the original building sites. The real rents actually paid by sub-tenants for houses, shops, stables and the like are only recorded for Southgate Street and the Mercery, and only incompletely for these. The landgable payments vary a great deal since the original burgages had become much sub-divided. Even so, they contrast strongly with the current house rents. For example, the Priory of St. Bartholomew paid the town authorities a landgable of 1s. 2d. for a certain tenement with a bakery in Southgate Street. The Abbey of Lanthony rented it from St Bartholomew's for 18s. and sub-let it to a baker who occupied it for 40s. William Butter paid 7¾d. landgable for two tenements in the Mercery and was able to get 12s. from a sub-tenant for one of them.

† A rare example of the terms of tenure of such a sub-tenant is as follows. The Hospitallers held a tenement in fee of the pittancer in Little Park Street and this was sub-let by the Hospital to John Preston for a term of years.

Although some houses were let for only a few shillings, clearly many houses in the middle of the town were let for £1 and over.

These examples of rents in the later middle ages have been quoted in order to show the contrast between the original ground rents and the rents which were paid for buildings in these sites. They show the possibilities of profit in site development, of which, as we have seen, the Stratford-on-Avon Holy Cross Gild took advantage. Such figures could be multiplied, not so much from rentals, which have their limitations and which are rather infrequent, but from charters and other deeds such as are to be found at Worcester Cathedral, in the Coventry or the Stratford municipal archives. The point, however, is rather a simple one, and leads to the more interesting problem of the importance of income from real property in medieval merchant fortunes. This is a problem that has already been posed by Professor W. G. Hoskins.[†] He quite rightly warns us against assuming that big real property accumulations were permanent, or even typical of the medieval merchant class. This caution seems justified by the evidence of some of these midland towns.

With this problem in view, let us return to the Coventry survey of 1280, drawn up at a period of rapid economic and population expansion. The sub-letting of properties within the original burgage tenements, to which we have drawn attention, points to the existence of a market in house property. It would be important if we could discover if this market in real property led to its concentration in few hands, to such an extent, for example, that income from real property could sustain, wholly or substantially, an important social group. The survey presents some technical difficulties, preventing us from being sure of an accurate count of all persons and all properties. For one thing, since the statute *Quia emptores terrarum* was not yet passed, a real sub-tenant cannot always be distinguished from a purchaser paying a quit rent. However, one must risk mistakes. It would seem that about five hundred persons or institutions occupied or had rights in real property in the town. There seem also to have been about seven hundred separate occupiable premises. The record, as we have seen, is unusual in that it records many sub-tenants, but the disparity between the number of tenants and the number of properties suggests that many other sub-tenants (or sub-sub-tenants) are unrecorded. Out of some two hundred and sixty or seventy burgages, one hundred and eighty are described as if undivided, an unlikely state of affairs. However this may be, the evidence suggests strongly that (below the chief lord, the Prior) there was very little concentration of properties in few hands. Only sixteen persons held more than the equivalent of five burgages. No religious house or other institu-

† 'English Provincial Towns in the Early Sixteenth Century', *Transactions of the Royal Historical Society*, 5th series, Vol. 6.

tion held as much as that.† Most significant, those people with the biggest real property holdings seem to have derived rather small net incomes from them. Master Richard Burton and his wife got 56s. 8d., Peter Baroun 39s. 2d., and others whom it would be tedious to enumerate, even less. In nearby Warwick, a much smaller town of course, the principal accumulators of real property were the Earl of Warwick with the equivalent of about twenty-seven burgages, and the Collegiate Church of St Mary with some seventeen burgages. By far the biggest individual owner among the burgesses was the Thomas Payn whom we have already mentioned. He had a net revenue from his holdings of only 14s. Thirteenth-century evidence from Stratford, Worcester and Gloucester, mostly charters and deeds, gives no indication there of big accumulations of real property.

This thirteenth-century evidence is too scanty to be conclusive, but what there is leads in the same direction. The more abundant fourteenth and fifteenth-century evidence suggests something of a trend towards a greater concentration of real property holdings, but mostly in the hands of institutions.

The mid-fifteenth-century rental of Gloucester enumerates some five hundred and eighty properties of different types. Of these, monasteries had about two hundred and seventy, town churches, chantries and religious gilds about a hundred, and the borough's stewards twenty-five or thirty. Individuals were much less endowed. Only ten had more than five tenements, the most important being Thomas Deerhurst with eighteen tenements and nine cottages. In Warwick by the fifteenth century the Collegiate Church of St Mary had probably increased its property holdings a good deal since 1280. At the earlier date, as we have seen it had about sixteen burgages; by 1424 its tenants held some sixty-five tenements, various cottages, crofts, gardens and the like. In 1482 the Earl (more like an institution than an urban personality) had more than a hundred and sixty tenants compared with his two dozen in 1280. Some of the Earl's tenants were themselves accumulators of property, holding from him and then (presumably) sub-letting. Such were John Huggeford, esquire, with ten burgages, eight messuages, three cottages, two barns, two gardens and half-a-dozen unoccupied sites. He was probably a tenant of St Mary's as well: his grandfather before him had held three tenements in 1424 from that institution. Another lesser tenant holding from the earl was the Warwick Gild which had two burgages, seven messuages, seven cottages and a croft. This gild probably played a part analogous to that of the Stratford Holy Cross Gild. But

† This fact may be attributed partly to the fact that Warwickshire was not a county dominated by big church land-owners, as were Worcestershire and Gloucestershire, and also to the late development of Coventry as a town.

the Holy Cross Gild, as we have suggested, emerged by the end of the fifteenth century as a considerable institutional property holder, with more than ninety tenements, cottages, shops and barns in the town.

At the end of the fifteenth century (1486), the Gild of the Holy Trinity in Coventry, by this time the most powerful institution in the town, was receiving rents from nearly four hundred tenants, many of whom, as we have mentioned, were leading merchants. This very sharply contrasts with the apparently wide distribution of real property in 1280. The early fifteenth-century priory rentals show that there were at this date some interesting individual accumulations. The biggest of these was in the hands of a draper, John Preston, who had five tenements in Cosford Street, two in Little Park Street, one each in Smithford Street, Great Park Street, and Westorchard, and some ridges, presumably of arable, in an enclosed croft at the bottom of a garden in St Nicholas Street. Unfortunately, we cannot tell what was the annual rental value to Preston. One of the tenements in Cosford Street which had been divided into four cottages was worth 40s., but there is inadequate data to enable the net income to be calculated. Another merchant, Robert Shipley, had holdings of similar extent, seven tenements and six cottages. William Lusterley, fishmonger, had four tenements and four cottages. John Lyrpole, butcher, had five tenements. Other individual holdings were smaller. Now these priory rentals are not necessarily comprehensive as was the 1280 survey, but they do in fact cover a good deal of ground. It cannot be said that individual property holdings show much advance, as far as concentration is concerned, compared with 1280. It would not seem that the net incomes from property would be very important to the individuals concerned.

Although the biggest individual property accumulators in early fifteenth-century Coventry were merchants, it is worth noting that non-mercantile types are also well represented. We know little about the mercantile community of thirteenth-century Coventry, but Mr Richard Burton as his title shows, probably was not part of it. He does not even appear as a witness in the borough court as does his contemporary and fellow accumulator, Peter Baroun. John Huggeford of Warwick was a member of a family whose principal function was to serve as officials to the Earls of Warwick.† Thomas Deerhurst of Gloucester was a lawyer. Whoever they were, one gets little evidence that any of them could have relied on their urban property holdings to give them an adequate income. Presumably mercantile and industrial profits were such as to attract the bulk of urban capital. Some capital may have been invested in rent charges, though on nothing like the scale found in continental

† *Ministers' Accounts of the Warwickshire Estates of Duke of Clarence*, ed. R. H. Hilton (Dugdale Society, 1952), p. XXIX.

towns. The main trend after the building expansion of the thirteenth century seems to have been towards institutional ownership of the bigger blocks of urban real property, safe investments, the income from which served the social purposes of these institutions. These purposes, of course, included the ritual functions of chantries and religious gilds, not to speak of monasteries; but the gilds also acted as credit institutions, burial clubs, political and social organizations. By no means enough is known about what they did with their incomes because few of them left accounts; and most of them, of course, were soon to be expropriated.

POTTAGE FOR FREEBORN
ENGLISHMEN: ATTITUDES TO
WAGE LABOUR IN THE SIXTEENTH
AND SEVENTEENTH CENTURIES

CHRISTOPHER HILL

'Wage-earning is not a career that men seek for its own sake'†

I

Recent controversies between 'optimists' and 'pessimists' concerning the effects of the Industrial Revolution have dealt mainly with the standard of living. Insufficient emphasis, it seems to me, has been placed upon the 'ideological' hostility to the status of wage labourer which many men and women felt in the eighteenth century. In our time, thanks to two centuries and more of trade union struggle, wage labour has won a self-respecting place in the community, and it is difficult for us to think ourselves back to a world in which, as Sir John Clapham wrote of the French *cahiers* of grievances in 1789, 'the position of *journalier* is seldom referred to except as a kind of hell into which peasants may fall if things are not bettered'.‡ This attitude was almost universal in the England of the Industrial Revolution, and it derived from at least two centuries of history. The object of this article is to recall some of the economic facts and social and legal theories which underlay the attitude.

II

Significant changes in the status of wage labour came with the rapid development of capitalism in the sixteenth century. Many of the wage-labourers (*servientes*) whom Professor Hilton records on Leicestershire estates in the late fourteenth and fifteenth centuries would have holdings of their own: they were not wholly dependent on wages for their existence. Indeed Froissart tells us that the rebels of 1381 demanded that 'if they laboured or did anything for their lords, they would have wages therefor

---

† E. H. Phelps Brown and Sheila Hopkins, *Economica*, N.S., Vol. xxiv (1957), p. 299.
‡ Sir John Clapham, *A Concise Economic History of Modern Britain from the earliest times to 1750* (Cambridge, 1951), p. 212.

as well as other'.† Wage labour meant freedom by contrast with serf-dom. But in the sixteenth century more and more of those who worked for wages were losing their land, and so were becoming wholly dependent on such earnings, together with their remaining rights in the common lands. The author of *A Discourse of the Common Weal* (1549) spoke of 'many a thousand cottagers in England...having no lands to live of their own but their handy labours and some refreshing upon the said commons'.‡

The assumption that wages were supplementary to an agricultural holding kept wages low:§ the rates which J.P.s authorized were rarely sufficient in themselves for the rearing of a family. Poor relief was there-fore needed in addition: full-time wage-earners were assumed to be paupers. There are many complaints against the introduction of a new industry into an area, on the grounds that it would lead to an influx of socially undesirable down-and-outs. Thus in 1606 the tenants of Broseley, Shropshire, protested that the owner of a new colliery was spoiling the manor by introducing 'a number of lewd persons, the scums and dregs of many [counties], from whence they have been driven'.|| Twelve years later Robert Reyce wrote of Suffolk that 'in those parts of this shire where the clothiers do dwell or have dwelt, there are found the greatest number of the poor'.¶ A similar remark was made two generations later. Industry creates poverty, for 'though it sets the poor on work where it finds them, yet it draws still more to the place; and their masters allow wages so mean that they are only preserved from starving whilst they can work; when age, sickness or death comes, themselves, their wives or their children are most commonly left upon the parish; which is the reason why those towns (as in the Weald of Kent) whence the clothing is departed, have fewer poor than they had before'.††

In these early days, when only the weakest would accept the status of full-time wage-labourer, there was little or no protection against the sort of abuses which were still prevalent in the eighteenth century—truck, delay in payment of wages and consequent indebtedness. In Sir Arthur Ingram's Yorkshire alum works wages in James I's reign were often 9 months in arrears. The workers complained that they were grossly overworked, paid in kind, with goods seriously over-valued, and that the contractors were deliberately aiming to ruin their credit locally so as to

† Froissart, *Chronicle*, translated by Sir John Bourchier, Lord Berners (London, 1901–3), Vol. III, p. 224.
‡ Ed. E. Lamond, *A Discourse of the Common Weal of this Realm of England* (Cambridge, 1893), pp. 49–50; cf. E. Lipson, *An Economic History of England* (London, 1943), Vol. II, pp. 66–8; T. G. Barnes, *Somerset, 1625–40* (Oxford, 1961), p. 3.
§ Adam Smith, *The Wealth of Nations* (World's Classics), Vol. I, pp. 131–2.
|| Quoted by J. U. Nef, *War and Human Progress* (London, 1950), p. 231.
¶ Robert Reyce, *The Breviary of Suffolk (1618)* (ed. Lord F. Hervey, London, 1902), p. 57.
†† [Anon.], *Reasons for a Limited Exportation of Wooll* (1677), quoted by A. Clark, *Working Life of Women in the Seventeenth Century* (London, 1919), p. 149.

reduce them to complete economic dependence.† In such circumstances men fought desperately to avoid the abyss of wage labour. In the Stannaries of Cornwall in the sixteenth and early seventeenth centuries, 'miners as a rule preferred the illusory independence of the tribute system rather than frank acceptance of the wage system', though this made them fall ever deeper into debt to usurious dealers. 'They have no profit of their tin if they be hired men'; once the status of free miner was lost, there was no hope of return.‡ 'Abandon hope all ye who enter here' was written over the portals of wage labour. Sir William Monson in James I's reign described how mariners preferred the 'liberty' (his word) of service on a privateer, where they shared in the profits and the risks, to the regular wages and floggings of the King's ships.§

Professor Nef pointed out that the rise of industrial specialization led to segregation from their communities of some wage labourers at least: this would be especially true of new industries staffed by immigrants, and of miners, whose work made them look and smell different from their neighbours. He also suggested that the falling standard of living of wage labourers in the sixteenth and early seventeenth centuries may have led to differences in physical appearance—a greater incidence of rickets among workers' children and an earlier loss of teeth in adults.‖ Professor Notestein believes that farm labourers seldom went to church in the seventeenth century, because they had no suitable clothes.¶ In this way too they would be excluded from the communities in which the lived. (One wonders indeed whether the baptisms, marriages and deaths of all labourers were included in all parish registers; or whether this, our main source of statistical information for sixteenth and seventeenth century population, may not be far from complete, in some parishes at least, at this early date. But these are dangerous speculations.)

The Statute of Artificers of 1563 accentuated the isolation of the poorest classes, since by it any man or woman without an agricultural holding could be condemned to semi-servile labour in industry or agriculture, whilst the children of paupers were compulsorily apprenticed. No labourer was to leave his employment without his employer's consent, under penalty of imprisonment until he submitted. These provisions had the effect of depressing wages and lowering the status of all wage labourers in town and country. This outcaste class was also liable to conscription for overseas service in army or navy. But wage labourers were

---

† A. F. Upton, *Sir Arthur Ingram* (Oxford, 1961), pp. 112, 128–32.

‡ G. R. Lewis, *The Stannaries: A Study of the English Tin Mines* (Harvard, 1924), pp. 211, 198.

§ Ed. M. Oppenheim, *The Naval Tracts of Sir William Monson* (Naval Records Soc.), Vol. II (London, 1902), p. 237.

‖ Nef, *op. cit.*, p. 229.

¶ Notestein, W. *The English People on the Eve of Colonization* (New York, 1954), p. 85.

normally excluded from service in the militia, the internal police force of the propertied class.†

It is hardly surprising that the rank and file of many early colonizing expeditions was composed of wage labourers, attracted by the prospect of winning the freehold land in America to which they could never aspire in England. Satirical verses of 1631 depict New England as the Land of Cokayne, that mediaeval Utopia in which wealth came without work.‡ Conversely propagandists for colonization put forward the argument that 'swarms of our rank multitude' might be exported.§ In 1622 a preacher told the Virginia Company of labourers rising early, working all day and going late to bed. They 'are scarce able to put bread in their mouths at the week's end, and clothes on their backs at the year's end'. Such men, starving in the London streets, would form a useful labour supply for the plantations.‖

III

Those entirely dependent on wage labour were so badly off in the six-teenth and seventeenth centuries that 'neither contemporary nor modern economists can explain how they lived'.¶ Children had to be put to work so early in life that there was no chance of educating them.†† Their poverty and helplessness was accompanied, as cause and effect, by an unfree status. Even the Levellers, the most radical of all seventeenth-century political groupings, would have excluded paupers and servants (i.e. wage-labourers) from the franchise, because they were unfree.‡‡ The Leveller franchise would have been restricted to 'freeborn Englishmen'. Wage labourers and paupers had lost their birthright because they had become economically dependent on others: they had lost their property in their own persons and labour. This view was held not only by the Leveller Richard Overton, but also by the Parliamentarian Henry Parker, who equated loss of property in one's self with 'a condition of servility'; and by the republican James Harrington, who not only denied

† Ed. F. J. Fisher, *Sir Thomas Wilson's State of England* (*1600*), Camden Miscellany, Vol. XVI (London, 1936), p. 20; ed. Sir C. Petrie, *Letters of King Charles I* (London, 1935), p. 84.

‡ P. A. Kennedy, 'Documents from the Nottinghamshire County Record Office', *A Nottinghamshire Miscellany*, Thoroton Soc. Record Series, Vol. XXI (Nottingham, 1962), p. 38.

§ W. Strachey, *For the Colony of Virginia Britannica* (1612), quoted by E. G. R. Taylor, *Late Tudor and Early Stuart Geography* (London, 1934), p. 163.

‖ P. Copland, *Virginias God be Thanked* (1622), quoted by P. Miller, *Errand into the Wilderness* (Harvard, 1956), p. 110.

¶ D. Ogg, *England in the Reign of Charles II* (Oxford, 1955), Vol. I, p. 55.

†† R. Crowley, *Select Works* (Early English Text Society, London, 1872), p. 166; J. Simon, *Education and Society in Tudor England* (Cambridge, 1966), p. 195.

‡‡ C. B. Macpherson, *The Political Theory of Possessive Individualism* (Oxford, 1962), chapter 4, *passim*. In the section which follows I draw heavily on this brilliant book. Some have queried Professor Macpherson's identification of 'servants' with wage labourers; but no evidence from seventeenth century usage has yet been produced which refutes him.

citizenship to servants but regarded them as a class outside the common-wealth.† Gregory King made the same point from the economist's point of view when he excluded cottagers, paupers and labourers from those who contributed to the wealth of the nation.

There is plenty of confirmatory evidence for Professor Macpherson's argument that in the sixteenth and seventeenth centuries those in receipt of wages were regarded as unfree. For Sir Thomas Smith in 1565 the commonwealth 'consisteth only of freemen'. 'Day labourers' and others who have no free land 'have no voice nor authority in our common-wealth, and no account is made of them but only to be ruled'. Those who 'be hired for wages...be called servants'.‡ For William Harrison yeo-men were 'freemen born English', who 'may dispend of their own free land in yearly revenue to the sum of 40s.'.§ In this sense Thomas Why-thorne felt himself 'as freeborn as he who may spend thousands of yearly inheritance', despite the fact that he earned wages as a musician: he differentiated sharply between 'the liberal arts', the arts of the freeborn, of gentlemen, and the 'drudgery' of 'servile and filthy trades'. Music was one of the former. ‖ Samuel Rowlands in 1614 thought that a 'free-bred muse' would despise poets who wrote 'for gold or silver pay'.¶ In 1615 one of the worst things that could be said of a stage player was that 'his wages and dependence prove him to be a servant of the people!'†† Ralegh in his *History of the World* wrote of 'factious and hireling histori-ans'.‡‡ The pejorative sense of 'hireling' and 'journeyman' is a comment on my theme. Martin Marprelate spoke of curates as 'journeymen hedge-priests'.§§ The separatist Henry Barrow thought priests were the 'waged servants of Anti-christ';‖‖ Milton and many others during the inter-regnum echoed this denunciation of 'hireling priests'.

† H. Parker, *Observations upon some of his Majesties late Answers and Expresses* (1642), p. 20, in W. Haller (ed.), *Tracts on Liberty in the Puritan Revolution* (New York, 1933),Vol. II, p. 186; Macpherson, *op. cit.* pp. 122–23, 140–41, 181–82.

‡ Ed. L. Alston, *De Republica Anglorum, A Discourse of the Commonwealth of England* (Cam-bridge, 1906), pp. 20–22, 46, 138.

§ W. Harrison, *Description of England*, in R. Holinshed, *Chronicles* (London, 1577), Sig. Di verso.

‖ Ed. J. M. Osborn, *The Autobiography of Thomas Whythorne* (Oxford, 1961), pp. 212, 237, 243, 248, 251.

¶ S. Rowlands, *A Fooles Bolt Is Soone Shott* (1614), in *Complete Works* (Hunterian Club, 1880), Vol. II, p. 5.

†† J. Cocke, *A Common Player* (1615), quoted by E. K. Chambers, *The Elizabethan Stage* (Oxford, 1923), Vol. IV, p. 256; cf. *A Health to the Gentlemanly Profession of Serving Men* (1598), quoted by M. C. Bradbrook, *The Rise of the Common Player* (London, 1962), p. 43.

‡‡ Sir W. Ralegh, *The History of the World*, quoted in the *Oxford English Dictionary*, under 'hireling'.

§§ M. Marprelate, *The Epistle* (ed. E. Arber, London, 1895), p. 30. First published 1588.

‖‖ H. Barrow, *A Briefe Discovery of the False Church* (1590), in *The Writings of Henry Barrow* (ed. L. H. Carlson, London, 1962), p. 505.

All political theorists assumed that 'servants' should be excluded from the franchise. The novelty with 'freeborn John' Lilburne and other Levellers was that they proposed so wide an extension of the franchise, beyond freehold landed proprietors and men free of corporations, that the inclusion of wage labourers and paupers had to be contemplated, at least as a logical possibility. Oliver Cromwell had to argue that it was absurd that 'men that have no interest but the interest of breathing' should have voices in elections.† Previously such persons had been deemed to be beyond the pale of the constitution. The only exception which I have found to this assumption that wage labourers were unfree comes in Hooker's *Synopsis Chorographical of Devonshire* (c. 1599–1600), which describes 'the daily worker or labourer in the tin works' and 'a daily labourer in husbandry and other servile works' as '*liberi homines* and of a free condition...albeit their labours be of the most inferior in degree'. But Hooker was contrasting this liberty specifically with the unfreedom of serfs, so there may be no contradiction.‡

Freedom in fact was a class concept. 'Privileges...made our fathers freemen', Sir John Eliot told the Commons in 1628:§ *libertas*, as Maitland put it, meant freedom to oppress others.|| Charles I spoke of 'the natural liberty all free men have' to choose their own advisers.¶ Rowland Vaughan in 1610 felt that 'being freeborn' gave him a superior nature as well as bluer blood.†† Forty years later Robert Heath contrasted 'freeborn birth' with 'peasant blood'.‡‡ It was royalist prisoners who in March 1659, as 'freeborn people of England', petitioned Parliament, 'the representative of the freeborn people of this nation', against being transported, put to forced labour and whipped.§§ Torture had been condemned by Smith as 'taken for servile in England',|||| and the Levellers regarded whipping as a punishment 'fit only for slaves or bondmen'.¶¶ 'Servants and labourers', a pamphlet of 1660 declared, 'are in the nature

† Ed. A. S. P. Woodhouse, *Puritanism and Liberty* (London, 1938), p. 59.
‡ W. J. Blake, 'Hooker's *Synopsis Chorographical of Devonshire*', *Reports and Transactions of the Devonshire Association for the Advancement of Science, Literature and Art*, Vol. XLVII (1915), p. 342. The importance of the distinction between servants and villeins was still being stressed by Edward Chamberlayne in his *Angliae Notitia* (London, 1669), pp. 515–16.
§ Quoted by C. V. Wedgwood, *Thomas Wentworth, First Earl of Strafford* (London, 1961), p. 62.
|| I have been unable to trace this sentence, which is quoted by G. G. Coulton, *Medieval Panorama* (Cambridge, 1945), p. 56.
¶ Edward, Earl of Clarendon, *The History of the Rebellion* (ed. W. D. Macray, Oxford, 1888), Vol. I, p. 437.
†† Ed. E. B. Wood, *Rowland Vaughan His Book* (London, 1897), p. 153.
‡‡ R. Heath, 'To one blaming my high-minded Love', *Clarastella* (1650), p. 13.
§§ Ed. J. T. Rutt, *Diary of Thomas Burton* (London, 1828), Vol. IV, pp. 255–57.
|||| Alston (Ed.), *De Republica Anglorum*, p. 105.
¶¶ *To the...Supreme Authority of this Nation, the Commons of England in Parliament Assembled* (1649), in D. M. Wolfe (ed.), *Leveller Manifestoes of the Puritan Revolution* (New York, 1944), p. 329.

CHRISTOPHER HILL

of vassals'.† In America no less than in old England, apart from Virginia between 1621 and 1655, servants had no vote. 'Free men' were freeholders.

During the interregnum others besides Levellers demanded an extension of the rights of 'freeborn Englishmen'. 'The Anabaptists are men that will not be shuffled out of their birthright as freeborn people of England', wrote one of their defenders in 1655.‡ We recall Bunyan's horror at selling his birthright.§ The Quaker Francis Howgill claimed in 1654 that he and Edward Burroughs were 'freeborn Englishmen, and have served the commonwealth in faithfulness'.‖ The latter said in the following year that the Quakers were a freeborn people, who should not be banished or taken for guilty until proved so, and in 1661 he described Quakers as freeborn, with a right to their lives, liberties and estates.¶ In 1656 George Fox said 'We are free men of England, freeborn; our rights and liberties are according to law and ought to be defended by it'.†† Lodowick Muggleton also called himself 'a freeborn Englishman'.‡‡

The word 'freeborn' in fact acquired a temporary notoriety as the catch phrase of political radicals. Marchamont Nedham, looking back from 1661 in his *Short History of the English Rebellion*, sang

> Farewell the glory of our land,
> For now the freeborn blades
> Our lives and our estates command,
> And ride us all like jades.§§

But the restoration changed all that. In February 1660 Lord Fairfax and other Yorkshire landowners were asserting their right as 'freeborn Englishmen' to be represented in Parliament.‖‖ Samuel Butler jeered at 'what freeborn consciences may do': no saint 'should be a slave to conscience'.¶¶ By 1669 'ranting like a freeborn subject' on behalf of

† [Anon.], *A Discourse for a King and a Parliament* (1660), pp. 1–2.

‡ [J. Sturgion], *Queries for His Highness to Answer* (1655), quoted by D. B. Heriot, 'Anabaptism in England during the 17th century', *Transactions of the Congregational History Soc.*, Vol. XIII (1937–39), p. 29.

§ J. Lindsay, *John Bunyan* (London, 1937), chapters 8 and 9, *passim*.

‖ W. and T. Evans, *Edward Burrough: A Memoir* (1857), p. 58.

¶ E. Burroughs, *The Memorable Works of a Son of Thunder and Consolation* (London, 1672), pp. 85, 89, 773.

†† Quoted by M. Coate, 'The Social Theories and Activities of English Dissenters in the 17th century', *The Way*, III (1941), p. 56.

‡‡ L. Muggleton, *The Acts of the Witnesses of the Spirit* (London, 1768), p. 160. First published 1699.

§§ In *Harleian Miscellany* (1744–46), Vol. II, p. 503.

‖‖ Ed. W. L. Sachse, *The Diurnal of Thomas Rugge* (Camden Third Series, Vol. XCI, 1961), pp. 40–41.

¶¶ S. Butler, *Hudibras*, Part II, Canto 2.

'privileges' was a subject for theatrical mockery.† Dryden in 1682 described the effects of Cromwell's rule as 'The free-born subject sunk into a slave'.‡ In Swift's *Discourse of the Contests and Dissensions between the Nobles in Athens and Rome* (1701), an elaborate series of parallels with recent English history, Servius Tullius (= Oliver Cromwell) was described as first introducing 'the custom of giving freedom to servants, so as to become citizens of equal privileges with the rest, which very much contributed to increase the power of the people'.§ The history is absurd; the implications however made very good sense for Swift's audience.

IV

Although the Levellers did not think the poorest classes capable of exercising the rights of freeborn Englishmen, there were those who did. But, significantly, such men opposed wage labour. In Spenser's *Mother Hubberd's Tale* (1591), the Ape asked the Fox:

> Shall we tie ourselves for certain years
> To any service?

and the Fox replied

> Why should he that is at liberty
> Make himself bond? Since then we are born free
> Let us all servile base subjection scorn...
> And challenge to ourselves our portions due
> Of all the patrimony which a few
> Now hold in hugger-mugger in their hand
> And all the rest do rob.

The Fox urged that the poor should no longer work to enrich others, but should revert to the condition of primitive equality in which there was not 'ought called mine or thine'.‖ Spenser must have heard something like that from a sixteenth-century agitator. A not dissimilar attack on the principle of wage labour can be read into words used by one of the Oxfordshire rebels of 1596. ('Care not for work, for we shall have a merrier world shortly...I will work one day and play the other...Servants were so held in and kept like dogs that they would be ready to cut their masters' throats.')¶

Just over 50 years later Gerrard Winstanley the Digger made a communist theory out of what must long have been muttered among the

---

† J. Lacy, *The Dumb Lady*, in *Dramatic Works* (London, 1875), pp. 18–19. Not published until 1672, but probably acted in 1669.

‡ J. Dryden, *The Medal* (1682), in *Poetical Works* (Globe ed., London, 1886), p. 130.

§ J. Swift, *Works* (Edinburgh, 1814), Vol. III, p. 283.

‖ E. Spenser, *Works* (Globe ed., London, 1924), p. 514.

¶ *Calendar of State Papers, Domestic, 1595–97*, pp. 317, 343–45.

exploited poor. Wage labour for him was slavery, a loss of man's birth-right freedom. 'Israel shall neither take hire, nor give hire. And if so, then certainly none shall say, This is my land, work for me, and I'll give you wages'.† 'Whosoever shall help that man to labour his proper earth, as he calls it for wages, the hand of the Lord shall be upon such labourers, for they...hold the creation still under bondage'.‡ 'If the common people have no more freedom in England but only to live among their elder brothers and work for them for hire, what freedom then have they in England more than we have in Turkey or France?...The poor that have no land are left still in the straits of beggary, and are shut out of all livelihood but what they shall pick out of sore bondage, by working for others as masters over them'. The civil war would have been fought in vain, would have given freedom only to the gentry and clergy, if there were not a far more radical reform than the men of property were pre-pared to envisage.§

A truly free and communist commonwealth, on the other hand, Winstanley argued, would 'unite the hearts of Englishmen together in love, so that if a foreign enemy endeavour to come in we shall all with joint consent rise up to defend our inheritance, and shall be true to one another. Whereas now the poor see, if they fight and should conquer the enemy, yet either they or their children are like to be slaves still, for the gentry will have all. And this is the cause why many run away and fail our armies in the time of need. And so through the gentry's hardness of heart against the poor the land may be left to a foreign enemy, for want of the poorers' love sticking to them. For, say they, we can as well live under a foreign enemy working for day wages as under our own brethren, with whom we ought to have equal freedom by the law of righteousness'.||
In Winstanley's utopia there would be a law that 'No man shall either give hire, or take hire for his work, for this brings in kingly bondage. If any freeman want help, there are young people, or such as are common servants [i.e. those under penal sentence] to do it, by the Overseer's appointment. He that gives and he that takes hire for work shall both lose their freedom and become servants for twelve months.'¶ The Digger colony on St George's Hill was intended to be the first stage in a sort of general strike against wage labour. As the Digger poet Robert Coster put it in December 1649, 'Rather than go with cap in hand and bended

† G. Winstanley, *The True Levellers Standard Advanced* (1649), p. 17, in *The Works of Gerrard Winstanley*, ed. G. H. Sabine (Cornell, 1941), p. 261.
‡ Winstanley, *The New Law of Righteousness* (1649), p. 55, in Sabine, *op. cit.* p. 195; cf. *ibid.* p. 262.
§ Winstanley, *A Letter to the Lord Fairfax and his Councell of War* (1649), p. 9, in Sabine, *op. cit.* p. 288.
|| Winstanley, *An Appeale to all Englishmen* (1650), broadside, in Sabine, *op. cit.* p. 414.
¶ Winstanley, *The Law of Freedom in a Platform* (1652), p. 85, in Sabine, *op. cit.* p. 595.

knee to gentlemen and farmers, begging and entreating to work with them for 8d. or 10d. a day, which doth give them an occasion to tyrannize over poor people (which are their fellow-creatures), if poor men would not go in such a slavish posture, but do as aforesaid, then rich farmers would be weary of renting so much land of the lords of manors', and 'down would fall the lordliness' of the spirits of the latter.†

<h1 style="text-align:center">V</h1>

The Diggers were of course an extreme example and a small group. But the other evidence collected in this article may help us to appreciate that their attitude towards wage labour was not unique among their class, though their remedies no doubt were. By the end of the century, at least, life-long wage labourers may well have been a majority of the population.‡

In the same centuries as the working class showed this hatred of wage labour, Puritans and others were evolving a doctrine of the dignity of labour. This began as part of the protestant critique of idle monks and begging friars. It soon became a primitive version of the labour theory of value, which seems to have been held, among others, by Bishop Jewell, William Perkins, Dod and Clever, Arthur Dent, John Preston, Richard Baxter, Milton, Hobbes and Sir William Petty, as well as by Peter Chamberlen and Gerrard Winstanley. These Puritan theories, which I have tried to discuss elsewhere,§ were aimed at free craftsmen: they take for granted that property in a man's own labour and person which wage labourers had lost. George Herbert's lines,

> A servant with this clause
> Makes drudgery divine;
> Who sweeps a room, as for thy laws,
> Makes that and the action fine,‖

represented a point of view more common among employers and independent craftsmen than among employees. When in 1751 Malachy Postlethwayt uttered his famous paean in praise of 'the ingenuity and dexterity of [England's] working artists and manufacturers, which have heretofore given credit and reputation to British wares in general',

† R. Coster, *A Mite Cast into the Common Treasury* (1649), p. 3, in Sabine, *op. cit.* pp. 656–57.

‡ Clapham, *op. cit.*, pp. 212–13; Macpherson, *op. cit.*, pp. 286–90.

§ Most of these names are quoted in my *Society and Puritanism in pre-revolutionary England* (London, 1964), chapter 4, esp. pp. 133–44; and in my *Puritanism and Revolution* (London, 1958), pp. 235–37. See also J. Milton, *Complete Prose Works* (Yale ed.), Vol. I, p. 804; T. Hobbes, *English Works* (ed. Sir W. Molesworth, London, 1840–45), Vol. VI, p. 321; *Economic Writings of Sir William Petty* (ed. C. H. Hull, Cambridge, 1899), Vol. I, pp. 43–49, 181–82.

‖ G. Herbert, 'The Elixer', *Works* (ed. R. A. Willmott, London, n.d.), p. 196.

his reference was precisely to such free craftsmen, whose skill was 'owing to that freedom and liberty they enjoy to divert themselves in their own way'. 'Were they obliged to toil the year round, the whole six days in the week, in a repetition of the same work, might it not blunt their ingenuity and render them stupid instead of alert and dexterous?'† What is freedom but choice? Milton had asked. And Hobbes agreed for once in defining a free man as 'he that in those things which by his strength and wit he is able to do, is not hindered to do what he has a will to do'.‡

Theories of the dignity of labour had little appeal for those who had evolved out of serfdom into wage labour. Such men in the sixteenth century sympathized with vagabonds and refused to prosecute thieving beggars. In the eighteenth century their descendants read the literature of roguery which glorified highwaymen and pirates, non-working heroes like Robin Hood and Dick Turpin, and they gave moral support to condemned criminals at Tyburn. In 1650 Abiezer Coppe the Ranter pictured God Almighty as a highwayman, 'demanding restitution from the rich like some urban Robin Hood: "Thou hast many bags of money, and behold I (the Lord) come as a thief in the night, with my sword drawn in my hand, and like a thief as I am—I say Deliver your purse, deliver sirrah! deliver or I'll cut thy throat".'§ All lower-class Utopias from the Land of Cokayne onwards aim to abolish labour altogether, or drastically to reduce the working day. This is the context in which we should see the French visitor's reference in 1694 to the Englishman's 'contempt of death and fear of labour'.|| Hanging seemed almost preferable if the alternative was enforced labour in unfreedom.

VI

This historical perspective may help to explain the attitude of those men and women who in the eighteenth century hated going into factories. Even if our 'optimists' could prove that workers would have been economically better off in factories than outside, men still did not live by bread alone. The relations of employer and wage labourer, wrote Dean Tucker in George II's reign, 'approach much nearer to that of a planter and slave in our American colonies than might be expected in

---

† M. Postlethwayt, *The Universal Dictionary of Trade and Commerce* (London, 4th ed., 1774), p. xiv.

‡ T. Hobbes, *Leviathan* (Everyman ed.), p. 110.

§ Abiezer Coppe, *The Fiery Flying Roll* (1650), Vol. II, p. 2, quoted, with useful comments, by A. L. Morton, *The Everlasting Gospel* (London, 1958), p. 63. Morton's *The English Utopia* (London, 1952) is also relevant.

|| B. L. de Muralt, *Lettres sur les Anglais et les Français*, quoted by L. Radzinowicz, *A History of English Criminal Law* (London, 1948), Vol. I, p. 720. Muralt's Letters were written in 1694 though first published in 1725.

such a country as England'.† Many factories looked like workhouses for paupers.‡ Self-respecting men fought against going into them, or sending their wives and children into them, just as to-day no one in his senses would go voluntarily into the army as an other rank if he could avoid it. Factory discipline must have seemed to the eighteenth century craftsman equally irrational, equally irrelevant to his interests, equally unfree. He clung on to his birthright, his property in his own person and labour.

One of Petty's favourite ideas for obtaining docile wage labour had been to transfer the bulk of the populations of Ireland and the Scottish Highlands to England.§ The early factories were in fact largely worked either by pauper children and women, or by Welshmen, Irishmen and Scots who lacked the English craftsman's 'notion, that as Englishmen they enjoy a birthright privilege of being more free and independent than in any country in Europe'. The anonymous author of *An Essay on Trade and Commerce* (1770) had little use for such a sentimental notion: 'the less the manufacturing poor have of it, certainly the better for themselves and the state...The cure will not be perfect till our manufacturing poor are contented to labour for six days for the same sum which they now earn in four days'. His remedy was a 'House of Terror' and 'ideal workhouse', where 'the poor shall work fourteen hours a day'. This House of Terror, Marx observed grimly, was realized a few years later, and was called the factory.‖ 'We make a nation of helots and have no free citizens', wrote Adam Ferguson, adding that 'manufactures...prosper most where the mind is least consulted, and where the workshop may, without any great effort of imagination, be considered as an engine, the parts of which are men'.¶

To Adam Smith it seemed obvious that a factory worker, from the nature of his toil, was 'altogether incapable of judging...the great and extensive interests of his country'. He contrasted the state of affairs in pre-industrial societies, where 'invention is kept alive, and the mind is not suffered to fall into that drowsy stupidity which, in a civilized society, seems to benumb the understanding of almost all the inferior ranks of people...Every man, too, is in some measure a statesman, and can form a tolerable judgement concerning the interest of the society, and the conduct of those who govern it'. Smith advocated state interference to ensure minimum standards of education.††

† Josiah Tucker, *Instructions for Travellers* (London, 1757), p. 25.

‡ S. Pollard, 'Factory Discipline in the Industrial Revolution', *Economic History Review*, Second Series, Vol. XVI (1963), p. 254.

§ Sir W. Petty, *Political Arithmetick* (1690), in *Economic Writings of Sir William Petty*, Vol. I, pp. 285–90.

‖ K. Marx, *Capital*, Vol. I (ed. D. Torr, London, 1946), 201–2.

¶ A. Ferguson, *An Essay on the History of Civil Society* (3rd ed., Edinburgh, 1768), pp. 309, 303.   †† Adam Smith, *The Wealth of Nations*, Vol. II, pp. 417–24.

Until 1875 the relations of wage-earners and employers were regulated by the Master and Servant Acts, whose title is a comment on my thesis. These placed wage labourers in a wholly inferior position to their employers.† We look back over two centuries in which wage labour has won freedom and self-respect, and are astonished (or some historians are) at the prejudices of those who were reluctant to enter the factories; men and women then looked back over two centuries and more of rejection of the slavery of wage labour. Liberty still included the concept of property in one's own labour (and that of one's family), of small proprietorship, of an agricultural holding to ward off starvation in unemployment, sickness and old age. This tradition helps to explain the overwhelming strength of the back-to-the-land movement right into the nineteenth century, even among the Chartists. To accept a merely wage status in the factories was a surrender of one's birthright, a loss of independence, security, liberty. 'It takes centuries', observed Marx, 'ere the "free" labourer, thanks to the development of capitalistic production, agrees, i.e. is compelled by social conditions, to sell the whole of his active life, his very capacity for work, for the price of the necessaries of life, his birthright for a mess of pottage.'‡

A historical approach suggests that Adam Smith and Marx got closer and more imaginatively to the heart of the matter than many recent historians interested primarily in the calory-content of the pottage. So did Wesley, who offered a birthright in heaven to those who had irretrievably lost it on earth. It was a long time before freeborn Englishmen could be convinced that the chains of factory discipline could in any way be justified. The acceptance of wage labour as a permanent system was accompanied, significantly, by the abandonment of the backward-looking ideal of the birthright, and even of the concept of the freeborn Englishman itself.

† D. Simon, 'Master and Servant', in *Democracy and the Labour Movement* (ed. J. Saville, London, 1954), pp. 160–200.

‡ Marx, *Capital*, Vol. I, p. 256.

A BIBLIOGRAPHY OF THE
WORKS OF MAURICE DOBB

A. BOOKS

Capitalist Enterprise and Social Progress. Routledge, 1925. Russian translation of historical chapters (1929), Japanese translation (1931).

Wages. With an Introduction by J. M. Keynes. Cambridge Economic Handbook 6. Nisbet, and Cambridge University Press, 1928; revised eds. 1938, 1946, 1956. Japanese translation (1931), Spanish translation (1941, 1949, 1957), Arabic translation (1957), Italian translation (1965).

Russian Economic Development since the Revolution. Assisted by H. C. Stevens. Routledge, 1928; 2nd ed. with a new Appendix, Labour Research Department, 1928.

Political Economy and Capitalism: Some Essays in Economic Tradition. Routledge, 1937; revised ed. 1940. American eds. (1939, 1945), Spanish translation (1945, 1961), Italian translation (1950), Japanese translation (1952), Korean translation (1955), Hungarian translation (1958), Serbo–Croat translation (1959).

Studies in the Development of Capitalism. Routledge, 1946; revised ed. 1963. Japanese translation (1946), American ed. (1947), revised American ed. (1963), Italian translation (1958), Serbo–Croat translation (1961), Polish translation (1964).

Soviet Economic Development since 1917. Routledge and Kegan Paul, 1948; revised and enlarged ed., 1966. American ed. (1948), revised American ed. (1967). Japanese translation (1955), Italian translation (1957).

Some Aspects of Economic Development: Three Lectures. Delhi School of Economics: Occasional Paper 3, Delhi, 1951. Japanese translation (1955).

On Economic Theory and Socialism: Collected Papers. Routledge and Kegan Paul, 1955. American ed. (1955), Japanese translation (1955), Polish translation (1959), Italian translation (1960).

An Essay on Economic Growth and Planning. Routledge and Kegan Paul, 1960. American ed. (1960), Japanese translation (1960), Italian translation (1963), Polish translation (1963).

Papers on Capitalism, Development and Planning. Routledge and Kegan Paul, 1967.

Works and Correspondence of David Ricardo. 10 Volumes. Edited by P. Sraffa, with the collaboration of M. H. Dobb. Cambridge University Press, for the Royal Economic Society, 1950–55.

B. POPULAR BOOKS AND PAMPHLETS

The Development of Modern Capitalism: an Outline Course for Classes and Study Circles. Labour Research Department, Syllabus Series, No. 2, 1922.

Ramsay Macdonald, seine Mitarbeiter die Labour Party und was Europa erwartet. Hans Seligo Verlag, Leipzig, 1924.

Money and Prices: an Outline Course for Students, Classes and Study Circles. Labour Research Department, Syllabus Series, No. 16, 1924.

An Outline of European History. Plebs League and National Council of Labour Colleges, 1926. Russian translation (1929), Danish translation (1932).

Modern Capitalism: its Origin and Growth: an Outline Course for Students, Classes and Study Circles. Labour Research Department, Syllabus Series, No. 20, 1928.

In Soviet Russia, Autumn 1930. Modern Books, 1930.

Russia Today and Tomorrow. Hogarth Press, 1930.

Soviet Russia and the World. Sidgwick and Jackson, 1932.

On Marxism Today. Hogarth Press, 1932.

The Press and the Moscow Trial. Friends of the Soviet Union, 1933.

Social Credit Discredited. Martin Lawrence, 1936.

Planning and Capitalism. Workers' Educational Trade Union Committee, 1937.

Trade Union Experience and Policy, 1914–18. An Outline. Labour Research Department. Lawrence & Wishart, 1940.

Production Front. Labour Monthly, 1941.

Soviet Economy and the War. Routledge, 1941.

How Soviet Trade Unions Work. Labour Research Department, 1941.

Soviet Planning and Labour in Peace and War: Four Studies. Routledge, 1942. Danish translation (1946).

U.S.S.R., Her Life and Her People. University of London Press, 1943.

Economics of Capitalism. An Introductory Outline. (A Marx House Syllabus). Lawrence & Wishart, 1943.

Marx as an Economist, an Essay. Lawrence & Wishart, 1943.

Social Insurance in the Soviet Union. National Council for British Soviet Unity, 1943.

Capitalism Yesterday and Today. Lawrence & Wishart, 1958. Japanese translation (1958), Indian ed. (1959), Polish translation (1960), Czech translation (1961), Italian translation (1962), American ed. (1962), Spanish translation (1964), Turkish translation (1965), Catalan translation (1966), Portuguese translation (1967).

Economic Growth and Underdeveloped Countries. Lawrence & Wishart, 1963. American ed. (1963), Italian translation (1964), Hebrew translation (1964), Spanish translation (1964), Japanese translation (1964), Brazilian translation (1964), Polish translation (1964), Turkish translation (1965), French translation (1965).

Argument on Socialism. Lawrence & Wishart, 1966.

354   BIBLIOGRAPHY

‡Introduction to Italian Edition of K. Marx, *Il Capitale*, Editori Riuniti, Rome, 1964. Translated into English in *Science and Society*, Vol. 31, No. 4, 1967.

Tendenze economiche del capitalismo europeo (Economic tendencies of European capitalism), in *Tendenze del capitalismo europeo* (a report of a conference in Rome, organised by the Gramsci Institute, 25–27 June 1965); Editori Riuniti, Rome, 1966.

D. ARTICLES§

†The entrepreneur myth. *Economica*, Vol. 4, February 1924.

The dynamics of capitalism: a reply. *Economica*, Vol. 6, June 1926.

Finansovoye polozheniye Velikobritanii (The financial position of Great Britain). *Planovoye khozyaistvo*, November 1929.

†A sceptical view of the theory of wages. *Economic Journal*, Vol. 39, December 1929.

A note concerning Mr. J. R. Hicks on 'The indeterminateness of wages'. *Economic Journal*, Vol. 41, March 1931.

Concerning a criticism of 'Recent criticisms of the theory of wages'. Manchester School of Economics and Social Studies, Vol. 2, No. 1, 1931.

The significance of the Five Year Plan. *Slavonic and East European Review*, Vol. 10, No. 28, June 1931.

†Economic theory and the problems of a socialist economy. *Economic Journal*, Vol. 43, December 1933.

Problems of Soviet finance. *Slavonic and East European Review*, Vol. 11, No. 33, April 1933.

Economic theory and socialist economy: a reply. *Review of Economic Studies*, Vol. 2, No. 2, February 1935.

A note in reply to 'Mr. Dobb and Marx's theory of value'. *Modern Quarterly*, Vol. 1, July 1938.

A note on some aspects of the economic theory of Marx. *Science and Society*, Vol. 2, No. 3, 1938.

†Economists and the economics of Socialism. R. *Modern Quarterly*, Vol. 2, No. 2, April 1939.

†A note on saving and investment in a socialist economy. *Economic Journal*, Vol. 49, December 1939.

Scientific method and the criticism of economics. R. *Science and Society*, Vol. 3, No. 3, 1939.

Reply to L. M. Fraser's 'Dissent from the Marxian theory of value'. *Science and Society*, Vol. 3, No. 4, 1939.

†A Lecture on Lenin. *The Slavonic Year-Book* (*Slavonic Review*, Vol. 19), 1939–40.

'Vulgar economics' and 'vulgar Marxism': a reply. *Journal of Political Economy*, Vol. 48, April 1940.

† Reprinted in *On Economic Theory and Socialism*.
‡ Reprinted in *Papers on Capitalism, Development and Planning*.
§ R.=Review article.

C. CONTRIBUTIONS TO BOOKS

Contributor to the *Encyclopaedia Britannica* (12th Edition); the *Encyclopaedia of the Social Sciences* (articles on Bolshevism, Entrepreneur, Cambridge School of Economics, Gosplan and Middleman); *Chambers's Encyclopaedia* (article on Communism); and the forthcoming *International Encyclopaedia of Social Sciences* (article on Socialist Thought).

An Introduction to Economics, in *The Outline of Modern Knowledge*. Gollancz, 1932. Reprinted as a booklet, Gollancz, 1932. Spanish translation (1938), Swedish translation (1939).

Edited (with a contribution to) *Britain Without Capitalists*. Lawrence & Wishart, 1936.

†The Economic Basis of Class Conflict, in *Class Conflict and Social Stratification*, ed. by T. H. Marshall. Le Play House Press, 1938.

Trade Unions in the U.S.S.R., in *Organised Labour in Four Continents 1918–1938*, by H. A. Marquand and others. Longmans Green, 1939.

†Bernard Shaw and Economics, in *G.B.S. 90: Aspects of Bernard Shaw's Life and Work*, ed. by S. Winsten. Hutchinson, 1946.

†On Some Tendencies in Modern Economic Theory, in *Philosophy for the Future*, ed. by R. W. Sellars, V. J. McGill and Martin Farber. Macmillan, N.Y. 1949.

Economic Planning and Planned Economies, in *Economics, Man and his Material Resources*, by W. A. Lewis and others. Odhams Press, 1949.

Foreword (with contributions) to *The Transition from Feudalism to Capitalism*, a Symposium by Paul M. Sweezy, Maurice Dobb, H. K. Takahashi, Rodney Hilton, Christopher Hill. Fore Publications, 1954. (Reprinted from *Science and Society*, Vol. 14, No. 2, 1950 and Vol. 17, No. 2, 1953.) American ed. (1955).

Foreword, and contribution to, *Keynesian Economics: a Symposium*. People's Publishing House, New Delhi, 1956.

Pianificazione, in *Dizionario di Economia Politica*, ed. by Claudio Napoleoni. Edizioni di Comunita, Milan, 1956.

Contribution to *Has Capitalism Changed? An International Symposium*, ed. by S. Tsuru. Iwanami Shoten Publishers, Tokyo, 1961. Japanese translation (1959).

Theories of Wages, and Methods of Wage-Payment, in *Industrial Labour in India*, ed. by V. B. Singh and A. K. Saran. Asia Publishing House, Bombay, 1960; revised and enlarged edition, 1963.

‡Some Further Comments on the Discussion about Socialist Price-Policy, in *On Political Economy and Econometrics, Essays in Honour of Oskar Lange*. Polish Scientific Publishers, Warsaw, 1964.

‡Some Reflections on the Theory of Investment, Planning and Economic Growth, in *Problems of Economic Dynamics and Planning, Essays in Honour of Michal Kalecki*. Polish Scientific Publishers, Warsaw, 1964.

† Reprinted in *On Economic Theory and Socialism*.
‡ Reprinted in *Papers on Capitalism, Development and Planning*.

A review of the discussion concerning economic theory in its application to a socialist economy. Iktisat Fakültesi Mecmuasi, Istanbul Universitesi, Vol. 2, No. 2, January 1941.

Economic planning in the Soviet Union. *Science and Society*, Vol. 6, No. 4, 1942.

The International Labour Conference. R. *Economic Journal*, Vol. 54, June–September 1944.

Aspects of Nazi economic policy. *Science and Society*, Vol. 8, No. 2, 1944.

Post-war economic prospects in the U.S.S.R. Oxford University Institute of Statistics Bulletin, Vol. 8, June 1944.

Marxism and the social sciences. *Modern Quarterly*, Vol. 3, No. 1, 1947.

Some recent tendencies in British economic thought. *Ekonomista*, Warsaw, 1947.

A comment on Soviet statistics. *Review of Economic Statistics*, Vol. 30, February 1948.

Marxism and economic theory. *Modern Quarterly*, Vol. 3, No. 2, 1948.

†Comment on Soviet economic statistics. *Soviet Studies*, Vol. 1, June 1949.

†Full employment and capitalism. *Modern Quarterly*, Vol. 5, No. 2, 1950.

Practice and theory of railway rates. *Soviet Studies*, Vol. 1, April 1950.

Reply to P. M. Sweezy's 'The transition from feudalism to capitalism'. *Science and Society*, Vol. 14, No. 2, 1950.

†A note on the discussion of the problem of choice between alternative investment projects. *Soviet Studies*, Vol. 2, January 1951.

†Historical materialism and the role of the economic factor. *History*, February and June 1951.

Soviet post-war reconstruction. *Science and Society*, Vol. 15, No. 2, 1951.

The problem of marginal-cost pricing reconsidered. *Indian Economic Review*, Vol. 1, No. 1, February 1952.

†The Accumulation of Capital. R. *Modern Quarterly*, Vol. 7, No. 2, 1952.

A note on turn-over tax and prices. *Soviet Studies*, Vol. 4, January 1953.

†Rates of growth under the five-year plans. *Soviet Studies*, Vol. 4, April 1953.

Comments on Professor H. K. Takahashi's 'Transition from feudalism to capitalism.' *Science and Society*, Vol. 17, No. 2, 1953.

Soviet economy: fact and fiction. *Science and Society*, Vol. 18, No. 2, 1954.

†Note sur le 'degré d'intensité capitaliste' des investissements dans les pays sous-developpés. (A note on the so-called 'degree of capital intensity' of investment in underdeveloped countries.) *Économie appliquée*, Paris, July–September 1954.

Capital accumulation: a note in reply to Professor Hideichi Horie. *Kyoto University Economic Review*, Vol. 25, No. 1, April 1955.

Comparative rates of growth in industry: a comment on Strumilin's article on expanded reproduction. *Soviet Studies*, Vol. 7, July 1955.

Some questions on economic growth. *Indian Journal of Economics*, Allahabad, Vol. 36, July 1955.

Comparative growth rates: a reply. *Soviet Studies*, Vol. 7, January 1956.

† Reprinted in *On Economic Theory and Socialism*.

A note on index-numbers and compensation criteria. *Oxford Economic Papers*, New Series, Vol. 8, February 1956.

Sobre algunas tendencias de la teoría económica moderna. (On some trends in modern economic theory). *Economía*, Santiago de Chile, April 1956.

A note on income distribution and the measurement of national income at market prices. *Economic Journal*, Vol. 66, June 1956.

Second thoughts on capital-intensity of investment. *Review of Economic Studies*, Vol. 24, No. 1, 1956.

Uwagi o roli prawa wartości i w gospodarce socjalistycznej i systemie cen. (Remarks on the role of the law of value in a socialist economy and on the price system.) *Gospodarka Planowa*, Warsaw, October 1956.

Marx and the so-called 'Law of Increasing Misery'. *The Economic Review*, Tokyo, Vol. 8, No. 1, 1957.

A further comment on the 'transformation problem'. *Economic Journal*, Vol. 67, September 1957.

Some economic revaluations. *The Marxist Quarterly*, Vol. 4, No. 1, 1957.

A comment on the discussion about price-policy. *Soviet Studies*, Vol. 9, October 1957.

Tendinte recente în domeniul teoriei economice în Anglia si U.S.A. (Recent trends of economic theory in England and the U.S.A.). *Probleme Economice*, Bucharest, November 1957.

Czy w kapitalizme nastapiły zmiany po drugiej wojnie światowej? (Did changes occur in capitalism after the second world war?) *Myśl Gospodarcza*, Krakow, No. 9, 1957.

Ancora sull'intensità capitalistica degli investimenti. (Once again on the capital intensity of investment.) *Informazioni Svimez*, Rome, April 1958.

Two modern theories of wages. *Indian Journal of Labour Economics*, October 1958.

The falling rate of profit. *Science and Society*, Vol. 23, No. 2, 1959.

Capitalism: How and when did it begin? R. *Monthly Review*, Vol. 11, Nos. 3–4, 1959.

Marxism and 'social laws'. *Monthly Review*, Vol. 11, No. 7, 1959.

‡The revival of theoretical discussion among Soviet economists. *Science and Society*, Vol. 24, No. 4, 1960.

Operational aspects of the Soviet economy. *Statsøkonomisk Tiddskrift*, Vol. 74, December 1960; Øst Økonomi, Oslo, 1961.

‡Notes on recent economic discussion. *Soviet Studies*, Vol. 12, No. 4, 1961.

Some problems in the theory of growth and planning policy. *Kyklos*, Vol. 14, 1961. Spanish translation, *Desarrollo Economico*, Vol. 1, No. 1, April 1961, and *El Trimestre Economico*, Vol. 28, October 1961.

The discussion about price-policy further considered. *Bulletin du Centre d'Etudes des Pays de l'Est*, Brussels, Vol. 3, No. 2, July 1962.

L'economia della Gran Bretagna e le sue difficoltà. (The British Economy and its difficulties.) *Critica Marxista*, Vol. 1, No. 4, July–August 1963.

‡ Reprinted in *Papers on Capitalism, Development and Planning*.

A further comment on the discussion of welfare criteria. *Economic Journal*, Vol. 73, December 1963.

A note on Professor Ishikawa's 'Choice of technique during the process of Socialist Indistrialisation'. *The Economic Review*, Tokyo, Vol. 13, No. 2, July 1962.

‡Alcuni questioni di storia del capitalismo. *Statistica*, Bologna, Vol. 22, No. 2, 1962. (Three lectures originally delivered at Bologna University in March 1962. Two of these lectures have been translated into English as 'Prelude to the industrial revolution'. *Science and Society*, Vol. 28, No. 1, 1964; and 'Some features of capitalism since the First World War'. *Science and Society*, Vol. 28, No. 2, 1964.)

Creative Marxism in political economy. R. *Science and Society*, Vol. 28, No. 4, 1964.

‡The discussions of the Twenties on planning and economic growth. *Soviet Studies*, Vol. 17, No. 2, October 1965.

Teorii occidentale moderne despre creşterea economică. (Recent Western theories of economic growth.) *Probleme Economice*, Bucharest, December 1965.

Discussions of the 1920's about economic policies for building socialism. *Annali 1967*, Milan.

E. BOOK REVIEWS

Control of Wages: Hamilton and May. *Economic Journal*, Vol. 39, December 1929.

Simonde de Sismondi as an economist: Mao-Lan Tuan. *Economic Journal*, Vol. 39, December 1929.

Fixation of Wages in Australia: Anderson. *Economic Journal*, Vol. 41, March 1931.

Theory of Collective Bargaining: Hutt. *Economic Journal*, Vol. 41, March 1931.

Collective Bargaining in the Pottery Industry: McCabe; Cooperative Banking: Barou. *Economic Journal*, Vol. 43, September 1933.

Political and Economic Theory: Cole; Studies in World Economics: Cole. *Economic Journal*, Vol. 45, June 1935.

Economic Planning in Soviet Russia: Brutzkus; Collectivist Economic Planning: Hayek. *Economic Journal*, Vol. 45, September 1935.

Second Five-Year Plan in the U.S.S.R.; Economic System in a Socialist State: Hall. *Economic Journal*, Vol. 47, June 1937.

Human Needs of Labour: Seebohm Rowntree; Condition of Britain: Cole, G. D. H. and M. I. *Economic Journal*, Vol. 47, September 1937.

Labour Contract: Shields; Labour Conditions in Western Europe, 1820–1935: Kuczynski. *Economic Journal*, Vol. 47, September 1937.

Science of Social Adjustment: Stamp. *Economic Journal*, Vol. 48, June 1938.

Growth of Collective Economy: Lawley. *Economic Journal*, Vol. 48, December 1938.

Anatomy of Revolution: Brinton. *Science and Society*, Vol. 3, No. 4, 1939.

‡ Reprinted in *Papers on Capitalism. Development and Planning.*

Critique of Russian Statistics: Clark. *Science and Society*, Vol. 4, No. 1, 1940.
Economics of Socialism: Dickinson. *Science and Society*, Vol. 4, No. 4, 1940.
Soviet Russia, Anatomy of Social History: Strauss. *Sociological Review*, Vol. 35, 1942.
Theory of Capitalist Development: Sweezy. *Science and Society*, Vol. 7, No. 3, 1943.
Economic Planning: Baldwin; Planning of Free Societies: Zweig. *Economic Journal*, Vol. 53, June–September 1943.
Price of Social Security: Williams. *Economic Journal*, Vol. 54, December 1944.
Wage Determination under Trade Unions: Dunlop. *Economic Journal*, Vol. 54, December 1944.
Soviet Labour and Industry: Hubbard; Work under Capitalism and Socialism: Leontiev. *Science and Society*, Vol. 8, No. 3, 1944.
Structure of Soviet Wages: Bergson; Management in Russian Industry and Agriculture: Bienstock. *Science and Society*, Vol. 9, No. 2, 1945.
Economics of Demobilisation: Howenstine. *Economic Journal*, Vol. 55, April 1945.
How Nazi Germany has Controlled Business: Hamburger. *Science and Society*, Vol. 9, No. 4, 1945.
Condition of the British People, 1911–45: Abrams. *Economic Journal*, Vol. 56, December 1946.
Spirit of Russian Economics: Normano. *Economic Journal*, Vol. 56, December 1946.
AEA Readings in the Theory of Income Distribution. *Economic Journal*, Vol. 57, March 1947.
Spirit of Post-war Russia: Schlesinger. *Economic Journal*, Vol. 57, December 1947.
Problèmes Théoriques et Pratiques de la Planification: Bettelheim. *Economic Journal*, Vol. 58, December 1948.
Comparative Economic Systems: Loucks and Weldon Hoot. *Economic Journal*, Vol. 59, September 1949.
Survey of Contemporary Economics: Ellis. *Science and Society*, Vol. 13, No. 4, 1949.
Economic Reconstruction of Europe: Crowther. *Science and Society*, Vol. 14, No. 1, 1950.
Soviet Handbook of Economic Statistics. *Soviet Studies*, Vol. 1, No. 2, 1950.
Budget of the Socialist State: Plotnikov. *Soviet Studies*, Vol. 2, No. 3, 1951.
Private Property: the History of an Idea: Richard Schlatter. *Economica*, February 1952.
Poverty and the Welfare State: Seebohm Rowntree and Lavers. *Economic Journal*, Vol. 62, March 1952.
Soviet Financial System: Condoide. *Economic Journal*, Vol. 62, December 1952.
History of Economic Theories, and Theories of Surplus Value: Marx. *American Economic Review*, December 1952.
Soviet Price System: Jasny; Soviet Financial System: Condoide. *Science and Society*, Vol. 17, No. 1, 1953.

IEA International Economic Papers, No. 4. *Economic Journal*, Vol. 65, September 1955.

Soviet National Income and Product, 1940–48: Bergson and Heymann. *Econometrica*, Vol. 23, No. 4, October, 1955.

Soviet Industrial Production, 1928–51: Hodgman. *Economic Journal*, Vol. 65, December 1955.

Management of the Industrial Firm in the U.S.S.R.: Granick. *Science and Society*, Vol. 19, No. 4, 1955.

Labour Policy in the U.S.S.R., 1917–28: Dewar; Incentives and Labour Productivity in Soviet Industry: Barker. *Economic Journal*, Vol. 66, December 1956.

Labour Productivity in Soviet and American Industry: Galenson. *Econometrica*, Vol. 25, No. 3, July 1957.

Key to Ricardo: St. Clair. *Economic Journal*, Vol. 67, September 1957.

Soviet Budgetary System: Davies. *Economic Journal*, Vol. 69, March 1959.

Ricardian Economics: Blaug. *Science and Society*, Vol. 23, No. 3, 1959.

‡Soviet Transportation Policy: Hunter. *Soviet Studies*, Vol. 11, No. 2, 1960.

‡Ocherki planovovo tsenoobrazovaniya v SSSR: Turetskii. *Soviet Studies*, Vol. 12, No. 1, 1961.

Choice of Techniques: Sen. *Kyklos*, Vol. 14, 1961.

European Socialism: Landauer. *American Economic Review*, Vol. 51, No. 3, June 1961.

Value and Plan in Eastern Europe: Grossman; Soviet Industrialisation Debate: Erlich. *Science and Society*, Vol. 26, No. 1, 1962.

Industrie Lourde en Union Soviétique: Mawrizki; Soviet Industrialisation Debate: Erlich. *Economic Journal*, Vol. 72, March 1962.

Soviet Statistics of Physical Output of Industrial Commodities: Grossman. *Econometrica*, Vol. 30, No. 2, April 1962.

Soviet Economy: Nove. *Economic Journal*, Vol. 72, June 1962.

Problemi politicheskoi ekonomii sotsializma, vypusk 1960 g.: ed. Kronrod. *American Economic Review*, Vol. 52, No. 4, September 1962.

Central Planning in Czechoslovakia: Michal; Hungarian Experience in Economic Planning: Balassa. *Economic Journal*, Vol. 72, December 1962.

Prices and Production of Machinery in the Soviet Union: Moorsteen; Real National Income of Soviet Russia: Bergson. *Science and Society*, Vol. 27, No. 3, 1963.

Theories of Economic Growth and Development: Adelman. *Economic Journal*, Vol. 73, June 1963.

Political Economy of Communism: Wiles. *Economic Journal*, Vol. 73, September 1963.

Malthus and Lauderdale: Paglin; Samuel Bailey and the Classical Theory of Value: Rauner. *Science and Society*, Vol. 27, No. 4, 1963.

After Imperialism: Barratt Brown. *Economica*, Vol. 21, May 1964.

Economies of the Soviet Bloc: Wellisz. *Economic Journal*, Vol. 74, September 1964.

‡ Reprinted in *Papers on Capitalism, Development and Planning.*

Economic Backwardness in Historical Perspective: Gerschenkron. *Economic Journal*, Vol. 74, December 1964.

Development and Underdevelopment: Celso Furtado. *Economica*, November 1965.

Problems of Economic Theory and Practice in Poland: eds. M. Falkowski and A. Lukaszewicz. *Economic Journal*, Vol. 76, June 1966.

Monopoly Capitalism: Paul Baran and P. M. Sweezy. *Science and Society*, Vol. 30, No. 4, 1966.

‡The Best Use of Economic Resources: L. V. Kantorovich. *Science and Society*, Vol. 31, No. 2, 1967.

‡ Reprinted in *Papers on Capitalism Development and Planning*.

INDEX